KING ALFRED'S COLLEGE
WINCHESTER

Library: 01962 827306

**To be returned on or before the day
marked below, subject to recall**

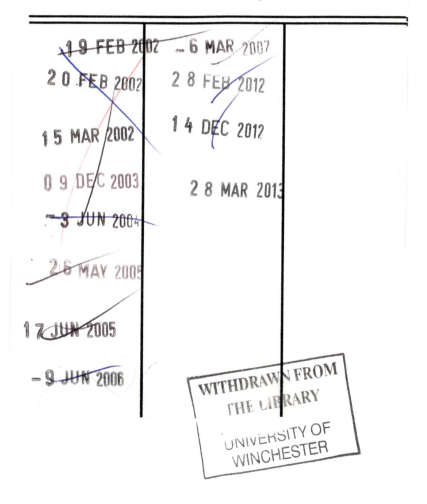

Lit Book Series

A series edited by Lee A. Jacobus and Regina Barreca
University of Connecticut, Storrs, USA

Volume 1
Hélène Cixous: Critical Impressions
Edited by Lee A. Jacobus and Regina Barreca

This book is part of a series. The publisher will accept continuation orders which may be cancelled at any time and which provide for automatic billing and shipping of each title in the series upon publication. Please write for details.

Hélène Cixous

Critical Impressions

Edited by

Lee A. Jacobus

and

Regina Barreca

*University
of Connecticut
Storrs*

Gordon and Breach Publishers
Australia Canada China France Germany India
Japan Luxembourg Malaysia The Netherlands
Russia Singapore Switzerland

Amsteldijk 166
1st Floor
1079 LH Amsterdam
The Netherlands

Some of the chapters in this book were published originally
in the journal *LIT: Literature Interpretation Theory*, volume 4,
number 1.

British Library Cataloguing in Publication Data

Hélène Cixous : critical impressions. – (Lit book series ; 1 –
    ISSN 1027-796X)
    1. Cixous, Hélène, 1937 -   – Criticism and interpretation
    I. Jacobus, Lee A. II. Barreca, Regina
    848. 9′14′09

    ISBN 90-5700-501-8

Contents

Introduction to the Series

Each volume in the *Lit Book Series* will contain a wide range of essays on a particular author, theme or genre. By offering a forum for oftentimes competing, but equally compelling, theoretical points of view within each volume, the editors hope to generate interest, debate, dissent, appreciation and attention for each volume's topic. The *Lit Book Series* will provide a valuable venue for scholars, writers and general readers to encounter, examine, produce and discuss insightful, sound scholarship about important fields of study.

Foreword

This international collection of essays regards the work of Hélène Cixous with all the complexity that she herself brings to her engagement with literature and psychology. Cixous is well known as an interpreter of Freudian and Lacanian theories, especially those connecting gender and the production of language. She is also a noted writer of fiction and drama as well as a distinguished theorist of literary feminism. Yet, she defies any categorization, just as her use of language often defies ordinary grammatical and lexical description. A protean force, like many of her characters, she was born in Oran, Algeria, in 1937 and is professor of literature at the University of Paris VIII, which she helped found in 1968. Scholars in France, the European community, the United States and elsewhere have been influenced by her work. Some authors in the present collection have had firsthand experience working with her; all have been responsive to her ideas.

Among the most influential of Cixous' critical works is "The Laugh of the Medusa," tr. Keith Cohen and Paula Cohen (1975; 1981), which investigates the source of feminine writing and examines Lacanian presumptions regarding creativity. Cixous' critical abilities reveal themselves powerfully in her early study *The Exile of James Joyce or the Art of Replacement*, tr. Sally Purcell (1972). *Reading with Clarice Lispector*, tr. Verena Andermatt Conley (1990) and *Readings: The Poetics of Blanchot, Joyce, Kafka, Kleist, Lispector, and Tsvetayeva*, ed. and tr. Verena Andermatt Conley (1991) further establish her power as an interpreter of texts. *Coming to*

Writing, tr. Deborah Jensen (1991), *Entre l'écriture* (1986), *Women in Movements Today and Tomorrow* (1993), and *Beethoven à jamais où l'existence de Dieu* (1993) demonstrate the range of her writing and influence. Her work continues to stimulate readers in both hemispheres and its power resounds through the essays that follow.

This collection, which inaugurates the *Lit Book Series*, began from a special issue of the journal *Lit: Literature Interpretation Theory*, volume 4, number 1 (1992), edited by Lee A. Jacobus and Regina Barreca. That issue included a section of Catherine A. F. Mac-Gillivray's translation of Cixous' "MANNA for the Mandelas for the Mandelstams," which was later published in its entirety by the University of Minnesota Press and does not appear in this volume. Essays by Anu Aneja, Robert Con Davis, Charlotte Canning, Martine Motard-Noar, Pamela A. Turner and Claudine Fisher appeared in that journal issue, dealing with a wide range of Cixousian ideas; they form the basis of this collection. To them have been added essays by Sissel Lie, Anne-Marie Picard, Mireille Calle-Gruber, Judith Still, Marilyn Manners, Christa Stevens, Rosette C. Lamont, Cynthia Running-Johnson, Liliana Alexandrescu and Violette Santellani. All have been organized into three sections: I. Cixous: Écrivain féminine; II. Cixous' Theorizing / Theorizing Cixous; and III. Portrayal and Performance. The essays in the first section define a Cixousian poetics, focusing on Cixous' écriture féminine and the philosophical implications of "writing the body." Section II explores the relationships among Cixous' theories and prose works, while the third section concentrates primarily upon Cixous' plays and her unique dramaturgic vision. Taken together, the chapters indicate a matrix of thematic associations embodying the intellectual richness and creative vigor of Cixous' work.

Introducing the opening section, Sissel Lie clarifies the relation between Cixous' pluralism and her ideal of writing in *La Vénue à l'écriture* (1977). Placing this text in an historical context, Lie demonstrates Cixous' innovations on André Breton's surrealism and discusses her primary theoretical/thematic concerns in *La Vénue*: woman's unconscious as jewel box; the tyranny of names; word as womb; the reclamation of the demonized man of 1970s feminism; and the relation of text to music. A diverse commentary, Lie's essay announces the collective issues that each of the subsequent essays in the first section will more particularly explore.

Anne-Marie Picard defines Cixous' central project as the textual reembodiment of the wounded, devalued souls of vanishing poet-heros in the womb of her word. These poet-heroes are Cixous' mother-men, the "maternal fathers" who give birth to nations and nurture martyred peoples just as the feminine father, a kind of male muse, gives birth to and nurtures Cixous in *Dedans* (1969) Anu Aneja represents and rebuts the central critiques of Cixous' thought that emerged after the publication of "La Rire de la Méduse" in 1975. Protesting that many of Cixous' critics are unfamiliar with the body of her work, Aneja challenges the argument that the utopianism of Cixous' writing, combined with its resistance to critical analysis, ultimately evince her indifference to the social and political "realities" of marginalized women. Closing section I, Mireille Calle-Gruber heralds a poetics improvised from the interrelated tropes of orality (music, breath, utterance and silence) and navigation (water, sailing, portaging and bridging) in Cixous' novel *Beethoven à jamais où l'existence de Dieu* (1993).

Devoted to theoretically contextualizing Cixous' prose fiction, the second section is aptly introduced by Martine Motard-Noar, who surveys the extent to which Cixous' fictional and critical writings interrelate. For Motard-Noar, the central challenge facing Cixous critics is the temporary delimitation of Cixous-the-writer as Cixous-the-critic. This necessary analytical task is made especially difficult given Cixous' sense of the indivisible union of fiction and criticism, her understanding that writing is rereading and that reading is writing.

Claudine Fisher continues exploration of Cixous' fiction, focusing on *Limonade tout était si infini* (1982). For Fisher, Cixous' fiction proves the theoretical premises announced in *The Laugh of the Medusa*, particularly her declaration that the writer's responsibility is not merely to create works of art but to offer up "works of being." Animate rather than static "works of being" do not arrest life in verbal taxonomies but offer us—through evocative portraiture—the gift of life itself.

In the first of three essays in section II to deal with Cixous' relation to other writers, Judith Still explores the theoretical relationship of a feminine gift economy to sexual difference in Cixous' work and Derrida's *Given Time: I* (1992). Marilyn Manners'

essay is located in a Derridean theoretical context where to bear a
proper name is to bear the law of the father against the nameless—
women, colonials, immigrants and slaves—whose identities are
forcefully appropriated within this law. Contextualizing Cixous'
work cross-culturally in relation to works by "othered" women
writers, Manners explores Cixous' (re)naming project where to
name is to give voice to the Other. This section concludes with
Robert Con Davis' critical comparison of Cixous and Spivak as
theorists that amplifies issues raised by Aneja in section I. According to Davis, while both theorists strive to draw from oppositional
theory a textual practice that may "lessen the effects of . . . the
patriarchal dimension of modern culture," Cixous' work "falls
short of having political significance" because, unlike Spivak, she
neglects to examine the socio-political foundations of oppositional
theory itself.

   That section III is the last and longest in this book speaks to
current intense interest in Cixous as playwright. The introductory
commentaries by Pamela Turner and Christa Stevens provide a
broad theoretical framework for issues of performance and portrayal that will be traced through specific plays in the volume's
remaining essays. Pamela Turner locates the dramatic impulse that
drives all of Cixous' writings regardless of genre. According to
Turner, critics typically regard Cixous as a producer of writings
rather than as a performer, emphasizing what she tries to say over
what she tries to do. Demonstrating how "The Laugh of the
Medusa" is "a performance in its . . . rhythm and movement
and . . . theatrical metaphor," Turner argues that performance
forms the heart of each of Cixous' texts. Christa Stevens examines
Cixous' "art of portraying" as a paradigm of her ethics and poetics
in *Portrait du soleil* (1973). Stevens argues that of all Cixous' texts,
Portrait most dramatically enacts the problematic transition
through which representation (portraiture) becomes a violent
wresting of subjectivity from subjects. For Stevens, this metatextual
enslavement is resolved in the moving force behind Cixous' work:
the search for the figure of the "lost father."

   Rosette Lamont offers lively production histories of both *Sihanouk* (1986) and *L'Indiade* (1987), attributing them to Cixous' fruitful
collaboration with playwright and director Ariane Mnouchkine.
Lamont's attention to the central themes and figures in each play
provides a clear, descriptive context for succeeding commentaries

by Cynthia Running-Johnson, Liliana Alexandrescu, Violette Santellani and Charlotte Canning.

In her essay, Running-Johnson describes Cixous' play as a turning point evincing the author's shift in focus from the body to
history, from self to others. Relating this transition to Cixous'
theoretical writings of the 1970s, Running-Johnson explores *Sihanouk*'s magnanimity and inclusivity, praising both "the success and
desirability of Cixous' project to inhabit a space in which 'the self
remains imperceptible'." Liliana Alexandrescu focuses on Cixous'
L'Indiade. For Alexandrescu, Cixous' vision of theater is a religious
one, where the purpose of dramatic form is to marry the terrestrial
to the celestial, the historical to the divine, and the temporal to the
eternal. Violette Santellani's reading of *L'Indiade* originates in her
personal response to the rehearsals for Ariane Mnouchkine's 1987
production of the play at Théâtre du Soleil. Working from her
rehearsal notes, Santellani argues that pregnancy and birth
comprise the central themes of *L'Indiade*, while its central hero
might be regarded as the androgynous spirit embodied in those
dual-gendered characters "pregnant with the future of India."

Rounding off discussion of Cixous-the-dramatist, Charlotte Canning insists on the essential "contiguity" of Cixous' plays and
criticism. Drawing upon her experience as "text analysis consultant" for Yale Drama School's 1991 production of Cixous' opera,
Canning examines how Cixous' feminist revision of the Oedipus
myth in *Le Nom* "transgresses the boundaries of theater and criticism" while "offering new ways to produce both." For Canning,
the successful production of Cixous' plays depends upon a close
reading of her criticism, which the plays illuminate.

The editors of this volume hope these collected essays will
contribute to continued insights and scholarship on Cixous' work.
The wide range of readings provided here certainly pay tribute to
the many insights Cixous has offered us—and will no doubt continue to offer us—throughout the years.

Barbara A. Suess
Catherine Nevil Parker

Acknowledgments

The editors would like to thank *Lit*'s past and present graduate editorial staff for their work on this project. We especially acknowledge Professor Tamarah Kohanski, who initiated the *Lit Book Series*; managing editor Barbara A. Suess, who took over the task of managing production of this volume; Catherine Nevil Parker; graduate assistants Julie Nash and Allison Hild; student assistants Stephanie Smith, John Caine, Wendy Brady and Luther Elliott for their research and clerical support; Aileen Phillips and Marie-Lise Charue for their translations; the book's reviewers; and the contributors for their continued patience. Please note that all translations are by the author unless otherwise noted.

1

Life Makes Text from My Body: A Reading of Hélène Cixous' *La Venue à l'écriture*

Sissel Lie

Why did Hélène Cixous' text *La Venue à l'écriture*[1] from 1976 have such echoes, first in France and later in English-speaking countries? Can the cause be the creative potential and the power Cixous sees in women? "Let yourself go! Let go of everything! Lose everything! ... Take to letters"(40) she writes and asks her readers to give themselves up to writing and to the flooding text to come. I read her texts, and this text in particular, as admonitions to me as a woman to use my own experience, listen to my own body and rethink old truths, and her faith in me has been of great encouragement to me as a reader and a writer of literary texts.

But first and foremost the essay talks about difference, complexity, plurality, in and between men and women, and between men and men, women and women. Sexuality is difference. "What is at stake is the definition of woman as other-than a non-man," says Rosi Braidotti (Brennan 91), about modern feminism. Cixous sees masculine and feminine in men and women; we are all different, with something in common.

Coming to Writing is not only a text for a specific historical situation. Its interest lies also in its poetical force, its ambiguity and playful, ironical attitude. Cixous herself recommends to both readers and writers to make love to their texts like she does. She mixes the genres of manifesto and autobiography, stressing the relationship between lived experience, rethinking and change. She is urging to action, illustrating her admonitions with examples from her own life, and she describes the transformational potential of the writing process departing from her own role as a writer, with one foot in psychoanalysis and one foot in the open.

Cixous attacks a language which maintains us in conventional concepts and dichotomies. A new way of writing can bring the body into the language, make us able to use our unconscious resources in a continuous exchange between conscious and unconscious. It is a question for both men and women of taking the plunge from what we know, what feels safe, but is oppressive, into the unknown, frightening and fascinating. Cixous' project of liberation is necessarily double. She wants to liberate the individual from the tyranny of rationality and liberate women from the image of "woman" in our culture.

Dare what you don't dare

The modernists tried from the end of the last century to extend the possibilities of the creative mind. Many artists saw their activity as revolutionary, as the new knowledge would create a new way of living. Cixous' text addresses itself to the feminist movement of the 70s, but "Let yourself go" is at the same time in Cixous' French version, "Lâche toi! Lâche tout!," a play with André Breton's text, when in 1924 he addressed himself to his male surrealist friends and asked them to let go of everything, especially of Dada. "Lâchez tout," he said, "Let go of everything. Let go of Dada....Let go of hope and fear....Set out on the roads" (Breton 263). He urged his friends to liberate themselves from family relations, from career and petty bourgeois habitudes, but also from former targets and from their fear of the unknown. Man, the lonely wanderer, must leave for the future and wins by so doing an inner and outer liberty.

Most important for Cixous is not to set out on the roads. She focuses on an inner liberation, obtained by transgressing one's own limits: "dare what you don't dare" (40). Cixous agrees with the former avant-garde movements on this point. She is relating to a tradition of rupture and revolt against the rationality of the Establishment, against conventional ideas about art and society. "I believed – up to the day that writing came to my lips – in Father, Husband, Family; and I paid dearly for it in the flesh" (49). Cixous has felt "bodily" what is means to be exposed to an ideology preventing the woman from becoming a subject. A fundamental difference between Cixous' text and the former avant-garde manifestoes is Cixous' conscious focusing on gender and on the oppression of women in our culture as both an integrated part of us and something hindering us from without. Her text can thus be read as a commentary on the former texts' blindness to gender.

Important thematic elements link, however, Cixous' "manifesto" to texts like Tristan Tzara's Dada-manifesto of 1918 and Breton's "Manifeste surréaliste" from 1924. Dada proclaims a total rupture with the past; anything happening before Dada is denied. Cixous goes even further, no need for the old body any more: "Listen: you owe nothing to the past, you owe nothing to the law...shed the old body, shake off the Law...take off, don't turn back: it's not worth it, there's nothing behind you, everything is yet to come" (40). What is new and unknown is a value in itself just as in Breton's manifesto. Apparently Cixous herself has no knowledge, no connections, no models. As for the surrealists, the romantic unrest leaves its stamp on the quest, never stay where you are, never be contented with what you have.

A tool for Breton as for Cixous in this quest is poetic writing, which creates contact with the unconscious, and is more than a tool – it is a way of living. Cixous exhorts her readers to write with one hand and experience pain with the other: "With one hand, suffering, living, putting your finger on pain, loss. But there is the other hand: the one that writes"(8). Life and writing become inseparable. She says in an interview in *Le Monde* in the same period that writing is as necessary as breathing: "When I don't write, it's as if I was dead" (Rambures).

Cixous' project resembles more of surrealism than of Dada. Dada was preoccupied with razing the established culture. Dadaists were also very sceptical about psychoanalysis. Tzara saw it as a way of taming the bourgeois. Breton and Cixous are explorers in

the inner and outer world, inspired by the split subject of psychoanalysis. In Breton's first surrealistic manifesto the unconscious is
the source of creative work, of understanding and change. Cixous
emphasizes the necessary and continuous communication between
the conscious and the unconscious. They both show us as capable
of getting closer to a "truth," an understanding, that reason alone
cannot reach, precisely because this "truth" comes from elsewhere,
from a place we cannot control rationally.

Contact with the unconscious is maintained mainly through
dreaming: "a blood tongue, a night tongue, a tongue that traverses
my regions in every direction, that lights their energy, urges them
on and makes my secret horizons speak" (43). This "night tongue"
is captured by the writer who is a medium for the unknown.
Cixous' description of the freely flooding text could indicate a
resemblance to the automatic writing of surrealism, but Breton
wants, in his first manifesto, the finished text to be an authentic
document and therefore untouched by reason. Only Cixous
describes a "double voice" where dream and consciousness alternately contribute to the writing process. In the cited interview from
Le Monde she describes her writing process thus:

> My good fortune is that I have a writing partner in my work who
> is no other than the dream. Immediately when I start on a book,
> a coupling is made automatically. I begin to dream in such a way
> that the dream and and the text are exchanged intermina-
> bly ... [I]t is as if I had a double voice .... The text that is on the
> point of becoming, writes effects in my unconscious. From here it
> is sent back to the text. It is like this that everything circulates
> between my life, my body, my unconscious, my history, my text,
> and it is all blended in me like my own blood.

In one of her later books, *Three Steps on the Ladder of Writing*,
published in 1993, the "School of Dreams" is still one of writing's
three ladders. Here she maintains that "Our dreams are the
greatest poets....The problem is that we usually destroy our
dreams the moment we wake up, or everyone would be a poet"
(80). The essay from 1976 voices the firm belief that women are
potential poets, even if the goal is liberty, not the status of literary
genius.[2]

Love is central in Breton's text as a force capable of contributing
to a final harmonizing and transcending of oppositions between

dream and reality, conscious and unconscious. Cixous accentuates that love is reaching towards the other, and towards writing and life in general. Both stress the role of the woman. Breton sees her as a guide for man on his way to the sources of imagination; Cixous accentuates women's strength to persuade her female readers to fight and write for themselves. If knowledge and poetical writing are closely connected to love, the male surrealists ponder erotic love, while Cixous idealizes maternal love and is preoccupied by the separation from the mother and its influence on all later love relationships. She makes writing an act of love and the maternal body the site of feminine subjectivity and poetic writing. Cixous describes the early mother-child dyad and the separation from it as her own relation to her mother, and as a basic psychic experience for everybody. In an interview from *Le Quotidien de Paris* from 1976 Cixous speaks of the universal themes related to women's love and the first separation from the mother:

> . . . the theme of separation, how a girl's body or a woman's body is marked by the separation, that is to say that another body disappears which is the nurturing body, the loved body which for the real little girl is the mother's, and later becomes the body of all mother substitutes, this means that one of the things I am working on is what is repressed in all sexual or love relationships which is played anew, because the mother is always in the beloved, man or woman.

It is the women in surrealism, not Breton, who are interested in the mother figure, both in texts and pictures. Some of them elevate the mother to a goddess (Bjørhovde). As does Cixous, they seem to seek a new definition of the female subject. Perhaps the strategy needed is idealization, necessary to counterbalance the misogyny of our culture? If Cixous in *Coming to Writing* makes ideals out of stereotypes of femininity, she presents maternal love as a dream of total and impossible abandonment, and this is all a part of the same strategy of making us think differently and means a valorization of what has been negated in our culture. The maternal can also be found in everyone to remind us of the hope and the goodness in the world:

> How would you survive that armed bestiality, Power, if you didn't always have for yourself, with yourself, in yourself, a bit

of the mother to remind you that evil doesn't always win out; if there weren't always a bit of the mother to give you peace, to keep a little of the milk of life through the ages and wars, a little of the soul's pleasure that regenerates? A taste of books, a taste of letters, to revive you? (48)

Breton describes how imagination is strangled through socialization, the adult having no contact any more with his creative powers. For both writers the child is the image of the free human being. In *Coming to Writing* Cixous focuses on the girl's education and describes how the young girl becomes edible:

They grab you by the breasts, they pluck your derrière, they stuff you in a pot, they sauté you with sperm, they grab you by the beak, they stick you in a house, they fatten you up on conjugal oil, they shut you up in your cage. And now, lay. How difficult they make it for us to become women, when becoming poultry is what that really means! (27–28)

Naturally a role such as this is impossible to combine with the urge to write. Cixous calls her desire to write "madness," but uses the word ironically. She wants "To be taken by surprise. To find in myself the possibility of the unexpected" (10–11), but this is considered as madness by the "Superuncles," who make the norms. The only alternative proposed to her is a form of realism which resembles the realism Breton was so harsh towards in 1924. She thus criticizes realism in the tradition of surrealism and of le Nouveau Roman from the 50s and the 60s. This realism she links to capitalism, and to the rulers' fear of the unknown, making any exploration and improvement dangerous and important to prevent. Cixous, on the contrary, seeks new ways of thinking, as Breton explored the real functioning of thought. The project in both cases is transformation, different thinking that could change the world.

The writing Cixous describes is different from the way of writing she designates as the norm, linked to works of scholars and the knowledge and thinking of the Enlightenment. She herself wants to communicate knowledge, but this is knowledge about the "forbidden" writing (45). The forbidden writing is, contrary to the other, lifegiving and liberating. It permits communication between inner and outer space, between the world, History and the individual, between the unconscious and the conscious.

Coming to Writing can be read as a manifesto, but is far from a copy of former manifestoes. Breton used a small part of psychoanalytic knowledge for his inspired proclamations. Cixous reads Freud and Lacan with a woman's perspective. In her effort to show us how we go about liberating our bodies by writing, Cixous can use the insights of psychoanalysis to describe the psychic development of the subject and at the same time let her story give examples of the innumerable obstacles a woman meets who wants to be a subject, and of how they can be overcome. She makes herself exemplary and studies herself with psychoanalysis as a model for explanation. The understanding, reached through her own experience, is the basis for a program valid for all her female readers. She, however, uses psychoanalysis no more than she needs and often makes fun of it. She challenges fundamental concepts in psychoanalysis and asks, for instance, if the castration complex concerns women at all.[3]

The jewelry box

Cixous wants to communicate to her readers not only what she comes up with, like Breton, but the hows and whys of this exploration to enable other women to do as she does. The women she talks about are her readers, women like herself, and the "woman" she is deconstructing is the definition of woman in our culture.

It is not uncommon in a manifesto to speak on behalf of others. In the quoted interview from *Le Monde* we can see how she also considers these women as her readers, writing being a way to share joy and energy with friendly readers:

> In fact I have a feeling that I am not alone, but that I write to the other and in the name of others. It is a kind of dialogue with the nearest: those who belong to memory and culture, on one side, those I love now and in the future on the other (and now especially, the women). Those with whom I want to share a special joy, a special energy.

This declaration is marked by generosity and by the wish to influence her readers. She does not address herself to her adversaries. Cixous' text appeals to the reader to identify with the writer's real history. She has learned something of importance that she wants to share. Her female readers can undergo the same metamorphosis as she does. These are the ones she admonishes in *Coming to Writing*, these are the ones who can be persuaded to do as she wants: "You are you too, a Jew-woman, trifling, diminutive, mouse among the mouse people, assigned to the fear of the big bad cat" (7). Man can also be integrated in her dialogue with the readers, but only if his femininity is not repressed: "Because he doesn't fantasize his sexuality around a faucet" (57). She ends up with a "we" where she is integrating these "feminine" men. Anatomical differences do not correspond with phantasmal representations of sexuality. In 1976 she uses "feminine" and "masculine" to make us think about their contents, but also to fill them with new meaning, whereas she later feels these concepts so laden by conventional ideas that she prefers to talk about "poetic" writing instead of "feminine" writing.

Writing seems a radical solution to the need in women to become subjects, so much discussed in the 70s. Women's possibilities are indefinite: "These pearls, these diamonds, these signifiers that flash with a thousand meanings, I admit it, I have often filched them from my unconscious. The jewelry box. We all know what it is. Every woman has one" (46). But her experience with poetic writing, a volcanic breath wanting to be born, should encourage every person with a closeness to the feminine in themselves, to write.

When writing deriving from the feminine in us, is delivered, it is flooding forth, a gift without any demand of a return, a real gift which will not create dependence, but freedom. A woman gives, protects and escapes with what she wants to steal from culture, she is the guardian of love in a world where love is threatened, but she also takes care of herself. So Cixous gives us back the best of maternity, but we are not to loose ourselves in sacrifice as the "perfect" mother was supposed to.

The dissolution of the preverbal mother-child dyad as described by psychoanalysis, is necessary to enter the symbolic order; but at the same time, to keep contact with the part of oneself that this dyad represents, as described by Cixous, is a condition for women of becoming a subject. Thus, if separation is necessary, it is not absolute. The song of the mother is a synonym of something fundamentally feminine in the unconscious of every individual, transmitted as a rhythm to the text.

Cixous is concerned by the capacity of language to transgress loss and lack by giving them a name, but also by the capacity of language to communicate traces of what is lost, because separation from the unconscious is neither definitive nor absolute. Memory of the separated maternal body is found in the unconscious as "the honey of my unconscious" (21) and can be delivered through a way of using language which comes naturally to women when they are not being watched and controlled. Thus the goal she puts up for women is the recovering of the "natural" flooding of words which is actually already there.

Be wary of names

Cixous' text can be seen as a contribution to a deconstruction and a rethinking of obsolete dichotomies of man/woman, female/male, feminine/masculine. If Lacan does not grant woman a position in the symbolic order, but sees her as a product of a collective male phantasm, Cixous does not consider this description neither as natural nor as final. Cixous' solution is to see woman as marginal, but not necessarily excluded from language. The woman is freer than the man because she has no responsibility for the norms; she can be more radical because she has an ironical position towards them. It does not cost her too much to reject norms that exclude her anyway. It is possible to write oneself through the norms, out of the concepts, the codes, to new freedom of the mind.

The text is raising the reader's consciousness of how concepts can prevent thinking: "I write 'mother.' What is the connection between mother and woman, daughter? I write 'woman.' What is the difference? This is what my body teaches me: first of all, be wary of names; they are nothing but social tools, rigid concepts, little cages of meaning assigned ..." (49). Concepts give capitalistic society a hold on the individual mind. The most important goal for Cixous seems to be eliminating the "names," "to unname" (49).

Women need to liberate themselves from the significations of what our culture calls "woman" to be able to discover a positive femininity, Cixous says. Only in this way will it be possible to feel love for oneself and for the Other. Cixous fills "woman" with the following content: "And woman? Woman, for me, is she who kills no one in herself, she who gives (herself) her own lives:

woman is always in a certain way 'mother' for herself and for the
other" (50).

The feminine is no fixed essence, but fleeting, not defineable,
whereas masculinity is linked both to rationality and power, often
in a negative sense. Masculinity, "helmeted phalloses" (48), means
wars and oppression. It would be easy to see this as a polarization
between man and woman, yet every individual can get a grasp on
"maternal goodness" (50) when he or she has written himself out
of conventional thinking. A part of this rethinking is giving all of
us the responsibility to liberate the feminine in ourselves, and at
the same time exhorting the historical women to battle against a
way of thinking that is maintaining them in oppression.

Is there a contradiction in the fact that Cixous exhorts women to
battle for a position as subjects in language, stating that they are
different from men, and the wish to eliminate the rigid limits of
gender? Oppression of women exists; it is our way of thinking
which has to change basically to make liberation possible. What
"woman" do we want? If we ponder the question, as Cixous asks
us to, we all have the experience of gender definitions not so
distinctly defined, and we know we can play all kinds of roles
for each other. If everyone can play all roles, if we recognize the
complexity of sexual difference, gender cannot be a reason to
oppress. "Haven't you been the father of your sister? Haven't
you, as a wife, been the husband of your spouse, and perhaps the
brother of your brother, or hasn't your brother been your big
sister?" (49).

The text is apparently constituted by dichotomies. However,
they are dissolved, modified, transcended. These dichotomies
often consist of images that magnify the master/slave dichotomy
implied. This makes the text polemic, but also playful and humor-
ous, for instance when the "I" of the text presents herself as a
mouse and the authorities she is confronted with in literature, as
prophets. The writing of the prophets is formulated on stone
tablets. Her writing is born out of a breath coming from her
body. "Between writing" (Cixous 1986) is an impossible position,
but possible to imagine, and women especially need to think differently about how they can write themselves a position in language.

Cixous uses no simplifying polarizations in *Coming to Writing*,
even if the text is also about society's oppression of women.

Women can shape their own lives, her own destiny testifies to this for us. She writes about herself as many times marginalized, being a French Jewess from Algeria, without a native country, without her own language. Her marginality gives her a nomadic liberty. She has no place to write from, so she can dash through the words and get out on the far side; she can be "between writing," because her place is not in the center where the norms are made. She has no language, because her mother's German tongue never became her written language, thus language is something strange, something one cannot take possession of, only love. If her identity is not one like she thought writers ought to be, it gives her texts many voices and makes them richer. In this way she turns obstacles into advantages for herself and makes this a model for her readers.

I am pregnant with beginnings

A common strategy amongst feminists in the 70s was the demonization of men. Cixous does not use means that simple. She describes women in Western culture as oppressed, and even exaggerates as when she says "A girl is being killed" (8) about the socialization of women. And she is not tender with the masters: "Who is the Superuncle who hasn't prevented a girl from flying, the flight of the thief, who has not bound her, not bandaged the feet of his little darling, so that they might be exquisitely petite, who hasn't mummified her into prettiness?" (8). But men are not given the responsibility alone, and all men are not alike.

Women have no rights, no reasons to write in our culture, affirms Cixous. The burning bush of the Bible does not address itself to women. The word is handed over, according to the Bible, by God to the prophet who had the "cheek to go claim [his] book from God on the mount Sinai" (9). Our culture does not give girls this feeling of an obvious right. But writing can be something other than to give words to the Law. If Cixous describes herself as a mouse looking up to Mount Sinai, she belongs to the "flying-stealing-mice."[4] In the end she stole what she needed and flew on.

One side of the dichotomy is clearly more powerful, that being, for example, prophets or Superuncles. The prophets belong to the

past and to literature; they are geniuses and have something ideal
and conciliatory about them. They seem to belong to Cixous'
models, after all. Superuncles are accused of murder and
censorship. There is a strong accusation against the masculine in
these dichotomies, of encroachment on women. Cixous states,
however, indirectly that she is the niece of those who make
norms. Women are involved with the systems which oppress
them.[5]

If Cixous portrays the woman in the dichotomy prophet/mouse
as insignificant, confined, timid, it is also evident that the plural
"I" she represents, with close contact to the unconscious, is the real
ideal. The irony lies in the certitude of the writer and the reader
that this powerful text is written by the fearful little mouse. She has
written herself a position in language in spite of her status as
mouse, or just because of that. Indirectly the text asks the female
reader what she has done with her own position as a mouse. Is
there a danger that Cixous does not change thinking but changes
the power positions, putting women in the center, making femininity the norm? She seeks to counteract this by showing the
ambiguity and complexity of all positions and not giving precise
definitions of what she wants to attain.

A woman's life is the journey the girl makes from her mother to
her grandmother, the Wolf. The housewives' daughters go astray
in the woods to be eaten in the end by the Grandmother-Wolf,
while the sons of the Book go on expeditions to the unknown,
"toward the never-yet-said" (14). Our vocation is to be swallowed,
says Cixous ironically, and accuses the myths of deceiving women.
Intuitively she puts herself early on the right path, because she
wanted just that, to write the never-yet-said.

The Superuncles make norms, but worse yet is the inner censor,
the Super-ego. She herself hinders the openness necessary to establish the direct relation between the writing and the unconscious;
the "breath" in her body is dependent on her giving up her
rational mastery of her mind. When the communication between
inner and outer space does not work, it is because she has internalized the image of the silent woman. Her description of how the
culture silences women will be well known by most of us, having
experienced it "in the flesh."

Cixous is on the side of the positive. There is no reason to linger
in the meaningless even if the meaningless exists, she says. Is this a

commentary to some of the modernistic literature absorbed by the absurdity of life? Anyway, she does not want even to ask the question of the meaning of life and looks for the advantages of being a woman. The strength of women is linked in the text to the image of giving birth. What interests Cixous is not the relationship between mother and child, but women's relationship to their own bodies, to bodies which when giving birth do what they have to, without any mastering by reason. This is a way of relating the feminine to the reality of women in their bodies.

Birth becomes an experience of the uncontrollable, a purely bodily experience which resembles the writing process, the "breath" which demands to be born. The body gives birth to a body text made in a kind of fundamental language, a "body language" (52). The birth of the text produces a new living being, as opposed to the realist literature Cixous criticizes for reproducing, repeating and reflecting what is already existing. The role of the artist is the role of the mother. When giving birth to the text, she takes care of those who need to be listened to: "for the fate of the living I have the untiring love of a mother, that is why I am everywhere, my cosmic womb, I work on my worldwide unconscious, I throw death out, it comes back, we begin again, I am pregnant with beginnings" (48).

To relate the image of birth to the writing process or to make the artist a mother is not contrary to the wish to transcend the limits of gender. Cixous does not want to fix women in an "essence" and contribute to maintaining oppression, but to find images illustrating the potentials of women. She proposes that a woman, having overcome inner and outer obstacles, should use a burst of laughter as her strategy, because the inner strength is a cheerful force and laughter is a way of outwitting Power. In relations between men and women, is laughter perhaps as efficient as violence? What happens to the warrior when the strange and horrible Medusa with serpents in her hair, does not threaten him, but is laughing?

Cixous uses, as we have seen, autobiographical elements in her research on "coming to writing." Already in her childhood Cixous saw how concepts such as mother and father did not correspond with concepts such as masculine and feminine. Her parents are the source of life, of love, of writing – the mother is her daughter, but she has also been God, just as her father: "I adored God my mother" (19). The father is maternal, and the mother is like a young man or girl, but stranger to "the calculating ferocity of the world of men" (29). The parents thus do not become models for a polarization between the sexes. The mother makes her want to be a man to be able to defend her against the world. This makes her ask herself what sexual identity she may have, for the armor of the chevalier is too heavy. Her positive description of her parents and her own hesitation in front of gender roles also shows her liberty from psychoanalytical explanations.

Cixous starts her writing process by giving birth to herself every day. But she is far from a foundling. She presents herself both as a daughter and a mother in *Coming to Writing*, a daughter that receives and a mother that gives love. Cixous situates herself, as we have seen, in a family context: both obstacles and benefits for her development as a writer come from "members of the family." The obstacles are never created by her parents. They are ascribed no responsibility for her marginality and insecure ego as a young girl, even if she felt her father failed her totally when he died.

Cixous' own liberating writing has its point of departure in the loss of the beloved. She says she is writing to dare "looking at life without dying of fear" (6). Writing is described as an individual strategy like the child's strategies for mastering separation, loss and death through replacing what is lost with words: "I write and you are not dead" (4).

The source of writing is not the person writing; it is love, life and death. Someone you love dies, making you write to survive. You yourself have to die to be able to write. Your own death is an image of a liberation from inner limits. If death is the death of the beloved or just the threat of separation, the answer of the writer to the anguish is the birth of the writer through writing. But writing is not motivated only by a need to work on separation and loss, but also springs forth from an abundance and a wish to reach for the other, the beloved.

Death as a metaphor is as important as love both in Cixous' own story and for writing in general. The mother figure is "our double mother" (38), because she represents both love and death. Not getting out of the preverbal mother/child dyad means the death of the "I." But Cixous links writing, maternal love, life and death, and stresses life.

Flesh that makes strangeness come through

The point of departure is the Other, in her and outside of her, Cixous says. "Cut out of History, observed by your witnesses, your magic book by more than one author, reality writes a part of it, strikes out, sorts out... your hundred origins program the dream-flesh" (55–56).

For Cixous the writing springs forth as a volcanic eruption, the lava coming from secret spots in the body. Writing has an inexhaustible source: "life becomes text starting out from my body" (52). The text is in the individual body, but is "constituted transculturally" (55). It means there is communication at an unconscious level, between women, but also with those men who recognize the feminine in themselves, and this communication between bodies makes women "morewomen" (55), confirms the self-respect, encourages a greater openness. To be more than oneself produces the necessary strength to risk being invaded, taken possession of, disappearing, a risk always run with total openness.

The result transcends by far the conscious capacity of the writer who is not responsible for the complexity of the text, only for adjusting the finished text. The text transmits "the secrets of human movements, the news of peoples you've never imagined" (55). Writing is a journey down into hell where the conscious "I" must step aside in a process she does not control: "To write is for me a descent to hell and the door is my body. It must retire so that this being in me that is writing can come forth" (Jean-Louis de Rambures).

Thus it is no dichotomy between body and mind that Cixous is seeking to cement. A "third body," something undefinable, strange, linked to the unconscious, is able to transcend this dichotomy and become text. The goal is to open the text for what the writer does not know consciously:

And so when you have lost everything, no more roads, no direction, no fixed signs, no ground, ... when you are lost, beside yourself, and you continue getting lost, when you become the panicky movement of getting lost, then that's when, where you are unwoven weft, flesh that lets strangeness come through. (38–39)

But the reward is high; we can all reach "the gardens of love." The moment when the "I" does not control and defend herself, but

abandons herself, she discovers that what was "this endless waste-
land, this ravaged space, your ruined states, without armies, without mastery, without ramparts...were the gardens of love" (39).
The image of a waste land, the end of values related to power and
mastery, gives the promise of different values close to love and
feminity for men and women.

The passive attitude Cixous recommends is passive only in
creating an openness to other voices than that of reason. Writing
is pouring out, as if the conscious "I" did not have any part in the
process: "Let yourself go, let the writing flow, let yourself steep;
bathe, relax, become the river... a practice of the greatest passivity" (57). The imagery in connection to this giving up of oneself
can be seen as an expression of a stereotype of femininity: the
woman abandoning herself passively to pleasure. I prefer to read
this as a conscious use of a stereotype, becoming an image of the
highest degree of preparedness and readiness toward oneself and
the other.

And when the conscious subject takes the risk of plunging,
floating with the current, all the time in danger of drowning,
being engulfed, invaded – pleasure is there also; one has to
give oneself up to the flooding of words and to make love to the
text. The "greatest passivity" is, as Cixous says, actually an active
openness and innocence, necessary to make the flood of
words reach the paper and not be prevented in its course. The
intervention of reason in a too early phase will stop the sponta-
neous unfolding which seems to be a condition to the birth of the
text.

Writing is a way of behaving in front of not only the death of
the other, but the menace of one's own obliteration, coming close
to it and removing from it. When writing is described as a
pleasure depending on an impending invasion of the I, Cixous'
text poses the question, is this a special female way of enjoying?
Cixous asserts that a voluptuous writing such as the one she
describes must differ depending on writing with a female or a
male body, even if a man can write in a feminine way and does
so, for pleasure is not the same in men and women. A resemblance
stems from the femininity and masculinity of both, and a
difference exists because women do not feel desire or pleasure in
the same way.

An opera inhabits me

The greatest provocation of this text is perhaps today as in 1976, repressed femininity being made a condition for liberating writing, so far as both men and women are concerned. Who is ready to accept the denigrated femininity in themselves? This femininity which cannot be grasped by a definition, but is characterized by words like "continuity" as opposed to separation, with abundance and generosity, in contradiction to what is stingy, controlling. "Feminine writing," "écriture féminine" was the name critics gave the poetic way of writing described by Cixous. It was interpreted by many as a writing reserved for women, even though the examples Cixous gave from the beginning were male writers such as Jean Genet. There is no doubt, however, that in the 1976 interview in *Le Monde* Cixous saw women as having a special potential for this kind of writing. Here the text is a "feminine flood" and the writing is like a woman's orgasm: "she [the woman] seeks to enjoy the writing in an erotic way. She really makes love to the text." But men and women alike can "let their femininity be expressed" as she says about James Joyce (Rambures).

Cixous was attacked especially in the U.S. for her essentialism, something that has for a long while hindered the reading of what is interesting in her text. Rosie Braidotti and Elizabeth Grosz have discussed feminist dilemmas concerning essentialism. Ideas can be called essentialist if they attribute to women "fixed characteristics, given attributes, and ahistorical functions," says Elizabeth Grosz (334). She asks how we can define specific positions for women within the social and the symbolic order, their relationship to power, language and meaning, and their sexual specificity without a theorization of their difference. A way to question the subordination of women is to take up positions linked to the "feminine" and use them in liberating strategies, as Cixous does. The binary logic that sustains the essentialist thinking is far from what Cixous is aiming at.

The text is a result of communication between reality in all its plurality and richness and the body: "the whole of reality worked upon in my flesh, intercepted by my nerves, by my senses, by the labor of all my cells, projected, analyzed, recomposed in a book" (52). Only the rhythm of the text is the signature of the body; the writer has otherwise no control of the form the

text will have. The breath that wants to be written, becomes a
body without limits, "without a frame, without skin, without
walls, the flesh that doesn't dry, doesn't stiffen, doesn't clot the
wild blood that wants to stream through it – forever" (10). How the
song, music becomes words is a "mystery" (56), something Cixous
does not try to explain. The cue for the writer is "listen": "Two
forces work on me at the same time, I am under the cosmic tent,
under the canvas of my body and I gaze out, I am the bosom of
happenings. And while I gaze, I listen. What happens takes place
simultaneously in song. In a certain way, an opera inhabits me" (53).

The conclusion of the text is triumphant, as Morag Schiach states
in her book on Cixous, but "this triumphant conclusion remains
remarkably fleeting, and slippery. Cixous' final image of women's
relation to writing is of fish swimming in water: reassuring, but
hard to pin down" (26). Fish inhabited by operas, that makes us
sirens, dangerous, alluring or just joyful as "poissons dans l'eau"
(Cixous 1986, 69)!

Are we all inhabited by operas? My answer as a writer is yes,
which of course does not mean that I shall, nor shall Cixous, hope
to present what comes spontaneously to paper without having
worked consciously on the text. Because, after the eruption
described, when the text is there on paper, "you execute the
dreamwork in a state of vigilance, you cheat, condense, compile,
you distill ..." (54). There is an important difference between text
and writing process. The text to a certain extent mimics the process
which proceeds it. However, the finished text is a reworked
version of the first overflow of text. The working on the words of
the text is related to "the hour of man" and to gardening: "Then, if
you want to write books, you equip yourself, you trim, you
filter, you go back over yourself, severe test, you tread on your
own flesh, you no longer fly, you no longer flow, you survey, you
garden, you dig, ah, you clean and assemble, this is the hour of
man" (54). To use one's own masculinity is not always negative, it
depends on where you are in the writing process. Femininity is
not supposed to compensate for masculinity; they are part of a
whole.

Cixous is caressed by a song and wants to transmit this song as a
caress. The writing process, as we have seen, has its source in the
love for the other, but also in the other's love for the writer. The
passive attitude is an active way of getting to know the unknown

and to transmit this knowledge to others: "an active way – of getting to know things by letting ourselves be known by them. You don't seek to master. But rather to transmit: to make things loved by making them known" (57).

The two most important stages in the writing process become abandonment, letting oneself be written "as if I were going to give birth through my throat, or come. And it's the same thing" (52), and then the giving of the text to make others love it. That is the reason why gardening is necessary, "masculine" rationality is used to weed and to tidy: because through the texts the readers must be reached. Those who only think they live, can be woken up to life, can learn to love again.

Walk into the text on bare feet

Cixous declares herself to be a poet, but she has often been read as a theoretician. She does not try to define new concepts, but to dissolve the limits for our minds made by the old concepts. We cannot accuse her of not being stringent when her poetic text is characterized by ambiguity and plurality, but rather ask ourselves if a devoted, amorous way of reading is more adapted to her texts than the mastering reading which can be accused of not letting the text be heard.

Coming to Writing also exemplifies Cixous' method: the writing is exploratory and addresses the questions that have preoccupied her throughout her work. On the cover of the book *Entre l'écriture*, ten years later, she states: "Here are collected moments of intense curiosity. I ask myself where artists come from – the writer, the painter, the musician, female male – this strange force which rushes you off into your work...." Characteristic for Cixous' production is the continuous circling around questions without definitive answers, linked to the role of the artist and the questioning of "this strange force" which makes us artists, capable of transcending a limiting rationality.

Cixous' texts tell me to explore the other, inside and outside me, transcending my fear. They give me a point of departure for my own thinking, not for applying concepts and principles. They tell me something about my existence, about my language and my body, as a literary text does, through images and figures, not concepts. And *Coming to Writing* is a spiral, always coming back to the same themes and developing them, playing with them. This does not prevent readers from letting themselves be inspired both to make philosophy and theory. Jacques Derrida said in a mini-seminar at Cixous' about his "loans" from Cixous' fiction: "It is in the literature that I find things that I later think I have found myself."[6] At the same seminar Cixous talked about the innocence needed in the relation to the text: "Take off knowledge, walk into it [the text] on bare feet." The utmost openness for the readers is perhaps to let the text talk for itself. But what Cixous says about writing can also be applied to our reading of her texts. Why not "let[ting] ourselves be known by them" (57)? When we read her texts, we can "Write, dream, enjoy, be dreamed, enjoyed, written" (56). Later on we can straighten up and tidy, to make our text capable of reaching our own readers!

Notes

1. I use the American translation, *Coming to Writing*, for all the citations from this text. The other translations are mine.
2. Verena Andermatt Conley states in *Hélène Cixous* that Cixous becomes more and more absorbed by the literary geniuses, "the Happy Few," and less by the writing of women in general.
3. See for instance "Le Rire de la Méduse."
4. This is my translation. "Voler" in French means both steal and fly and Cixous plays with both meanings in "souris volantes."
5. Martine Motard-Noar points to the following citation from Marianne Hirsch,"Father Owns the Words," *Sunday New York Times*, (7 Dec. 1986): 70, where Cixous underlines the fact that there's no easy way out of the name of the Father: "To my stupefaction as a 'feminist,'... I had to come to the realization that in fact I *was* in the name of my father. Women who have written are women who have been phallicized by their father, that is to say whom the father allowed and did not prohibit to write" (186).
6. Miniseminar at Hélène Cixous' with Jacques Derrida, 27.3.93. From my own notes.

Works Cited

Braidotti, Rosi. "The Politics of Ontological Difference." *Between Feminism and Psychoanalysis*. Ed. Teresa Brennan. London and New York: Routledge, 1989.

Breton, André. *Oeuvres complètes*, T.I. Paris: Gallimard, 1988.

Cixous, Hélène. *La Venue à l'écriture*. Paris: Union Générales d'Edition, 1977.

——. *Entre l'écriture*. Paris: des femmes, 1986.

——. *Coming to Writing*. Trans. Deborah Jensen. Cambridge: Harvard UP, 1991.

——. "Le Rire de la Méduse." *L'Arc* (1975): 39 – 54.

——. *Three Steps on the Ladder of Writing*. Trans. Sarah Cornell and Susan Sellers. New York: Columbia UP, 1993.

Conley,Verena Andermatt. *Hélène Cixous*. London: Harvester Wheatsheaf, 1992.

de Rambures, Jean-Louis. Interview with H.Cixous. *Le Monde* 9.4 (1976): 20.

Grosz, Elizabeth. "Conclusion. A note on essentialism and difference." *Feminist Knowledge. Critique and Construct*. Ed. Snedja Gunew. London and New York: Routledge, 1990. 332-344.

Lie, Sissel. "ryttersker, poeter og dronninger." Kvinner i surrealismen. *Gå mot vinden*. Ed. Bjørhovde, des Bouvrie, Steinfeld. Oslo: Universitets-forlaget, 1993: 164 – 76.

Motard-Noar, Martine. *The fictions d'Hélène Cixous. Une autre langue de femme*. Lexington: French Forum, 1991.

Schiach, Morag. *Hélène Cixous. A Politics of Writing*. London: Routledge, 1991.

2

Le Père de l'Écriture:
Writing Within the Secret Father

Anne-Marie Picard

Tout est là: quand la séparation ne sépare pas; quand l'absence est animée, reprise au silence, à l'immobilité. Dans l'assaut que donne l'amour au néant. Ma voix repousse la mort; ma mort; ta mort; ma voix est mon autre. J'écris et tu n'es pas mort. Si j'écris l'autre est sauf.
(La Venue à l'écriture 12)

This is what matters: when separation does not separate; when absence is animated, taken away from silence, from immobility. In the assault made by love against nothingness. My life pushes away death; my death; your death; my voice is my other. I write and you are dead no longer. If I write, the other is safe.

La Fragilité du corps de mon père[1]

Sihanouk, Gandhi, Mandela, Mandelstam, Celan, Dostoïevski, Kafka, Hesse, von Kleist, Genet, Rilke, Hofmannsthal, Pouchkine, Shakespeare, Beckett, Freud...: the frailty of men, the vulnerability of princes...We know that Hélène has set a task for herself which is titanesque: she must protect the princes and the poets before they become corpses, corpses of young men. She must tell the stories of peoples before they disappear into oblivion, before their traces are erased by time and ignorance. Hélène is writing before silence, before darkness, theirs and hers: *L'Indiade ou l'Inde de* leurs *rêves*. Whose dreams?[2] *L'Histoire terrible mais inachevée de Norodom Sihanouk, roi du Cambodge*. Whose story? Her letters, her words are life-lines for the princes to emerge once more from the earth, from the soil where their bodies are rotting:

> J'écris l'encore. Encore ici, j'écris vie. La vie: ce qui touche à la mort; j'écris tout contre elle mes / *Lettres du Qui-Vive:...(La Venue* 12)

> Still further I write. Here, still I write life. Life: what touches death; against it I write all my / *Letters for dear life:...*

Etre sur le qui-vive par l'écriture...et par la lecture aussi: to be on the lookout, tense, in a state of apprehension and impatience, of extreme urgency and of utmost attention to save the lives of the souls, the unique wounded souls of poets who are among the wealthiest humans: such is the endeavour and the ideal that Hélène wants to teach and tell the world, before, she says, writing itself becomes obsolete, for "[l]a mort du texte est en chemin" ["the text's death is on the way"] ("Entretien avec Hélène Cixous" 65). Because her writing is rooted in an overwhelming sense of loss, it has become a feat of transforming *bereavement* into *benediction:*[3]

> Et quand j'écris un texte de fiction, c'est un acte double pour moi. D'une part, j'essaie justement de protéger, d'inscrire, de rappeler, de faire un travail de remémoration d'un thème qui est toujours ténu, mais qui, pour moi, est essentiel. Et en même temps, j'essaie de sauver le moyen de le sauver, c'est-à-dire l'écriture elle-même. J'ai appelé ma préoccupation, la préoccupation du précaire – du précaire, c'est-à-dire de ce qu'il faut prier, qui attire la prière, qui est de l'ordre de la prière et qui est précaire. Et quand j'écris pour le théâtre, je défends les mêmes valeurs...("Entretien avec Hélène Cixous" 65)

> Writing a text of fiction is, for me, a double gesture. On the one hand, I try precisely to protect, inscribe, recall, to accomplish a labor of recollection of a theme which is always tenuous but which, for me, is essential. And simultaneously I try to save the means to save it, that is to say writing itself. I have called my preoccupations that of the precarious – the precarious that is to say that which needs to be prayed, beseeched, which attracts

prayer, that which is a prayer and which is precarious. And when I write for theater, I defend the same values.

Precarity and prayers both depend on the will of an other: transforming the precarious into the precatory turns the arbitrary and the uncertain fate into an appeal which is an attempt at entering a relation with that fate, by first of all embodying it as an omnipotent Other who can hear. It seems, then, that Hélène is toiling on a rapprochement, a reduction of the distance between that supernatural force, which she does name God, and humans. But her prayers are written words. These words will indeed allow the precarious to become an inscription and therefore attain a state of relative permanence. But the threatening Other who is beseeched and even worshipped is the one ultimately addressed: in the process, "He" is created as a fixed space and, in fact, made more distant, pushed away and controlled by the very writing. While "He" is listening to Hélène's story and appeal, he is not striking at random princes and peoples. Therefore the desire for closeness, which is the very nature of the prayer, mutates into an ability to preserve what is essential *for the writer*: the prayer becomes above all an ability to safeguard oneself as separate from that Other (be it God or History, hazard or fate). Keeping the Other at bay by telling stories protects the writer and the ones she identifies with: the vulnerable "species": "Je me soucie des espèces qui sont menacées d'extinction: les poètes, certains peuples, les hippopotames, les éléphants, les femmes – et qui sait, les hommes-mères?" ["I care about species threatened by extinction: poets, certain peoples, hippopotami, elephants, women – and who knows, mother-men?"] ("Entretien avec Hélène Cixous" 65).

Hélène then writes to save minute and fragile things and people, ideas and relationships; primarily a means of distanciation, writing becomes the only way to avoid complete diappearance. Having had herself to suffer so much from the arbitrariness of History, she knows about the menace of disappearance and the morbid effects of loss. It is that very knowledge that makes her a poet, because:

Au prix de l'Enfer, on a idée du Paradis: tout est redoutablement ambivalent. Celui qui sait le plus de choses de la liberté, c'est le prisonnier. Celui qui sait mieux parler le Paradis, c'est celui qui a vu le monde se dissoudre devant lui, celui qui a vu le monde se taire. (*Le Sacrifice dans l'oeuvre littéraire*, Seminar of Jan. 9th 1988)

At the expense of Hell, one gets an idea of Paradise. Everything is fearfully ambivalent: the one who knows the most about freedom is the prisoner; the one who can best speak of Paradise is the one who has seen the world dissolve in front of him; the one who has seen the world lapse into silence.

It is this very sensitive and always frail positivity of the loss and of the alteration the self must submit to to become the other – on whom and for whom one will write – that I shall try to relate here. Hélène Cixous' ethics and almost mystical approach to alterity, her benevolence and kindheartedness, obvious to anyone who has had the chance to talk to her, stems from an extraordinary intuition for others' anguish and desires. Her own imagined people of angels whom she embodies in her fiction and her theatre, to whom she lends her personal pronouns, are her "guides," as she calls them in *L'Ange au secret* (33): "Sans anges on ne part pas pour l'Apocalypse. / On ne part pas sans anges pour l'Apocalypse.... il nous faut bien des anges afin de nous relever chaque fois que nous nous écroulons par terre à moitié morts comme les poètes" ["Without angels one does not leave for the Apocalypse. / One does not leave without angels for the Apocalypse.... We need quite a few angels to stand up again each time we collapse to the ground half dead like poets."] (*L'Ange au secret* 33–34). But we know that her first angel, the *mother* to them all and the prototype of all the frail young men of her epopoeia, was her father. He is the first one Hélène has wanted to protect from fate.

The father is indeed the first other, place and locus from where the writing subject was born, as related in *Dedans*: the father is the name of that place and the beginning. The walls of the first book are pages on which to read and retrace the suffering and the darkness from which Hélène, as a prince threatened by disappearance herself, has risen from the dead. *Dedans* is above all the now symbolic body of that young man, a warm place that she could have inhabited for ever, eaten up by grief, all sense of identity, of the limits of her own body, of her own history, lost. The birth from a *newly written body of the father* is and will always be the point of departure. It will keep being recounted in all her stories of poets and wounded men, *feminine* men: men who give birth to nations, who are mothers to sacrificial peoples, just like her feminized father gave birth to her in *Dedans*.

Dedans le Symbolique

Finding words to make the secret father alive again: here is the dream of the little girl and the light burning in Hélène's écriture:

> *Dedans* was necessarily written within the father, in seeking him right up to death and *revenant* (coming back, ghostly). There is something simple and mysterious in the origin of writing: "I" am in the father I carry within me, he haunts me, I live him. There is a rapport between the father and language, the father and the "symbolic." ("From the Scene of the Unconscious" 4)

Because it is a body, a quantity of body which has been lost, one will have to restore something which also pertains to the body.[4] And it is not only a matter of creating a textual body of words, but of inventing the father's body as a place, a three-dimensional volume, a house within the house of the city of Oran. A series of painful and blissful experiences will make the mourning daughter imagine, touch, lay beside and then actually inhabit her father's body as a place from which later she will be born metaphorically: a birth from the father's veins which mimes the coming to writing, the father's body becoming in the process the original site of all metaphors.

Like Athena's – whose birth through her father's ear serves one main function, says Loraux: to relate the origin without having to go through women (13) – the subject of *Dedans* imagines herself as a caterpillar moving along the father's body and then along his veins:

> J'aurais voulu être née de toi, avoir vécu longtemps sinueuse dans tes veines au creux du genou, bercée dans ton sang, lovée dans une membrane transparente, moïse au nil rouge. La fille du pharaon le regarde glisser entre les roseaux, et c'est Moïse qui décide d'approcher la rive où l'attend la femme vêtue de blanc. C'est moi moïse en ton sang mais je ne veux pas aborder. (*Dedans* 94–5)

If I'd have my way I would have been born out of you, I would
have lived for a long time creeping through your veins in the
hollow of your knees, rocked by your blood, coiled in a transparent membrane, Moses in the red sea. The pharaoh's daughter
watches him slip between the reeds, and it is Moses who decides
to approach the shore where the woman wearing white awaits
him. I am the Moses in your blood but I do not wish to reach the
shore. (*Inside* 62)

As Monique Schneider reminds us too, the discovery of Moïse
floating on the river is also a myth which eliminates from the origin
all needs for intimacy with a woman (Schneider 76). In the same
way the heroine makes her mother disappear from the story in
violent capital letters: PARCE QUE JE LA HAIS, MA MÈRE N'EST
PLUS ["BECAUSE I HATE HER, MY MOTHER IS NO MORE"]
(*Inside* 65). This necessity to eliminate the mother stems from a
principle which needs to be described and understood within the
phallic reality principle:

Le poète sait.... S'il ne devient héros et créateur de langue pour
les autres hommes, soit prêtre, soit père, il se condamne à
l'impuissance de l'identification maternelle dans la jouissance
féminine. L'enjeu de l'écrit est là. (Lemoine-Luccioni 139)

The poet knows.... If he does not become a hero and a creator of
language for the other men, or a priest, or a father, he condemns
himself to the impotency/ powerlessness of maternal identification in feminine *jouissance*. Such are the stakes of writing.

When Hélène writes *Dedans*, she is aiming at being a poet, a neutral
if not a male offspring to her father. Numerous occasions in *Dedans*
show this neutralization, an androgyny represented both in the
relationship of the heroine with her brother (as same) and her
identification with the imaginary father, an identification which
happens before sexual difference is "realized." The latter will be
represented later in her writings through a desire to speak as a
subject in a female body. The premise shown (if not consciously
"expressed") in her *oeuvre* is that a *symbolic for women* – the expression *écriture féminine* has been so deformed and overused that a
new way of approaching the question needs to be invented – has to
imitate if not "branch out" from what is usually considered the

son's identification to the Father; in the same way, the French Women's Movement stemmed out of the sons' rebellion against the Father and their claim of their share of *jouissance*. "The Father" is of course a metaphoric position to be understood within the reality principle where both daughters and sons have to go through the "recognition of the Father" as Ego Ideal to enter the Symbolic.[5]

In 1969, when Cixous comes into writing (and its institutions), she has to do so (unconsciously and later knowingly) from/within the Father and his Law: she will however position herself in her first book not as a dutiful daughter (as Simone de Beauvoir had) but as a seductive and loving one. This "positioning" is to be understood as a Symbolic structuring which may also be appropriated by poets in male bodies – an identification with the daughter's position towards the Father can be read in Mallarmé, for instance.[6] Without exploring further a question which would need a thorough exposé of the work and function of writing within the phallic reality principle, let's posit here that *Dedans* allows Hélène to become "Cixous" and therefore to occupy the Father's place, to introject the Name-of-the-Father and make it her own. We will see how this process is represented in her poetic novel.

L'empreinte du corps de mon père dans mon âme[7]

Hier le temps, le monde, l'Histoire, la vie, toutes les sciences étaient dans la tête de mon père, et j'étais dans ses mains, et je n'avais besoin de rien. Je n'avais rien à faire que grandir. Je ne possédais rien que mon enfance. (*Dedans* 27)

Yesterday time, world, History, life, all forms of knowledge were in my father's head, and I was in his hands, and there was nothing I needed. The only thing I had to do was grow up. The only thing I owned was my childhood. (*Inside* 17)

Peut-être aussi que le vide laissé par mon père s'était empli de sens dès la nouvelle sue? Peut-être que je crois à tort avoir choisi, et que c'est l'empreinte du corps de mon père dans mon âme qui a moulé mon projet? Peut-être que les mots ont seulement suivi

la courbe silencieuse que la voix de mon père avait gravé en
moi? (*Dedans* 16-17)

Was it, perhaps, too, that the void left by my father had taken
on meaning once the news known? Could it be perhaps
that I'm wrong to think I have chosen, and that it's my
father's body imprinted in my soul that has shaped my plan?
Could it be perhaps that the words have only followed the
silent curve which my father's voice had engraved in me? (*Inside*
23)

Scanty fragments of childhood, imagined episodes of blessful car-
esses, declarations of love will function as the starting point for a
real work of reconstruction. The subject-in-process begins her quest
for her Self with actual memories of her real, concrete father which
she interweaves with inventions of encounters with what she calls
her "secret father" – if he is secret, it is because he is made of
words. The secret father is the one who speaks to her, even after
the real father's death, and keeps her alive. It is this father who is
continually lost and regained, coming back as a ghost (*revenant*)
only to disappear again: "Mon enfance est morte, mes deux pères
sont morts. . . . Je ne dirai à personne que mon père n'est pas mort.
C'est une de ces vérités pour lesquelles je n'ai pas encore de mots"
(38). ["My childhood is dead, my two fathers are dead. . . . I won't
tell anyone my father isn't dead. It's one of those truths for which I
don't yet have words"] (*Inside* 23). Once the real father has dis-
appeared, it is this secret father who will stay within the daughter
and acquire the status of being the site of knowledge. It is a
difficult process based on the full realization of the (first real)
father's death. For the transformation of the father into a sublime
figure, his death has to be put into words, objectified, so that the
loss of his body may be mourned and his daughter born again into
the field of desire.

   Like an exorcism which works as a regression back to the father's
own *conception* – and the theme of the father's conception works as
metaphor for his objectification – the "little girl"[8] will first cuddle
in her father's place in bed near "his wife," re-enact his *sortie*
from his mother's body,[9] ask the latter what she remembers of
her pregnancy, and finally regress back one more generation to
become her father's mother and father and speak with their
voices. Through the symbolisation of the two preceding genera-

tions, the subject is creating lineage. But before becoming a clear structure which would also figure the subject's place in the History of the Jewish people,[10] the "I" will lose its particular referent, become blurred: the ancestors start speaking with one single voice and so loudly that the subject is deafened by their screams:

> résister aux cent voix de la mémoire qui se démènent dans la corne de bélier et beuglent et lacèrent ma peau vibrante...la chambre s'incurve et se met à tourner sous la voix de tous mes pères...le gouffre où souffle la voix pour dégorger tout mon sang en fuite vers le passé....(*Dedans* 119)

> resisting the hundred voices of memory that are thrashing about in the ram's horn, bellowing and lacerating my pulsing flesh...the room curves inward and starts to reel under the voices of my fathers...the abyss where the voices are blowing to disgorge all my blood escaping toward the past...(*Inside* 77-78)

What happens is that the enunciator has to lend her own body to the Dead so that they may give a symbolic birth to her father and then to her through the telling of their suffering. The process is a painful exorcism because it is necessary to expulse the undying father from within her body. It aims at creating a representation of the past, a burdened and terrible past which tends to pull the subject backward "within a heavy space which has no limits to contain me" (*Dedans* 119; 78). She has to submit as "ear of the last generation"(*Dedans* 120; 78), only so that she may be named "child of our child" (*Dedans* 120; 78) and witness the birth of her father and *his* father and herself (*Dedans* 121; 79). After genealogy becomes written as a syntactic line, something fundamental is *realized*: "the only incontestable difference is not that of sex or age or strength, but that of the living and the dead; the former have all the power, which they don't always know how to use, the others have only knowledge without power" (*Dedans* 121; 79).

The process of regression has worked in a very specific way: the subject-daughter has had to speak with her ancestors' voice and become a collective enunciating subject so that she could "bear her father" as a word, give "him" birth symbolically as a character in her story. Consequently, the subject is separated from the secret image of the haunting ghost. Writing the story of the father (as other) is only possible after the realization that "he is my grandmother's child and he is dead." Through this tearing-apart, father and daughter become two positionings in langage and two separate points on a temporal line and, ultimately, two elements in two irreconciliable paradigms: that of the dead and that of the living. However, what makes the reading of Cixous' text difficult is the fact that she is telling us simultaneously about the father (therefore already separate) and about the moment of realization that such a separation is necessary, even if never fully accomplished. The different status and natures of the father figure are not chronologically organized (they could not be) but written through free associations, memories and inventions, dialogues and appeals leading to one another. What seems in a simple way to function as a distanciation through narrativity is in fact also a way to *restore the father* and avoid his disappearance: as point of arrival of multiple ancestral stories, the father acquires the status of link to the past. The imaginary father gives place to a symbolic father. Giving a form, a contour to the first by inventing his birth for and from herself (so that he may also and finally die), is a way to make him one particular individual in a lineage, an element in a structure – even if he has to remain on the wrong side of the wall of what she calls the ultimate difference.

On the level of Hélène's project, *Dedans* writes the father's body by primarily representing and realizing its frailty, making it fully dead[11] so that he may be given a proper sepulture and of course an altar. What the (writing of the) text does is then recall and control within a symbolic space the limitless dangerous imaginary father who, like the ogre of fairy tales, could keep engulfing the self of his daughter for ever, pretending not to be dead and therefore remaining inseparable from her (on the same side of the wall), pulling her towards a psychological death and an unbearable melancholia:

A travers mon père je vois tout.... [M]es yeux dans ses orbites voient le noir, mon coeur cesse de battre, ma peau de résister, et je sors et ma vie rejoint sa mort. (*Dedans* 75-76)

I can see everything through my father... [M]y eyes in his orbits see the blackness, my heart stops beating, my skin stops resisting, and I emerge and my life rejoins his death. (*Inside* 48-49)

Mais si nous étions un, il n'y aurait plus d'espace entre nous, où Dieu pourrait se glisser. Si j'étais lui, s'il était moi, s'il était moi, si j'étais lui, qui aurait pu nous interrompre? (*Dedans* 81-82)

But if we were one, there would be no more space between the two of us, for God to creep in. If I were he, if we were me, if we were me, if I were he, *who could have broken us apart*? (*Inside* 53)[12]

This desire to disappear, to keep dying with the father, is what is being described and worked through in *Dedans*. It can be thought of as an initiation in the feminine, a writing-cure which succeeds in making the father's death "real" and the daughter enter language equipped with her own desire to live.

Finding limits, that is an identity, comes after the symbolic burial of the father into a final dwelling. Once there, having been given his final form, he may be worshipped: such is the process of bereavement and of sublimation on which all writing is rooted. *Dedans* tells and shows the metamorphoses of the imaginary limitless father into an object (a "rotten body") which can be mourned and made sublime as a sensual textual body.

Hélène Cixous has drawn numerous and intricate knots with which she is still working, twenty-five years after her first book. Hélène's aims and desires in writing are complex and not all decipherable in the first stages of readings because she is *showing* and *telling* simultaneously, the scene of enunciation not being separated from what the subject of the enunced, the character, is going through. The work is done after all with and from the repetitive and anhistoric temporality of the Unconscious. The imaging of childhood memories and feelings and their relative rationalization and interpretation by the young adult are interwoven and inseparable. To simplify for the purpose of our own rationalization, let us say that:

1) at the level of the enunced (the signified, the story), *Dedans* is a) showing the father-daughter relationship (before,

during and after his death) but also, b) telling the story
of the daughter's coming to langage, to speech and writing;
and

2) at the level of the enunciation (the subject in the *here* and *now*
of writing, that is of encountering the signifiers, therefore a
desiring subject), what is said and made readable is that the
construction of the father as dead – here meaning "other" – to
the subject (point 1. a) *is* the condition for the coming to
writing (point 1. b).

Therefore *Dedans* (as thing) is the result of that process and (as
meaning) it is also and simultaneously the telling of that same
difficult process: that of creating words from a feeling of absence
and loss in the shape of a text. The enunciation provides the space
for this explanation of the unconscious drives at work in the *writing
of the coming to writing*.

Dedans, to be simultaneously read as a word and seen as a text-
thing, is therefore the symbolic tomb for the father. As the necessary
ritual of burial, an exorcism which brings death into discourse, it in
fact functions like the writing of History for a people, as Michel de
Certeau has shown in *L'Ecriture de l'Histoire*.[13] He summarizes this
idea by saying, *"L'écriture construit un «tombeau» pour le mort"*
["writing builds a tomb for the dead"] (119); writing, when taken
as a passage into symbolisation, is what allows the subject "to
situate [her]self by giving [her]self a past through and by langage.
It therefore opens a proper space for the present," says de Certeau.
Because "by creating a place for the dead, one is determining
negatively what remains *to be done*." And consequently burying
the dead through narrativity becomes "a means to provide a
space for the living." Hélène Cixous's first text is indeed the found-
ing ritual of her personal history. The challenge that the poet has
taken up to continue to exist in spite of and from the loss will stem
from the discovery that one can rebuild the lost body with words.
The nostalgic subject chooses not to die but to live through and by
the illusion of the letter, a letter actually drawn on the father's body,
as we shall see. In becoming the symbolic father, the paternal figure
has acceded to a position, has been made into a site on which an
altar will be built: the God to be worshipped will be one who knows
langage and the *real* meaning of words.

Cette tombe est une source. Cette pierre écoute et répond[14]

Mon père qui pourrit n'est pas dans l'appartement de granit, il est là où il est. J'ai de la peine pour la vieille bête [sa mère] qui gronde le cadavre par habitude. Je lui dis:
– Il n'est pas mort *ton fils*, pourquoi gronder un tas pourri, ton fils est dans toi, si tu ne le sens pas, demande à ton ventre, il doit le sentir, lui, la chair est moins bête que l'esprit, elle n'oublie pas. Dans l'appartement, il y a une poupée en métamorphose, c'est pas mon père, c'est pas ton fils. (*Dedans* 87-88)

Combien de millions de millions de particules étais-tu, mon amour? Celles qui entendaient sont-elles vives encore? J'ai quelque chose à te dire avant que n'explosent les derniers centres, patiente un instant, je t'en prie, j'attends qu'ils nous laissent seuls, attends, je t'en supplie, ne t'éloigne pas en cet instant, forme de mon père, oreille soeur de ma bouche, si tu as tenu jusqu'ici, patiente, mon amour, tu as toute ta mort devant toi, attends, attends-moi, si peu. (88-89)

My father who's rotting is not in that granite apartment, he is where he is. I feel sorry for the old beast [his mother] scolding the corpse out of habit. I tell her: / -*Your son* is not dead, why are you scolding a rotting pile, your son is in you, if you don't feel him, ask your womb, *it* must feel him, the body is not as big a fool as the mind, it doesn't forget. Inside that apartment, there's a doll in the process of metamorphosis, it's not my father, it's not your son.[15]

How many millions of particles were you, my love? Are the ones that could hear still alive? I have something to tell you before the last centers explode, just wait a moment please, I'm waiting for them to leave us alone, wait, I beg you, don't go away at this very moment, form of my father, sister ear to my mouth, if you have held out this far, be patient, my love, you have all your death before you, wait, wait for me, just a little longer. (*Inside* 57-58).

Attends-moi, entends-moi . . . The beauty and tenderness of the words spoken to the father, the appeal to his love and also to his knowledge are the most moving passages in *Dedans*. They are essential ones: because the father died before giving the whole secret of langage, he will have, in and through *Dedans*, to be made into a (still secret) interlocutor who will play as her mentor and initiate her into langage – it is after all through langage that she will become a *newly born woman*. The *venue à l'écriture* will then happen as an appropriation by the daughter of the constructed "father's place," his (new) imagined position as master of language, as enunciator of the first and all signifiers.

[Mon père] s'était tu, sans me donner d'explications, et il se reposait en silence, allongé, immobile sur le lit. Alors je le convoquai en secret, et quand il apparut, dans son costume clair, j'eus le sentiment poignant que je trahissais celui qui se reposait en silence sur le lit.

Mon père secret et moi, nous eûmes pourtant un dialogue heureux, mais nous chuchotions pour ne pas aller contre la nécessité du réel. Je tendais l'oreille, je n'arrivais pas à comprendre le sens des mots; ils étaient tous nouveaux. . . . Tout ce que je pus saisir du murmure c'était les sons les plus caressants que j'aie jamais entendus, et qui insufflaient à mon corps un feu tel que je le pris pour cette joie qui permet aux êtres humains de voler. Les mots de mon père étaient donc faits avec le vent qui transporte et dont je ne connaissais pas le nom? Je m'élançai. (*Dedans* 31)

[My father] had lapsed into silence, without giving me any explanation, and he lay quietly resting, motionless on the bed. So I summoned him in secret, and when he appeared in his light-colored suit, I had the agonizing feeling that I was betraying the man who lay silently on the bed.

My secret father and I had a good talk however, though we whispered in order not to contradict the need of what was real. I strained to hear him, I couldn't grasp the meaning of his words; they were all new. . . . All I could make of his murmurings were the most loving sounds I'd ever heard, which breathed such fire into my body that I took it for that joy which allows human beings to fly. Could it be that my father's words were made of the wind that carries us away, the wind whose name I did not know? I took off. (*Inside* 19)

The father's now absent voice is remembered as producing caressing sounds, making the ear the privileged organ in the whole story: "Le bonheur me pénétrait par l'oreille" ["I'd be penetrated by happiness through my ear"] (94). The father used to name the world, give her that world and his words – words which needed to be tasted by the ear, rolled around on all sides like new strange objects tamed and adopted, slowly. Her father's words were body words, given as sensual presents.[16] They remain as her treasure and because they were so attached to the father's voice, look and touch, speaking them will be like bringing him back to life: he is in the words just like Marcel's Combray is in the madeleine. The words bring back the father's caress.

If the father's death was a threat for the daughter that she will never be able to know all of the words, it is by making him into a reader[17] and interestingly into a speaker that nobody would listen to[18], a lonely "I" therefore, that she will be able to create him as an Ego Ideal and identify with him. The daughter engenders a new ideal father ["il ressemblait à Dieu"] (116),[19] mother himself to all the other fathers she will give herself. How is this done? The daughter has first to appropriate the father as her own and dismiss all other "intrepretations," figurations of who he *was*. She has to prove that she is the only one who really knows him and that he was the only one who really knew her.

C'était lui? Il était immobile, je courais, je ne l'approchai pas, je poursuivis, il était devant moi. Peut-être était-il dans mes yeux, ou peut-être n'étais-je qu'une image qu'il avait laissé traîner derrière lui, et j'étais accrochée à lui par un regard? (*Dedans* 34)

Was it he? He was motionless, I was running, I couldn't get close to him, I pressed on, he was in front of me. Was he perhaps in my eyes, or was I perhaps but an image he'd let trail behind him, and I was attached to him by a look? (*Inside* 31)

The Ego Ideal, who has looked at and recognized the subject as One (in the Lacanian mirror-stage) is imagined as having witnessed the (lost) plenitude of the subject and therefore as being "itself" within this plenitude and, consequently, as knowing truth, the true words to speak the real Self. *Dedans* starts as the daughter's demand to her father (dead and now idealizable) to bring her back *within*, where she used to be "with him," that is true to her Self: "J'oubliais les limites, j'oubliai le début, je confondis la fin avec la courbe de ses bras, je croyais être au centre inaltérable" (33). ["I forgot the limits, I forgot the beginning, I mixed up the end with the curve of his arms, thinking I was in the inalterable center"] (*Inside* 21). He would achieve this lost plenitude by looking at her once more, by answering her look and her call beyond death:

> Il s'allongeait et s'étalait, il envahissait l'horizon et cependant je ne l'approchai pas. Peu à peu je cessais de vouloir l'approcher, il était devenu trop grand. Je le reconnaissais, je le contemplais, mais.
>
> Je me mis à l'appeler, j'essayais tous les noms: «Toi! hé là!» criai-je... «L'homme! oh là! l'homme.»
>
> – Papa! je pleurai, je pleurai.
>
> – Dieu! , Dieu! hurlai-je en jetant le mot comme une pierre dans les eaux noires où il ricocha, Dieu, dieu, dieu, di.
>
> Alors il s'arrêta et se retourna, et je le vis: la face de Dieu était une main. (*Dedans* 34-35)

> He was growing taller and spreading out over everything, he was invading the horizon and still I was getting no closer to him. Little by little I stopped wanting to reach him, he had become too big. I recognized him, I contemplated him, but. / I began to call him, trying every name: "You! hey there! you!" I cried;... "Man! Over here! Man." / "Papa!" I wept, I wept. / "God! God!" I shouted, hurling the word like a stone into the black waters where it ricocheted, God, god, god, go... / Then he stopped and turned around, and I saw him: the face of God was a hand.[20] (*Inside* 21)

She wants to find the name which will support her claim that he is still her father, make him seen and seeable, One, whole, so that he may do so with her. In this nightmarish scene, the desired look is barred by the hand of God, forbidden: the subject is left alone with the dead father striken by fate: "He wasn't holding me anymore ....No one here knew" (36; 22). Once the father disappears as Ego Ideal, the subject remains "in the centre of the gaping world full of disorder and chaos" (36; 22), because nobody "knows" her. The trick will then to make the father figure pass from *Dieu* to *Di*, that is to say from a godlike omnipotent Ego Ideal/Superego, to a piece of the name of God which says the spoken word (*dit*), but which is also the premise of an injunction, an address and an appeal for an answer: "*Dis!*"

Near the end of the book, the character of *Dedans* has to state her identity and her reason for *being here* to an emigration officer. This leads to the (fragmented) retelling of a primary scene of mutual recognition, making her identity associated a posteriori if not born from a look and a specific sign on her father's body:

'Quand êtes-vous née? Où êtes-vous née? Quel est le motif de votre visite?....' Je suis née il y a deux cents ans en Westpha-lie...il y a six cents ans en Palestine...et depuis, une ou deux fois ici et là.... (Je me suis sauvée, j'avais peur de mourir; ou de naître; j'ai pensé: là-bas il n'y a plus rien ni personne, on peut arriver; on peut trouver; moi? non pas moi, mais qui sait, une trace.) Jamais; une fois, très jeune, j'ai cru; je voulais, j'ai voulu; deux fois, avec lui; il était là, je l'ai reconnu, il avait tous les signes. Une étoile brillait entre ses seins. Un rire luisait entre ces cils..... (*Dedans* 149-150)

"When were you born? Where were you born? What is the reason for your visit?..." I was born a hundred years ago in Westphalia...six hundred years ago in Palestine...and since then, once or twice here and there;...(I ran away, I was afraid of dying; or of being born; I thought: over there there's no longer anything nor anyone, you can reach it; you can find it; me? no not me, but who knows, a trace.) Never; once, when I was very young, I believed; I wished, I wanted; twice, with him; he was there, I recognized him, he bore all the signs. A star shone between his breasts. Laughter gleamed through his lashes...(*Inside* 97)

The look ("rire entre les cils") comes next to another mark of distinction, that one inscribed on the very surface of the father's body: "Une étoile brillait entre ses seins." The fragile Self who cannot answer the officer remembers a time and place where she has felt One, identical to herself. "[M]oi? non pas moi, mais qui sait, une trace": the subject is a trace and it is erasable. However she remembers having existed as "believing" and "wanting" when she had been "with him": "une fois, très jeune, j'ai cru; je voulais, j'ai voulu: deux fois, avec lui." It is the very recognition of "all the signs" which had made her believe in "me," in a stable image of herself. The father is here not an image but the vehicle of a "pass-mark" (not yet a pass-word) traced on his body: a star shining between his breasts, a smile, a look adressed to her, a pleasure of which she is the source, which makes her feel more than a mere trace. As symbol of all these signs, the "star" in fact *marks the father*, makes him unique and *One*; because it is invested by affect ("brillait," "luisait"), the *star-gaze* makes the "seeing subject" recognize and identify with its Oneness. In the center of the father's body, the mark "read" only by the daughter is *a sign for the subject* and constitutes her as identifiable to the very unicity of the star: that is to say, the two conjugated signs (look and birthmark) are "readable" in so far as they are always-already *signs for the (loved) daughter* and constitute her as "whole," adressed as One by those signs. This passage illustrates what Lacan has called the "symbolic identification," that is the identification of the subject to a signifier or rather to a simple "mark," a minimal trace, which he will name the *trait unaire* after Freud (*Einziger Zug*, the single stroke). It plays in the story of the little girl of *Dedans* at being the one feature which transforms the atemporal and possibly overbearing ("envahissant") Ideal Ego into the *support*[21] of the signifier: the star is the metonymy of the whole body and the first trace of a possible first word never pronounced (which Lacan calls the primary signifier). The star had in fact already appeared once and very early in the story to illustrate the idea that the girl was "the first," that is "the one and only," to have seen this special feature of her father's body – which consequently made the father hers only, known and owned by her only:

> JE L'AI CONNU, mieux que sa propre mère, mieux que sa femme. Je ne dirai à personne que c'est moi qui l'ai vue la première, la petite tache en forme d'étoile que les cousines ont su découvrir sur son ventre. (*Dedans* 43)

> I KNEW HIM, better than his own mother, better than his wife, I won't tell anyone that I was the first to see it, the little spot on his

belly in the shape of a star which my girl cousins thought they had discovered. (*Inside* 27)

This star which marks the body of the (Jewish) father is therefore a trace both of uniqueness and unicity with which the daughter acquires a stable identity, still linked to the father's gaze however, the loss of which will be "compensated" by imagining him addressing her with words, looking at her as co-enunciator, as we shall see.

Even if very different paternal figures are intermingled in the story, the final configuration of the father will appear no longer as a form perceivable as a whole (a looming faceless image) but as the carrier of a *God-written sign*. The star drawn on the flesh is not only a *birthmark* for the father but also for the subject reader: it is the first trace of the first letter of the destiny of the subject who has identified with it – her love objects will have to be carriers/wearers of this *trait unaire* so that she can identify with them as knowing of her lost plenitude and thus desire their desires: "car mon amour et mon père sont un" (*Dedans* 161).

L'Etoile d'Oran

We will transgress a little away from the reading of *Dedans*, to note, even in passing, that when Hélène wants to tell the story of her *venue au théâtre*, her father's star seems to reappear as symbol of Oneness and serve directly as a metonymy for "universality" and "humanity" and as a symbol for their mystery:

J'ai besoin du ciel pour que le théâtre soit. Et que la scène terrestre se mire dans la scène céleste. Nuages, ciel, soleil du coeur humain.

Ce n'est pas seulement une métaphore. C'est aussi une définition: le théâtre est l'espace où l'être humain s'éprouve comme un atome du cosmos, comme une minute du Temps, comme une question dans le multimillénaire dialogue des hommes avec les Dieux, comme un des milliards de «pourquoi» lancés dans le mystère de la question parlante en direction du Mystère sans forme, de la Cause sans corps.

Il y a les étoiles.

Les étoiles célestes et les étoiles terrestres. L'homme, dans

l'Indiade, n'est pas sans les étoiles. Sans la conscience de la
hauteur, de l'éloignement, de la lumière et de la nuit, de l'incompréhensible. Voyant les étoiles et vu par les étoiles, il prend la
mesure de sa petitesse et de sa grandeur, de l'immensité de ses
possibilités et de ses impossibilités. Il veut les étoiles.... ("Ecrits
sur le théâtre" 247-48)

I need the sky for the theatre to be. I need the terrestrial scene
to be mirrored in the celestial scene. Clouds, sky, sun of the
human heart.

It is not only a metaphor. It is also a definition: theatre is the
space where the human being can experience her-himself as an
atom of the cosmos, as a minute of Time, as a question in the age-
old dialogue between men and the Gods, as one of the billions of
"why" sent out in the mystery of the speaking question directed
to the formless Mystery, the bodiless Cause.

There are the stars.

Celestial stars and terrestrial stars. Man, in *l'Indiade*, cannot be
without the stars. Without an awareness of height, distance, light
and night, of the incomprehensible. As he sees the stars and is
seen by the stars, he gets the measure of his smallness, of his
greatness, of the vastness of what is possible, of what is impossible to him. He wants the stars.

Isn't "this Cause without a body" a spiritual and mysterious Cause
for everything which is not anchored in matter? Something divine,
source and origin for the Whole which can be seen but which also
sees "Man"? What is it? *The stars*, answers Hélène. *Man wants the
stars*. Man is a *star gazer*. Indeed.

Our intuition that the star on the father's belly functions as a *trait
unaire* for the subject of writing born in *Dedans* (and maybe the *degree
0* for Hélène as writer), seems to receive more grounding when one
examines the way the poet's aesthetics and ethics privilege figures
of "Holy men," saints who seem to represent "wholeness," plenitude and certainly work as idealized figures. This idea of "wholeness" recurs in the universal categories that Hélène uses to speak of
her art. In "Ecrits sur le théâtre," for instance, we find
numerous capitalized words: the Mystery, the Enigma, the Tomb
(147-48) and also the She-Bear, *L'Ourse* – which in French is also *La
Grande Ourse*, a stellar constellation. The She-Bear is strong and
motherly and equivalent to a "black star." It also seems to

encompass the whole world, its inhabitants together with their desire for Paradise:

> Une force de vie, une force de mort, un être enchaîné, déchaîné. Une étoile noire qui arpente la terre. De l'amour. Un géant poilu dans lequel habite une petite fée. Notre mystère.... Ah! Comme nous aimons l'innocence de la créature vivante, comme nous regrettons le Paradis, et comme, en caressant l'Ourse, nous grattons à la porte de Dieu. ("Ecrits sur le théâtre" 249)

> A life force, a death force, a being who has been chained up and unleashed. A black star which paces up and down the earth. Love. A hairy giant inside whom lives a small fairy. Our mystery .... Oh how much we love the innocence of the living creature, how much we regret Paradise, and how, when caressing the She-Bear, it is at God's gate that we scratch.

In *Dedans*, isn't Hélène that small fairy inhabiting the She-Bear, a "black star" bearer of the mystery of desire, the enigma of humanity who has lost its Paradise, its Plenitude? Isn't the father then the real She-Bear and the primal and primary star bearer? Don't we all feel the absence and loss of our father's bodies, of tender *male mothers*? Are tenderness and strength what both daughters and sons long for? Hélène is giving us back the She-Bear and the star. She asks:

> Et le montreur de l'Ourse? C'est l'Oedipe transfiguré en le fils-père, l'amant de l'animale. Il tient enchaînée la part sauvage et douce de lui-même, Mais elle lui échappe. Elle le tient enchaîné par un charme sans nom. Et il montre ce qu'il cache. L'amour de la Bête. Nous n'avons pas fini de nous raconter les secrets de la Belle et de la Bête. ("Ecrits sur le théâtre" 250)

> And the She-bear leader? It is Oedipus transfigured into the father-son, the animal's lover. He keeps that wild and soft part of himself chained up. But it escapes from him. It keeps him bound by a nameless spell. And then he has to show what he is hiding. The love of the Beast. We will go on forever telling the secrets of the Beauty and the Beast.

Dedans is indeed the story of Beauty and the Beast, of a little sexless fairy who inhabits a hairy giant. She and her father become One, they are born together from the star of his belly, from the gaze they exchange. Her writing seems to want to come back to the lost Star, metaphor for the lost Paradise of her father's arms.

If the star was and still is something else than what it is (being inscribed on the father's body and a sign for and of his daughter), it plays at being the first hieroglyph which is not quite a signifier (the latter getting its value from negativity and difference). There is however a second hieroglyph in Hélène's own story of writing: ORAN, the capital of the fatherland:

> I lost myself often within the city of my birth. It was a veiled woman. It was a signifier. It was ORAN.... The first of my treasures was the name of my native city which was Oran. It was my first lesson. I had heard the name Oran and through Oran I discovered the secret of language.... Then I lost Oran. Then I discovered it, white, gold, and dust for eternity in my memory and I never went back. In order to keep it. It became my writing. Like my father. It became a magic door opening onto the other world. ("The Scene of the Unconscious" 2)

"[T]he city of my birth.... was a signifier. It became my writing. Like my father." ORAN has become invested by the writer as the very locus where the Imaginary and the Symbolic meet, where they form a knot; for it is simultaneously the secret pass word to the lost being (ORAN comes before JE) and the city of the birth of the body, the form around the treasure of the seed ("the mystery of fruit") ("The Scene of the Unconscious" 2), the mystery also of the star as seed of Hélène's identity: *I am (in) the star which is (on) the father's body which is (in) Oran....*

ORAN is then reified, imagined as a container for all words, an emblem for the richness of language, the birth place of all meta-phors. Hélène says she writes from and within this *word-thing*: it is thought as a materiality which can be sculpted, deformed (*Or-An*: Golden Year; *Hors-En*: Outside-in) ("The Scene of the Uncon-scious" 2). Its deformation and reformation represent a wishful thinking, a dream: that language can be made into something; a thing which, in its turn, can be made to represent the real of the subject, can be shaped into a figure, a story. ORAN will only instaure the play of difference when placed next to the "star." But by being secondary to the star (*the binary signifier*), it erases it, represses it into the Unconscious (which occurs and gets structured

from this primary secret signifier, says Lacan): the subject's destiny
is then born from this primal minimal chain, the first term of which
remains secret. ORAN is indeed the birthplace of Hélène as desiring subject. If the poet knows so, it is because she had had to
undergo a forced exile, an uprooting; for

> L'Exil ouvre le paradoxe de l'origine au singulier; puisqu'une
> origine il faut bien s'en constituer une pour pouvoir en faire le
> deuil, afin d'autrement habiter le nom et le corps que collé à la
> glue identificatoire des romances culturalistes.... L'exil peut dire
> ce trajet qui amène à une réouverture et une écriture de la
> métaphore paternelle et des arcanes identitaires pour en écrire
> une nouvelle sublimation. (Douville 88, 90)

> Exile opens onto the paradox of a a singular origin; since an
> origin has to be constituted to allow for its loss and mourning, so
> that the name and the body can be inhabited in a different way
> than stuck to the glue of identification of culturalist romances
> .... Exile allows this trajectory to be told, a trajectory which leads
> to a reopening and a writing of the paternal metaphor and of the
> mystery of identity so that a new sublimation can be written.

In Hélène's imaginary, the (guiding) star comes back with different names but always functions as a symbol for truth, wish,
origin, gaze, Oneness...In the same way, ORAN is the symbolic
birthplace, because it plays as the second term which has engaged
the difference which allows the star to be: the centre of ORAN will
then always be marked by an invisible star which had to be erased,
the same way as the father's body had to be buried so that Hélène
could enter the Symbolic.

Etre Dedans: Enters the other

Once *within*, inside the father's star, inside the word ORAN, she is
inside the skin and bones of langage, inside the lost voice of a frail
young man who has become the king of a story, a prince idealized
as a secret angel,[22] a model for all her others, all the sacrificial
lambs of her lyrical poetry and literature. The process was a difficult one and the ambivalence of the grammatical subject in *Dedans*
as to its referent(s) shows this very painful but necessary tearing

apart of the "I" from the "Him" – this ambivalence remains in
Hélène's ethics where the other is always given precedence on the
"I." The father's body has had to disappear to become the background, the page on which a star was first traced by God, then read
by the daughter. The star as signifier of Oneness having allowed
identity, the subject may then call herself "Je" and later, as we
know, "juifemme" – the star acquiring here its full meaning and
force of destiny. The poet's initial loss once represented as the
Oneness of the star is the secret meaning of the "I." Mourning is
accomplished when the real father is finally buried under the name
on the tombstone so that he may become alive again:

> Mets ta main sur ta mort, ô humain, distingue entre l'essentiel
> et l'insignifiant, et à partir de là, tu sauras dans quelle
> direction est la vie. Car de cette tombe où git quelqu'un qui fut
> joyeux, n'émane que de la pensée de vie. . . ("Ecrits sur le
> théâtre" 251)

> Put your hand on your death, oh human, distinguish between
> what is essential and what is insignificant, once this is done, you
> will know in which direction life is. For, from this tomb where
> someone who was joyful lies, only lifeful thoughts emanate. . .

The altar is built on the tomb. The rite will be one of love and the
prayers spoken to Him who has become the first other among all
others: the loved father who can now be addressed as "You." Not a
"secret" father any longer, but a worshipped partner. A sublime
body of words, of tender names, can now fill the emptiness of the
tomb. Can the body of writing as a whole then acquire the status of
a melancholic *ersatz* to the body of the young father?

> Forgive me for having given you a name to call you towards me.
> Forget it, I beg you. . . .
>   I say to you: come. Come without a name between us. There
> will be no place for a name when you are near me. (*Ou l'art de
> l'innocence* 309)[23]

The name is full of nostalgia because it plays the role of a transi-
tional object – that is an object which takes the place (*tient-lieu*),
symbolizes the site of the lost presence; it allows sublimation,
metaphorization but will always be felt as a simulacrum. The
empty grave under the tombstone is the space for the writing of

his name and ultimately for the book/word *Dedans*, a book of love to be given, addressed. For,

> [i]l ne suffit pas en effet de dire de la sublimation qu'elle *idéalise* son objet. L'objet sublimé est proprement dénaturé, du seul fait que sa charge de haine est positivée. . . . La perte de l'objet est métamorphosée en don du moi, la haine transmuée en serment d'amour, si tant est que l'amour consiste bien, comme le dit Lacan, à donner ce que l'on n'a pas. (Pécaut 164)

> [i]t is not enough to say of sublimation that it idealizes its object. The nature of the sublimated object is actually changed only because its charge of hatred is made positive. . . . The loss of the object is metamorphosed into a gift of the self, hatred transmuted into vows of love, if indeed love consists, as Lacan tells us, in giving what one does not have.

The sublimation of the loss which is *Dedans* is the condition for the "creation" of alterity within, and therefore for the coming to generosity and love, two recurring features in Hélène's ethics. It is through the introduction of intersubjectivity in the field of the powerful Other, that love and writing have happened.[24] The father, after being buried and resuscitated as Ego Ideal – lost so that he may be restored and worshipped, made a bearer of the birthmark of his daughter – finally accedes to a more permanent position: that of a "companion" in language, a partner in writing. He then enters the daughter's Self, becomes the focal point and the condition of her desire to write.

When her father is worshipped as the bearer of the star and site of knowledge, he still does not speak to her (he remains as the all desirable Other). It is only by becoming a "You," a partner in the scene of enunciation, to whom all messages may be finally addressed, that the father will be restored and kept *within* the daughter, herself within language. Because speech told and heard by the "reader" – a position into which the secret father ultimately steps, becoming therefore universal – streams together the dispersed fragments of the childhood memories and of the suffering. These fragments are collected respectfully and safely by the imagined "listener" who, as other, is a position which has to be built into the telling for any telling to exist; it serves as *telos*, direction and aim, and enables the fragile, anguished enunciator to assume a discourse which is no longer a private delirium but which aims at communicating, even if it is that very story of anguish and loss. Such is the work of sublimation (or symbolization). The desire to "write oneself" is founded on the presupposition and construction of that "other" who will/would read. It consequently makes that otherness organize the chain of signifiers for "itself." By playing at "being the other" to whom she is speaking, by creating a "Tu" (the reader/the father), the subject will also and then be able to accept the "je" as her name, assume her place in the chains of signifiers and the Symbolic (next to the "Tu"). By this acceptance, she becomes a speaking subject, that is an "other" signified by language.

It is indeed only through an identification with the father as speaker, reader, proprietor and master of language that she will become a writer. Imagining a secret speaking father elevates the woman-in-becoming, makes her accede the sublime, away from death and the ineluctable separation. Her secret father will then keep the figure of *a speaking God*: simultaneously an idealized lover-mentor and an inhabitant of language, the all-powerful but benevolent guardian of the signifiers.

Cesser de mourir

Taking the father's place, becoming the father by writing, was paradoxically a way to be separated, to get rid of the inhabitant of her soul to make him into an other so that she can then preserve him and worship him as her center, her symbolic place of birth: the star, Oran, the father of *Dedans* were points on a quest for the writing of the Self. Not to be the dead man's daughter any longer: such was the first step towards sublimation, self-representation, even if the latter started by being done with images of decay and insignificance:

> Dans le filet de ma peau je me transformai sans cesse, ne laissant pas à mon âme le temps de retrouver ma forme humaine. Mieux valait être chien, ou lézard, que moi-même. Mieux valait être poussière, chat crevé, ou noyau de pêche, qu'être la fille du mort. (27)

Inside the web of my skin I went on transforming myself,
never allowing my soul the time to get back to my human
form. Better to be a dog, or a lizard, than myself. Better to be
dust, a dead cat, or a peach pit, than the daughter of the dead
man. (*Inside* 17)[25]

"[C]hien, ou lézard .... poussière, chat crevé, ou noyau de pêche":
better disguise myself with words, be somewhere else than here,
other than the name given to me: "the dead man's daughter." It is
that very process of being other through metaphorization which
had marked the premise to separatedness and sublimation. What
we witnessed with and all through *Dedans* is what Eugénie
Lemoine-Luccioni calls very appropriately: "L'enfantement de
l'auteur par la littérature" ["The author being given birth to by
literature"] (129). Hélène re-invented her birth as poet as that
moment when she discovered that the loss of the real father
could be made sublime and recuperated through language,
language becoming therefore the only salvation, the first and final
place for inscribing identity and existence: the rest is illusion. The
only truth then becomes the very desire of the poet to keep
imagining and writing in order to, one day, create the definitive
metaphor, engrave a definite "I" on a monument. *Dedans* tells of
that discovery of truth as desire.

In *Dedans*, the true story to be told is that of the painful
realization and metamorphoses the heroine had to undergo to
become that screaming voice who, at the end, manages to write
"merde merde merde à la mort" (208). This negation of death
shows how the writing of the book has lifted the denial of the
father's death, allowing the daughter to become the writer that
she is, master of the signifier. By constituting the father as a lost
object, that is by recovering her past self as now separate from the
father, the daughter has "realized" her own mortality and her own
desire. In that insult shouted at death, the overpowering death
drive which was at work in the character's wish to become her
father and disappear inside him, is metabolized into an affirmation
of the power of language: *merde merde merde*, if I keep speaking,
repeating, death will be pushed away – and it works literally
because as a written word DEATH is indeed being pushed along
the synctactic line and away from the *I*. Becoming other than the
dead man's daughter by putting him *inside* his tomb is indeed

the frightening but necessary challenge of mourning related in
Dedans.

Following the final violent scream against death, Hélène will end
her novel by "quoting" her "father's words," beautiful words
which engage her with her future writing. In doing so she becomes
her father's favorite interlocutor in an everending dialogue
with him:

> Viens, dit-il, allons en prison, nous deux ensemble, sans elle sans
> eux, moi tout seul je te ferai seule toi seule tu feras la nuit de tes
> lèvres sur mes yeux.... Si tu veux de moi je t'étreindrai et nous
> créerons de nouvelles histoires.... Tu seras en haut et en bas et
> je serai dedans. Dehors le mystère des choses s'assèchera, les
> générations reflueront morts sur mots sous le soleil, mais dedans
> nous aurons cessé de mourir. (*Dedans* 209)

> Come, says he, let's away to prison, we two alone, without her
> without them, alone I will make you alone, alone you will make
> the night with your lips on my eyes...If you will have me I will
> hold you in my arms and we shall create new tales....You will
> be up above and down below and I shall be inside. Ouside, the
> mystery of things will dry up, under the sun the generations will
> wash up worlds over words, but inside we shall have stopped
> dying. (*Inside* 236)[26]

The Sun as the father-star opens the book and closes it, announcing
the death of death. "[L]es générations reflueront *morts sur mots*
sous le soleil, mais *dedans nous aurons cessé de mourir*": to cease to
die, to extirpate oneself from death, from the overpowering body
of the imaginary father by covering that body with a tombstone
and the stone with the letters of his name: such is the ultimate
challenge of the writing of History and the alpha of all *écriture*,
daughters' and sons' alike.

1. *Dedans*, 81.
2. We develop this question in "L'Indiade ou l'Inde de *leurs* rêves," *Dalhousie French Studies*.
3. From the title of one of her seminars given at Paris VIII and the Collège de Philosophie, 1983–84.
4. "[R]efaire du corps puisqu'il y avait du corps perdu" ["Reconstruct something of the body since it was something of the body which was lost"] (Lemoine-Luccioni 134) .
5. A recognition based on the fact that the father is the one who gives his name to the child and above all that he "deprives" him/her of the mother: "father" and "mother" have to be understood as functions; See Lacan, Jacques, "Remarque sur le rapport de Daniel Lagache," 680–683; and also "Situation de la psychanalyse en 1956," 459–491, where Lacan reminds us that by murdering the primordial father in *Totem and Taboo*, Freud aims at maintaining the father as a signifier whose function "appears then unequivocally in the affirmation thus produced that the true father, the symbolic father is the dead father," 469: in our cultural unconscious, the Law will therefore refer to an idealized instance or, better still, to a pure signifier. Within the psycho-analytic paradigm, we will therefore aim at avoiding the confusion between structure and ideology; by the same token we will not take the phallus for its cultural and historical representations – an erect penis, detached from any body, for example. The phallus, as Lacan has shown us, is the desirable and the desiring and may also be imagined as a double knot: partly erection, partly aspiring hole – a hole without borders, limits; that is where the difficulty lies. . and where Lacan's topography was leading him to (as Marc-Leopold

Levy, a now prominent psychoanalyst and theoretician who attended
Lacan's seminars, declared in a private conversation).

6. See Lemoine-Luccioni, 138, and Lacan, "Lituraterre."
7. *Dedans*, 16.
8. "C'EST MON TOUR. JE ROULE DANS LE CREUX du lit tiède. Hier
c'était mon tour. Autrefois c'était le tour de mon père. Les draps ne
savent pas. On les lave et on les plie, ils ne gardent rien. Mon père
n'avait pas d'odeur, quand il vivait. Dans les draps monte l'odeur de
ma mère, de ses orteils jusqu'à ses bras. La tête est dehors, à plat.
Dedans il fait brun, et chaud, nous sommes seuls, le corps et moi"
(*Dedans* 63) ["IT'S MY TURN. I ROLL INTO THE HOLLOW of the
warm bed. Yesterday it was my turn. In the past, it was my father's.
The sheets don't know. They're washed and folded, retaining nothing.
When he was alive, my father had no smell. Inside the sheets the smell
of my mother rises, from her toes to her arms. Her head is outside,
lying flat. Inside it's dark, and warm, we're alone, her body and me"]
(*Inside* 40).
9. "Enfin la rage délivre une douleur féroce.... / A quatre pattes, ma
grand-mère rugit; tout le monde s'est sauvé sauf moi.... Nous sommes
seules. Alors je fais ce que je voulais faire, je me glisse doucement
derrière la bête qui glapit, et je m'aplatis comme un ver, mon petit
corps sinueux se faufile entre les quatre pattes rigides, et je repose sur
le dos, les yeux ouverts, je suis dans le caveau de mes pères, au centre
du malheur, là où soufflent le passé et l'esprit de ma race. / Je ne suis
pas née. Je suis bien. Encore" (*Dedans* 67–8) ["At last her fury delivers
a ferocious grief.... / Down on her four paws, my grandmother roars;
everyone has run away but me.... We are alone. So I do what I've been
wanting to do, I slide gently behind the yelping beast, and flatten
myself like a worm, my sinuous little body edging between the four
stiff paws, and I rest quietly, on my back, eyes open, I am in the vault
of my fathers, in the very centre of misfortune, there where the past
and the spirit of my race breathe. / I'm not born. I like it here. Still"]
(*Inside* 43–4).
10. Which will lead here to affirming her collective identity: "Je suis née il
y a deux cents ans en Westphalie et il y a trois cents ans en Espagne, il
y a six cents ans en Palestine, il y a cent ans en Afrique, et depuis, une
ou deux fois ici et là" (*Dedans* 149) ["I was born two hundred years ago
in Westphalia and three hundred years ago in Spain, six hundred years
agon Palestine, a hundred years ago in Africa, and since then, once or
twice here and there..."]. (*Inside* 97).
11. Sometimes brutally: "ET MON PÈRE POURRIT. . ." (26) ["AND MY
FATHER IS ROTTING"] (*Inside* 16).
12. The italics indicate a slight change from Barko's version: "who could
have come between us?," the non-interruption between father and
daughter being here a leit-motif.
13. As writes Michel de Certeau in *L'Ecriture de l'histoire*: "D'une part,
l'écriture joue le rôle d'un *rite d'enterrement*; elle exorcise la mort en
l'introduisant dans le discours. D'autre part, elle a une fonction *sym-*

bolisatrice; elle permet . . . de se situer en se donnant dans le langage un passé, et elle ouvre ainsi au présent un espace propre: «marquer» un passé, c'est faire une place au mort, mais aussi redistribuer l'espace des possibles, déterminer négativement ce qui est *à faire*, et par conséquent utiliser la narrativité qui enterre les morts comme moyen de fixer une place aux vivants" (118). ["On one hand, writing functions as a burial rite; it exorcises death while introducing it into discourse. On the other hand, writing has a symbolic function; it permits us to situate it while giving to it, through language, a past; and to open it, in this manner, to a present in its own space: "to mark" a past is to make a place for death, but also to redistribute the space of the possible, to antithetically determine what is *to be made*, and consequently, to use narrativity, which inters the dead as a means to fix a place for the living"] (Editors' translation).

14. "This tomb is a spring. This stone listens and answers" ("Ecrits sur le théâtre" 251).

15. I have replaced "the old beast" with "the old cow" because Brako's words sounded too much like an insult – which the French does not really – and above all because the word "beast" tends to have a positive value in Cixous; see *Dedans* (67) and *Inside* (47), and my later discussion on the "She-Bear."

16. "D'abord j'écoutais le bruit du mot nouveau que mon père prononçait; pendant plusieurs jours je le laissais mûrir dans l'air, sans le toucher. Nous nous habituions l'un à l'autre. Jamais je n'ai forcé un mot trop vite. J'attendais qu'il trouve lui-même sa place parmi les familiers" (*Dedans* 52) ["First, I'd listen to the sound of the new word my father pronounced; for several days I'd let it ripen in the air, not touching it. We would get accustomed to each other. Never would I force a word too quickly. I'd wait for it to find its place among the familiar ones"] (*Inside* 32).

17. He has left traces of his reading in books: "Quelqu'un a lu André Chénier. Debout au milieu de la chambre du lecteur mort, je crie à mon frère les lignes soulignées sur les pages jaunes" (50–1) ["Someone has read André Chénier. Standing in the middle of the room of the dead reader, I call out to my brother the underscored lines on the yellowed pages"] (*Inside* 31).

18. To her mother: "'-Pourquoi, dis-je, Heine est-il immortel, si mon père est mortel? -Ton père n'a rien écrit.» Elle ment, je sais qu'il a vécu et parlé, c'est elle qui n'écoutait pas" (50) ["'-Why, I ask, is Heine immortal, if my father is mortal? -Your father didn't write anything." She lies, I know he lived and spoke, it was she who didn't listen"] (*Inside* 31).

19. Let's recall what had been accomplished earlier in the text: "Je commençai par révoquer Dieu, dont l'inutilité n'était que trop manifeste, et je le remplaçai par mon père. Ensuite j'abolis la différence entre l'homme et la femme, qui me semblait être l'excuse de toutes les paresses" (19) ["I began by dismissing God, whose uselessness was only too apparent, and replaced him by my father. Then I abolished

the distinction between man and woman, which seemed to me to be an excuse for every kind of sloth"] (*Inside* 12).

20. The play on *Dieu* and *di* (say/said) is of course completely missed in English where *God...go* give another meaning altogether to the scene.

21. As in the French *support* which is at the same time medium and stand, a materiality carrying and anchoring an abstraction as in "la lettre est le support du signifiant."

22. Let's note that by being a metaphor for the entry into the Symbolic and a "sortie" out of the death drive and silence, the father remains a sexless body which is more an envelope of flesh and bones around a voice than an objectified and possibly seductive male body.

23. Translated by Mairéad Hanrahan with the approval of Hélène Cixous: *Writing Differences*, 115.

24. We will quote Pécaut again: "La sublimation permet d'introduire dans le champ de l'Autre une masse d'*intersubjectivité* qui se vit au travers d'une relation à deux, sans les inconvénients du chiffre deux. Dès lors que la mort est mise du côté de l'Autre...le sujet peut se ressourcer à loisir à un réel d'où toute hypothèque est levée. Tout en poursuivant sa quête infinie du père, comme un but irréprochable..., un but social qui ne soulève dès lors plus la moindre objection" (*La Matrice du mythe*, 165) ["Sublimation allows for the introduction in the field of the Other of a mass of *intersubjectivity* which is experienced through a relationship between two subjects, without the inconvenience of the figure 'two'. As long as death is placed on the side of the Other...the subject can leisurely replenish herself into a real from which all the mortgage has been cleared. While still on an infinite quest for the father, now an irreproachable aim..., a social aim which does not raise any objection any longer"]

25. I have replaced Brako's "a dead man" by the original "the dead man," as he is a specific object of discourse, the negative hero of the story being told.

26. Cixous plays with the words *mort* and *mot* all through the book; it is lost in English in what is the very last sentence of the book; we should remember that this is what is at stake in *Dedans*: to wash up the dead with the word.

Works Cited

Certeau, Michel, de. *L'Ecriture de l'histoire*. Paris: Gallimard, 1975.

Cixous, Hélène. *Dedans*. 1969. Paris: Editions des Femmes, 1986.

——. "Entretien avec Hélène Cixous." With Pascale Hassoun, Chantal Maillet, Claude Rabant. "L'Autre sexe." *Patio / Psychanalyse* 10. Montpellier, France: Editions de l'Eclat, 1988. 61-76.

——. "From the Scene of the Unconscious to the Scene of History." *The Future of Literary Theory*. Ed. by Ralph Cohen. London: Routledge, 1989. 1-18.

——. *L'Indiade ou l'Inde de leurs rêves, et quelques écrits sur le théâtre*. Paris: Théâtre du Soleil, 1987.

——. *Inside*. Trans. Carol Barko. New York: Schocken, 1986.

——. "On ne part pas sans anges." *L'Ange au secret*. Paris: Editions des Femmes, 1991. 31–58.

——. *Le Sacrifice dans l'oeuvre littéraire*. Notes from the seminar (1987–88). Unpublished.

——. "La Venue à l'écriture." *La Venue à l'écriture*. In collaboration with Madeleine Gagnon and Annie Leclerc. Paris: Union Générale d'Edition, 1977. 9–62.

——. *Writing Differences: Readings from the Seminar of Hélène Cixous*. Ed. Susan Sellers. New York: St. Martin's, 1988.

Lacan, Jacques. *Ecrits*. Paris: Seuil, 1966.

——. "Lituraterre." *Bulletin de L'Association Freudienne* 14 (Sept. 1985): 4–13.

Lemoine-Luccioni, Eugénie. *Le Rêve du cosmonaute*. Paris: Seuil, 1980.

Loraux, Nicole. *Les Enfants d'Athéna*. Paris: Maspéro, 1981.

Pécaut, Myriam. *La Matrice du mythe*. Paris: Aubier Montaigne, 1982.

Picard, Anne-Marie. "Voir ou dire le corps du père: filiation et narration." *Cahiers du Centre de narratologie appliquée* 5 (Université de Nice 1992): 219–28.

——. "L'Indiade ou l'Inde de leurs rêves." *Dalhousie French Studies* 17 (Fall-Winter 1989): 17–26.

Schneider, Monique. "La Paternité comme lieu de carrefour." *Le Père: Métaphore paternelle et fonctions du père: L'Interdit, la Filiation, la Transmission.* Paris: Denoël, 1989. 71–86.

3

The Medusa's Slip: Hélène Cixous and the Underpinnings of Écriture Féminine

Anu Aneja

Ever since the publication of *"Le Rire de la Méduse,"* in 1975, Hélène Cixous' Medusa has continuously given the slip to critics of *"écriture féminine."* Rewriting the horrifying Medusa of a masculist mythology, Cixous creates a laughing Medusa who, in the role of hysteric, resists the male view of her sexuality in becoming incomprehensible, unclassifiable, as one finds her only "in the divide." Through the image of the Medusa, and in some earlier essays, Cixous writes about a feminine scriptive space where women can learn to approach their own forbidden bodies. The construction of such a femininity has, of course, led to ongoing debates about the "essentializing" tendencies of Cixous' methods. To engage in one more discussion of the "theoretical" works of Cixous, in 1992, seems at first glance rather anachronistic since Cixous, a prolific writer, has continued to produce a plethora of creative prose and drama which far exceeds her "theoretical" writings from the 1970's. Because Cixous' creative fiction remains largely untranslated into English, and because she remains accessible to only a select francophile audience, the critical appraisal of her works

presents a perspective that is curiously askew. Even those outside
of France who do read Cixous' other fictional works seem to glean
much more out of the essays, perhaps owing to their easier cooptation into critical prose. Despite some of the sharp debates that
have emerged in the past two decades, the extent to which feminists are willing to be convinced by the transformational power of
"écriture féminine" remains unresolved. For all the above reasons, it
would seem appropriate to recapitulate both sides of the debate
about *"écriture féminine"* as represented in Cixous' texts, so that we
can move the debate closer to a clear appreciation of the problematic surrounding Cixous' theories.

In *"Le Rire de la Méduse,"* as in *La Venue à l'écriture,* Cixous invites
women to explore their repressed sexualities and "come" to a writing that lies outside the parameters of phallogocentric discourse.
Because patriarchal social-economic systems have kept women at a
distance from their own bodies, Cixous sees traditional writing as
closely identified with a singular "neutral" discourse which speaks
about the female body but will not let it speak (for) itself. Thus
Cixous tells women to "write the body" (*écrire le corps*) and asks
them to reclaim the "dark continent" of their sexuality. Writing is
never very far removed from desire, from sexuality, and the pulsions that locate themselves in writing may be marked by either a
feminine or a masculine libidinal economy. The feminine libidinal
economy, according to Cixous, does not establish itself around
capitalist structures of investment and return but expends itself,
communicating and begetting pleasure from the act of giving. *"Écriture féminine"* thus has a close affinity to *"le don"* (the gift), as well as
to the archaic voice of the mother before its semiotic pulsions are
interrupted by the advent of the symbolic: "Ecrire au féminin c'est
faire passer ce qui est coupé par le symbolique, c'est à dire la voix de
la mère, c'est faire passer ce qu'il y a de plus archaïque" ("sexe" 14)
["Writing in the feminine is passing on what is cut out by the
Symbolic, the voice of the mother, passing on what is most archaic"]
("Castration or Decapitation" 54). Drawing itself out of a tactile and
sensual continuum of touching, speaking and listening, *"écriture
féminine"* sets itself up as an alternate way of writing, distinct from
the castrated discourse of phallocentric speech.

It must be pointed out at the very outset that Cixous repeatedly
clarifies that the "masculine" and "feminine" attributes, as she

proposes them, are distinct from any representation of differentiation between the genders:

> My own position is to insist always on the fact that libidinal femininity is not the *propre* of women and that libidinal masculinity is not the *propre* of men. What is most important for me, what allows me to continue to live and not to despair, is precisely the conviction that it does not depend on the anatomical sex, not on the role of man and of woman but that it depends on life's chance which is every individual's responsibility. ("voice i" 54)

Instead Cixous speaks of a bisexuality available to men and women alike, not a classic neutralization of genders, but an "other bisexuality" which works with differences, rather than with oppositions. For historical and cultural reasons, however, it is women who are seen as benefitting more from this bisexuality, since they are not subjected to the culturally induced fear of castration in the way that men are. Thus it is that Cixous can say: "d'une certaine façon, 'la femme est bisexuelle'" ("Rire" 46), ["In a certain way, 'woman is bisexual'"] ("Laugh" 254), a statement that has caused obvious discomfort amongst those most suspicious of a gendered differentiation in Cixous' discourse. Writing, according to Cixous, works in the in-between spaces of feminine and masculine desires and economies. The differences between women and men are not inherent or "natural." Rather, "sexual difference develops out of bisexuality which is the original condition of every individual and is subsequently displaced, transformed by culture" (Makward 22).

Despite Cixous' caveats against the setting up of a rigid and binary structure of sexual attributes, feminist critics in the US and in England have grown increasingly wary of what they deem to be an essentializing praxis in Cixous' discourse. Among those who have most emphatically decried these tendencies are Gayatri Spivak, Toril Moi, and Ann Rosalind Jones, while others such as Robert Con Davis, Hélène Vivian Wenzel, Parveen Adams, Beverly Brown and Domna Stanton have tried to caution against the use of the female body as a central metaphor, and the subsequent biologism and essentialistic binarity within French "*écriture féminine*."

More recently, other feminists have been searching for alternate and more sympathetic ways of reading Cixous. Christiane Makward, Naomi Schor and Barbara Freeman have made a case for *"écriture féminine,"* while Morag Schiach's recent book on Cixous proposes a defense of her politics. Barbara Freeman, in an interesting account of the "mind-body problem" as it relates to Cixous' work, underlines two main lines of attack that have been used to pin down *"écriture féminine:"* "First, they accuse her of essentialism because they think that in her work the body functions as an origin which has a direct unmediated relation to feminine writing.... Secondly, Cixous's alleged conceptualization of the body is criticized as not only conservative but even as fundamentally dangerous to feminist political change" (Freeman 59–60). Freeman attempts to show that in Cixous' works, contrary to these critics' beliefs, the body lies not outside culture but is always implicated within it, and that the body appears not prior to the text but is textually enmeshed.

To these two main objections – that of essentialism and its potential negative impact on social change – I would like to review three other accusations commonly hurled against Cixous: her supposed neglect of social and political realities and of "other" women, the idealism and utopianism of her writing, and the resistance that her work offers to critical analysis. Adherence in these beliefs has led critics to doubt the subversive impact, the efficacy and the transformational abilities of *"écriture féminine."* An additional misgiving, according to Ann Rosalind Jones, is that instead of working with differences among women, *"écriture féminine"* will only serve to efface those differences and resurrect a singular, homogeneous aesthetic that will dethrone and replace the dominant ideology already in place.

The main case against Cixous – that of manifesting some kind of essential feminine by placing the body at the heart of a definition of feminine writing has been recurrently made. For instance, Hélène Vivian Wenzel is apprehensive about the regressive move towards powerlessness that such an essentialism might entail, while Gayatri Spivak expresses dissatisfaction with the revolutionary potential of Cixous' discourse because of its apparent ties to avant-garde feminism. Spivak sees both Hélène Cixous and Julia Kristeva as writing a "High Feminism" which essentializes the female body according to western psychoanalytical practices and imposes this essence on all women while ignoring the heterogeneity of class, caste, race and other socio-economic factors that separate women from each other. Similarly, Toril Moi discusses the biologism and the "slippage" from "feminine" to "female" and "masculine" to "male" in Cixous' essays, while Ann Rosalind Jones questions the theoretical consistency of her work, and fears, as does Domna Stanton, the glorification of motherhood in "*écriture féminine*."

The claim of a "slippage" towards biologism in Cixous' texts is not completely unfounded. Although Cixous has tried to use the terms "feminine" and "masculine" in contexts independent of anatomical distinctions, she often speaks of a feminine writing in its specific relationship to women. My purpose here is not to re-enforce the same argument against Cixous but rather to explore why such an essentialism manifests itself in a writing that otherwise wants to avoid any immobilizing of meaning. In her discussion of Moi's attack on Cixous, Naomi Schor, while acknowledging that Cixous speaks "a dialect of essentialese" (Schor 98), suggests that instead of being alarmed by the supposed consequences of such a dialect, we should be prepared to analyze why, in the work of some women writers, a "femininity beyond deconstruction" is being produced (Schor 99). Although Schor herself refrains from developing such an analysis, the question that she poses is an interesting one.

Rather than defending essentialism I would venture firstly that what critics perceive to be an inherent "slippage" in Cixous' essays, especially in "Le Rire de la Méduse," is a distinct "slipperiness" which constantly attempts to speak both *of the "feminine'* and *to women* and simultaneously refuses to be pinned down by critical discourse. Laughing, the Medusa gives the slip to those who, armed with the torch of reason, would chase her down the labyrinth of her (bi)sexualities. Cixous' discourse about femininity constantly shifts between the two functions it tries to fulfill: i) the revalorizing of the feminine (as libidinal economy and in its various metaphorical associations) in both women's and men's texts and ii) speaking to and about women so that they can carve a way out of cultural repression, and reclaim for themselves the ability to speak and to write their identities into political reality through a work on language. Because both of these functions are operating simultaneously in Cixous' texts, the feminine often does locate itself in the female, an event which acts as the catalyst to the fear of essentialism.

What is in question here is whether when "slipping" from the feminine to the female, Cixous commits an inadvertent but dangerous error, as Moi, Jones and others would have us believe, or whether the shifting locus of femininity emphasizes gender differences induced by culture. The answer is perhaps best found in Cixous' own work where she repeatedly tries to locate gender differences within a cultural framework. Speaking of sexual opposition, in "Le Rire de La Méduse," she says: "l'opposition sexuelle qui s'est toujours faite au profit de l'homme, au point de réduire l'écriture aussi à ses lois, n'est qu'*une limite historico-culturelle*" ("Rire" 45) ["sexual opposition, which has always worked for man's profit to the point of reducing writing, too, to his laws, is only a historico-cultural limit"] ("Laugh" 253). Thus, beginning as sexual difference and the play of bisexuality within both men and women, the dynamic between feminine and masculine drives gets reinscribed as the opposition between genders owing to the work that culture performs upon the human psyche. If there is a "slippage," therefore, it is already evident in culture, and in writing about sexualities, one can hardly refrain from duplicating some of the slips.

Of course, instead of reinscribing culturally imposed oppositions, the feminist writer and critic must seek to dissociate the body from any essentializing praxis. But since *"écriture féminine"* wants to posit certain feminine attributes as positive avenues that women can explore for their own benefit, and as avenues that are available to all, it will always stop short of rejecting the feminine in ways that, for instance, Monique Witting and others might prefer. The subversive impact of *"écriture féminine"* would thus arise out of its affirmation of traditionally devalued terms, rather than through an escaping out of what some other feminist critics might view as a feminine mythology. Since such an escape would keep women from enjoying (*jouir de*) their inherent femininity (like the taboo against femininity already established for men), it is viewed as a phallocentric response to the patriarchal control of the female body. Cixous would want us to write directly against the proposition that since patriarchy nurtures feminine attributes in oppressive ways, we buy our freedom by playing the game of the Father, and that we move away from bisexuality towards the "masculine" in order to acquire greater political power.

Instead, Cixous speaks of other kinds of powers that women can find pleasure in: "une exploration des pouvoirs de la femme: de son pouvoir, de sa puissance, de sa force toujours redoutée et des régions de la feminité" ("sexe" 13). ["an exploration of woman's powers: of her power, her potency, her ever-dreaded strength, of the regions of femininity"] ("Castration or Decapitation" 52). At the same time she rejects the bid for the kind of power within political structures that feminism sees as one of its goals, since she views feminism's endeavours as informed by a patriarchal philosophy, a perspective which leads her to declare: "Je ne suis pas feministe" ["I am not a feminist"] (van Rossum-Guyon 482). In the same interview she distinguishes between a power identified with patriarchal principles which she sees as "un pouvoir sur d'autres" [a power over others] and the power that women can avail in and of themselves, which is a "pouvoir sur soi" [a power over oneself] (van Rossum-Guyon 483–84).

These differences in the way that femininity is perceived in its rapport with the female body and with patriarchal control over the body become the cause of a major divide between practitioners of "écriture féminine" and those feminist critics more concerned with bringing about immediate changes within the socio-political arena of women's lives. The objection that Cixous ignores political realities has been made by Gayatri Spivak, Domna Stanton, and Hélène Wenzel, among others, while Ann Rosalind Jones and Toril Moi complain that Cixous uses a select and privileged discourse which does not speak to all women. Since Cixous' discourse relies heavily on western psychoanalytical methods of constructing femininity, which include the rapport of the female body to the Imaginary and the manifestation of an originary voice through the semiotic interruptions of phallic law, it is apparent that many third world women will remain at a distance from such a discourse.

This typically French concern with the interactions of language and psychoanalysis, and the linguistic implications of the unconscious insertions of sexuality into the text, is however made over in Cixous' writing because of a careful steering away from any kind of metalanguage about the body. Cixous works rather on sensuality, the language of touching, smelling, and devouring words through a text that remains umbilically linked to the body of the writer. Such a focus on the melodic affiliations between the body and the text underscores Cixous' predilection for the poetic over

the political. However, to accuse Cixous of being completely
apolitical would be like saying that the poetic does not interrupt
or interact with the political. In fact, Cixous herself views
writing as the place where political changes commence: *"l'écriture
est la possibilité même du changement,* l'espace d'où peut s'élancer
une pensée subversive, le mouvement avant coureur d'une transformation des structures sociales et culturelles" ("Rire" 42) ["Writing is precisely *the very possibility of change,* the space that can serve
as a springboard for subversive thought, the precursory movement
of a transformation of social and cultural structures"] ("Laugh"
249).

To the extent that the lyrical is a refracted mimesis of the real,
and that it transforms history into myth and the real into the
imaginary, political reality is going to be apparently absent from
poetic discourse. When it does come down to a choice between the
poetic and the political, Cixous does not hesitate to reveal that she
is on the side of the poetic: "I would lie if I said that I am a political
woman, not at all. In fact I have to assemble the two words,
political and poetic. Not to lie to you I must confess that I put the
accent on poetic . . . I think that I am constantly guilty, for example,
of having the privilege of being able to console myself poetically"
("voice i" 58). It is only in deconstructing the absolute differences
between poetry and political reality that we can eventually move to
a closer understanding of how political changes can be generated
through a work on language, which is probably the most valuable
insight that *"écriture féminine"* is currently furnishing.

Due to the widespread mistrust of essentialism and its "real"
dangers, all those aspects of Cixous' theories that might aid in
constructing such an essentialism are approached with equal
vigilance. Cixous' focus on the maternal metaphor and the rapport
between the writing self and the archaic presence of the mother's
voice in the writer's psyche has caused much discomfort among
Anglo-American critics. Domna Stanton, in her discussion of the
maternal metaphor in Cixous' works writes about the phallic
potential of the metaphor as literary trope: "But the moment the
maternal emerges as a new dominance, it must be put into question
before it congeals as feminine essence, as unchanging in-difference" (Stanton 174). To avoid the congealing of maternity into
essence, Stanton suggests a move towards metonymy. Similarly,
Jones warns against the dangers of the drive towards gestation that

impels Cixous' discourse: "I myself feel highly flattered by Cixous's praise for the nurturant perceptions of women, but when she
speaks of a drive toward gestation, I begin to hear echoes of the
coercive glorification of motherhood that has plagued women for
centuries" (Jones, "Writing the Body" 368–69).

That Cixous sees maternity as metaphor, and in its various
possible representations, appears to be ignored by Jones and others
who seem to rush towards a positing of the worst possible scenarios for women based on a literal interpretation of the maternal
metaphor. Even Stanton, who considers metaphoricity as a literary
trope seems to believe that despite its plurimodal manifestations in
Cixous' texts, the metaphor will come back to haunt the female
body. It is precisely this "taboo of the pregnant woman" ("Laugh"
261) that Cixous wants to unveil as phallocratically imposed terror.
At the same time she declares that

> Il y a mille facons de vivre une grossesse; d'avoir ou pas avec cet
> autre encore invisible une relation d'une autre intensité. Et si tu
> n'as pas cette envie-là, cela ne signifie pas que tu en manques.
> Chaque corps distribue de façon singulière, sans modèle,
> sans norme, la totalité non finie et changeante de ses désires.
> ("Rire" 52)

> There are thousands of ways of living one's pregnancy; to have
> or not to have with the still invisible other a relationship of
> another intensity. And if you don't have that particular yearning,
> it doesn't mean that you're in any way lacking. Each body
> distributes in its own special way, without model or norm, the
> nonfinite and changing totality of its desires. ("Laugh" 262)

Despite this rather loose and pluralistic use of the maternal
metaphor which can manifest itself through the body, the text, or
in interpersonal relations, the metaphor continues to be read in all
its literal ramifications. Such readings seem to reveal the culturally
induced terror of motherhood and its imprisoning dimensions that
we, as women, have internalized. Displacing the maternal temporarily while we wait for an access to "political" power might
betray our own complicity with the disdain of the patriarchal
viewpoint towards the pregnant female body and feminine
powers, and our willingness to adopt masculist perceptions in
order to accede to political empowerment. The extrication of

maternity from the stereotypical space into which it has been ensconced for centuries can only be performed by means of a discourse that works on linguistic, and by extension, cultural connotations of the maternal. In the process of such discursive transformations, apprehensions about the congealing of maternity as feminine essence are bound to surface, but these need to be placed in perspective so that a move towards the completion of a transformational process is not obstructed.

Because Cixous speaks of a textual engendering in its relationship to the drive for gestation, while she displaces the masculine, capitalist economy of investment and return with a feminine economy of libidinal giving and loving, her writing does tend towards the positing of an ideal universe. Cixous has therefore been accused of a "utopic" writing. In this regard, Toril Moi makes concessions for what she sees as the "contradictory aspects" of Cixous' texts because of the presence of a "conflict between an already contradictory patriarchal ideology and the utopian thought that struggles to free itself from that patriarchal stranglehold" (Moi 122). However, she cannot excuse Cixous for the elements that go into the making of such a utopia: "It is just this absence of any specific analysis of the material factors preventing women from writing that constitutes a major weakness of Cixous's utopia. Within her poetic mythology, writing is posited as an absolute activity of which all women *qua* women automatically partake" (Moi 123).

Although it is true that Cixous' writing focuses much more on the issue of how women (can) write rather than who can write, she seems to be well aware of those who cannot. Speaking of third world women in an interview with Verena Andermatt Conley, she says that "there is a part of the world which cannot write and which will always only write in silence." ("voice i" 59) Some third world women will obviously read in this statement a hint of patronizing privilege, and will resent being spoken for, that is, silenced on the presupposition that they can only ever be silent. Despite the awareness of the (different) situation of third world women therefore, French feminism's assumed privileged position irks those, especially Marxist feminists, like Gayatri Spivak, who would much rather see actual work upon women's conditions rather than work upon language and its deferred effects.

However, it needs to be noted that "Le Rire de la Méduse" as well as *La Jeune Née* were both published in 1975, "Le sexe ou la tête" in 1976, and *La Venue à l'écriture* in 1977. Since the publication of these early writings, Cixous has moved in many new directions, which continue to be overlooked by critics of *"écriture féminine."* Since then, Cixous has published several fictional works including two plays about Cambodia and India which present sensitive readings of political situations in the third world and a widening interest in the story of the other, rather than a focus on the self. Perhaps because these texts appear in the guise of fiction rather than critical theory, certain critics are more wary of speaking about them since the earlier "theoretical" essays provide an easier access (and route of attack) into *"écriture féminine."* Based on these early readings, critics continue to flog the back of *"écriture féminine."*

The fact that Cixous tries to create in her texts a world where women, unafraid of their (bi)sexualities, live in harmony, has been seen as an urge towards a return to the womb, and a nostalgia for an archaic past and an ancient mythology grounded in the impossible. But it must be conceded that although utopias are inherently "impossible" places, and are based on idealistic mythologies, the positing of ideals may not be necessarily detrimental. In fact, such a positing may be an essential precondition for the reconstruction of the real, as long as it works upon the real in effective ways. As Nicole Ward Jouve says, "our utopia, yes, but utopias are written so that things will come to pass" (Jouve 72).

Similarly, Robert Con Davis' reading of Cixous' utopic strategies in terms of a "failure" due to their appeal to "oppositionalism" is concurrent with the objections raised by Jones, Stanton, and others, that Cixous' writing remains caught in the trap of binarity. Such an objection is founded on the view that in Cixous' discourse, femininity is always placed in opposition and in reference to the male ideology which it tries to subvert, and which in turn never stops determining its design. But since Cixous' work is on difference rather than on oppositions, and the distinctions made are between the feminine and masculine aspects of a bisexual psyche, the assumption about binarity might reveal the critics' own slippage from bisexuality to binarity, and hence the imposition of dualism and oppositionalism upon a place where only difference is at play.

Robert Con Davis, in his discussion of oppositionalism in its relation to Cixous' work, conceals his own accusations behind those of a woman (Ann Rosalind Jones):

> Cixous' discourse, then – actually an agent of what it opposes – inadvertently returns to and re-enforces the masculine discourse *it was supposed to go beyond and subvert*. Cixous-as-oppositional-reader, as Jones summarizes, *misunderstood* the inherent *dangers* of oppositional criticism and, accordingly, was *lured* by the appearance of analytical clarity into the *trap* of accepting a patri-archal ethos. Cixous' oppositional reading is *confined* and *neutra-lized* in effectiveness, therefore, by the patriarchal frame – the male form of reading – she chose to employ. (274, emphasis added)

Reading difference as opposition, the ludic play of bisexuality as the fault line between men and women, Davis blames Cixous for not having understood the intricacies of the male game. So he concludes that Cixous, despite her good revolutionary intentions, is duped by the logic of the patriarchal logos, "lured" as Eve was, into the "trap" of "the male form of reading." Unable to match the cerebral sophistication of the "patriarchal ethos," Cixous' dis-course ends up in "failure" according to Davis. Davis' reading of Cixous thus betrays an inability to accept the possibility of an "other" discourse, one that perhaps slips just out of reach of the patriarchal framework into which he wishes so hard to make it fit. Thus, his desire to co-opt Cixous' difference into the oppositional-ism of the "male form of reading" results in an attempt at confine-ment. Performing the jailor's role literally, Davis uses A. J. Greimas' "semiotic square" to split up and reduce Cixous' lyrical discourse into four terms which inhabit the four corners of the square. Fortunately for us, the fourth term, the Mother, "goes beyond the square by recognizing female power" (Davis 277). Even though he concedes the power of this strange "irruption" of the Mother out of the four-cornered room, he maintains that Cix-ous "does not (cannot) change culture directly" (Davis 279). This bizarre desire to place within the parameters of a geometrical space that which will continually slip beyond might signal a reluctance to accept the fact that there can be a discourse beyond the reductive binary square.

Since Cixous' discourse, like the Medusa's body, does slip out of reach, in its deliberate attempt to create a beyond where femininity may gambol freely, it presents resistance to any analytical system which would wish to codify and explain it in terms of its own structures. The slipperiness of Cixous' lyricism is thus resented by those who, like Toril Moi, want to penetrate the nexus of *"écriture féminine."* Meeting the fierce resistance offered by this discourse, Moi says about Cixous: "Her style is often intensely metaphorical, poetic and explicitly anti-theoretical, and her central images create a dense web of signifiers that offers no obvious edge to seize hold of for the analytically minded critic. It is not easy to *operate cuts into, open vistas in or draw maps of Cixous' textual jungle* (Moi 102, emphasis added). Jones, too, complains about the inaccessibility of French feminism because it "resists any easy pluralistic assimilation" (Jones, "Inscribing Femininity" 93).

In their call for theoretical consistency however, critics such as Moi, Jones, Davis and Spivak end up resurrecting their own oppositional discourse which poses theory as the master out to know the lyrical other and bespeaks an impatience with the poetic whenever it eludes the master's consistent logic. Moi, like Spivak, blames Cixous for her individualism because her discourse depends on poetry: "Cixous' poetic vision of writing as the very enactment of liberation, rather than the mere vehicle of it, carries the same individualistic overtones" (Moi 125). One wonders at the origins of this widespread scepticism towards the poetic, as though the lyrical could be nothing but a romantic mirage seducing us towards the lure of a dangerous femininity.

In their desire to emphasize the need for "real" changes in socio-political structures, critics such as Moi and Spivak end up relegating poetry to the back seat of feminist discourse. This gap between theory and poetry is one that Cixous herself wants to undo. Her "theoretical" writings are never very far removed from creative prose, while the fiction speaks and provides an access to the "theory." In maintaining the discourse of oppositionalism, critics of *"écriture féminine"* inadvertently re-enforce the binary system which sets up the theoretical and the poetic at opposing ends and privileges the abstract and analytical powers of the theoretical as the more competent discourse – that is, more capable of speaking about the "real" situation of women. The danger of such binary thought is apparent since it presumes that theoretical discourse provides a superior or more cogent way of accomplishing an overhauling of patriarchal culture. It also implies that as long as such internalized suppositions stay in place, we will not be able to liberate ourselves from the phallogocentric rhetoric that wants to "operate cuts" into our femininity and balks at the slipperiness of our agile movements.

Thus, while we need to remain aware of the silencing effects of the patronage extended by *"écriture féminine"* towards third world women, it is perhaps also time that we examine our own complicity with patriarchal prejudices against the feminine and direct our attention to the "gift" of potential empowerment that Cixous proffers to women through her work on language. Since the Medusa's tongue, like language itself, is inherently slippery, the only way of avoiding the Medusa's slip on her/our way to a liberating feminine discourse is to follow her in genial ways, rather than hindering her nimble steps by an unrelenting interrogation of her (in)consistencies.

Works Cited

Cixous, Hélène. "Le Rire de la Méduse." *L'Arc* 61(1975): 39–54.

———."The Laugh of the Medusa." Trans. Keith Cohen and Paula Cohen. In *New French Feminisms*. Ed. Elaine Marks and Isabelle de Courtivron. New York: Schocken Books, 1981. 245–264.

———."Le sexe ou la tête?" *Les Cahiers du Grif* 13 (October 1976): 5–15.

———."Castration or Decapitation?" Trans. Annette Kuhn. *Signs* 7(Autumn 1981): 41–55.

Conley, Verena Andermatt. "Voice i..." (Interview With Hélène Cixous.) *Boundary 2* 12 (1984): 51–67.

Davis, Robert Con. "Woman as Oppositional Reader: Cixous on Discourse." *Papers on Language and Literature* 24 (Summer 1988): 265–282.

Freeman, Barbara. "Plus corps donc plus écriture: Hélène Cixous and the mind-body problem." *Paragraph* 11 (1988): 58–70.

Jones, Ann Rosalind. "Writing the Body: Toward an Understanding of Écriture Féminine." *New Feminist Criticism*. Ed. Elaine Showalter. New York: Pantheon, 1985. 361–377.

———."Inscribing Femininity: French Theories of the Feminine." *Making a Difference*. Ed. Gayle Greene and Coppélia Kahn. London: Methuen, 1985. 80–112.

Jouve, Nicole Ward. *White Woman Speaks with Forked Tongue*. London: Routledge, 1991.

Makward, Christiane. "Interview with Hélène Cixous." *Sub-stance* 13 (1976): 19–37.

Moi, Toril. "Hélène Cixous: an Imaginary Utopia." In *Sexual/Textual Politics*. London: Methuen, 1985. 102–126.

Schor, Naomi. "Introducing Feminism." *Paragraph* 8 (October 1986): 94–101.

Shiach, Morag. *Hélène Cixous: A Politics of Writing*. London: Routledge, 1991.

Spivak, Gayatri. "French Feminism in an International Frame." *In Other Worlds*. New York: Methuen, 1987. 134–153.

Stanton, Domna. "Difference on Trial: A Critique of the Maternal Metaphor in Cixous, Irigaray, and Kristeva." *The Poetics of Gender*. Ed. Nancy K. Miller. New York: Columbia UP, 1986. 157–182.

van Rossum-Guyon, Françoise van. "Entretien arec Françoise van Rossum-Guyon." *Revue des Sciences Humaines* XLIV(168)(1977): 479–493.

Wenzel, Hélène Vivian. "The Text as Body/Politics: An Appreciation of Monique Wittig's Writings in Context." *Feminist Studies* 7 (1981): 264–287.

Works Cited

Andermatt, Verena. "Hélène Cixous and the Uncovery of a Feminine Language." *Women and Literature* 7 (1979): 38–48.

Brown, Beverly and Parveen Adams. "The Feminine Body and Feminist politics." *M/F* 3 (1979): 35–50.

———. 'Editorial" *M/F* 2 (1978): 2–4.

Cixous, Hélène. *La Jeune Née*. Paris: Union Générale d'Editions, 1975.

———. *La Venue à l'écriture* with Madeleine Gagnon and Annie Leclerc. Paris: Union Générale d'Editions, Collection "10/18," 1977.

Duren, Brian. "Cixous' Exorbitant Texts." *Sub-Stance* 32 (1981): 39–51.

Féral, Josette. "Towards a Theory of Displacement." *Sub-Stance* 32 (1981): 52–64.

Fisher, Claudine. *La Cosmogonie d'Hélène Cixous*. Amsterdam: Rodopi, 1988.

Gibbs, Anna. "Hélène Cixous and Gertrude Stein: New Directions in Feminist Criticism." *Meanjin Quarterly* 38 (1979): 281–293.

Heilbrun, Carolyn G. "A Response to Writing and Sexual Difference." *Critical Inquiry* 8 (Summer 1982): 805–811.

Makward, Christiane. "To be or not to Be..A Feminist Speaker." *The Future of Difference*. Ed. Eisenstein and Jardine. Trans. Marlene Barsoum, Alice Jardine and Hester Eisenstein. Boston: G. K. Hall, 1980. 95–105.

Marks, Elaine. "Women and Literature in France." *Signs* 3 (Summer 1978): 832–842.

Marks, Elaine and Isabelle de Courtrivron. *New French Feminisms*. New York: Schocken Books, 1981.

Radhakrishnan, R. "Feminist Historiography and Post-Structuralist Thought." *The Difference Within*. Ed. Elizabeth Meese and Alice Parkes. Philadelphia: John Benjamins, 1989. 189–205.

Richman, Michele. "Sex and Signs: The Language of French Feminist Criticism." *Language and Style* 13 (1980): 62–80.

Running-Johnson, Cynthia. "The Medusa's Tale;" Feminine writing and "La Genet." *Romanic Review* 80 (May 1989): 483–95.

Sellers, Susan. *Writing Differences*. New York: St. Martin's, 1988.

Sherzer, Dina. *Representation in Contemporary French Fiction*. Lincoln: U of Nebraska P, 1986.

Stanton, Domna C. "Language and Revolution: The Franco-American Dis-Connection." *The Future of Difference*. Ed. Eisenstein, Hester and Jardine. Boston: G. K. Hall, 1980. 73–87.

4

Hélène Cixous: Music Forever or Short Treatise on a Poetics for a Story To Be Sung

Mireille Calle-Gruber

Ma pensée ne peut se passer de la parole à qui je parle dans ma parole
Ni ma vie de la musique de son fil

– Hélène Cixous, *Beethoven à jamais*

My thoughts cannot do without the speech to which I speak in my
speech/Nor my life of the music of its stream

With *Beethoven à jamais ou l'existence de Dieu*, Hélène Cixous takes the
oath of music. Promise, faith, credit, belief, memory: these are a matter
of time, an adventure of time, in the course of time akin to music.

The writer gives her word, and music soars. Music flows from
(her) speech. What is there to *say*, what is there to *write*, when, in
giving your word, giving it up, you follow the thread of writing?
This question is precisely what is at stake in the process of
thinking: follow the clue, follow the right clue, lose the clue. For
thought is inherent speech: ponderous thought bearing the burden
of words, measurable in terms of the tension that keeps them
suspended; or measurable in terms of the friction of air
against the arrow of meanings; the blank surrounded with letters
and the blank "autour d'eux deux" [around both of them] (121);

sound or silences surrounded with signification, "toi mon être le plus cher – ma nue – inconnue" [you my dearest – naked cloud – unknown] (103). And thought nonetheless coming across, that cannot afford not to ford the word around, word after word, paving the way, giving the password, distilling, one drop at a time, the effects of absence: the advance consisting of oblivion and promise entangled.

The Metaphor, "Portageur"

It is hardly surprising that Hélène Cixous' favorite means of transportation is the metaphor since this trope draws, spins, and threads its way across page more easily than any other. Metaphor, "navette d'or" [a golden shuttle], makes the wildest crossings (60); it takes language on board, temporarily granting it a passage. Respiration-like, metaphor is the staggering telephoned breath which shifts features:

> Elle était là ensemble avec les faims dans le four à pain sans pain, dans la faim. La faim est le cercle de l'enfer. L'enfer est *dans pour dans*. (79, my italics)

> She was there together with hunger buried in the stale oven, in hunger. Hunger draws a circle around hell. Hell is a tooth for a tooth.

Ethereal in essence, the metaphor provides wings which are essential to get acquainted with what is closest: the "dedansdehors" [insideoutside], "Ellelui" [S/he] (93), "tantôt terre tantôt ciel, interresticiellement à Eumême" [sometimes earth sometimes heaven, interearthly to Themself] (121).

Metaphor is not merely passage, or a means, but also what *portages* – as the Amerindians from Quebec would describe fording between two lakes or two rivers with the canoe carried by men. Hélène Cixous' metaphor occasionally becomes a *portageur*. Her metaphor supports the vehicle of language which is in turn carried by the feet and legs of letters, illumined by their flashes of lightning, making bridgeheads out of syllables and providing footbridges: "ces neuf mots tu-vis-avec-quelqu'un-qui-part-tout-le-temps – séparément, ensemble, d'un trait" [this nine-letter word   you-live-with-someone-who-leaves-all-the-time   –   apart, together, in one line] (150), which echoes with new meaning, carrying along, in effect(s), page after page, the echo of infinite sentences:

sans le faire exprès il lui a donné : tu vis + avec + tu vis avec + tu vis avec quelqu'un + tu vis avec quelqu'un qui d'un côté vit-avec-toi, de l'autre côté part-tout-le-temps. (151–52)

without doing it on purpose he gave it to her: you live + you live with + you live with someone + you live with someone who on the one hand lives-with-you, and on the other hand, leaves all the time.

Here, the device exemplifies what linguists and semanticians have been telling us for some time: that the meaning of a sentence is not merely the sum of its elements. Hélène Cixous exemplarily knows how to boost the poetic benefit: her writing uses the opening breaches to pursue its career and substantially reexperiences its visionary outlook. Obviously, writing is less mathematical than magical, consists less in juxtaposition than in magnetism, where computation becomes an unaccountable gift without doing it on purpose, a fructiferous depositary, an overture score, where indeed, *plus fait plus*: "vivre *plus*," "avec *plus*," "quelqu'un *plus*" [more makes more, to live more, with more, someone more].

The sign of (de)composition (+) enters a new (re)composition phase, where it appears as a sign of magnanimity, a sign of abundance: the miracle of the text is thus celebrated, behind the scenes, under the veil of unified elements. The advent/event of the miracle is a multiplication changing − into +, and + into x, thus adding weight, trait, belief and meaning. The miracle of the textual heurism, which is granted a life warrant from a body of words and which leads to a substantial promulgation in terms of symbolical meaning, is a kind of transubstantiation intrinsic to the future of literal substance. The miracle changes desert into desire, hunger into bread, stones into springs, drought into melodious floods, deafness into high-sounding offsprings − " j'entends ma surdité pousser ses énormes silences inaudibles jusqu'au ciel," [I can hear my deafness sighing its inaudible silence to heaven] (107) − turning absence into presence-of-absence and weaving the web of a collective communion, a would-be union, on the page.

The most miraculous aspect, however, is to be found in this heurism of the text which gives full body and meaning to the frantic speech of the writer, draws its (re)gain of strength precisely from the lack of strength; the extra letter, "les lettres qu'elle ne lui avait jamais écrites" [the letters that she never wrote to him] (157), the *being more* wells up unexpectedly amidst the lapses of syntactic memory, of narrative reason, and the inter-letter blanks.

While taking every risk, this is a means to express the fragile notation of speech opening up in the book: everything is achieved on a tightrope, along the line – no matter how *sinu*ous it is, "c'est une ligne *si nu*e [it is such a bare line] (193, my italics). A line drawn despite/over the blanks which are part and parcel of the sentence: where everything seems lost, and where everything is suddenly returned to us, in a flash, a hundred-fold.

Such work permits going astray, crossing the desert when "le *sec*ret est devenu *sec*" [the secret has become desiccated, dese-crated] (137, my italics). Language needs to be grasped at any cost till it bursts and is forced to produce a song:

O toi par qui tous les présents m'arrivent, les uns
présents, les uns absents, les uns partants, les uns
venants, tous vivants. (152)

You through whom I receive all these presents, some
of which are present, others absent, others leaving, others
coming, all alive.

Then the sentence sails away; and the sentence waves.

A metaphor is two-fold. A metaphor is a metaphor and this metaphor is akin to a mountain. You ride on a mountain.

On one of the metaphoric mountain slopes lies the syndrome of the staircase, desert, and death. Climbing up the slope is a rough experience, where one may face falls, aridity, fireburns, boldness, alteration. Above all, this mountain bears landslides. Legend lies on the other slope: legends embedded in music, a mythical ocean, in food, or in quench-thirsting fluidity. It is a locus that allows flowing. And from one-land to the other-sea (sea of sounds, of "millions de cris" [millions of cries] (105), one may find the ridge, some superhuman limitation, where the sentence utters its

highest note. Ecstasy. (A B. – "Ton B": which sounds like "Tomber" (161).[1] Cixous writes: "la musique est ma limite et ma vie
surhumaine" [music is my limitation and my life is superhuman]
(71):

> De l'autre côté c'est le contraire. La musique est partout, un
> océan balance ses longs houloulements me disant "ça va passer,
> ça va passer, je reste, je reste".... Maintenant viennent des
> pluies pour moi, les pluies pleurent longtemps, pleurent les
> larmes pour mes yeux assoiffés, et pendant ce temps-là je me
> passe, je m'écoule.... (139).

> On the other side it is the opposite. Music is foaming, a billowy
> ocean rocks at length, telling me "it will go by, it will go by, I am
> staying, I am staying"....There comes the rain for me, it is
> pouring rain, shedding tears for my thirsty eyes, and in the
> mean time, I pass by, I drift away....

When metaphor sails us away and allows us to feel greater than
we actually are (70), it rolls down, as it claims, its own slope: flux,
flood, a stream of ink and cries, of rain and music. The metaphor,
whether it be ravishing or arresting, does not long forget to make
its portage of letters heard: the foot of the letter literally takes the
wrong footing as it introduces its impulse "tromper/tremper" [to
mislead/to drench].[2] "Heureusement qu'il y a la musique pour
tremper l'attente" [Happily, there is music to drench expectation]
(139), and then, allowing its identity as bold target, the metaphor
suddenly becomes tangible and thin like a sounding and graphic
bow by means of alliteration, rhyme, paronomasia cast against the
blank sheet:

> ô lève lèvres libre livre lait lèche veuille et je veux (137)[3]

> o lift lips free book milk lick wish and I want.

Portage and transportation, motion and emotion, crumbling and
flowing, are intrinsically at work in turns. Writing sometimes consists in pulling the text-life-boat and is at times carried away by its
magical trans-power: words welling up – forever. The narrative
thread which is addressing us (*to* us, *from* us) is Life, the life that
clings onto one *fil*ament, one thread, a palindrome, a double
bloody body of meaning.[4]

The Infinite Sentence

The Cixousian sentence becomes infinite, unveiling inexplicit signs, unmarked paths, unwritten letters that may pop up at any moment amidst the disjointed pavement of the page. The book itself is one long sentence, the work itself is a single sentence, panting, breathless, gasping for breath, and yet unbegun, unaccomplished, still underway like a castaway, a being with no other origin besides enduring participation in the casting, the throw – a gesture emblematic of a *separation from*, which maintains writing like living within in an unmemorable race with its own undiscovered forces, a gesture emblematic of the unknown target.

From the outset, *Beethoven à jamais* is once more part of the trend in progress:

> Nous vivons au milieu de la vie, les côtés du milieu, on ne les voit jamais, il vaut mieux ne pas les voir. Ainsi la vie nous apparaît sans fin et c'est ainsi qu'elle l'est. Tant que dure le vol. (11)

> For the better, we live in the midst of life, the bands of the middle can never be seen. So life appears to us to be endless, and it is indeed so. For as long as the ride will last.

To *live* is to be understood as the infinit(ive) act per se: "Je veux vivre, je ne veux pas 'la vie'" [I want to live, I do not want "the life"] (171). Not the substantive, but the verb, not the definite possession, but the course of action that sweeps everything away.

The Cixousian sentence is manipulated from back to front by its intrinsic infinity: the sentence is no longer a logical unit, a synthetic entity, a pause in the concept, but a stream with no banks or external constraints, a stream that does not allow any direction(s) other than its own. Hollowing itself from inside into fractions of divided sections, the Cixousian sentence multiplies limitations and oversteps them from inside. Writing has no other choice than to conceive in this manner from then on. While passing by. With interruptions, going back and forth.

The scissiparity of syntax which, more than ever before at work in *Beethoven*, undoubtedly gives Hélène Cixous' speech a particular tone of intimacy, a meaning-beating close to the heart, throbbing within the heart like the pain of anguish. The Cixousian sentence is inexhaustible because it stems from its own tearing-apart, making negation, interruption, and syncope feel present. The sentence requires a justification for each word, i.e., a *Rhyme*, i.e., a call for a *hymn*. The sign of division proliferates: the linearity of writing undergoes deep cuts, is broken into segments because of the massive use of hyphens.

c'est qu'il faut s'éloigner de ce qu'on aime – pour entendre –
haletant – le présent – revenir-sur nos pas

Tu entends – ma joie – ma tendre –
Est-ce que tu m'entends –
C'est toi-même si près – si présente –
A l'oeuvre dans mon rocher –
Entre un ange – et me frappe –
C'est toi l'ange – et me frappe – plus fort –
Plus fort plus fort – je veux entendre les morts –
Aller – Allons –
A la joie
Ceci est mon alléluia – aura été mon hymne
Je commence à t'écrire ce 6 juillet – l'hymne qui ne sera pas
entendu de mon vivant – (102)

We have to drift away from the loved ones-to listen –
panting – to the present – come back – on our steps

You hear-my joy – my tender –
Can you hear me –
It is you so close – so present –
At the? work in my rock –
Between an angel-that knocks me –
You are the angel – that knocks me – harder –
Harder harder – I want to hear the dead –
Go – Let's go
To the joy
This is my alleluia – will have been my hymn
I am starting to write to you on this July 6th – the hymn that
will not
be heard in my life time –

The hyphen, so positioned, opens the abysses of the unrecountable, the high depths of the text. Below the bar of the hyphen, blank activity starts. And ferments. Like a poetic flag digging for the justification of the text in prose, it provides words along with enough space to make them sound, resound in the echo chamber preserved by writing:[5] the vocalic and syllabic revivals (entends, ma tendre, m'entends [hear, my tender, hear me]), dissemination (aller, allons, alléluia [go, let's go, alleluia]), the rhythmic progression (si près, si présente [so close, so present]) and the thematic designation of the principle of what is in progress, all these devices organize an outstanding poetical strike. Nurtured on its own accents, present to itself, in the vigor of its course: it is the voice – the guiding voice of lyrical singing.

Both a means of union and separation, the hyphen separates as well as links, draws apart as well as together. It polarizes and organizes magnetic fields, electric arcs, in a type of writing that wonderfully exemplifies the game of opposites: "Tout ce qui vit est oxymorique" [Everything that lives is oxymoric] (172). Though the hyphen reveals tensions that may not be suspected, it also provides the proper outcome of writing by which the word shall be ashes before being reborn as fire; there is a constant fear of writing "à feu trop doux" [on the back burner] (42) since that would not provide enough fuel for the future. Following the advent of a trajectory which is as yet still aimlessly targeted, a premonition open to interpretation like a door left ajar, an advance which only feeds its adventurous, firm step from its very advance, Cixous is in search of "ma pensée d'avant ma pensée – et devant moi l'attelage d'alizés plus rapide que l'orage" [my thoughts before my thoughts – and in front of me a winsome team more rapid than storm] (106).

Given such a process, the sentence evinces the conformation of a caterpillar, a sectioned body akin to an all-terrain vehicle, able to adapt to the potholes and inequalities of the language-ground. For, indeed, language no longer enjoys the principle of equivalency which levels the signs of everyday life. Hyphens intervening between words tear the syntax to shreds and return the memory of its oblivion to language. For what is written with this sporadic hyphen reenacts its origins in the upstream gesture of throwing that conceives the castaway and, consequently, forever maintains the *process of separation*. From this process, a white on black reversal where the page supersedes and pulls away from the sentence like a gulf it can neither approach nor span, emerges the oblivion that writing usually thrives to forget under its disguise of black-hooded mastery, of unfailing logic. The Cixousian sentence is, on the contrary, pierced right through, perforated; moving the breath in rests and quarter-rests, it creates suspirations of air and aria; it embodies the rhythm of meaning, systole/diastole, the cadence of nerves; it derives its inspiration from the volume of the lungs.

We understand better why the writer thrives to give (her) voice to language; for while the multiplication of many individual voices disperses standards of univocal meaning, it *affects* living meaning at the same time. Hence the importance that the text be, little by little, like the bellows of a huge forge where unprecedented alloys and alliances alchemize. This is a way for Hélène Cixous to catalyze the secret of love – "partager – l'éloignement – [to share – being apart] (99) – which is also the mystery of creation whether in musical art or poetry, a symphony by Beethoven or a symphony from the text. The creative incantation: "Mon impuissance est le secret de mon génie" [My powerlessness is the secret of my genius] (69).

Where the Story Utters its Deepest Shrills

The following sequence, *powerlessness – secret – genius*, provides "trois clefs" [three keys] which are, according to the text (namely, *the Author*), "or, argent et diamant" [gold, silver and diamond] (69). Consequently, this sequence, simultaneously precious and magical, animates the oxymoric mechanism. The secret, which holds center place, represents the paradoxical axis articulating the inarticulable, the key tuning what jars: "mon impuissance – mon génie" [my powerlessness – my genius].

Such is the tensional principle at stake in the book, that is in the wounds of the story, of "l'Histoire sans intrigue, et avec un minimum de personnages" [the Story without a plot, with a minimum of characters] (41). Here there is no narrative teleology – simply a plot and hence, an unfolding, a protagonist and hence, a destiny, a realistic anchoring and hence, a lesson – dictating from the outside its own laws of verisimilitude. Everything in the Cixousian story is *elementary*, constituted of elements to be (re)composed indefinitely. Mimesis is used sparingly so as neither to regulate nor take over the elements by force nor arrange the effects of the text according to a conventional meaning or schema. Instead, the rules for combining elements are intrinsic to writing itself and are submitted to its extravagant efflorescence of polysemy and polymorphism, to its commanding multiplicity of aspects which, equally, work.

So much so that the story uses indirection as a steering-wheel, agrees to listen to its weakness, to its potentials rather than to its powers; and this story is doomed to *genius*. This word has several meanings, all of them crucial here. Genius primarily implies the constructive and communicative, bridge and footbridge, in short, the art of passage. And this engineering, this ingeniousness, thrive to produce, to bring forth in keeping with the "génie des langues" [spirit of languages] (in reference to the hidden treasures of linguistic fields and undergrounds) new relationships, crossings and openings. This is the locus where an endless dialogue originates, "la parole à qui je parle dans ma parole" [the speech I am addressing in my speech] spurred by a vivacity of thinking constantly on the move. Thoughts are at stake within language itself and enjoy playing with words, ever playing on words: they are restless; they embody successive appearances.

From this restless embodiment evolves the second meaning of *genius*: demon, guardian angel, spirit. This genius means freedom: freedom of thought which, along with thinking, also comprises dreaming, feeling, relishing. Language spins out breaches for thoughts to slip through. Just listen to it: the Spirit is "ton alliée née" [your born ally] (57).[6]

> L'Esprit se fiche de l'heure, des habitudes, des frontières reconnues de la culture, des nations, des lois de l'époque, des murailles mentales.
> L'Esprit montre le passage invisible qui traverse les montagnes. C'est la Voix de l'Autre. (57)

> The Spirit could not care less about time, habits, acknowledged limits of culture, nations, laws of the epoch, mental walls.
> The Spirit cuts the invisible passage through mountains. It is the Voice of the Other.

The genius of powerlessness is precisely to build passages at will, provided that the third meaning of genius not be omitted: *inclination*. This is the locus for the inclined-being who yields, bends to its ultimate limit on the verge of accepting a turning point, a U-turn. This genius is ready to accept the Other: an acceptance-renunciation dichotomy enhanced by blindfolded freedom and weak strength. All this proves that the industrious genius does not bring the story to a dialectic resolution: there is always something left aside, a secret around the secret – the separated-being, separation itself, the intrinsic secret. My powerlessness/my genius. Due to secrecy's magical aspect – incomputable, unrepeatable, unmasterable – it is precisely in the locus of separation that opposites agree. *Separation leads to harmony*, though it does not unite. It does not tone down discrepancy or suffering:

> Je veux les fils de la séparation
> Je veux le tissu de la séparation
> Je veux mon hors
> Je te veux, je veux nos deux hors . . . .
> Sans éloignement pas d'espérance
> Et de même sans féminin pas de masculin. (172)

> I want the threads of separation
> I want the material of separation
> I want my outside
> I want you, I want both our outsides . . . .
> Without distance and no hope
> And similarly no feminine without a masculine.

Never will a book *tell* the secret. Neither would an opus. Nor will they abolish the secret of a powerlessness of genius. For the story resorts to other means to come across and transcend itself. The secret cannot plainly be told: it has to be sung. More precisely, the secret *sings*. Intransitively. These words are "non dites mais retenties" [not spoken but resonated] (59).

As a result, with the genius of powerlessness, an unpremeditated way of writing is indeed arriving; writing like crossing rocky territories of irreducible language, mounts of meaning, and meaning's remains, writing that denomination, denotation, connotation, logical abstraction cannot harmonize in an intelligence of representation:

Les choses avaient une légère emphase....Elles restaient.
Elles avaient du reste en elle. Un poids impondérable qui
empêchera la bise d'oubli de les balayer. (43)

Things had a slight emphasis....They stayed.
They had something left in her. An imponderable weight
which will prevent oblivion's kiss from sweeping them away.

Writing a story which sings, a story to be sung, will similarly
consist in granting to the sentence the imponderable weight of a
slight emphasis which, weighed down with words of a particular
echo, will prevent them from vanishing amidst the chain of mean-
ingful propositions as soon as they are read. Writing will consist in
freeing syntax, leaving the lexis some room in which to maneuver
(with blanks, hyphens, indentations, free versification in prose),
and impeaching logical sequences with counter-propositions:

Trente années, et ils avaient toujours eu confiance –
Trente années et ils n'avaient jamais eu confiance –
Les deux propositions étaient également vraies. (172)

Thirty years, and they had always granted each other trust –
Thirty years, and they had always denied each other trust –
Both clauses were equally true.

Writing will consist in throwing the story from the top of the
mountain ranges of narration to the pits of dialogue where voices
falter, "portées sur le bout des langues, au-dessus de l'abîme"
[carried on the tips of their languages, over the abyss] (81).

Consequently, writing will mean accentuation, stressing, mark-
ing the accent in language; the accentuation of affects and urges in
the veins, body, and vocal cords, every particular of which is heard
in the story as "Deux voix un seul chant" [Two voices one single
song] (170), their consequent agreement. Their secret agreement,
since the agreement is always secret and grants the miracle of
separation. The exceptional, unexpected gift – also called grace. It
comes and takes over where there is some powerlessness. It *cannot
be*. It has to be *wanted*, desire.

O vie revenant, ô vie miséricorde, caprice, ô espérée et accordée,
toi qui parfois n'accordes pas et tournes vers nous un visage

mort, toi qui parfois accorde avec la grâce de qui accorde toujours tout et pour toujours, ô mystérieuse, terrible adorable, toi
qui me dis oui aujourd'hui et non hier, et jamais non à jamais,
mer aux marées irrégulières chantait-elle, balancée d'Ouest en
est, entre la lune et la musique, ivre, le corps ivre, le cerveau
rougissant sous le front, des elfes courent à deux mètres devant
moi et sur leurs traces, des éclats de rire. (233)

O life coming back, O life forgiving, whimsical, O hoped for and
granted, you who sometimes do not grant and face us with a
dead face, you who sometimes granted with the grace of what
always grants all and forever, O mysterious, terribly adorable,
you who tell me yes one day and no the day before, and never no
forever, sea with irregular tides she sung, swinging from West to
East, between the moon and music, drunk, the body drunk, brain
blushing under forehead, elves running two meters ahead of me
and along their foot traces, bursts of laughter.

Throughout these lines, the story utters its deepest shrills as an
invocation – out of surprise, in time, in double-time, like panting,
like ebbing and flowing, like the said and denied, like endless
reversibility ("jamais non à jamais" [never no forever]), up to the
point of being misinterpreted, of becoming litany, echolalia, up to
the point of depriving the trope of every categorization.

We understand that what attempts to be heard in the metatextual and metaphoric openings of the story is not just a poetics at
work, but also the limitations and overflowing of art. The art of
life-and-death. The art of struggle. Hence, the narrative ambition
can no longer be realistic in order to speak; it must be superhuman
in order to "rendre chantable" [become singable] (94). Narrative
voice and the voice of desire are intermingled in Hélène Cixous'
book, and they both weave interruptions and revivals for one
another. They are combined so as to satisfy the demands of art
and the changes of the heart.

Writing through the music of speech means giving up and giving in. *In advance*. "La musique, c'est toujours d'avance" [Music is
ever in advance, advancing] (59). Giving up and giving in becomes
a representation of a strange availability featuring extreme attention and tension. Wait, expect (everything); to drop, to let oneself
drift (nothing yet). It is *writing without a precedent*. Experience and

work are necessary, however, as well as poetic treatment to train the eyes and ears; in this respect, Hélène Cixous' works provide an excellent stimulation for reading. The musique of creation, when it wells up, however, *never appears on purpose*. It is given as a plus. It is above the know-how.

Beethoven à jamais holds its breath over this revelation in the book's last sentence: "Ils se taisent pour entendre respirer la créa-tion que tous deux viennent de créer sans l'avoir même fait exprès" [They keep quiet to hear breathe the creation that both of them just created without intending to do so]. This may be considered the secret of secrets: perpetual, though slight, separation; the agree-ment – not on purpose. Something left-over (-), a + (plus): singing as the grace of writing.

Notes

* I would like to thank Queen's University at Kingston for its support.
1. "Ton B" or your B, sounds like the French verb *tomber*, to fall.
2. The pronunciation of *tromper* and *tremper* is identical.
3. Notice how orthographic resemblance carries metaphoric resemblance in Cixous' word pairs, a resemblance that English translation cannot approximate.
4. In the original French *vie* ["life"] and *fil* ["thread"] carry an implied orthographic resemblance (see the alphabetic history of "f" and "v") and hence, a metaphoric resemblance. An English/French pair expresses this resemblance palindromically as in *life/ fil*.
5. See in particular, Mireille Calle-Gruber and Hélène Cixous, *Hélène Cixous, Photos de Racines*, "On est déjà dans la gueule du livre" [We are already in the book's mouth] (Interviews) and the section entitled "L'écriture se reprend quand elle s'entend" [Hearing itself, writing is correcting itself.]
6. Here, the pun, *alliée née*, which implies alliance and at-one-ment, defeats *l'aliénée*, madness and alienation.

Works Cited

Calle-Gruber, Mireille and Hélène Cixous. *Hélène Cixous, Photos de racines.* Paris: Editions des Femmes, 1994. Rootprints. London/New York: Routledge, 1997.

Cixous, Hélène. *Beethoven à jamais ou l'existence de Dieu.* Paris: Editions des Femmes, 1993.

5

Reading and Writing the Other: Criticism as Felicity

Martine Motard-Noar

Hélène Cixous has always worked against any systematic approach to life and writing. This makes it difficult and ironic for anyone – especially a critic – to quickly and conveniently summarize the bodies of literary and art criticism in the works of a writer also well-known for her fictional talent. Therefore, any attempt at finding a simple rationale for both her fictional and critical writing is apparently destined to fail. Another difficulty resides in the fact that her criticism – particularly in its form and values – seems to have made any critical comment over the personal, sometimes consciously intimate expression of her reading an absurd academic exercise. Yet, both the quality and quantity of her critical production require that it be studied for its attempt at unconventional, non-systematic ways of reading. Besides, her claim of not entering the realm of "categorical accesses to language and experience" (Gray 174) needs to be studied in relation to her criticism. Thus, to what extent are her fictional writing and her critical writing related?

It is first interesting to note that Cixous' standing as a critic is in fact what distinguishes her from all other "New French Feminist" writers, as they are often called. Neither Monique Wittig nor Chantal Chawaf, two prominent fiction writers of Cixous' generation to whom she has been compared many times, have been

known for either formal or informal criticism. Her critical works
then stand out to the reader and critic as a rare opportunity to
watch the application of some personal beliefs and approaches
onto another writer's verbalization of feelings and emotions. This
is an unusual challenge in French feminist literature, a display of
the real, and not simply claimed, relationship between writing and
reading.

Cixous had to propose a critical approach that could be seen as
neither a contradiction of claimed feminist values (repression of
speech) nor some biased and castrating gesture toward a good
number of male writers whom she has chosen to study, such as
James Joyce, Henry James, Edgar Poe, Kafka, Kleist, Hoffman,
Heidegger, Freud, Jean Genêt, or more recently Jacques Derrida
and Thomas Bernhard. This is all the more important since the
critic in Cixous has indeed been obvious since the early years of her
career and accounts for a substantial part of her overall production.
In fact, one could consider her doctoral dissertation, *L'Exil de James
Joyce ou l'art du remplacement*, published in 1968 in the middle of a
cultural and political revolution in France, as a landmark study on
Joyce. A proof of this might be that it was translated into English
soon after its publication. Cixous has also been a regular contribu-
tor to famous French reviews such as *Poétique*. However, it was
probably only in 1975, with "The Laugh of the Medusa," then a
true French feminist[1] bombshell which has now become a classic
manifesto, that Cixous was crowned as a non-fictional writer. Her
critical works have been published on a regular basis ever since.
From the late 70s on, most of Cixous' readings have been those of
Clarice Lispector, a Brazilian writer who works on questions of
femininity, power, writing, life and death. Meanwhile, ever since
the late 60s, Cixous has concurrently published some twenty-six
novels and works of short fiction. Thus, the difficult task for the
critic's critic remains that of defining and limiting Cixous as a critic
only, especially as she believes that writing is a constant rereading,
and that reading is writing, in this way stressing their similarities
in dealing with crucial issues. A description of these issues will be
the focus of this study.

As for many French "feminist" writers of her generation, Cixous
relates her desire for reading (Cixous' form of criticism) and
writing to a personal revolt originating from her early childhood.
There are several steps that cause her defiant gesture. The first one

relates religious prejudice to an overall feeling of being deprived of any access to the Book, i.e. reading or writing for a myriad of reasons. Her constant state of marginality as a Jew in a then French colony, Algeria, as a German speaker (her mother's native language), and as a woman may explain much of her bitterness and, at the same time as is usual with Cixous, much of her joyful exuberance. An example of these complex and apparently opposite feelings can be found in an essay entitled "Coming to Writing," where, as in several other texts, she accuses the church as the bastion of phallocentrism:

> One summer I got thrown out of the cathedral.... It's true that I had bare arms; or was it a bare head? A priest kicks me out. Naked. I felt naked for being Jewish, Jewish for being naked, naked for being a woman, Jewish for being flesh and joyful! – So I'll take all your books. But the cathedrals I'll leave behind. Their stone is sad and male. The texts I ate, sucked, suckled, kissed. I am the innumerable child of their masses. (12)

The second step corresponds to a later realization about the nature of the sum of knowledge that she, as a Woman, has been allowed to revere. Claudine Herrmann, another French feminist writer, could be read here as merely echoing Cixous' words when she writes:

> I have tried to record here certain of the stupefactions that were mine when I attempted to initiate myself into virile knowledge and culture. I had excellent teachers. They enraptured me all the more because their voices seemed to reach me from an unreal world, as foreign as the world of *The Arabian Nights*. Nothing was more beautiful than a law course or a lesson in philosophy: there, obvious truths were deliberately put aside to make way for astonishing architectural constructions wherein I frequently got lost... for they seemed to me entirely arbitrary. I contemplated these beautiful systems from afar;... I never succeeded in entering them. (*The Tongue Snatchers* 135–36)

That seems to be the exact story of Cixous who, because of social and cultural forces among other reasons, had to submit to the critical approaches of pre-1968 French academia while she was preparing for her doctoral dissertation on Joyce. Despite the magisterial size of her thesis (over eight hundred pages), it manages to

propose a new interpretation of Joyce's characters and shows a
fascination with the signified at a time when mainline critics
were mostly concerned with the signifier. Surprisingly enough for
those days, Cixous managed and was allowed to stay away from
all grandiose construction to keep the "divisibility"[2] of Joyce's text.
This was her first distinct success against the type of discourse
Hermann accused in *The Tongue Snatchers*.

Another "raison d'être" of Cixous' desire to read and have access
to criticism stems from pure outrage towards the contents of some
of her early readings – all belonging to the canonical French literature of the 50s, and for the most part, of today. In *Coming to
Writing* she gives the example of her reaction to Mallarmé, and, in
a sense, remembers here her first piece of (mental) criticism:

> I remember, at the age of twelve or thirteen, reading the follow-
> ing sentence: "The flesh is sad, alas, and I have read all the
> books." I was struck with astonishment mingled with scorn
> and disgust. As if a tomb had spoken. What a lie! And beyond,
> what truth: for the flesh is a book. A body "read," finished? A
> book – a decaying carcass? Stench and falsity. The flesh is writ-
> ing, and writing is never read: it always remains to be read,
> studied, sought, invented. (24)

This, of course, leads Cixous to a full discussion of canon formation both in our society and our "reading" (in the broad sense of
the word) of literature. *The Newly Born Woman*, an early theoretical
text "that combines essay, autobiography, and poetic-prophetic
prose," (*New French Feminisms*, Note, 90) offers a feminist critical
basis as the origin of many, if not all, of Cixous' decisions to seek
texts and thoughts to criticize:

> if you examine literary history, it's the same story. It all refers
> back to man to *his* torment, his desire to be (at) the origin. Back to
> the father. There is an intrinsic bond between the philosophical
> and the literary ... and phallocentrism. The philosophical con-
> structs itself starting with the abasement of woman. ("Sorties,"
> *New French Feminisms* 92)

As can be seen in that passage and the first one from "*Coming to
Writing*" quoted in this article, Cixous links the religious, the
philosophical, the literary, and, in final analysis, all forms of interpretation, to phallocentrism. Her lucidity and bitterness in

particular toward the literary establishment as a notorious representative of phallocentrism has not decreased. All the way into the
80s and 90s, she has stressed her precarious situation as a female
critic, theorist, and fiction writer, as well as university professor at
the Collège International de Philosophie/University of Paris VIII.
Although she was allowed to establish and run the "Centre de
Recherches en Etudes Féminines" there in 1974, she has had a
difficult time maintaining her mode of displacement within the
university system:

> we're completely crushed, especially in places like universities,
> by the highly repressive operations of metalanguage, the opera-
> tion that sees to it that the moment women open their
> mouths...they are immediately asked in whose name and
> from what theoretical standpoint they are speaking, who is
> their master and where they are coming from: they have, in
> short, to salute...and show their identity papers. ("Castration
> or Decapitation?" quoted in *When the Moon Waxes Red* 20–21)

Working against such behavior means working towards the
deauthorization and "degrammaticalization" (*Reading* 4) of her
critical discourse in order to lead to the transgression of defensive
language. The stress – meant by "degrammaticalization" – placed
by Cixous on the signified may explain her attraction to foreign
texts and transcultural reading, from Irish literature (Joyce) to
American literature (Poe, Henry James), from French literature
(Jean Genêt) to German literature (Hoffman, Kleist, Kafka, Rilke,
Ingeborg Bachman, Thomas Bernhard) to Russian literature (Tsve-
taeva), and finally, but not least, to Brazilian literature with Clarice
Lispector. After twenty-five years of critical writing and publishing, the list is far from being closed. In fact, as a "Jewoman"
belonging to no country, raised at the crossroad between several
languages, why should Cixous feel faithful to a specific country of
words and syntax? Moreover, since mastery is being questioned,
she also presents critiques of psychoanalysis, and studies of paintings (Rembrandt, Monet) and music (Rossini), without being a
psychoanalyst or an art critic.

However, reading foreign literature alone is not sufficient to
account for more than exoticism. But these texts and voices are
approached in a fashion that tries to keep them from being
colonized by the critic, or rather reader, a name that fits Cixous'

practice and attitude much better. And in order to read, one has to decide how to, as if setting out on a great journey. For that reason Cixous, again in unison with Herrmann, sings a new concept: that of slow motion reading. Herrmann had been specific and ironic on traditional approaches to the text: "speed-reading... evokes only hell: a place where the time to dream is abolished" ("In Favor of Slow Motion Reading" 2). Slow motion reading stands then as the first step against the "reductive properties of modernity and mass culture... at the expense of knowledge and understanding" (Shiach 62). Slow motion reading is what Cixous will revere in Clarice Lispector's writing and her reading of it: "At the school of Clarice Lispector, we learn the approach. We take lessons of things. The lessons of calling, letting ourselves to be called. The lessons of letting come, receiving" (*Coming to Writing* 60–61). Hence the title of Cixous' book *Coming to Writing* (in French *La Venue à l'écriture*) which alludes, especially in the French noun "La Venue," to a slow movement as it is happening, to a non-aggressive or at least not overtly aggressive approach. This might explain why a majority of Cixous' written criticism resembles the delivery of her criticism during her seminars at the Collège International de Philosophie in Paris. Although very carefully prepared, her critical, oral meditations there express still on-going thinking and a search for the most appropriate words and expressions. Her words are weighed carefully and thoughtfully, probably because her criticism is truly a theoretical practice where a general philosophy of the subject is enacted.

Yet, Verena Andermatt Conley, who translated some of Cixous' seminar lectures of the early 1980s, notices in the latter ones the presence of a phrase not often found in her written criticism and traditionally considered the most common and vulgar phrases in the French language (and therefore not one to use in any literary discourse) : "il y a" (there is/there are). Yet, instead of understanding this as a weakness or an oral mannerism, in very much the same way as her search for a limitless vocabulary, this recurrent expression (even when it is mostly found in the recording of her seminars) may:

> impl[y] a theoretical position that refers to Heidegger's *es gibt*, "there is (to give)," an utterance that is charged with theological and philosophical undertones. It inaugurates an originary

moment by calling to attention the positioning of an individual in the world. The words suggest that as a collectivity we have the great grace and privilege of being born into the world through an act of language, simply put, that comes with and is enclosed within all... *there is*. (*Reading* ix)

This act of language for Cixous stands both as a simple and a complex one in oral and sometimes written criticism. For her, coming to reading and writing can be compared to straying into the forest of language. "There is" evokes precisely the birth of an approach to a discourse in its general indistinct direction. Identification with the "other," a highlight of her philosophy of the subject, stands as the only textual certainty, placing the reader back into the arena of writing: " 'We, character, reader, author, circulate between 'I am not her,' and 'I could be her.' as we advance along the most powerful path of meditation that we can take in thinking of the other' " (Jenson "Coming to Reading Hélène Cixous" 187). The feminine pronoun "her" relates to a character in one of Lispector's novels and possibly Lispector herself. Cixous has in fact come to admire the Brazilian writer and her writing for their constant investment of the self, although the word "investment" has unfortunately an economic ring to it, something that Cixous would reject. Nevertheless, Cixous loves in her a non-defensive writing which can be matched with non-defensive readings, for "Lispector is a writer who 'knows nothing,' because her work is not the stasis of cognition; it is the journey of 're-cognition.' As such, her work 'puts us back in the world school' of unceasing, 'equal' attention" (Jenson 186–87). In such a school, there is no room, according to Cixous, for a critical perspective that would assume a privileged situation for the character, the author, and the reader as well. Cixous makes clear her ideals of writing and, indirectly, of reading in her study of Lispector:

In an interview, Clarice says... that she does not rewrite or touch up words. This is both true and untrue. As she says, she lets her hand write and puts herself into an intense relationship of listening. She is tuned into her unconscious and becomes a scribe. She transmits. At that moment, she is in a relation of respect, of sacralization with what she writes. She considers that she is not the one that writes but that the word is already a thing in itself.

So when I say that it is not true that she does not rewrite, it is because the operation of rewriting precedes. At the moment when she puts herself into this state of writing she is already rewriting....What is happening in this formidable impulse is such that she will probably have gone as far, at a given moment, as to destroy the frame, the kind of writing practiced in an office, on paper, because for her, when writing comes, it comes. She notes on pieces of paper, in the present, at the very moment it presents itself. (*Reading* 14)

Although this concept of writing as a pure listening/self-reading exercise can be understood as automatic writing, Cixous seems to not identify it as such, but rather as a capacity for improvisation. In fact, Lispector's account of her writing process rejoins Cixous' own writing process as a fictional writer. This might make it easier for Cixous to pursue her fictional and critical goal, namely of constantly changing points of view in order to stay away from theoretical reduction. This occurs in her criticism as well, although in a more obviously conscious manner. This allows for both writing and reading to be a matter of pleasure, of personal, emotional spending and giving – a feminine "economy" which Cixous has defined in opposition to a masculine economy, driven by concerns about taking, saving, and profit. Of course, Cixous does not limit her definition of feminine economy to females or of male economy to men since, according to her, many women have adopted the masculine economy which some men have managed to resist. Spending as a central notion in her philosophy of the subject, and therefore, of writing and reading, all included in criticism, gives birth to a set of positive values in Cixous' eyes, much beyond any question of *genre*. It is her concept of life as poetry:

poetry, with its over determinations, replaces the univocity of a concept that reappropriates, creates new exclusions, hierarchies, repressions. In the context of the French debate of the subject that focuses on difference and alterity...Cixous is most attuned to Lispector's ways of inscribing textual interruptions, into meditations about the "self," that is, of masking limits, of linking self and other at all levels. (Andermatt Conley *Reading* xii)

Cixous' detailed reading of Lispector and other writers tries to revalorize the living "her story" (consequently the story) thus privileging the signified. What matters is not only how it is told but what is being told. There is no indifference on her part as to the philosophy emanating from this "inmost" writing. A sentence, a paragraph, a page by Lispector or any of the authors whom she has recently read often leads to several pages or hours (in the case of her seminars) of play on their discordance, on their absence of justification or demonstration. In a way, Cixous could be considered in the end as the author of the text which she reads as she journeys through philosophical questions. In this communicative pleasure of the writing, minute reading builds up a passage to the infinite.

To those disturbed by her utopian thinking, Cixous proposes practical examples of it in life and in her "criticism"/reading. The best example of it stems out of her reading of one of Lispector's books, *Felicidade Clandestina*,[3] the story of a little girl waiting for a book to be lent to her from another little girl, her friend. After waiting for several weeks, her friend's mother finally hands it over to her. On the moral of the story, Cixous writes:

> She *has* the book; what must she do to have it? A present must be invented that will not stop presenting itself. This is where she begins to enjoy what she has and not what she desires. By a sort of fabulous intuition she stages the having, makes it palpitate, move slightly, vibrate, she does not consume it, she does not devour it: first making a sandwich, coming and going between the kitchen and the book, the bread sandwich and the textual sandwich that she does not devour, sitting down in a hammock with her book on her knees, she literally rocks it, and she does not read, does not read, not yet – and then she goes off again. And she finds all the most profound, delicate, subtle ruses to continue having what she has eternally, to not lose having, to be pregnant with having, is – guesses – the text, already, in the child, in the woman,... happy already to have something to enjoy, happy that there is, in the world, the to be–enjoyed,... "clandestine felicity." (*"Coming to Writing"* 160)

Cixous' oral and written reading tends to be an analysis of ideas as well as a psychoanalysis for herself and her audience. To recognize and admit one's closeness to the text is how to find the proper distance. For this reason, Cixous does not hesitate to use the first person in her critical approaches. An example of such personal investment in the issues brought up by the text can be found again in an analysis of a story by Lispector. When Lispector writes: "My fear was that, out of impatience with the slowness that I have in understanding myself, I would be hurrying to bring about a meaning before its time" (*Reading* 104), Cixous chooses to not really explore the Brazilian writer's position as a traditional, autobiographical piece of information or as a literary topos. On the contrary, she totally engages herself into the account:

> If I mark this sentence down, I have to hear that something has to be understood in me. It means that I have to understand myself, I have to envelop myself. There is an egg in me and I do not have to hurry its birth. I also have to undertake the astonishing trajectory of my own comprehension, of entering into myself and being my own egg. (*Reading* 104)

According to Cixous, the place of the pseudo-objective, distant, and, in the end, phallocentric reader/critic cannot be assumed. Involvement in the text is a necessary condition of her reading as well as her writing. In fact, she may be so invested in these texts because she herself has spent much energy in fictional writing. Cixous has indeed published an average of at least one fictional text per year in the last quarter century since she started publishing. Thus, it might be considered that her reading/criticism stands as a pleasurable attempt toward understanding put in close proximity to her forever on-going search as a writer, to the point where it is difficult to disassociate them.

Some critics may see this aspect in Cixous' reading/criticism as a chosen strength or admitted weakness, since she obviously decides only to recognize and analyze inspiring texts, texts that definitely converge, directly or indirectly, with her own interest. And Cixous clearly identifies such similarity in, for instance, Lispector's passion for questioning. In the following passage, she summarizes her concerns in a study of Lispector's writing:

> How do we behave with the other in the major experiences of life-experiences of separation, experiences, in love, of possession and dispossession, of incorporation and non incorporation; experiences of mourning by allusion, of real mourning, all the experiences governed by economies, variable structures? How do we lose? How do we keep? Do we remember? Do we forget? Do we take? Do we receive? (*Coming to Writing* 155)

In the same way, the concept of the egg – a mysterious one – to be understood as a questioning of offering and writing in Lispector's work is partially made of similar questions of life and death, of the figure of the Father and his disappearance, of problems of filiation[4] which are all leitmotifs in Cixous' work. Her seminars follow that same critical rationale – that of interest, inspiration, and exchange, away from outside indifference, pseudo-objectivity, or mastering of a discourse based on the importance of the signifier over the signified.

The ultimate testimony of such "unreserved" discourse can be found in *To Live the Orange* where Cixous' reading/criticism of Lispector is intricately woven into Cixous' writing and quest. *To Live the Orange* is a chant to Lispector's writing which "Came with an angel's footsteps" (10), and beyond that to all women. Cixous' personal concerns reach out into the realm of the Revelation for all women; the first person is constantly used with the third one:

> in these times of inertia, when we forgot the listening and the hearing,...we hold still under a silence without nearness....I wandered ten glacial years in over published solitude, without seeing a single human woman's face,...I took the last book before death, and behold, it was Clarice, the writing. (48)

When reading is writing and writing reading, Cixous opens her texts to a wide field of personalized discourse (including her testimony as a published writer and scholar) and, concurrently, decentralizes concerns in a visionary mode. *To Live the Orange* is the perfect example of this. It is reminiscent of an ode to the conjuration and presence of women in Lispector's and Cixous' writing ("I feel women writing in my writing" (34)), in all of its repetitions, phrasing, reiterated belief, and images.

Such total exchange between writer and reader, reader and writer, is in no way an easy task to achieve since Cixous' goal in reading/interpreting/writing is to "save the approach that opens and leaves space for *the other*" (*Coming to Writing* 62). Despite the fact that such statements seem to be always elaborated around Cixous' criticism of Lispector and sound very idealistic and calm for a writer otherwise well-known as a wonderful polemicist, they have been part of her philosophy ever since the 1970s. Her famous essay, "The Laugh of the Medusa," has already enunciated this same desire for the Other, a genuine "ouverture" in both senses of the word in French, i.e. an opening as well as a musical overture, quite comparable to the way she chants Lispector among others. Yet, many readers are uncomfortable with a word like "opening" that could convey usual images associated with Woman, defined as the one awaiting physical and mental fulfillment by Man. However, Cixous never proposed to dispose of sexual difference in her definition of a feminine practice of writing, and thus of reading too. Consequently, opening space for the other, according to her, stands as the prime realization of an inexhaustible and forever present desire which represents neither a lack nor a need for castration. She clearly explains her position against any Freudian interpretation of her quest:

> Woman be unafraid of any other place, of any same, or any other. My eyes, my tongue, my ears, my skin, my mouth, my body-for-(the)-other – not that I long for it in order to fill up a hole, to provide against some defect of mine, or because as fate would have it, I'm spurred on by feminine "jealousy." (*New French Feminisms* 260)

The laugh of the medusa is precisely encompassed, in this declaration, of love for living, writing, and reading the Other, male and female, in her/his bisexuality which makes her/him a subject belonging to the erotic universe:

> isn't it evident that the penis gets around in my texts, that I give it a place and appeal? Of course I do. I want all. I want all of me with all of him. Why should I deprive myself of a part of us? I want all of us. Woman of course has a desire for a "loving desire" and not a jealous one. But not because she is gelded; not because she's deprived and needs to be filled out....I don't want a penis to decorate my body with. But I do desire the other for the other, whole and entire, male or female, because living means wanting everything that is, everything that lives, and wanting it alive. Castration? Let others toy with it. What's a desire originating from a lack? A pretty meager desire. (262)

Cixous opposes such meager desire and drive to a traditionally masculine economy, as she studies it sometimes in Freud, an economy characterized by "immense detours, this formidable expenditure to get to a pleasure" (*Reading* 125) – in other words, an economy of attraction that leads to and lives on agitation, repulsion, retention, and release. Few of these moments, if any, are joyous in the holy "dire-jouir-interdire" (say-enjoy-forbid) trinity.

The progression in Cixous' critical thought since the 1970s has directed her toward the exemplification of her theory through criticism. Lispector has certainly been an important presence, which has allowed her to push her theoretical praxis to the limit since the late 1970s, as her essays become more meditative and imbued with a mystical tone. Her first essay on Lispector, "Clarice Lispector: the Approach," published in French in 1979, had already lost most of the exuberant attacks and satirical puns that made Cixous the writer of the "Feminist" Manifesto ("The Laugh of the Medusa") just four years earlier. But Cixous' apparent appeasement should not be mistaken; it represents a springboard to a further questioning of the voyage toward and with the other. She has come to define the next step of the approach:

> *To allow a thing to enter in its strangeness*, light from the soul has to be put into each look, and the exterior light mixed with the interior light...seeing to see and see....It is the science of the other! An art in itself; and all the ways of letting all the beings with their different strangenesses enter our proximity are regions that ask to be appreciated, each with an appropriate patience. (*Coming to Writing* 66)

This visionary philosophy finds an extended field of study in art criticism, specifically, that of painting. "The Last Painting or the Portrait of God," published in French in 1983, examines the artist's dilemma between representation and physical knowledge as the best way to love. Here Cixous goes further in her definition of love and the other, and of spatial relationship. She takes an anecdote from the life of the French painter Monet whom she has been studying. One day, Monet received an apple so splendid that he never dared to eat it; instead he offered it to someone else. Cixous' reaction to this anecdote is without hesitation:

> I would have eaten it....I am different...in my need to touch the apple without seeing it. To know it in the dark. With my fingers, with my lips, with my tongue. In my need to share with you the food, the bread, the words, the painted food. In my need to make use of my right hand to hold the pen and write, and of my two hands to hold nothing, to caress and to pray. (130–31)

This passage clearly expresses an enlargement of Cixous' earlier claim to an aura of love for the other, where opening would in no way symbolize a lack, a precarious condition or a desire to anni- hilate and engulf. What prevails here in looking at the other is nonfear of the other, the inside and the entering, as well as being entered. In a 1989 essay, Cixous proposes to see the limit, the extreme in Lispector's work, a limit which Cixous herself has explored in a majority of her fictional texts: to be the most other possible for all women is to pass into the masculine (and the opposite for all men):

> the most other possible involved passing into the masculine, *passing by way of a man.* Paradoxical step. So, to approach this almost-woman, one sees in the text how (Clarice)-I has not shaved for several days, has not played football, and so on. "I" goes into the masculine, and this particular masculinity impov- erishes her.... But like every process of impoverishment with Clarice Lispector, it is a positive movement, a form of asceticism, a way of bridling a part of pleasure, to attain a strange joy. Moreover, in his turn this man "monasterizes" himself, deprives himself, bows down. Double impoverishment. (142–43)

As usual in Cixous, the philosophy of the sexes, while engender- ing a more intense pleasure for bisexuality, reaches out into the realm of critical writing and writing at large. There is much pleas- ure in the intense questioning of Lispector's text:

> Who is the "Man" who writes this text? No. Who is the man who writes this text? No. What sex is the writer who is capable of writing this text? No. What sex, then, am I who can write this text? Or: does the text decide the sex of the author? I mean the sex hidden in the sex, the imaginary sex. Or: who is the author of the author? I mean: who makes the author? This is what happens to the author who sees him(her)self constrained to ask by an extremely demanding subject: Who am I, who are I, at this very moment? A flight of questions beating two she-wings one black one white one he-r one h-ymn one s-he one (s)he-sitation ... Mad is the wo(man) who wants to know who I ... (143)

Ultimately, Cixous works on the unreadability of the text, on a love for the not-I, the "Clarisk" (76) when words do not attempt to replace things, in a movement of nonexclusive difference, a

"Blanc-dire," a white speech (*Reading* 118) that would let even ugliness be.[5] This might be the reason why she still dreams of a further limit to writing: by definition, the Limit, i.e. the last text. The proximity of death brings the writer closer to this edge: "no one" (*Coming to Writing* 136). There exactly can be placed the relationship between Cixous as a writer and Cixous as a reader/ critic, in the search for vertigo, for the mysterious splendor of life and its writing, in apparent unreadability:

> One day I wrote a book called *Lemonade Everything Was So Infinite* – it was a book of meditation on one of Kafka's last phrases, a phrase he wrote down on a sheet of paper, just before his death. During this time he no longer spoke out loud, because of the burning in his throat. A phrase came from that unuttered zone where, mute but distinct, the most essential things are said, minuscule things, infinite things, inexpressible outside in the sharp air, because of their fragility and beauty. This phrase is *Limonade es war alles so grenzenlos*. For me this is *The Poem*, the ecstasy and the regret, the very simple heart of life. It is the end. And the end of the end. And the first refreshment. (*Coming to Writing* 136–37)

Again writing and reading, or fiction and criticism, seem to join in a fascinating pursuit of the biggest secret: truth. Cixous places it as close to death as possible, at the limit between the one (i.e. life) and the other (i.e. death) in its most radical representation. Kafka's last sentence is to be put in parallel with most of the underlying concerns found in her fiction. From *Inside*, her first novel published in French in 1969, to *L'Ange au secret*, published in 1991, her fictional writing has attempted to inscribe and analyze her father's death when she was still a child. One of its chapters in particular, "Nos Morts – nos assassins,"[6] is entirely dedicated to the exploration of the meaning of his death.

Many reproaches could be extended to Cixous for reading texts partially based on their French translation.[7] There is much irony too in this article which itself relies on English translations of Cixous' French texts! Cixous could also be accused of over simplistic universalist comparisons in her ahistorical, acultural concept and practice of reading foreign texts. However, her "mode of attention [is] comparativist rather than universalist; attuned to changes and contrasts instead of to 'covering laws'" ("Social

Criticism without Philosophy" 101), to apply Nancy Fraser and Linda Nicholson's theory to Cixous' attempt. Cixous' criticism runs away from all systems in its praxis. Unfortunately, this praxis, always in search of the Last Words, the ultimate ones – and the theme of her recent text *L'Ange au secret* – might not be able to escape its own mortality, for Cixous' defiance resides in her passing into the other as her definition of poetry, criticism, and Clandestine Felicity. The ecstasy and provocation are certainly limitless as she defines her work in this way: "Ce que l'on dit lire, qui sait si ce n'est vivre? Ou bien si ce n'est mourir pour se passer plus loin?"[8] [What we call reading, who knows if it is not living? Or if it is not dying in order to happen further down?] (*Déluge* 12).

Notes

1. I shall characterize Cixous' works as "feminist" in this article, although she has consistently rejected this description, like several other women writers. Her hostility to the term seems to result from semantics (feminism would be defined as the exclusion of men and the replacement of their power by another tyranny – that of women) and from her desire to distance herself from any political group or agenda. However, I shall use the term "feminist" in a broader sense as expressing a focus on issues of gender as well as a belief in women's voices.
2. For more details, see Motard-Noar, *Les Fictions d'Hélène Cixous*, 126.
3. Title of a text written by Clarice Lispector and studied by Cixous.
4. See, for instance, " 'Sunday, before falling sleep': A Primal Scene," in *Reading*, 3–10.
5. This is at the basis of an interesting antithetic comparison by Cixous of Rilke and Lispector in *Coming to Writing*, 75.
6. "Our Dead – our murderers."
7. Cixous has also been using native speakers with whom she works in her seminars in order to refine her understanding of the language used in foreign texts. She is also fluent in English and German.

Works Cited

Cixous, Hélène. *L'Ange au secret*. Paris: Des femmes, 1991.
——. "Castration or Decapitation?" *Out There: Marginalization and Contemporary Culture*. Ed. Russell Ferguson, *et al*. New York: The New Museum of Contemporary Art and M.I.T., 1989.
——. *"Coming to Writing" and Other Essays*. Trans. Sarah Cornell, *et al*. Cambridge: Harvard UP, 1991.
——. *Déluge*. Paris: Des femmes, 1992.
——. *L'Exil de James Joyce ou l'art du remplacement*. Paris: Grasset, 1968.
——. *The Exile of James Joyce or the Art of Replacement*. Trans. Sally Purcell. New York: David Lewis, 1972.
——. *Inside*. Trans. C. Barko. New York: Schocken, 1986.
——. *The Newly Born Woman*. Trans. Betsy Wing. Minneapolis: U of Minnesota P, 1986.
——. *Reading with Clarice Lispector*. Trans. Verena Andermatt Conley. Minneapolis: U of Minnesota P, 1990.
——. "Le Rire de la Méduse." *L'Arc* (1975): 39–54.
——. "The Laugh of the Medusa." Trans. Keith Cohen and Paula Cohen. *Signs* 1 (Summer 1976): 876–99.
——. *Vivre l'orange/To Live the Orange*. Paris: Des femmes, 1979.
Fraser, Nancy & Linda Nicholson. "Social Criticism without Philosophy: An Encounter between Feminism and Post-modernism." *Universal Abandon? The Politics of Post-modernism*. Ed. Andrew Ross. Minneapolis: U of Minnesota P, 1988.
Gray, Nancy. *Language Unbound: On Experimental Writing by Women*. Urbana: U of Illinois P, 1992.
Herrmann, Claudine. "In Favor of Slow Motion Reading." Trans. Nancy Kline. *Boston University Journal* 20 (1972): 2–5.
——. *The Tongue Snatchers*. Trans. Nancy Kline. Lincoln: Nebraska UP, 1989.

Jenson, Deborah. "Coming to Reading Hélène Cixous." *"Coming to Writing" and Other Essays*. Cambridge: Harvard UP, 1991.

Lispector, Clarice. *Felicidate Clandestina*. Rio de Janeiro: Nova Fronteira, 1971.

Marks, Elaine, and Isabelle de Courtivron, ed. *New French Feminisms*. New York: Schocken Books, 1981.

Motard-Noar, Martine. *Les Fictions d'Hélène Cixous: Une autre langue de femme*. Lexington, KY: French Forum, 1991.

Shiach, Morag. *Hélène Cixous: A Politics of Writing*. New York: Routledge, 1991.

Trinh Minh-Ha. *When the Moon Waxes Red: Representation, Gender and Cultural Politics*. New York: Routledge, 1991.

6

Cixous' Concept of "Brushing" as a Gift

Claudine Fisher

Le Rire de la Méduse was published in France in 1975, a crucial date for the MLF (Movement of Liberation of Women) and a culminating point in Cixous' critical feminist theory. This corresponded as well to a turning point in Cixous' fictional writings. She started writing less theoretical texts per se, and more consistently blended her theory into the core of her fiction in the last two decades. Cixous is a prolific writer with a consistent output of a book each year, the latest being *L'Ange au secret*. It is obvious that interest in Cixous' writings and criticism, far from waning in the United States, seems to be gaining momentum. In *The Laugh of the Medusa*, Cixous had already something to say on the concept of gift. In her early writings, she recognized the importance of the problematics of the gift, as seen by some as "the gift-that-takes." She differentiated it from the true other gift, the "gift-that-gives."

> I shall have a great deal to say about the whole deceptive problematic of the gift. Woman is obviously not that woman Nietzsche dreamed of who gives only in order to. Who could ever think of the gift as a gift-that-takes? Who else but man, precisely the one who would like to take everything? (Adams 317)

I would like to look into Cixous' fictional texts, especially *Limonade tout était si infini*, to show that all the premises of *The Laugh of the Medusa* still hold true in Cixous' fiction, and that she went on to define more precisely her concept on artists and their "works of art," and on artists-in-life as a reflection of their "works of being." The important relationship which exists between the work and the artist is never enough for Cixous. As an avid reader, Cixous keeps delving into the biographies of famous painters and writers who fascinate her, and some happen to be males. She finds in the lives of a few men an "other" relationship which exists between the man and his life, that "other" relationship taking precedence for Cixous over the "work of art" itself. In this relationship, Cixous sees an "other," sees a being capable of the ultimate gesture of giving, a "blessing" or "brushing" which she associates with love, and the access to a second innocence. The concept of "brushing" belongs to the realm of the gift and silence, whereas the act of writing extols the desire to dare to speak. *Lemon Soda all was so Infinite* merges both desires into a whole.

Recurring sentences from Kafka and Dostoevski are used as leitmotiv in Hélène Cixous' fiction, *Limonade tout était si infini*. The gesture which appropriates someone else's writing, thanks to several striking poetic words, reflects the ultimate gesture of "gift" for Cixous, linking the writers through the centuries, and linking the different tongues between all communities of writers or artists. In Cixous' writing, general intertextuality stands as a homage to the writers quoted or discussed. It is also used as a displacement, illustrating Cixous' feminist stand on the problematic of the true gift.

Cixous structures her books in several layers. Often, there exists in her fiction a diffuse "exterior" line with no real plot which evolves, paralleling an "inside" adventure of the mind within the female protagonist. Moreover, a philosophical motif is woven into strong semantic threads reinforcing the premises. The various layers gradually converge into a coherent whole at the end of the novel, debating the questions of law, love, freedom, innocence regained, writing, and the true artist.

In *Limonade tout était si infini*, it is Kafka's phrase set in the title, "Lemon Soda all was so Infinite," which gives its tone to the book. By the same token, Cixous used a sentence by Kafka in her title, *Préparatifs de noces au-delà de l'abîme* (Nuptial Preparations Beyond the Abyss) in order to displace and serve as echo to Kafka's text,

Préparatifs de noces à la Campagne (Nuptial Preparations in the Country). In *Angst*, a Kafka-like novel of feminine anguish, a man called "K." happens to be one of the protagonists. K. is a man once loved, that is the writer Kafka, as well as a disguise for the name of the protagonists's male lover in the novel. Thirdly, K. stands for a place as forbidding as that of *The Castle*, where misfortune and unhappiness are bound to happen, a locus of writing where the dilemma of the forbidden shifts to a transgression of love and law. The same connotation exists in the little-known political essay, *Un K. Incomphéhensible: Pierre Goldman*, where Cixous questions the French justice system by using the "case" of Goldman, a man accused of a hold-up in 1969 and tried in 1974. With the play on the word "case" ("cas" in French, thus "K." with an identical pronunciation), Cixous shows that the "Law" can be as nightmarish in modern France as during the time of *The Castle* by Kafka.

The sentence from Kafka in *Limonade tout était si infini*, contrary to *Angst*, conjures up a world of happiness and innocence in which the light and bubbly taste of lemon soda dominates. By its transparence, lemon soda resembles pure water; by its bubbles the soda evokes lightness; by its sweet-sour taste and light tartness, it gives pleasure. All the connotations merge to remind the protagonist of a beloved woman of whom she speaks and to whom the book is transmitted.

Taste and thirst, the philosophical highlights of the novel, are shown to be in direct relationship to the "taste" of the thoughts themselves. Semantically and symbolically for Cixous, thirst corresponds to the gift of freedom given and received in total liberty. The premise of thirst must be considered with extreme attention since Cixous links it to the first "Thirst" (with a capital letter) and tries to discover its mystery:

> ...soudain la première Soif sort de l'eau en brillant, la première Adoration revient une telle Soif on ne l'a connue qu'au paradis, sort ruisselante, la Passion retrouvée, une Soif exaltante comme l'amour, tend les paumes pleines d'eau, quand on s'incline, soudain, dans le conte, tout l'endormi est réveillé, l'immergé surgit, les paumes sont pleines de mémoire, on avait oublié le secret de l'eau, mais quand de tout son être on la désire, on l'aime à nouveau comme on l'aimait au commencement. (*Limonade* 13)

Suddenly the first Thirst comes glistening out of the water, the
first Adoration comes back, such a Thirst was only known in
paradise, coming out dripping wet, Passion recovered, a Thirst
as exciting as love, holding up both palms full of water; in the
tale when one bows, it is, all of a sudden, the sleepiness which
awakens, the submerged which arises, the palms are full of
memory, the secret of water was forgotten, but when one wishes
for it with all of one's being, one loves it anew as it was loved at
the beginning.

Cixous here insists on the close link of thirst to water which goes
through both body and soul. The hands make the gesture of giving
as it must have been for the "first" thirst. The liquid matter calls for
the thirst and the thirst calls for the act of drinking. In its symbolic
meaning, the liquid element implies the maternal side, the source of
life. For Cixous, the exchange thirst/drink is in direct proximity to
the concept of "one" to the "other," in a perfect equilibrium of
understanding oneness and "alterity." One can become the other
by the absorption of the liquid, water or lemon soda. Cixous differ-
entiates between the analytical stands of thirst and hunger. Drinking
water implies caring for one's body as well as an acknowledgement
of the other, a reconnaissance of alterity, and a gratefulness (as in
the double French meaning of "reconnaissance") toward the other.
Hunger, on the contrary, is total absorption of the "other," as in a
mythical "cannibalism"; that is, one must eat the other in order to
survive. The consequence of hunger for the other is best illustrated
for Cixous in love, particularly in passionate love, the epitome of a
cannibalistic gesture. A good example of "cannibalistic" passions,
can be a brutal and violent loss and fall as seen in the love of
Achilles and the Amazon in Kleist's *Penthesilea*. Hunger often can
be equated with relationships of devourer/devoured or that of
victim and oppressor, whereas thirst for the other presupposes a
freedom on both sides for Cixous. There is absorption with integrity, respect and comprehension, but no destruction. The double
harmonious movement of the ritual of offering and receiving a
drink becomes a sign of corporeal and mental equality. In the
theoretical Cixousian space, there exists in thirst a transmutation
which does not have the total-absorption implications of hunger.

The structure of *Limonade tout était si infini* is thus inscribed in the
desire for thirst between the poles of "Because" enhanced in the

first part of the book, and of "Why" in the second part. Each part represents a different facet of the meditation on thirst. The title of the first half of the text, *First Letter*, refers to the double meaning of "first letter": it is the letter A from the alphabet as well as the first mail sent to the beloved, a young woman named Elli. This young person lives in the same house as the woman narrator who surprises herself with her unusual gesture of addressing mail to a person living intimately under her own roof. The hidden identity of Elli is slowly revealed all along the text through stylistic clues, yet also remains hidden throughout the text. Elli seems to be an anagram for the word "daughter" ("fille" in French transposed and inverted, with the suppression of the first "f"). This explanation fits the double meaning of the text perfectly, since the title of the first part is *First Letter* (that which is said in silence, that which is omitted in the anagram, [f]ille-Elli; and the first mail sent to the young woman as a true adult and no longer a teenager). The narrator mails the letter and, at the same time, the author sends the book as her "ultimate" gesture to her own daughter, both a gesture of love and a gift of freedom. The second part of the novel, entitled *La Dernière phrase* [The Last Sentence], explicates the last phrases of other protagonists, Kafka and Dostoevski included: beloved phrases for they have been remembered and gathered after their deaths, then used again in Cixous' text to explain her own novels.

The message, in the second part of the Cixousian novel, is carried through instances in the lives of Kafka and Dostoevski. Cixous delves into their lives in order to elucidate the dilemma between living and writing, and to see how the writers of the past have walked that tightrope. *Limonade tout était si infini* therefore presents hidden messages left in literature and in the arts about the private lives of famous persons, as well as through the life of Cixous' own narrator/mother and the narrator/writer. The question of origin shifts to a meditation at several levels: the origin of the non-said, thus silence; the origin of exceptional written sentences; the origin of the narrator's daughter; the origin of works of art (oeuvres d'art) as well as "works of being" (oeuvres d'être), both works of art/être sharing deep signifying and signified implications.

This text, as with many others by Cixous, is consistently oriented toward a textual unconscious, and evokes the allegorical scene of the origin of life. The origin, quite often in Cixous' most recent texts, means rediscovering a special moment of awareness where one "dies" in the mind, so to speak, and discards the encumbrances of everyday life in order to be reborn into a second innocence with a heightened sense of "true" life. Cixous does not place this rebirth within a religious framework, but outside it, and seems to believe that a "happy few" are capable of reaching that stage. A few artists or writers have been able to live this reprieve of physical death to pass on to the side of authentic life. Cixous selects three specific moments in the lives of three artists to illustrate the existence of "life beyond death" in everyday life: these are crucial happenings in the life of Kafka, in that of Dostoevski, and finally, in the life of the woman protagonist.

The exceptional phrases used form a poem at the very end of the novel to represent "eggs freshly laid" (306) which keeps their circular mystery. These "eggs" of thought can be weighed and out-weighed, but will always escape comprehension even if an intuitive apprehension of their value can exist. Kafka's sentence, "lemon soda all was so infinite," expresses an exceptional "life-gesture" addressed to someone known, while still keeping anonymity, a gesture which appears suspended in time between life and death, and is full of grace. The mysterious beauty of the moment makes the gesture particularly enigmatic. To quote from her seminars, Cixous calls this special instant of "frôlement," of lightness of touch and of being, a "brushing":

> I insist on the value of movement, of mobility, and of good viscosity. I also repeat that grace can only be in movement. One never *has* grace, it is always given. Grace is life itself. In other words, it is an incessant need, but even if it is given, like life itself, this does not mean that it will be received.... The brushing makes the difference between an innocent innocence that we do not know – like that of Adam and Eve before they were expelled from paradise – and another for which we have to look, at the other end of the world.... That is when we arrive at the second innocence that, contrary to the first, does not *not* know itself. This second innocence is precisely the grace one gives to oneself. (*Readings* 67)

The chosen sentences in the novel are keys for the reader and the phonic, linguistic, and symbolic signs allow for a better understanding of Cixous' "meandering" style, as she approaches obliquely the visible and the invisible aspects of the allegorical primitive scene:

> Je veux étudier, toute ma vie, les mystères des arts délicats. Je veux travailler près des mystères qui assurent la vie de la vie. (*Limonade* 41)

> I want to study the mystery of delicate arts my whole life. I want to work close to mysteries which guarantee the life of life.

Kafka and Dostoevski have influenced her fiction, but in *Limonade tout était si infini* Cixous deliberately chooses texts outside their output to make the following points. Works of art are important, indeed; so Cixous proceeds in analyzing the paintings of Leonardo da Vinci and those of Rembrandt. However, Cixous shows that the pictorial or literary masterpieces which speak mostly to the soul are the works of art which are simultaneously works of art and works of "being." In Cixous' mind, Rembrandt is above de Vinci because of his works of art/being, whereas Leonardo da Vinci creates only works of art. This "art of being" is shown through Rembrandt's brush strokes when he expresses his love for his companion, Saskia. The "human beings" [êtres humains] represented are transformed into "hand beings" [êtres à mains] (Cixous plays with the double entendre human/hand beings in French, with almost the same sounds). In Rembrandt's case, Cixous shows that she responds more sensitively to an artist who succeeds in expressing in his art "the geography of happiness" (53); Cixous alludes to "hand beings," such as Saskia, in the etymological sense of the Latin word "manus," which is in the root of the French word "mansuétude," gentleness or mansuetude, as the meaning can be encountered in Clarice Lispector's works. The gesture would be the two palms holding water, and offered upward. The "hand beings" are more apt to be sensitive to touch; they tend to offer the gift of the self with a gesture of a hand, in silence, far from the maddening words. Elli is such a being; she holds in her hand the head of the narrator when they are lounging together in the garden, showing her love in complete silence, and offering her all possible mansuetude in all freedom possible. It is through the thirst of the other, with their hands, and with mansuetude that the beloved communicate in a silence loaded with meaning, akin to a "benediction" or a blessing:

Dans le sein des mains, (elle) méditait sur cette étrange histoire
des mains pleines de mots muets.
Le bien dire le plus pur était muet. (158–9)

In the bosom of the hands, she meditated on this strange story of
hands filled with silent words.
The purest well-said words were silent.

For the narrator, her best "work of being" is her daughter, Elli,
and she is gratified by receiving the "non-said" words offered by
her daughter through the silent gesture of blessing of her hand on
the narrator's head.

Cixous takes a similar example in Kafka's life to enhance the
weight of the silent gesture and to add another dimension to the
story of her "brushing" philosophy. The anecdote takes
place between F., M., and O., or to clarify the story, between
Franz Kafka, Max Brod and Oskar Baum. (It is interesting to note
once more than Cixous does not use Kafka the writer, but Kafka
the man to recount the tale.) The conversations with Kafka and the
two other men were recorded by Januch, a seventeen-year-old
young man at the time he knew Kafka, two or three years before
Kafka's death. Januch remembered hundreds of conversations he
had with Kafka and reconstituted them onto paper thirty years
later. Those conversations are thus "hors-oeuvre," or "outside
the work of art," since this is a crucial point to Cixous' thesis.
Asfor Max Brod, Kafka's friend, he is the man who will undertake
the publication of Kafka's stories and *Journal*. But it is through
Januch that Cixous will use the anecdote in *Limonade tout était si
infini*.

In the anecdote, Kafka was invited to meet a man that he
admired very much, Oskar Baum, a blind man. Max Brod made
the formal introductions when the three men were present. Franz
Kafka greeted Oskar Baum silently, and to show his respect bowed
to salute him. Kafka's bow in front of Oskar Baum expresses the
utmost respect, and is a completely gratuitous gesture, since Oskar
Baum is blind, and cannot see the bow. The secret gesture shows
that Kafka treats the blind man as a man who can see, thus giving
him back all his lighted dignity. Oskar Baum would never have
seen the gesture if it were not for a crucial fact at the very moment
of the bow. By chance, Kafka's hair slightly "brushed" Oskar

Baum. Thus, this extremely tactful gesture gave Oskar Baum his sight back, symbolically speaking, since Kafka treated him as a man who could see. The silent gesture of tactfulness remained a secret between the two men and the witness to the scene, Max Brod. None of the three men ever talked about it, except that Kafka had told it to Januch, who recorded the gesture thirty years later. Kafka's action symbolizes for Cixous the silent gesture par excellence, the gesture carrying in its wake the sign of the invisible gift. For Cixous, Kafka gave the blind man back his sight by treating him as a seeing man.

Feodor Dostoevski, like Kafka, lived a crucial moment in his personal history. The moment of silence and gift for Dostoevski centers around the instant when he was condemned to death on December 22, 1849, at the age of twenty-eight. Dostoevski waited for his execution for three days. Dostoevski was lucky, since he was pardoned after the three-day period, and went to Siberia instead, where he lived to the year 1881, when he was sixty. Cixous points out that the Russian writer's awareness of his imminent death at such a young age allowed him to pass from life to death while living, to know death when alive, to experience the passage from everyday life to a higher life of suffering, with death lived within. The gift received by Dostoevski was the perception of the existence of that other life, more real than the normal life, which is a kind of death. That is how the Russian writer was able to become a "student of being" (*Limonade* 212) in his art. That instant of silence before his condemnation was told through the silence of time much later on by a woman who remembered, and who was capable of transmitting the secret message of Dostoevski's awareness. There always exists the kindness of an intermediary person to recount the tale of the moment of "brushing," the gaining of second innocence through intense experience.

In the personal history of the narrator of *Limonade*, three characters share the secret about the origin of the daughter, Elli: the narrator or future mother, and two other people able to keep the secret. Later on, when Elli is an adult, her mother and father meet again, and this is the first time that Elli meets her real father, and that, for the first time, the three meet. At that very instant, the minute of silence is loaded with meaning, loaded with tactfulness as nothing is explained, but everything is understood between the three people present. The instant of silence at the edge of life and death is the moment of gift and "brushing" which Cixous develops in the novel. This silence allows the true life to be reborn at the deepest level. Instead of giving death, the moment gives life anew, since there is knowledge, reconnaissance of the importance of the moment, and understanding, and later an effacing ("efface-ment"), an erasure or a fading away of the persons who know the truth.

The whole book is interspersed with sentences that are linked to Kafka and to the evocation of the lemon soda. The thirst represents the person able to give the essential "water," able to quench the desire in an altruistic gesture, totally devoid of self-interest, appro-priation and the devouring of the other.

The young woman appears in the text through poetic metaphors, such as the water-nymph, dragon-fly or libellula, butterfly, then swallow, and peony, each with its symbolic message. Elli receives the delicate message in total tactfulness (the French word, "délica-tesse"), in the same delicate way it is given to her as a gift. This novel plays on delicate touches and insists on the meeting points of some exceptional human beings who can hear the "pure call" (143) of life, which is the very matrix of real life. Cixous writes on the origins and on the gift with a delicate écriture which intends to "approach" and to "withdraw," to get near and to move away all at the same time, because to state "too much" or to stay "too close" could kill the secret which is not said, but understood. By silent words as light as "seagull feathers" ("mouette" is the seagull and "muette" is the silent woman) and by sentences which seem like "bird-phrases" (263), the secret can shine and can be tasted like the lemon soda mentioned in the title. The lemon soda drink reminds the narrator of her childhood, when she used to drink lemon soda with her father at the café in Oran, the town of her birth, and of the first "virgin" innocence. The narrator remembers the lemon soda from her childhood at the instant of her "nonvirgin" second inno-cence. "Le vivre n'est pas donné" (206), "the living is not given," Cixous reminds the reader, or, in other words:

> The thematics of my reading deal with innocence, or with what I would call a "second innocence." There are at least two types of innocence. I could speak of a virgin innocence and of an inno-cence regained, even if it seems tautological. Is there a nonvirgin innocence? Yes, I think so. (*Readings* 41)

The act of living is not a given due, but a gift earned by the persons who are able to enter their own rooms within, as did Dostoevski, who went first through false life to reach true life:

> ... il [Dostoevski] vint au monde grâce à un renversement subit et absolu. D'où il sut que c'est seulement ainsi, par renversements complets, que l'on peut espérer passer de mort à vie, de faux à vrai. Et toute la vie n'est-elle pas le série des renversements de la mort? (*Limonade* 257)

> Dostoevski came to the world with a sudden and absolute reversing. From this he knew that it can only be through complete reversing that one can hope to pass from death to life, from fake to true. And is not all life but a series of reversings of death?

Cixous, through the three examples taken from Kafka, Dostoevski, and from her own narrative, proves that writers must not be content to create works of art, but that they need to strive to create "works of being." "Works of being" are superior, for they do not talk of the semblance of life, or the "gift-that-takes." On the contrary, such works open up to the true "gift" through the portrait of a bird, or the portrait of a young woman, or the portrait of delicate touch near the essence of being. This strives for the immortal. And for Cixous, all the rest is mortal.

Works Cited

Adams, Hazard, and Leroy Searle, eds. *Critical Theory Since 1965*. Tallahassee: Florida State UP, 1986. 309–320.

Cixous, Hélène, *Angst*. Paris: Des Femmes, 1977.

——. *L'Ange au secret*. Paris: Des Femmes, 1991.

——. "Le Rire de la Méduse." *L'Arc* (1975): 39–54. Translated by Keith Cohen and Paula Cohen. *Signs I* (Summer 1976): 875–99.

——. *Limonade tout était si infini*. Paris: Des Femmes, 1982. All quotations from this book translated by Claudine G. Fisher.

——. *Préparatifs de noces au delà de l'abîme*. Paris: Des Femmes, 1978.

——. *Readings. The Poetics of Blanchot, Joyce, Kafka, Kleist, Lispector, and Tsvetayeva*. Ed., trans. and intro. Verena Andermatt Conley. Minneapolis: U of Minnesota P, 1991.

7

The Gift: Hélène Cixous and Jacques Derrida

Judith Still

The importance of the gift in the thinking of Hélène Cixous around sexual difference is quite generally acknowledged by her readers; this is no doubt influenced by strong statements in some of her best-known works: in *The Newly Born Woman* she writes: "All the difference determining history's movement as property's movement is articulated between two economies [the feminine and the masculine] that are defined in relation to the problematic of the gift" (80).[1] I would argue that the gift is equally important in the thinking of her compatriot, Jacques Derrida, although it is not so regularly signposted by his commentators.[2] To some critics of Cixous the alignment of Cixous and Derrida may seem strange: she has been charged with a number of suspect tendencies (essentialism, biologism and so on) which appear quite alien to deconstruction. And yet, even before considering conceptual similarities as well as differences in their writing, we might note that in terms of strategic public practices they have been united in a number of significant ways, for example: Derrida as the key speaker alongside Cixous at her first *Etudes féminines* conference in 1990 or Derrida interviewed in a *Boundary 2* special issue on Cixous, the piece entitled "voice ii," after the interview with Cixous entitled "voice i."[3] Cixous and Derrida have much in common: a certain background, a range of cultural and philosophical references, a radical

questioning of much of what had gone without saying in intellectual debate prior to the late sixties, and certain aspirations in the
ethical and political domain – all these inflect upon their preoccupation with the gift. However, Cixous' domain is that of the creative writer and the literary critic while Derrida's is that of the
philosopher. Both have worked to make their respective domains
permeable to a range of discourses to the point where the reminder
of disciplinary boundaries may seem quite inappropriate; and yet, I
would argue, the difference in the disciplines with which each
struggles is part of the gap between them. This article will attempt
to bring together some of Cixous' references to a possible feminine
gift economy with Derrida's theorisation of the impossibility (and
necessity) of the gift, in particular in the recently published
Given Time: I and in his writings on sexual difference.[4] Cixous
herself brings them together with respect to their interrogations
of the gift in an interview with Verena Andermatt Conley:

> The question of the gift is a question on which we have worked a
> lot, marking it and following it, if one may say, with a step as
> light and as airy, as "feminine" as possible. The question is of
> course the following: Is it possible that there is a gift? It is a
> question that has been treated at length by Derrida in a seminar
> on the philosophical mode, etc. Is there such a thing as a gift; can
> the gift take place? At the limit, one can ask oneself about the
> possibility of a real gift, a pure gift, a gift that would not be
> annulled by what one could call a countergift. That is also what
> Derrida worked on. (158)

One: An Intertextual Economy

Relations between texts (or between "authors") can themselves be
modelled according to different economies – hence Cixous' characterisation of certain writing as *écriture féminine* on account of its
generous relation to "the other." Harold Bloom's theory of the
anxiety of influence might be regarded as an account of writing
both as fighting over property and fighting with property (an
expression sometimes used to designate potlatch). This intertextual
relation between Cixous and Derrida could engender and dissem-
inate: it could produce references (direct or indirect) to a series of

other intertexts. I want to suggest that this is also a sexed relation between a male philosopher and a female writer – although each of these designations can be called into question.[5] It may even seem that this evocation of intersexuality as well as intertextuality is gratuitous; however, the very question of gratuitousness is itself interrogated by these texts.

There has been some debate over Cixous' characterisation of two (libidinal) economies as "masculine" and "feminine" – whether these are applied to writing, social relations or intrapsychic structures. Derrida suggests that these cannot be bound to men and women ("voice ii" 88-89), and much in Cixous' writing would support such a claim whether it be her celebration of a feminine economy in a number of male writers from Shakespeare to Mandelstam or certain of her explicit statements. Nevertheless, in *The Newly Born Woman*, for example, Cixous argues that until there is radical political, economic, ideological change, and a change in sexuality, most men and women will be caught in a web of cultural determinations which make men more afraid of loss such that

> in the development of desire, of exchange, he [the traditional man] is the en-grossing party: loss and expense are stuck in the commercial deal that always turns the gift into a gift-that-takes. The gift brings in a return. Loss, at the end of a curved line, is turned into its opposite and comes back to him as profit. (87)

Woman, on the other hand, "doesn't try to 'recover her expenses.' She is able not to return to herself, never settling down, pouring out, going everywhere to the other" (87). The feminine, between Cixous and Derrida, slips from a bond with women to an evocation of something which is before or beyond sexual opposition.

Derrida's *Given Time* is explicitly highly intertextual in its analysis of the problematic of the gift: Heidegger, Mauss and Baudelaire are his chief points of refererence, but many others are evoked (Marshall Sahlins, Lévi-Strauss, Poe, Freud, Lacan, Balzac, Gide) – we might even call this network of male writers a homosocial textual economy. Although I should confess (confession being part of the problematic of the gift) that he begins with a letter from one woman to another (Mme de Maintenon to a friend) which bemoans the fact that the Sun-King takes all her time –

leaving only "the rest" for Saint-Cyr – when she would like to give it *all* to Saint-Cyr – the foundation for impoverished young girls.[6] As Derrida explains, only the death of the King will allow that; the King, we might suggest, is the paternal figure of the Law *par excellence* who usurps the "natural" place of superabundant generosity, establishing its pattern. Derrida analyses such solar economies in "Economimesis."

I do not suggest that Derrida is innocently homosocial in his choice of texts: in *Given Time* his analysis of Baudelaire's *Petits poèmes en prose* (in particular *La fausse monnaie*) is explicit about the libidinal charge between male friends as one speculates on the other's gift and feels betrayed by his confession that the apparent gift is a counterfeit coin. Derrida informs us that in writing about the gift there must be gift, or at least a sign or pledge to give – thus Mauss's *The Gift* is gift, even if only insofar as it fails to talk on the gift; thus it is what it says even as it is counterfeit. And the reader (Derrida cites Lévi-Strauss' hommage to Mauss) will betray it even as he feels betrayed. Derrida's own desire could thus be related intertextually to that of another "great man" he cites – Montaigne. Instead of the essay Derrida cites, we could choose a different, but equally relevant one, "On three kinds of relationships," which ranks commerce, relationship, intercourse with the great male dead writers above other kinds of *commerce* with the living. *Given Time* is indeed a more analytical and "philosophical" work than, for instance, some of Derrida's writings on sexual differences. And yet its willful generosity towards Mauss, its refusal to feel betrayed as Mauss fails to produce the gift even as he insists that there is gift, cannot be reduced to a "masculine economy."

Cixous has an avowedly passionate relationship with her intertexts, and her delight at the discovery of Clarice Lispector is well-known. At the same time her work is exceptionally open to male writers (such as Joyce or Genet) and political figures (such as Mandela) in whom she can sense a feminine. In, for example, "La Venue à l'écriture" she (a writer, and therefore a reader) is alternately mother, child, lover, beloved, giving and receiving sustenance in an abundance of fantasmatic relationships which do seem before or beyond any stable economy of sexual opposition, and which she terms "feminine."

Two: The Gift

Given Time is also highly intertextual with respect to Derrida's own *oeuvre*, obsessively auto-erotically footnoted – revealed to have been obsessively concerned with the gift. The reader is not surprised that cultures very distant from us in time or space, classical Rome (where Seneca wrote a lengthy treatise on beneficence) or the "primitive" cultures studied by the anthropologist Mauss, are exercised by questions such as "what constitutes a gift?" and "what is the best way of giving?" However, today so much has been given over to market or state – even central and fundamental gestures such as giving shelter, food and drink, at one extreme, are marketed hospitality (hotels and restaurants, cafés and pubs) and, at the other extreme, State safety nets ("Income Support" at subsistence level). But vestiges, remnants remain – there is some excess which overspills the ever–encroaching market and the care of the dwindling Welfare State. And poststructuralist thinkers – such as Derrida as given to us, displayed, in his footnotes – are fascinated by this impossible thing (not a thing of course), the gift.

French "feminists" – Hélène Cixous who writes about the *économie féminine* or the Realm of the Gift, or Luce Irigaray concerned with exchange between women – have been particularly, politically, dynamically utopianly evoking the gift. In *Elemental Passions*, Irigaray writes:

> The gift has no goal. No for. And no object. The gift – is given. Before any division into donor and recipient. Before any separate identities of giver and receiver. Even before the gift. Giving oneself, that giving – a transition which undoes the properties of our enclosures, the frame or envelope of our identities. I love you makes, makes me, an other. Loving you, I am no longer; loved, you are different. Loving, I give myself you. I become you. But I remain, as well, to love you still. And as an effect of that act. Unfinishable. Always in-finite. (73-74)

The gift has no object – in both senses. It is disinterested and it is not the gift of a commodity. It is pre-essential, prior to any division into giver and receiver, and yet, while undoing division, it prizes (sexual) difference. There is *je* and *toi* – even as I become you, I must be I in order to love you. It is becoming (and loving) which are the modes of relation between I and you – not being. I am not you. But I am not fixed as "not you."[7] As a text *Elemental Passions* is highly poetic more often than it is philosophical, it is a love song to the other although the love is frequently presented as mortal combat.

In "La Venue à l'écriture," Cixous exhorts us:

> *Gagne* ta liberté: rends tout, vomis tout, donne tout. Donne absolument tout, entends-moi, *tout*, donne tes biens, est-ce fait? Ne garde rien, ce à quoi tu tiens, donne-le y es-tu? (46)

> *Win* your freedom: give everything up, vomit everything up, give everything away. Give absolutely everything away, do you hear, *everything*, give your goods away, is it done? Don't keep anything, give away what you hold dear, are you there?

And later, she muses on the gift of milk, of nourishment in writing (giving and taking nourishment); hatred eats you alive, she tells us, and:

> Celui qui garde la richesse et la nourriture pour lui-même est empoisonné. Mystère du don: le don-poison: si tu donnes, tu reçois. Ce que tu ne donnes pas, l'antidon, se retourne contre toi et te pourrit. Plus tu donnes, plus tu jouis, comment ne le savent-ils pas? (54)

> Anyone who keeps wealth and nourishment for himself is poisoned. The mystery of the gift: the gift-poison: if you give, you receive. What you don't give, the anti-gift, turns against you and destroys you. The more you give, the more pleasure overwhelms you, how can they not know that?[8]

Three: The Impossibility of the Gift

These references to the gift focus on the psychic benefit to the subject of superabundant generosity. At another time, Cixous is more troubled by the relational aspect of the gift: what relation must there be to the recipient for a gift to take place (can a gift ever take place?). She asks:

How does one give? It starts in a very simple way: in order for a gift to be, *I* must not be the one to give. A gift has to be like grace, it has to fall from the sky. If there are traces of origin of the *I* give, there is no gift – there is an I-give. Which also signifies: say "thank you," even if the other does not ask you to say it. As soon as we say thank you, we give back part or the whole gift. We have been brought up in the space of the debt, and so we say thank you. Is it possible to imagine that there can be a gift? (Conley 158-59)

For me Derrida's *Given Time* helps to elucidate why the problematic of the gift has been so problematic, and why our position with respect to Cixous' (or Irigaray's) text might be an ungrateful one. Frequently the reader response to texts on the gift has been to conjure the gift away, refusing its magic or madness in the name of reason, of reducing everything to economic exchange. One example which Derrida gives is Lévi-Strauss reading Mauss;[9] another is those readers of Irigaray or Cixous who wish to reduce the gift in the feminine to unpaid domestic labour. One major difference between Cixous and Derrida has frequently been taken to be sexual difference – Derrida's alleged unwillingness to admit that he is a man, that he cannot write in the feminine,[10] that his evocation of woman may be another patriarchal colonisation taking the place of women who might speak for themselves, that his supposed deconstruction of the subject is a deconstruction of the male/masculine subject while a female/feminine subject is yet to see the light of day.[11] While I am not convinced that these charges are absolutely defendable when laid against the letter of Derrida's texts, it might be helpful to note that if male and female writers do not have the same place of enunciation then a dialogue between them could open up the symbolic possibilities of sexual difference.

Readers and students of Cixous are primarily women – women who are concerned with women: this can be a kind of specular circle, and an uncomfortable one.[12] The donor or dative movement of Cixous' writing is towards women. Feminist readers can be particularly demanding because of the urgency of a political agenda, and this demand can be a productive one. And yet Baudelaire amongst others tells us how the supplicating eyes of the poor, the dispossessed, with their unquenchable thirst for gifts, can arouse aggressivity in the benefactor. This aggressivity can be projected onto the writer figured as maternal benefactor in the reading transference. One great fear of feminist readers has been the fall back into essentialism, biology, the nature of woman. Mother Nature herself is of course the great model for superabundant generosity, and the maternal nature of women might seem to be what makes them dedicated to the gift. Thus the discourse on the gift would be poison or counterfeit coin, and we readers would be betrayed. (If it were openly counterfeit, fiction giving itself for fiction, metaphor for metaphor, then readers might be more comfortable – although not necessarily, since even metaphor can suggest a natural bond.) A gift cannot secure itself/be secured against the possibility of the counterfeit or because of this very calculation and hence security there is no longer gift. Legitimation, the King with a title to stamp the coin (as the Father stamps the child in a certain mythical biology), corrodes the gift. The gift is not, in any case (according to Seneca, Rousseau, the great thinkers of the gift) the object or content, *what* is given, but the desire, the thought and the act – what Derrida would call the work as textual or poetic performance (*Given Time* 57). And, Derrida argues in *Given Time*, that performance has to be an engaged one, an ethical one of *il faut* or *on doit*, an opting for the gift; although that very taking on of responsibility can seem in the paradox of the gift to slide back into economy (62): an inevitable fall. The theoretical-ethical demands a response in time, and the demand for a response may seem like a demand for a counter-gift.

At times Cixous seems to agree about the difficulty of the gift – the fall from grace into graces (in the French) or more grace (in the Portuguese) – a slide into quantification (*Readings* 35). She tells us that you can never have grace – "it is always given" (*Readings* 67) – and that what must be given is something to be taken; love has a part of hatred:

> According to philosophers such as Jacques Derrida, there is no pure gift. One could say, though, that if a gift is to take place, it would be in these scenes of a very heavily symbolized maternity [in Lispector's "The Foreign Legion"] that goes much beyond an anatomic maternity and consists in letting oneself be taken by the other. It is the most difficult thing in the world. What needs to be given is a gift to take, not a gift of something that is already

there. The possibility, the violent right to take something that has been accorded has to be given. ("Apprenticeship and Alienation," *Readings* 84)

Cixous seems here to suggest that a gift cannot be given, only the possibility of taking can be given. Derrida states clearly the paradox of the gift as impossible, as trapped in a double bind of gift and obligation (*Given Time* 27) – which hits us in a familiar form in the impossibility of perfect altruism or a disinterested (unmotivated) gratuitous act. There is no gift without bond, but no gift that does not have to untie itself from obligation. The gift must and must not be recognised by both benefactor and beneficiary, must and must not be forgotten (36). Any recognition (13), self-recognition (14), gratitude, could motivate the gift, become a binding contract, a repayment, interest. But how can one desire to forget the good of the gift (17)? How can one say that gifts should not circulate (7)? Because circulation is economic, is an Odyssean return to the home, or hearth – where women find their *non* place.

Four: Dreaming of Giving and of Sexual Difference

Both Cixous, and perhaps to an even greater extent Derrida, are struck by the "impossibility" of the gift: "there is no 'free' gift" (*The Newly Born Woman* 87). Equally both are aware of the social constraints which necessitate our recognition of sexual opposition – even if sometimes we claim that we are only doing so as a short-term strategy. In "Choreographies," Derrida recognises the crucial importance of patient laborious feminist struggle (strategy) even as he pleads for it to be interrupted by "dance"; in "voice ii" he reminds us that strategy is an effect of the same contract, the same old system which produces sexual opposition: "Terrible, n'est-ce pas, qu'il faille encore calculer son discours, en acceptant les règles d'une stratégie sans fin au moment où on aimerait mettre bas les armes, où l'on n'aime qu'à mettre bas les armes" (86). [Isn't it terrible that it is still necessary to calculate what we say [referring to "masculine" and "feminine"] by accepting the rules of an endless strategy at the moment when we would love to lay down our weapons, when we only love if we lay down our weapons.] Is there a gap in strategic calculation, a space for dreaming and giving?

Cixous is lyrical about the aggressive and amorous exchange between Kleist's Penthesilea and Achilles or Tasso's Tancredi and Clorinda or Rossini's Tancredi and Armenaida; her admiration is partly inspired by the shifting masculine and feminine economies – whether Clorinda is assumed to be a man or Tancredi sung by a mezzo soprano.[13] This last example brings us to the question of voice. Since the first publication of *Of Grammatology* in 1967, Derrida has often been represented as the champion of writing against speech. His careful analysis of the privileging of speech (and indeed song) as a less or even un-mediated form of self-expression and communication in a certain philosophical tradition has sometimes been over-simplified to an alarming degree. This simplification can be used to set him against Cixous who has not been afraid to refer in a positive fashion to voice. . . .

In "voice ii" (and "Choreographies"), Derrida refers to a dream of a multiplicity of sexually-marked voices, to the way in which the voice is both attached to and detached from the body (78-79), and can even give birth to another body.[14] He refers to a *writing of the voice* which "se donne à entendre," translated by Conley as "lets itself be heard" (80). The question of translation runs through Derrida's thoughts on sexual difference here, and through his thoughts on the gift in *Given Time* – for instance the legitimacy of the translations which allow Mauss to recognise gifts in a variety of very different cultures (25). This example from Conley is a fine and accurate translation which must nevertheless lose *se donner* which literally means either "to give oneself" or (in the passive voice) "to be given." This vocal writing "speaks otherwise," outside representation, in opposition to the brutality which assigns difference to opposition (sex as a binary). (Thus we cannot escape opposition as we oppose it, other than in the pleasure of the dream.) How does the voice help sexual opposition become sexual differences or sexual differance? "Perhaps because where there is voice, sex becomes undecided (*le sexe s'indécide*)" (78) – another (unfamiliar) reflexive passive voice in the French. Derrida tells his female interlocutor and translator: "Vous voyez, pour moi, la traduction entre des langues ou entre des sexes, c'est presque la même chose: à la fois très facile, impossible en toute rigueur, livrée à l'aléa" (78). ["You see, for me translation between languages or between sexes is just about the same thing: both very simple and impossible in any rigorous way, once given over to chance" (79,81).] I could re-translate this as "translation between tongues or between sexes is almost the same thing: at once very easy, impossible in a strict sense, a prey to chance." This re-translation begins to mark what need not be marked: *langue* and *sexe* both refer to bodily organs as well as metonymically (synecdochally?) to categories. Is the relation between your sexual organ(s) and your sex category at once as certain and as uncertain as the relation between your tongue and the language you (naturally? normally?) speak? And what, if any, is the relation between your sex and your tongue – or someone else's?

Cixous, like Derrida, asserts the feminine as something other and radical; however, neither ties the feminine to the biological female. Derrida in addition makes clear – for example in "Women in the Beehive" – that the counter-privileging of the feminine as undecidablity is a provisional strategy which is a useful point of insertion when confronted with a textual privileging of rational decidability. Derrida tries to open up thinking on sexual difference which would not be "sealed by a two" ("Geschlecht" 80).[15]

Derrida's way of opening up, and I want to suggest that it is Cixous' too, is an act of faith – the "transcendental illusion of the gift" (*Given Time* 30) – is (sexual) differance, the rhythm of the gift, the move in and out of the economic, the setting going (displacement) of the circle. Mauss stubbornly refuses to get rid of the notion of the gift despite all economistic pressures to replace it with, say, the logic of credit (*Given Time* 42), and this very stubbornness is a kind of textual performance, an act of faith. In *Readings*, Cixous talks about the *coup de grâce* (63) in the act of love between Achilles and Penthesilea: "There is an ephemeral moment of equilibrium that could be called the moment of grace. It is followed by disequilibrium and loss that do not have one and only one cause. One can say – and that is where the question of the other is vital – that Achilles did take the necessary leap." I from should like to juxtapose this with a final quotation from Derrida:

But whereas only a problematic of the trace or dissemination can pose the question of the gift, and forgiveness, this does not imply that writing is *generous* or that the writing subject is a *giving subject*. As an identifiable, bordered, posed subject, the one who

writes and his or her writing never gives anything without
calculating, consciously or unconsciously, its reappropriation,
its exchange, or its circular return – and by definition this
means reappropriation with surplus-value, a certain capitaliza-
tion. We will even venture to say that this is the very definition
of the *subject as such*. One cannot discern the subject except as the
subject of this operation of capital. But throughout and despite
this circulation and this production of surplus-value, despite this
labor of the subject, there where there is trace and dissemination,
if only there is any, a gift can take place, along with the excessive
forgetting or the forgetful excess that. . . is radically implicated in
the gift. The death of the donor agency (and here we are calling
death the fatality that destines a gift *not to return* to the donor
agency) is not a natural accident external to the donor agency; it
is only thinkable on the basis of, setting out from the gift. This
does not mean simply that only death or the dead can give. No,
only a "life" can give, but a life in which this economy of death
presents itself and lets itself be exceeded. Neither death nor
immortal life can ever give anything, only a singular *surviving*
can give. (*Given Time* 101-102)

$$\boxed{\text{Notes}}$$

1 See Brian Duren's "Cixous' Exorbitant Texts" on *propre* and *impropre* and Bataille's influence on Cixous' use of the gift; see also Judith Still,"A Feminine Economy."

2 It has not been completely ignored, and yet if I look in the indexes of three books on Derrida taken from my shelves (by Rodolphe Gasché, Christopher Johnson and Christopher Norris) I find no entry for "gift."

3. Since writing this article I have read Calle-Gruber's *Hélène Cixous Photos de Racine* in which Cixous refers insistently to a great debt to Derrida, the person to whom she chose to send her earliest writings. Derrida's paper from the *Etudes féminines* conference is reproduced in the middle of the book.

4. See, for example, "voice ii"; "Choreographies"; *Spurs Nietzsche's Styles*; and "Women in the Beehive: A Seminar with Jacques Derrida."

5. In "voice ii," Conley claims that Derrida has chosen philosophical discourse, which is strongly marked as masculine; he replies that he is not so sure that he has made that choice (90/91) although he agrees that some of his early work appears to prove her right. In "voice ii" itself (and, say, in "Choreographies") he presents himself as a dreamer more than as a philosopher – a choice which brings him close to Cixous.

6. Derrida cites Lacan's formualation that to love is to give what one does not have (*Given Time* 2), thus Mme de Maintenon's paradoxical expression is part of a different economy and a different logic.

7 References to the gift may be found throughout Irigaray's work. I shall give just one additional example here:

> But what if these "commodities" refused to go to "market"? What if they maintained "another" kind of commerce, among themselves?

Exchanges without identifiable terms, without accounts, without end...Without additions and accumulations, one plus one, woman after woman...Without sequence or number. Without standard or yardstick...Nature's resources would be expended without depletion, exchanged without labour, freely given, exempt from masculine transactions: enjoyment without a fee, well-being without pain, pleasure without possession....

Utopia? Perhaps. Unless this mode of exchange has undermined the order of commerce from the beginning – while the *necessity of keeping incest in the realm of pure pretense* has stood in the way of a certain economy of abundance. (*This Sex* 196-97)

8. Many more examples of Cixous' evocation of the gift can be found in *The Newly-Born Woman*. See especially 87 and 140.

9. A further instance is Derrida's essay on Nietzsche, *Spurs/Eperons*, in which he highlights woman's ability to "se donner pour" even as she "se donne." This functions to prevent a hypostasization of the absolute gift of self since, in giving herself with superabundant generosity, woman also acts that gift. Gayatri Spivak reads this as a (somewhat literal) statement about the female ability to fake orgasms. (It has become a commonplace in certain corners of deconstructionist mythological biology to assert that men cannot fake orgasms.) When one thinks about it, however, they obviously can; this marks quite a fascinating lapsus into the social. (Or perhaps deliberately or otherwise rests on a potent masturbatory fantasy of visible ejaculation.) See Spivak's "Displacement and the Discourse of Woman."

10. In "voices ii" Derrida gently questions Conley's assertion that he cannot assume a feminine position (92-93). Conley argues:

Without awaking you from your dream of a multiplicity of voices – to which one should add of course that of timbre, rhythm, tone, etc. – one could say that those qualifiers about which I spoke to you, "masculine" and "feminine", should at the limit disappear. Then, "man" would no longer repress his libidinal economy said to be "feminine." But we are far from it and in these times of transformation which engage each being in her or his singularity in a daily endeavor of questioning, negotiating, etc., rather than simply bypassing, or discarding "femininity" as a masculine construct, should one not at least give woman a chance to speak herself, to write herself from *her* border before acceding to a beyond? (73)

11. Cf debates in which Gayatri Spivak ("Displacement") and Alice Jardine (*Gynesis*) have engaged. Luce Irigaray's position is elucidated in Margaret Whitford's *Luce Irigaray Philosophy in the Feminine* in which she suggests that Derrida's dream of sexual multiplicity is a utopian fantasy which bypasses sexual difference.

12. Cixous has evoked quite a polarised reading response. While there are examples of judicious and analytical appreciations of her work, such as Morag Shiach's *Hélène Cixous: A Politics of Writing* and Anu Aneja's

"The Medusa's Slip: Hélène Cixous and the Underpinnings of *Ecriture Féminine*," many readers fall into either a hostile or an amorous mode. Many examples of hostility have already been cited in the *LIT* special issue on Cixous. Examples of amorous miming would include some of the essays in *Hélène Cixous, chemins d'une écriture*.

13. See, for example, Cixous' *Readings*, "Tancredi continues," and *The Newly Born Woman* (112-22).

14. A point of reference here for Derrida is opera. Cixous gives us the example of Rossini; we could look earlier in time to operas written when some of the greatest singers were castrati – their roles now sung by counter-tenors. Barthes's *S/Z* reminds us how a voice can give birth to a body and unsettle fixed economies not only in the sexual, but also in the linguistic and financial sense.

15. See also "Women in the Beehive: A Seminar with Jacques Derrida":

When we speak here of sexual difference, we must distinguish between opposition and difference. Opposition is two, opposition is man/woman. Difference on the other hand, can be an indefinite number of sexes and once there is sexual difference in its classical sense – an opposition of two – the arrangement is such that the gift is impossible. All that you can call "gift" – love, *jouissance* – is absolutely forbidden, is forbidden by the dual opposition. (198)

Works Cited

Aneja, Anu. "The Medusa's Slip: Hélène Cixous and the Underpinnings of *Ecriture Féminine*. *LIT* 4.1 (1992): 17–27.

Barthes, Roland. *S/Z. An Essay.*Trans. Richard Miller. New York: Hill and Wang, 1974.

Calle-Gruber, Mireille and Hélène Cixous. *Hélène Cixous, Photos de Racine*. Paris: Editions des Femmes, 1994.

Cixous, Hélène. *Readings. The Poetics of Blanchot, Joyce, Kafka, Kleist, Lispector and Tsvetayeva*. Trans. and Ed. Verena Andermatt Conley. Minneapolis: U of Minnesota P, 1991.

——. "Tancredi continues." Trans. Ann Liddle and Susan Sellers. *Writing Differences: Readings from the Seminar of Hélène Cixous*. Ed. Susan Sellers. Milton Keynes: Open UP, 1988. 37–53.

——. "La Venue à l'écriture." *La Venue à l'écriture*. In collaboration with Madeleine Gagnon and Annie Leclerc. Paris: Union Générale d'Edition, 1977. 9–62.

Cixous, Hélène and Catherine Clément. *The Newly Born Woman*. Trans. Betsy Wing. Minneapolis: U of Minnesota P, 1986.

Conley, Verena Andermatt. *Hélène Cixous, Writing the Feminine*. Expanded ed. Lincoln: U of Nebraska P, 1991.

Derrida, Jacques. "Choreographies." Interview by Christie McDonald. *The Ear of the Other*. Trans. Peggy Kamuf. Lincoln: U of Nebraska P, 1988. 163–85.

——. "Economimesis." *Diacritics: A Review of Contemporary Criticism* 11.2 (Summer, 1981): 3–25.

——. "Geschlecht: sexual difference, ontological difference." Trans. Reuben Berezdivin. *Research in Phenomenology* 13 (1983): 65–83.

——. *Given Time. I: Counterfeit Money.* Trans. Peggy Kamuf. Chicago: U of Chicago P, 1992.

——. *Of Grammatology.* Trans. Gayatri Chakravorty Spivak. 1st American ed. Baltimore: Johns Hopkins UP, 1976.

——. *Spurs: Nietzsche's Styles.* Trans. Barbara Harlow. Chicago: U of Chicago P, 1979.

——. "voice ii." Interview by Verena Andermatt Conley. *Boundary 2* 12 (1984): 68–93.

——. "Women in the Beehive: A Seminar with Jacques Derrida." *Men in Feminism.* Ed. Alice Jardine and Paul Smith. London: Routledge, 1989.

Duren, Brian. "Cixous' Exorbitant Texts." *Sub-Stance* 10 (1981): 39–51.

Irigaray, Luce. *Elemental Passsions.* Trans. Judith Still and Joanne Collie. London: Athlone, 1992.

——. *This Sex Which Is Not One.* Trans. Catherine Porter. Ithaca: Cornell UP, 1985.

Jardine, Alice. *Gynesis: Configurations of Woman and Modernity.* Ithaca: Cornell UP, 1985.

Shiach, Morag. *Hélène Cixous: A Politics of Writing.* London: Routledge, 1991.

Spivak, Gayatri Chakravorty. "Displacement and the Discourse of Woman." *Displacement: Derrida and After.* Ed. Mark Krupnick. Bloomington: Indiana UP, 1983. 169–95.

Still, Judith. "A Feminine Economy: Some Preliminary Thoughts." *The Body and the Text: Hélène Cixous, Reading and Teaching.* Ed. Helen Wilcox et. al. New York: Harvester Wheatsheaf, 1990. 49–60.

van Rossum-Guyon, Françoise and Myriam Díaz-Diocaretz, eds. *Hélène Cixous, chemins d'une écriture.* Amsterdam: Rodopi, 1990.

Whitford, Margaret. *Luce Irigaray: Philosophy in the Feminine.* London: Routledge, 1991.

8

Hélène Cixous Names Woman, Mother, Other : "a feminine plural like me"

Marilyn Manners

Il y a longtemps que les noms qui ne sont propres qu'à l'envie de posséder ne sont plus propres à nommer l'être qui s'égale à la Vie. Tous les noms de la Vie lui vont, tous les noms ensemble ne suffisent pas à le désigner.

For a long time now, the names that are only right for the urge to possess have not been right for naming the being who equals life. All the names of Life suit it, all the names put together don't suffice to designate it.

Aimer: garder en vie: nommer.

Loving: keeping alive: naming.[1]

– Hélène Cixous

The (Derridean, deconstructionist) project of theorizing the proper name has concerned itself with disentangling the carefully-woven veil of the "natural" and the "normal" which disguises its hold on right, power, and might. Its emphasis, therefore, has been on the bearers of the name (of the law), rather than on the nameless or those with improper names. To go in want of a name, to be unnamed, in Western culture is very much like being unmanned: men with power, both fathers and sons, are bearers of the proper name. Everyone else – women, mothers and daughters, but also immigrants and the colonized, and certainly slaves – have been forcibly given, have had to align themselves with, a proper name and thus, with the Selfsame who define, hold, and transmit property and propriety.

Hélène Cixous has, over the course of two decades, both participated in this critical project and gone beyond it, enlarging its parameters and implications. My purpose here will be first to trace the contours of her extended naming project and then to contextualize it somewhat differently. Examination of Cixous' (re)naming project allows for, indeed insists upon, consideration of issues having to do with naming the Other; naming (self and other) and the ability to speak (and, crucially, be heard) are closely related. Attendant to Cixous' own call that we behave with "delicacy with regard to the other,"[2] I contextualize her work cross-culturally, by examining it with that of Other Women, others who have also struggled with the patronymic and who attempt to name female subjectivity (which is to name subjectivity differently) by grappling with the interlocking problems of naming and speaking for(th).

I. Woman

> Ecrire et traverser les noms, c'est le même geste nécessaire. . .
> ("Venue" 60)

> Writing and traversing names are the same necessary gesture. . .
> ("Writing" 49)

One of Cixous' long-term projects then has been to chip away at the monolithic block of the proper name[3] while at the same time theorizing the improper name and the given name, le prénom (not incidentally, in English, otherwise known as the Christian name). This work began very early in Cixous' writing, sometimes through titles: Le Prénom de Dieu and Prénoms de personne. As Claudine Guégan Fisher points out, irony lies in the fact that God is the only one who does not have or need a first name (6). Of course, God does not have one because he *is* one (One); he *is* the First Name. Regarding Cixous' *Prénoms de personne*, Verena Conley writes:

> *Prénoms*: first names, not last names that would inscribe the subject into a patrilinear genealogy, a plurality of first names, multiplying the effects of the subject; and *pré-nom*, that which is before the noun, before something is named, given unity. *Personne*, as both somebody and nobody...remains undecidable....The loss of one's name, the divisibility of the self, the inscription of masculine and feminine are read in Freud, Kleist, Joyce, Hoffmann...Poe. (14–15)

Inarguably the case, and *yet*, there is a difference: these authors' names are not (either for Conley or Cixous) Sigmund, Heinrich, James, Ernst, Edgar. That other kind of naming will mark a break in what Conley calls Cixous' "canon" (15),[4] and will come five years later (twelve years after the publication of *Le Prénom de Dieu*), in 1979, with Cixous' discovery of Clarice Lispector. At this time, naming, or more accurately perhaps, pre-naming, will take on a life of its own in Cixous' writing. Rigorous play with the name of Clarice and the naming of Clarice (Lispector) takes another tact:

> Clarice est le nom d'une femme qui appelle la vie par son prénom. Et toutes les femmes qui rappellent la vie à nous rappellent Clarice; appellent la vie du nom de Clarice. La vie s'appelle Clarice, mais ce n'est pas son seul nom (j'appelle aussi la vie du nom de : Amie). Chaque fois que nous rappelons d'aimer, Clarice revient. Clarice est un nom rare, mais commun. Un nom qui ne s'est jamais trompé. Un nom d'orange qui se dévoile. Par fidélité à elle-même. Quand une femme s'appelle Clarice, elle n'oublie pas. (*Vivre l'orange* 99)

> Clarice is the name of a woman who calls life by its first name. And all women that remind us of life remind us of Clarice; call life by the name of Clarice. Life is called Clarice, but this is not its only name. I also call life by the name of Amie. Each time that we remember to love, Clarice comes back. Clarice is a rare but common name. A name that has never been mistaken. The orange name that unveils itself. Out of fidelity to herself. When a woman is called Clarice, she does not forget. (*To Live the Orange* 98)

Cixous' naming project structures the political poetics of *Vivre l'orange*, a companion piece to "Poésie, e(s)t Politique?" Emphasis has not only shifted to the first name, of a woman, but also to a woman who "calls life by its first name," a woman, therefore, like Cixous herself, who purposefully confuses boundaries and categories by attributing "proper" names to common nouns ("Amie," "call[ing] life by its first name"). This is a woman too who values life over death, who remembers – all issues that remain central in Cixous' work. Neither a simple lyricism nor entirely new with her writings on Lispector, the problematic of naming emerged early in Cixous' work, and significantly, for example, in her exchange with Catherine Clément at the end of *La Jeune Née* [*The Newly Born Woman*]:

> C. Ecoute, tu aimes bien Dora, mais à moi, elle ne m'est jamais apparue comme un personnage révolutionnaire.
> H. Je me fous de Dora, je ne la fétichise pas. Elle est le nom d'une certaine force dérangeante, qui fait que le petit cirque ne marche plus. (289)

> C: Listen, you love Dora, but to me she never seemed a revolutionary character.
> H: I don't give a damn about Dora; I don't fetishize her. She is the name of a certain force, which makes the little circus not work anymore. (157)

"Dora" is the pseudonym, of course, for Freud's most famous (and infamously unsuccessful) case history in hysteria. Dora, the name and the very figure of hysteria, is to be found not only in Clément's and Cixous' *La Jeune née*, but also in Cixous' *Portrait du Soleil* and as the basis for her play *Portrait de Dora*. As their exchange demonstrates, Clément and Cixous disagree not simply over whether one should read Dora positively or negatively, but over whether the name itself can have, or can be, a disruptive force.

In Cixous' 1976 essay "La Venue à l'écriture," translated into English as "Coming to Writing" (1991), her work on the name becomes more explicitly elaborated. Cixous begins with her own name, or rather, her own *names*, Cixous and Hélène:

Cixous un nom lui-même tumultueux, indocile. Ça un "nom"?
Ce mot bizarre, barbare, et si mal supporté par la langue française, c'était ça "mon" "nom". Un nom impossible.
   On pouvait me faire mal à la lettre, à ma lettre. Et sur la peau
des possédées on imprimait une lettre. J'étais donc personne;
mais un corps sillonné de foudres et de lettres.
   . . . Avec un nom pareil, comment ne pas être en rapport avec
la lettre? Ne pas avoir l'oreille à vif? Ne pas avoir compris qu'un
corps est toujours substance à inscription? Que la chair écrit et
qu'elle est donnée à lire; et à écrire. (35–36)

Cixous – itself a tumultuous, indocile name. That, a "name"?
This bizarre, barbarous word, so poorly borne by the French
tongue, this was "my" "name." An impossible name.
   They could give me a pain in the letter, in my letter. And on
the skin of the possessed, they branded a letter. So I was no one;
merely a body scored by thunderbolts and letters.
   . . . With such a name, how could one not have been concerned
with letters? Not have sharp ears? Not have understood that a
body is always a substance for inscription? That the flesh writes
and is given to be read; and to be written. (25–26)

The genesis, as it were, of "writing the body" is strikingly different
from its eventual polemics: pain instead of exuberance, passivity
instead of activity, humiliation rather than *jouissance*. "Cixous" is
inscribed. Her "barbarous" family name allows only *others* to play
("Avec Cixous, les imbéciles . . . font des sous. Et du sous" [36]);
this also leads to her wishing for its opposite – which is also her
name – a classical name, the signifier of beauty:

J'aurais pu m'appeler Hélène, j'aurais été belle, et unique, la
seule. Mais je fus Cixous. En tant que souris enragée. J'étais si
loin d'Hélène, nom qui me fut d'ailleurs innocemment transmis
depuis une arrière-grand-mère allemande. ("Venue" 36)

I could have been called Hélène; I would have been beautiful,
and unique, the only one. But I was Cixous. As an enraged
mouse. I was so far from Hélène, a name which had actually
been innocently transmitted to me from a German great-grandmother. ("Writing" 26)

A number of crucial elements have been put into play: classical *versus* "barbarous" (and Hellenic *versus* Semitic), writing *versus* being written, French *versus* German, unity *versus* multiplicity, paternal *versus* maternal, high (Helen also means "moon") *versus* low (souris, sous), unique beauty *versus* the "tumultuous, indocile," "bizarre," "enraged." For Hélène/Cixous, however, this confusion of signs and tongues does not represent a (sorry) state to be overcome or transcended, but rather one to be explored, and indeed played with: "Pas de langue sérieuse déclarée. En allemand je pleure, en anglais je joue, en français je vole, je suis voleuse. Pas d'hommicile fixe" ["No serious declared language. In German, I weep; in English, I play; in French, I fly, I am a thief. No per*man*ent residence"] ("Venue" 46 / "Writing" 36).

Naming, however, is by no means bound only to Cixous' own names. She also argues that *naming* gender, a practice which varies from language to language, is precisely one of the elements which constructs rigidly dualistic genders, and from a very early age:

> J'étais ce "das Kind" que nous n'avons pas la sagesse de laisser errer en français. Car cette langue range dare-dare les nouveau-nés d'un côté ou de l'autre du genre.... Dans d'autres langues, on vous laisse divaguer, et l'enfant est d'un neutre, en sursis de décision sexuelle. Ce qui ne veut pas dire que le refoulement de la féminité serait moindre là où on parle allemand ou anglais. Il est autre, il intervient en d'autres termes. Mais il reste quelque chose, dans ces langues, d'indécis, l'espace pour une hésitation de la subjectivité. ("Venue" 36–37)

> I was "das Kind" this child that we don't have the wisdom to let circulate in French. For this language swiftly assigns the newborn to one side or the other of gender.... In other languages you are allowed to digress, and the child remains a kind of neuter, in reprieve from sexual decision. Which doesn't mean that the repression of femininity is less significant where German or English is spoken. It's different, it intervenes in other terms. But there remains something undecided, a space for the hesitation of subjectivity, in these languages. ("Writing" 26-27)

In this essay in general, in fact, Cixous elaborates fairly explicitly on the political significance of language. Here she also names

Woman/women as the nexus of history and the trans-historical, of births, deaths, and rebirths. Woman is presented as a complex, and unstable, "category":

> Etais-je une femme? C'est toute l'Histoire des femmes que j'interpelle en ranimant cette question. Une Histoire faite de millions d'histoires singulières, mais traversée des mêmes questions, des mêmes effrois, des mêmes incertitudes. ("Venue" 37)

> Was I a woman? I am challenging the entire History of women in reviving this question. A History made up of millions of singular stories, but traversed by the same questions, the same fears, the same uncertainties. ("Writing" 27)

She argues also that Woman can indicate the dead weight of signification itself as well as the refusal to bear that weight any longer, along with the refusal of names *given*:

> La femme est énigmatique paraît-il. Les maîtres nous l'enseignent. Elle est même, disent-ils, l'énigme en personne.
> L'énigme? Comment l'être? Qui a le secret? Elle. Qui elle? Je n'étais pas Elle. Ni une Elle, ni aucune. ("Venue" 38)

> Woman is enigmatic, it seems. This is what the masters teach us. She is even, they say, enigma personified.
> Enigma? How do you set about being that? Who has the secret? She does. She who? I wasn't Her. Nor a She, nor anyone. ("Writing" 28)

An often-mentioned, and equally important aspect of Cixous' naming, re-naming, and un-naming concerns undoing the name(s) of the Family, its hierarchy, its laws, its rigidity, its roles:

> J'écris – mère. Quel rapport entre mère et femme, fille? j'écris – femme. Quelle différence? Voici ce que mon corps m'apprend: tout d'abord, *méfie-toi des noms*: ils ne sont que des outils sociaux, des concepts rigides, petites cages à sens qu'on met en place comme tu sais, pour que nous ne nous mélangions pas les uns les autres sans quoi la Société à Ponctionnement Cacapitaliste ne tiendrait pas. Mais, amie, prends le temps de te dé-nommer une minute. ("Venue" 60)

I write "mother." What is the connection between mother and woman, daughter? I write "woman." What is the difference? This is what my body teaches me: first of all, *be wary of names*; they are nothing but social tools, rigid concepts, little cages of meaning assigned, as you know, to keep us from getting mixed up with each other, without which the Society of Cacapitalist Siphoning would collapse. But, my friend, take the time to unname yourself for a moment. ("Writing" 49, emphasis added)

II. Mother

Est-ce qu'un homme maternel est une femme? Dis-toi plutôt: il est assez grand et plusieurs pour être capable de la bonté maternelle. ("Venue" 61)

Is a maternal man a woman? Tell yourself rather: He is big enough and plural enough to be capable of maternal goodness. ("Writing" 50)

Les comédiens sont des mères. Et les mères sont bonnes ou mauvaises comme d'habitude. Certaines défendent leurs enfants selon l'amour, d'autres selon l'orgueil.... ("De la scène de l'Inconscient à la scène de l'Histoire" 29)

Actors are mothers. And the mothers are good or bad as usual. Some defend their children through love, and others through pride.... ("Scene" 13)

Amid this general disruption and flux, there is, however, the hint of a still-solid bedrock supporting it all, and that *function*, if not actual nor necessarily female *person*, redounds – when has it ever not? – on Mother, or perhaps even more precisely, on the Good Mother. Cixous in no way suggests that all biological mothers fulfill the maternal function, but neither does she see that as a positive departure, even potentially; she reads it rather as a lack of what North American feminists once regularly named sisterhood: "il y a des mères qui ne sont pas maternelles, qui sont des soeurs jalouses" ["there are mothers who are not maternal, who

are jealous sisters"]("Venue" 61 / "Writing" 50). Yet, "Il y a de la
mère en toute femme" ["There is something of the mother in every
woman"] (60 / 50) seems to stabilize maternal meaning in the
female body; this, however, is immediately dislocated: "Malheur-
euse la 'femme' qui s'est laissé enfermer dans un rôle à un seul
degré!" ["Unhappy the 'woman' who has let herself be shut up in
the role of a single degree of kinship!"] (61-62 / 50). Nevertheless,
"Il y a de la mère en toi si tu t'aimes. Si tu aimes" ["There is
something of the mother in you if you love yourself. If you love"]
(62 / 51). In her theory too, "there is something of" a flux, a
playfulness, an ambiguity, some would say contradiction, which
has tended, until fairly recently, to confound or entice her readers
into searching for firm ground by privileging one mode of Cixous'
statements over another and therefore necessarily naming it
either/or; feminist/not feminist; political/non-political; essential-
ist/non-essentialist.

I would argue for a different orientation. In her attempts to write
her way out of an economy based on lack/castration, Cixous
describes (discovers, constructs) an alternative libidinal economy
structured on diffusion, multiplicity, giving, loving, nurturing,
naming differences, naming differently. I agree with Anu Aneja
that not enough attention has been given to Cixous' texts' "refu-
s[al] to be pinned down by critical discourse" (20). Indeed, Cixous
herself has sometimes been quite explicit on this point: "Impossible
de *définir* une pratique féminine de l'écriture, d'une impossibilité
qui se maintiendra car on ne pourra jamais *théoriser* cette pratique,
l'enfermer, la coder, ce qui ne signifie pas qu'elle n'existe pas" ["It
is impossible to *define* a feminine practice of writing, and this is an
impossibility that will remain, for this practice can never be
theorized, enclosed, coded – which doesn't mean that it doesn't
exist"] ("Le Rire" 45 / "Laugh" 253); or, as she warns in "De la
scène de l'Inconscient à la scène de l'Histoire," "dans le domaine
des femmes rien n'est théorisable.... La seule chose que l'on
peut dire c'est que l'écriture peut, non pas en dire ou en
théoriser, mais en jouer ou en chanter. En discourir c'est être
atteinte par la réduction théorique" ["in the domain of women
nothing can be theorized.... The only thing one can say is that
writing can, not tell or theorize it, but play with it or sing it. To
hold discourse on it is to be overtaken by theoretical reduction"]
(27 / "Scene" 11–12).

Indeed, it is Cixous' writing's resistance to theoretical classification (or summary, for that matter) which undermines Domna
Stanton's often-cited critique of the maternal in Cixous' work.
Stanton underestimates the relation of Cixous' work to "presence"
and thus to Derrida. She reads Cixous' work as "a break with the
symbolic father" (Derrida), but believes that "it remains a lyrical
gesture that paradoxically reaffirms the phallophilosophy of presence which the maternal feminine is designed to efface" (163). Here
I would disagree: Cixous does not so much break with as fly in the
face of Derridean deconstruction on this point. She very consciously over-writes the absent (I continue here with Stanton's
use of Derrida's terms) which makes possible "phallophilosophy";
that is, Cixous' maternal *presence* is flagrant: her manoeuvre is
offensive, not defensive (or simply ignorant). Cixous seeks to (re-)
write the maternal as activity, as a presence that undoes the logic
(the presence) of the Same, which can *only* be Phallic.[5] (And it
should not be forgotten that in terms of Cixous' overall project,
men have as much to gain as do women by nurturing, loving,
giving, thawing out of the Phallic mold.) To break radically from
the law of the father necessitates, furthermore, breaking with those
breaks which recuperate the scene of killing the father. And we
cannot, as Stanton does, continue to call upon the word of the
father, however congenial a father he (Derrida, for example)
might be, in order to critique attempts to go beyond, fly and
steal, speak otherwise.

What strikes me as the snag in Cixous' open maternal weave,
however, is not that Cixous prescribes that all women become
biological mothers (she clearly does not; see, for example, "Le
Rire" 51 / "Laugh" 261), but that she *names* her polemical
model *Mother*. And Mother, beloved or hated ground of all
grounds, tends to freeze the flow, arrest transformation, stop
change in its tracks (by which I do not mean that *mothers* do).
The word, the name – the myth, more precisely – is still too
powerful to be used "freely." Beyond symbol or metaphor – and
certainly beyond the real – Mother (*la mère*) is less sea (*la mer*)
than maelstrom, pulling into itself all that tries to fly off in other
directions. This is not a case of over-determination (there is no
subject here to be subject *to* determination) but rather of excessive condensation: Mother is the great black hole of myth, effacing the outlines of its construction as quickly as they are

delineated. It (not she) remains out of even metaphorical control, but because mothers (and Cixous herself is one) continue not only to live the myth but to think and write it, it begins, little by little, to take on somewhat human dimensions, to enter history, to play.[6] At present, however, it cannot yet serve as shorthand or a shortcut: it is still a *cut* (which includes unnecessary episiotomies and caesareans)[7]; the gap between Mother and mothers is too great. To undo Mother, and to give "birth," let us say, to mothers, someone (if not necessarily Cixous herself) must be able to say, as Hélène Cixous said of Dora: "I don't give a damn about [the mother]; I don't fetishize her. She is the name of a certain force" ["le nom d'une certaine force dérangeante"].

In "Aller à la mer" (1977), Cixous compares her 'newly-staged' actor's body specifically, albeit implicitly, to the figure of Woman as Mother: "Corps en travail" ["A body in labour"] (19 / 547), a body therefore in process of changing and giving. It could be argued that part of the problem with Cixous' figure/name Mother is that it anthropomorphizes – more accurately, gynamorphizes – her "concept" of "Le don sans retour" ["the gift without return,"]("La Venue" 60 / "Writing" 49), and thus unnecessarily stabilizes a trope which is characterized by/as process, without end/goal. On the other hand, her re-writing of proper names (both historical and literary) often has the opposite effect: her readings, her interpretation, her *writing* of them *become the gift* (without return).

It is precisely in and on these terms that I balk at what is often called Cixous' maternal "metaphor": women cannot be accused of not having lived "it" certainly, nor even entirely of not having theorized "it," but we may want to begin to consider why we have done so little to make these activities congruent. Why do there remain such chasms between the strength of a woman in labor (see "La Venue" 40-41/ "Writing" 30-31) and the helplessness of a woman in labor, between maternal desire and the difficulties of mothering? I argue here neither for the primacy of experience (or theory) nor for a transparent language which would finally describe what mothering "really" is and means; I argue instead, as does Teresa de Lauretis in "Semiotics and Experience" for a theory of experience. It is in this spirit that I draw attention to Cixous' use of the maternal. The matter is both more simple and more complex: Mother is still everything and nothing,

still provides the ground for, and at the same time exceeds, signification. Although Mother overlaps the position of Woman and
other Others in the Symbolic, Imaginary, and Real, Mother remains
an exceptional case in that, for women, who have the potential for
biological maternity, and for the others, who have the potential for
a positive – (but here already the ground shakes: what is positive?
for whom? how much is too much? not enough?) – "maternal"
libidinal economy, there has been as yet almost no overlap between
the maternal as lived and the maternal as still rather
impressionistically theorized. The Medusa may be laughing, but
is the Mother?

III. Other

> Naming is a serious process. It has been of crucial concern for
> many individuals within oppressed groups who struggle for
> self-recovery, for self-determination. (hooks 166)

> A trois ans j'ai su...qu'on pouvait tuer pour un nom ou
> une différence. ("De la scène de l'Inconscient à la scène de
> l'Histoire" 16)

> At the age of three I knew...that one could kill for a name, for a
> difference. ("Scene" 2).

Cixous has written a great deal on the Other, and Woman and
Mother are certainly othered in Western Culture. Here, however, I
want to focus on her work on the cultural Other: on the one hand,
because she has, with good reason, named herself culturally other,
and, on the other, because her work in the theater since the mid-
1980s has prompted her to talk explicitly about other cultures. One
of the strengths of Cixous' theory has been her insistence on differ-
ence(s) and an appreciation of subjective heterogeneity. Yet in her
work, she sometimes, although not always, extends more courtesy
– or "delicacy," as she might say – to her own differences than to
those of different cultures – except insofar as they illuminate dif-
ference(s) in relation to Cixous herself.
   In the final section of "De la scène de l'Inconscient à la scène de
l'Histoire" ["From the Scene of the Unconscious to the Scene of

History"] entitled "Le voyage en Orient" – translated into English, significantly, as "The Voyage in Oriant" – Cixous asks and answers "Pourquoi l'Asie, l'Orient? Parce que ce n'est pas moi, parce que c'est moi, parce que c'est le monde différent de moi qui m'apprend moi, ma différence qui me fait sentir ma/sa différence" ["Why Asia, why the Orient? Because it is not me, because it is me, because it is the world different from myself that teaches me myself, my difference, that makes me feel my/its difference"] (33 /17). Yet in stark contrast to Cixous' relentless insistence (in both content and form) on heterogeneity elsewhere, here she answers questions concerning why she wrote her play about Cambodia, *L'Histoire terrible mais inachevée de Norodom Sihanouk roi du Cambodge*, somewhat "differently":

> parce que l'Asie est religieuse dans son âme.... parce qu'elle est notre préhistoire et notre passé présent. Parce qu'il y a des masques: en Asie on croit aux masques, au visage-âme, à l'autre; parce que les femmes continuent à bouger en Asie avec la lente grâce des rivières, parce qu'elles continuent. C'est une réalité qui existe par milliards. Parce qu'il y a tellement de mort et donc tellement de vie. ("De la scène" 33)

> because Asia is religious in its soul.... because it is our pre-history and our present past. Because there are masks: in Asia they believe in masks, in the visage-soul, in the other, because women continue to move in Asia with the slow grace of rivers, because they continue. It's a reality that exists in billions. Because there is so much death and thus so much life. ("Scene" 17)

Morag Shiach has suggested that Cixous' work on the cultural Other can border on orientalism (65-66, 122-23), and Aneja notes how problematic some of Cixous' statements might be for Third World women (21, 23). Shiach's and Aneja's criticisms, although based on other texts, are certainly appropriate here. The fluidity of Cixous' quicksilver statements regarding woman or even mother here turns to stone. The Other is pulled up short several times in each statement via totalizing abstractions that belie, both empirically and theoretically, the heterogeneity of – and the differences in process within – each term: "Asia," "religious," "soul," "masks," "other," "reality," "exists." It would be too generous to name this simply a "blind spot" in a text which elsewhere emphasizes the difficulties of attempting to speak for the Other: "Mais comment les laisser parler? Comment ne pas mettre ma langue devant leur langue?" ["But how does one let them speak? How to avoid putting my tongue before their tongue?"] ("De la scène" 24 / "Scene" 9). Yet it may not be particularly useful in this case to distinguish which of Cixous' statements regarding the cultural Other display a greater complexity from those in which she veers close to a similarly totalizing in-difference, though these too exist: in "Le Droit de légende," she compares "la vraie grandeur primitive" [the true primitive grandeur] of the West's past to the present state of various "Indes" [India/Indies] (4).[8]

Those of us who have come to read Cixous in a primarily or originally Western context need also to recognize the complexity of Self/Other relationships both as they have to do with the "West" and its "Others" and within the "West's" "Other(s)." A minimal recognition would account for, even if we limit our discussion to women, different post- and neo-colonial and diasporic situations as well as class differences, for example, which might range from the "subaltern" to highly educated and privileged academics. The complexity of the situation also requires recognizing that Cixous' discourse does not operate alone, or only in terms of her own theoretical influences (Freud and Derrida) or those influencing the authors she reads (Lispector, for instance), but in a more global sense, within a discourse in which the "Other" has been speaking, talking back, playing, and naming for quite some time.

One might begin investigating Cixous' answer to the question "Why Asia?" by considering Spivak's critique of Kristeva's *On Chinese Women*: "Her question, in the face of those silent women, is about her *own* identity rather than theirs" ("French Feminisms" 137)[9]. One might then move on to Spivak's own questions: "not merely who am I? but who is the other woman? How am I naming her? How does she name me?" (150). Such questions could not be fully addressed without keeping in mind, as appropriate, Trinh's un-formulaic formulation: "She is this Inappropriate Other/Same who moves about with always at least two/four gestures: that of affirming 'I am like you' while persisting in her difference; and that of reminding 'I am different' while unsettling every definition of otherness arrived at" (*Moon* 74). At some point, such an investigation would also of necessity include thinking back – that is, remembering – the ethnographic, colonial origins of French theories' work on such concepts as the gift. In a discussion of African cultures, Jamaica Kincaid remembers her own Antiguan culture:

> prostitution was not known in Africa until Europeans came. An African woman would have many lovers, but there was no money exchanged. A man would bring a gift, but it wasn't in exchange for sex. It was to show affection. And I think there's something like that where I come from, and so almost all the most basic arrangements are made on that basis: *no exchange, just a gift*. (Perry 509, emphasis added)

Dead Daughters?

> Comment écrire de ceux qui ne savent pas écrire?
> ...L'idéal: de moins en moins de moi de plus en plus de toi.
>   ("De la scène" 24)

> How to write about those who do not write?
> ...The ideal: less and less of me and more and more of you.
> ("Scene" 9)

> Some jump down wells, others hang themselves. (Xiao Hong 57)

Cixous' work in the theater has produced the context and necessity for her theoretical comments on the cultural Other, but in "Aller à la mer," an early text in which she discusses her shift to the theater, Cixous also recalls two names from the English theater, Ophelia and Cordelia; here, they represent for her the female spectator of traditional theater as "victim":

> Ophélie trois fois condamnée à être enterrée vivante, par les trois pères jaloux (Polonius-Laërtes-Hamlet) qui ne s'entendent qu'à lui faire la loi....Si elle est Ophélie, le corps interdit, l'âme violée, elle n'aura jamais vécu. Et si elle trouve la force de Cordélia pour affirmer une féminité non asservie au rôle de miroir du délire paternel, elle mourra. Car il y a en tout homme un roi Lear découronné qui exige de sa fille qu'elle l'idéalise à coups de mots gros d'amour, et l'érige, si aplati soit-il, tel qu'il veut être vu.... (19)

> like Ophelia, she is three times condemned to be buried alive
> by the three jealous father-figures – Polonius, Laertes and
> Hamlet – who are in agreement only in laying down the law
> to her.... If she is Ophelia, her body banned and her soul
> violated, she will never have lived. And if, like Cordelia, she
> finds the strength to assert a femininity which refuses to be the
> mirror of her father's raving, she will die. For in every man
> there is a dethroned King Lear who requires his daughter to
> idealize him by her loving words and build him up, however
> flat he may have fallen, into the man he wishes to
> appear.... (546)

In other texts ("La Venue" 50, 60 /"Writing" 40, 58, for example),
Cixous has both problematized and revised in various ways
women's deaths/silences (by "drowning" or "hanging") in much
the same way that she problematized and revised the Medusa.
Medusa is no longer deadly (petrifying); because her laugh shat-
ters, it gives life rather than brings death. In a similar way, the
paralyzing daughter-deaths of Ophelia and Cordelia mentioned in
"Aller à la mer" have long been implicitly re-named in Cixous'
theory: drowning and hanging become transformed into swimming and flying:

> à son bénéfice joyeux elle est érogène, elle est l'érogénéité de
> l'hétérogène; ce n'est pas à elle-même qu'elle tient, la
> nageuse aérienne, la voleuse. Dispersable, prodigue, étourdis-
> sante, désireuse et capable d'autre, de l'autre femme qu'elle
> sera, de l'autre femme qu'elle n'est pas, de lui, de toi. ("Le
> Rire" 51)

> For her joyous benefits she is erogenous; she is the erotogeneity
> of the heterogeneous: airborne swimmer, in flight, she does not
> cling to herself; she is dispersible, prodigious, stunning, desirous
> and capable of others, of the other woman that she will be, of the
> other woman she isn't, of him, of you. ("Laugh" 260)

This re-naming is of course itself a stealing: of language from the
realm of the Phallus, of life from the "jaws" of death; her naming is
both process and gift, process *as* gift (without return).

Numerous other women have been revising as well. That a
woman's *heroic* death by suicide (in this case, hanging) could be

re-named passive and stereotypical (by suppression and willful forgetfulness) is one of the points made by Spivak in "Can the Subaltern Speak?" (307-8). There exist also, however, "Other" texts which recall women very like Ophelia and Cordelia in order to re-name them, to write their stories otherwise – much as Cixous herself has not been the only woman writer revising Medusa.[10] My aim here is not to catalogue or tally up a list of works by non-Western female writers which employ strategies revising female deaths comparable to those of Western figures such as Ophelia and Cordelia; I have, however, been repeatedly struck by other attempts to re-write such stories and re-name such women. Nor am I suggesting that these writers are consciously or even unconsciously re-naming "archetypal" Western female death-figures (although neither would I be at all surprised that most and probably all these writers would be well aware of Ophelia and Cordelia). I suggest rather that a cross-cultural investigation, however cursory, of women re-writing such traditional and passive daughter-deaths will help explain why *not* recognizing the Other's differences and specificities, as Cixous has done, mutes the Other, makes her a type of Ophelia/Cordelia: drowned, hanged, silenced, suppressed, dead, Other(ed).

In 1940, Xiao Hong, from Northeast China, remembered the "same old story" differently. In *Tales of Hulan River*, she describes arranged marriages and how easily they may fail; in such cases, she says, wives often find themselves trapped between two families who do not want them, and "bewildered, cannot understand why they must suffer such a fate, and so tragedy is often the result; *some jump down wells, others hang themselves*" (57, emphasis added). A "classic" case, apparently, "West" or "East," "Ophelia" or "Cordelia." Unwilling to leave the complexities of this resolution to a reader's enfeebled imagination, however, Xiao Hong with characteristic irony re-writes this old story and names it heroic:

An old saying goes: "A battlefield is no place for a woman." Actually, that's not a fair statement; those wells are terribly deep, and if you were to casually ask a man whether or not he would dare to jump down one, I'm afraid the answer would be "no." But a young woman, on the other hand, would certainly do so. Now while an appearance on a battlefield doesn't necessarily lead to death, and in fact might even result in an official position later, there's not much chance of someone emerging alive after jumping down a well – most never do.

   Then why is it that no words of praise for the courage of these women who jump down wells are included in the memorial arches for a chaste woman? That is because they have all been intentionally omitted by the compilers of such memorials, nearly all of whom are men, each with a wife at home. They are afraid that if they write such things, then one day when they beat their own wife, she too may jump down a well; if she did she would leave behind a brood of children, and what would these men do then? (57–58)

Yet Xiao Hong's is not the only such re-naming. Nawal El Sada-awi's *Woman at Point Zero* (1975) retraces the story of a woman, a prostitute about to be hanged for murdering a pimp. This woman, Firdaus, insists upon the "suicide" which her own death becomes (she refuses to request pardon). This is the only avenue for speech allowed her, since she is well aware of the sins of the Law of the Father(s): "No woman can be a criminal. To be a criminal one must be a man" (100).

   Maxine Hong Kingston's "No Name Woman" in *The Woman Warrior* (1975) is significant here for a number of reasons. The aunt whose name must not be spoken drowned herself and her illegitimate child in the family well in China. This "spite suicide" (16) haunts the family in more ways than one: the narrator's mother has specifically told her this story in order that the same kind of disgrace not fall on the family again and on the condition that her daughter "not tell anyone" (3). As "No Name Woman" is, of course, that very telling, published moreover, there is another type of "spite" here: "there is more to this silence: they want me to participate in her punishment. And I have" (16). This is an un-naming ("no-name") which paradoxically re-names the other; by remembering her aunt and speaking her (no)name, as well as inventing stories about her, the narrator gives the aunt life, and a name of sorts.[11]

   These three texts reinscribe, in very different ways, potentially passive and forgotten female deaths by drowning and hanging as heroic, active deaths – actions with the potential to transform – although, of course, the "suicidal" protagonists themselves do in fact die. With regard to each text, however, Cixous has made statements to the point in "De la scène de l'Inconscient à la scène de l'Histoire" which might indicate a potential reciprocity, though not necessarily a congruence, in a larger, cross-cultural discourse: "Je rêve de protéger les vivants et les morts. Car on peut aussi tuer les morts, on peut les enterrer, les effacer à l'infini" ["One must protect the living and the dead. For it is possible to kill the dead, too, one can bury them, erase them to infinity"] (20 / "Scene" 6) and "Il faut ne pas oublier. L'écriture ce n'est au fond qu'un anti-oubli" ["One must not forget. Writing is in the end only an *anti-oubli*"] (22 / "Scene" 7).

Re-Call

"Ce n'est pas moi qui suis muette, je suis tue par ta surdité."
– Cixous, speaking for Dora ("Aller à la mer"19)

"I'm not the one who is dumb. I am silenced by your inability to hear"(547)

To name, other than oneself, is always in some way to *speak for* the other. Speaking for the other necessarily risks silencing her. The extraordinary suppleness which resulted from what Aneja calls Cixous' "slipperiness" in theorizing Woman may well become restricted when she names those who give-without-return (Mother), but her naming project stiffens into rigidity when she others the Other by "un-naming" it/them/her as faceless masses. An utterly indifferent swarm of the living and the dying, they are by definition voiceless as well. But indeed and in fact, "they" are no more nameless or faceless than voiceless: they have been speaking as eloquently and to some of the same points as Cixous for quite some time.

If Cixous' homogenization of the Other which "is" "Asia" arrests the flow of her own theory, it also casts the Other into a pre-discursive, pre-linguistic paralysis: without speech; without agency; without change, process, or play. Certainly without laughter. Her theory, then, at such a moment resembles the pre-Cixousian Medusa: it metamorphoses the other into (silenced) stone; it un-names and de-humanizes; it is monstrous, not beautiful and laughing. Much as speech unheard petrifies into silence, a gift unrecognized becomes not gift but loss. Not to listen to the Other, to refuse her gift, is indeed monstrous, an allegiance with death. That other women have been re-writing and re-naming the deathly traps of female silence has produced a creative reverberation, one which resembles laughter, the reverberating laughter of a calling back and forth that recognizes differences as well as similarities, that looks at the Medusa/Other with a shock of delighted recognition: I am like her and/yet I am unlike her. To close by switching imagistic tracks: Cixous once defended her theoretical subject-position by reminding us that "We live in a post-Freudian, Derridean age of electricity and the aeroplane. So let's do as modern people do, let's use the contemporary means of transport" ("Conversations" 144-45). I would suggest as well that there are other planes to catch, other calls to make, other calls waiting.

Notes

1. First and third passages are from "La Venue à l'écriture," 55 and 11; second and fourth passages from "Coming to Writing," 44 and 2.
2. The original context concerns Kafka's respectful bow to Oscar Baum: "C'est la scène même de la délicatesse à l'égard de l'autre" (De la scène de l'Inconscient à la scène de l'Histoire" 25). The passage which follows is relevant to the argument of this essay: "Arriver à la délicatesse de Kafka n'est pas donné à tout le monde, c'est seulement à l'horizon de ce que l'on peut espérer. Mais c'est lorsque l'on a pu atteindre le moment de s'ouvrir totalement à l'autre que va pouvoir prendre place de manière très vaste la scène de l'autre qui est en particulier la scène de l'Histoire. Je ne dis pas que je l'ai atteint par moi-même. J'ai reçu beaucoup de leçons d'autres. J'apprends..." (ellipsis in original) ["Coming to the delicacy of Kafka is not given to everyone, it is only on the horizon of what one can hope for. But it is when one has been able to reach the moment of opening oneself completely to the other that the scene of the other, which is more specifically the scene of History, will be able to take place in a very vast way. I don't say I have reached this by myself. I have had many lessons from others" ("Scene" 10)]. Cixous' final "I am learning..." is not included in the English translation.
3. Brian Duren discusses the multiple aspects of the *propre* in "Cixous' Exorbitant Texts": property, the proper, the self (same), the denotative, and so forth; I will concentrate here on multiple aspects of naming and re-naming.
4. The quotation marks are Conley's as well as mine.
5. See also Cixous' comments on her relation to philosophy and her use of its terms, in Conley, 151–52.

6. Suleiman, in a different context, is also concerned that mothers should play and laugh ("Feminist Intertextuality and the Laugh of the Mother" 141–80).
7. Compare Cixous "toutes les femmes sentent... ce qu'aucun homme ne peut éprouver à leur place, les incisions, les naissances, les explosions dans la libido, les ruptures, les pertes, les jouissances dans nos rythmes" ["all women feel... what no man can experience in their place, the incisions, the births, the explosions in libido, the ruptures, the losses, the pleasures in our rhythms" ("La Venue" 67 / "Writing" 56).
8. Shiach cites a very similar case, 122.
9. See also Spivak's reading and critique of Cixous in the same essay.
10. For one overview, see the conclusion of Paula Bennett's *My Life a Loaded Gun*.
11. There are, moreover, other texts which rewrite such deaths (potential or actual within the narrative) differently, which inscribe them to emblematize relations among women, mothers, daughters. Anita Desai's *Clear Light of Day* (1980) is based and structured on remembering; it employs the central motif of drowning in a well, though the drowning victim is, in this case, a mother cow. Beyond its function as a symbol of memory, this image is used to underscore the problematic of motherhood in the text. The drowned cow is associated with an Aunt Mira who mothers (active verb, emphasizing process) a group of children whom a biological mother – a Westernized, bourgeois wife who plays with cards rather than with her children – will not, cannot mother. In Buchi Emecheta's *The Joys of Motherhood* (1979), the mother Nnu Ego attempts drowning because her son dies; her drowning is thwarted only that she live long enough, narratively speaking, to prove the irony of the novel's title. Similarly, Fleur Pillager, in Louise Erdrich's *Tracks* (1988), is a quasi-mythical woman, as well as a mother, whose power is so great that she defies drowning, though her maternal joys are also bitter.

Works Cited

Aneja, Anu. "The Medusa's Slip: Hélène Cixous and the Underpinnings of *Ecriture Féminine*. *LIT* 4 (1993): 17–27.

Bennett, Paula. *My Life a Loaded Gun: Dickinson, Plath, Rich, and Female Creativity.* Urbana/Chicago: U of Illinois P, 1986.

Cixous, Hélène. "Aller à la mer." *Le Monde* 28 April, 1977: 19.

———. "Aller à la mer." Trans. Barbara Kerslake. *Modern Drama* 27 (1984): 546–48.

———. "Le Droit de légende." *L'Avant- Scène de théâtre* 745 (1984): 4–5.

———. *La Jeune Née.* Paris: Union Générale d'Editions, 1975.

———. *The Newly Born Woman.* Trans. Betsy Wing. Minneapolis: U of Minnesota P, 1986.

———."Le Rire de la Méduse." *L'Arc* 61 (1975): 39–54.

———. "The Laugh of the Medusa." Trans. Keith Cohen and Paula Cohen. *New French Feminisms.* Ed. Elaine Marks and Isabelle de Courtivron. New York: Schocken, 1981. 245-64.

———. "De la scène de l'Inconscient à la scène de l'Histoire: Chemin d'une écriture." *Hélène Cixous, chemins d'une écriture.* Ed. Françoise van Rossum-Guyon and Myriam Díaz-Diocaretz. Amsterdam: Rodopi, 1990. 15-34.

———. "From the Scene of the Unconscious to the Scene of History." Trans. Deborah W. Carpenter. *The Future of Literary Theory.* Ed. Raph Cohen. New York/London: Routledge, 1989. 1–18.

———."La Venue à l'écriture." *Entre l'Ecriture.* Paris: des femmes, 1986. 7–69.

———. "Coming to Writing." *"Coming to Writing" and Other Essays.* Trans. Sarah Cornell et. al. Ed. Deborah Jenson. Cambridge: Harvard UP, 1991. 1-58.

——. *Vivre l'orange/To Live the Orange.* Bilingual text. Trans. with Ann Liddle and Sarah Cornell. Paris: des femmes, 1979.

——. "Conversations with Hélène Cixous and Members of the Centre d'Etudes Féminines." *Writing Differences: Readings from the Seminar of Hélène Cixous.* Ed. Susan Sellars. New York: St. Martin's, 1988.

Conley, Verena Andermatt. *Hélène Cixous: Writing the Feminine.* Lincoln: U of Nebraska P, 1984.

de Lauretis, Teresa. *Alice Doesn't: Feminism, Semiotics, Cinema.* Bloomington: Indiana UP, 1984.

Desai, Anita. *Clear Light of Day.* New York: Penguin, 1980.

Duren, Brian. "Cixous' Exorbitant Texts." *Sub-Stance* 32 (1981): 39-51.

Emecheta, Buchi. *The Joys of Motherhood.* New York: Beorge Braziller, 1979.

Erdrich, Louise. *Tracks.* New York: Harper & Row, 1988.

Fisher, Claudine Guégan. *La Cosmogonie d'Hélène Cixous.* Amsterdam: Rodopi, 1988.

hooks, bell. *Talking Back: Thinking Feminist, Thinking Black.* Boston: South End, 1989.

Kingston, Maxine Hong. *The Woman Warrior: Memoirs of a Girlhood Among Ghosts.* New York: Vintage, 1975.

Perry, Donna. "An Interview with Jamaica Kincaid." *Reading Black, Reading Feminist.* Ed. Henry Louis Gates, Jr. New York: Meridian, 1990.

El Saadawi, Nawal. *Woman at Point Zero.* Trans. Sherif Hetata. London: Zed Books, 1975.

Shiach, Morag. *Hélène Cixous: A Politics of Writing.* London/New York: Routledge, 1991.

Spivak, Gayatri Chakravorty. "Can the Subaltern Speak?" *Marxism and the Interpretation of Culture.* Ed. Cary Nelson and Lawrence Grossberg. U of Illinois P, 1988. 271-313.

——. "French Feminism in an International Frame." *In Other Worlds: Essays in Cultural Politics.* New York / London: Routledge, 1987. 134-53.

Stanton, Domna. "Difference on Trial: A Critique of the Maternal Metaphor in Cixous, Irigaray, and Kristeva." *The Poetics of Gender.* Ed. Nancy K. Miller. New York: Columbia UP, 1986. 157-82.

Suleiman, Susan Rubin. *Subversive Intent: Gender, Politics, and the Avant-Garde.* Cambridge: Harvard UP, 1990.

Trinh T. Minh-ha. *When the Moon Waxes Red: Representation, Gender, and Cultural Politics.* New York/London: Routledge, 1991.

——. *Woman, Native, Other: Writing Postcoloniality and Feminism.* Bloomington: Indiana UP, 1989.

Xiao Hong (Zhang Naiying). *Tales of Hulan River.* Trans. Howard Goldblatt. Hong Kong: Joint Publishing, 1988.

9

Cixous, Spivak, and Oppositional Theory

Robert Con Davis

In what follows, I want to explore the political dimension of cultural theory. I do not mean a dogged and mechanical politicizing of aesthetics but the extent to which cultural theory needs to engage with politics in order to be coherent. I have in mind the exemplary cases of Hélène Cixous and Gayatri Chakravorty Spivak, theorists who consistently have addressed strategies and the potential for effective cultural change. My argument is that Cixous self-consciously advances an oppositional theory of culture that critiques patriarchal practices but does so in a way that falls short of having political significance. Spivak, on the other hand, critiques the very foundations for oppositional theory within a social context, the very context that Cixous assumes to be in place in her formulation of *écriture féminine* as cultural critique. When we see Cixous' work in light of Spivak's critique, we come out with a focus not only on the political dimension of cultural theory but on the possibility of complicity with the dominant culture that is being critiqued – on the difficulties, that is, of speaking outside of the dimensions of patriarchal values even when we aim to oppose them. The problematics of complicity with an oppressive practice, the possible inevitability of ideological "collaboration" with what is being critiqued, bear directly on the possibilities of changing culture. Cixous and Spivak, in other words, both attempt – at different levels of success – to enact an oppositional cultural theory as well as the textual practice it engenders in order to lessen the effects of, if possible to disarm, the patriarchal dimension of modern culture.

To grasp the scope of what these two theorists are attempting, we need to see them in relation to current feminist critiques, especially issues concerning the effectiveness of critique, the risks of essentialism, definitions of the "feminine" and the "masculine," history, ideology, complicity in analysis, and so on. Let us take the example of one controversy involving Peggy Kamuf and Nancy K. Miller, played out initially in Kamuf's "Replacing Feminist Criticism" and Miller's "The Text's Heroine: A Feminist Critic and Her Fiction." In these texts, Kamuf and Miller take sharply opposed positions in relation to the possibility of an oppositional theory of culture and the question of effective cultural change. The issue is whether culture can be rationally critiqued and then transformed, or whether such deliberate attempts at change necessarily negate themselves and end up accomplishing something completely unintended. Kamuf summarizes the question of oppositional practices for feminist cultural theory when she says: "If one concludes that...there is nothing beyond oppositional modes of thought and being, no outside from which something else can intervene which is not already programmed by the dialectical machine, then indeed one's oppositional strategy must fully espouse the logic of change (of history made possible there and in those terms" ("Parisian Letters" 125). Kamuf's own stance is that while "one cannot take up a position against [the idea of ideological] positions" (125), effective "oppositional tactics" must necessarily keep "open a space for possible dislocation." Kamuf wants to give "the traces of the non-opposable other a chance to make their mark before they are too quickly reduced to recognizable positions and thereby made available to dialectical reason and its institutions" (126).

Kamuf's critique of oppositionalism suggests that modes of rational critique may only be able, finally, to reiterate the terms of the ideology they are critiquing. Judith Butler argues the same point about the encompassing nature of patriarchal discourse when she says that "the masculine sex" necessarily "*appears* to originate meanings and thereby to signify" as an effect with ideological ends (45). Within patriarchal discourse, or so her argument runs, woman will always and only be seen as "the masculine sex *encore* (and *en corps*) parading in the mode of otherness" (12). These are the same frustrating impasses that many left-leaning cultural theorists repeatedly encounter as they work for change from within institutions.

Diana Fuss argues, however, that such debates as Kamuf and Miller's demonstrate that oppositional discourse is not so much an argument to be resolved as it is itself a "conflictual" model of a particularly productive form of feminist discourse. Perennially in conflict and changing, feminist discourse is a critique grounded on cultural values that, in turn, must continue to be critiqued, and critiqued repeatedly thereafter. This willingness to submit itself to change is the traditional strength of feminist cultural critique. Fuss argues for this view of feminist critique as able to remain dynamic and in "conflict" when she says that " 'essentially speaking' . . . we need both to speak and, simultaneously, to deconstruct these spaces [of discourse] to keep them from solidifying" (118). "Such a double gesture," she goes on, "involves once again the responsibility to historicize, to examine each deployment of essence, each appeal to experience, each claim to identity in the complicated contextual frame in which it is made" (118).

Cixous enters precisely this discussion about oppositional theory through her formulation of *écriture féminine*. In her role as "oppositional critic" she self-consciously chooses a style of confrontation with dominant culture practices in order to understand and change patriarchal dominance. Cixous reads the discourses of contemporary culture to expose crucial oppositions as misleading formulations of truth and error, key binarities – such as father/mother, man/woman, active/passive, nature/culture, superior/inferior, etc. – that govern the exercise of power. Cixous' primary strategy has been to alter the effect of gender relations in the way people read. She attempts to do this in her classroom, criticism, and fiction – at least into the middle 1980s – through her own innovative reading and writing of cultural texts, her goal being to expose, and even to begin to dismantle, patriarchal dominance in the academy and in the institution of cultural criticism and theory. She strives to create for her students and readers, in short, a revolutionary cultural frame which legitimizes a feminine dimension of textuality and shifts the cultural relations of power between male and female. Her work, in this way, has been in the avant garde both in the literary and political sense.

Ann Rosalind Jones, Monique Wittig, and various other feminist critics describe Cixous' teaching and writing in this way, too, but they also worry that the intensity of her "oppositional" reading of culture may have the hidden weakness of, at the same time, imprisoning her work within "the very ideological system [of 'oppositional' thinking] feminists want to destroy" – in this case, the patriarchy (Jones 369). The fact is that in the late 1980s Cixous and her strategies for instituting and understanding "feminine discourse" – a theoretical definition of "feminine" reading and writing – were of far less urgency to those thinking and writing about women's issues in literary or in cultural studies. Many critics committed to *"theories of writing and reading,"* as Alice Jardine reports, actually "posit themselves and their work as hostile to, or "beyond," feminism" such as Cixous' (20), there being a strong commitment in the late 1980s, as Jones says, "to move outside that male-centered, binary logic [which I identify ultimately with Aristotle but which is here tied to Cixous] altogether" (369).

However, given the extent of Cixous' intervention in literary and cultural studies, and the uncommon strength and appeal of her work, she has to be considered a nearly ideal initiator of cultural change from within an institution. If she, working on so many fronts, could not initiate change, then we must wonder who can? Thus, Jones' and others' judgment of Cixous' apparent "failure" to inform and influence women's studies in the 1980s and 1990s raises disturbing questions about the ideological commitments of oppositionalism in contemporary culture – about the potential to subvert and change culture from within, the goal common to Western intellectuals in the late 1960s through the middle 1980s (most prominently Michel Foucault and Noam Chomsky – see Paul Bové's *Intellectuals in Power*).

The medium of Cixous' "oppositionalism" is "feminine writing." In the middle 1970s Cixous, Luce Irigaray, Julia Kristeva, Michele Montrelay, and Catherine Clément, among others, developed a body of thought about reading women's texts in particular contexts of women's experience. The general strategy of this thought reflects Virginia Woolf's notion of a feminine writing that does not rely on a biological conception of the sexes – a "given" essence of male and female characteristics – but on culturally-determined features, such as "openness" in feminine texts as a lack of repressive patterning in discourse and a tendency to retain a sense of the indeterminant and the random. Such would be a designation as applicable to the reading of Marcel Proust as

Virginia Woolf. These theorists tried to accomplish three things: (1) to expose the mechanism by which Western texts (literary and otherwise) have been written to advance the prestige of patriarchal culture, (2) to understand how women's writing has been effaced and suppressed by male discourse, and (3) finally to recover, or reinvent, a way of reading feminine writing (including writing *by* women) that does not duplicate and advance the paternal romance. Such theorizing, pursued in the atmosphere of post-May 1968 France and deconstruction, predictably asked questions about the relations of writing, politics, and gender – what "writing" is, how texts deploy power, how to read a feminine (non-patriarchal) text, and (with even greater urgency) what the "feminine" is?

Common among these critics, whose ideas are otherwise divergent, is that feminine writing (*écriture féminine*) – both escaping and situated within patriarchal culture – is best understood in metaphors related to "orgasm" (*jouissance*) or, in Cixous' case, *sortie*, which means "excess" (again suggestive of *jouissance*) and the "way out," "exit," or a "leaving" (see "Sorties" in *the Newly-Born Woman*). Taken together, these metaphors suggest the common aim, through an underlying metaphor, of finding a "beyond" or "way out" from patriarchal discourse and the analytical double binds it fosters. Cixous, for example, calls for "leaving" behind "the signs of sexual opposition" all together ("Laugh" 311), that is, simply abandoning the binarity of gender as a way of defeating the Western tendency to elevate men and efface women in oppositions she formulates as man/woman, activity/passivity, great/small, nature/history, transformation/inertia, white/black, etc., where the second term in each case is effaced or made peripheral. Patriarchal (Western) culture, Cixous argues, is generated out of these oppositions based ultimately on what she calls "the power relation between a fantasized obligatory virility meant to invade, to colonize, and the consequential phantasm of woman as a 'dark continent' to penetrate and to 'pacify' ("Laugh" 310, also "Castration" 44). Cixous focuses on these oppositions, which all "come back to the man/woman opposition" anyway, as requiring fundamental adjustments in language and "discourse," changes in the linguistic and social context of language use ("Castration" 44).

"Laugh of the Medusa" and "Castration or Decapitation?" present Cixous' case for the reading of feminine writing. In "Laugh," for example, she presents the scenario of writing as structured by a "sexual opposition" favoring men, one that "has always worked for man's profit to the point of reducing writing...to his laws" (313). She means that writing is constituted in a "discourse" of relations social, political, and linguistic in makeup – and these relations can be characterized in a masculine or feminine "economy." The masculine, traditionally dominant in the West, is a system of militant exclusion wherein patterns of linearity and exclusion (patriarchal "logic") overemphasize the hierarchical nature of (sexual) difference in discourse and give a "grossly exaggerated" view of the "sexual opposition" actually inherent to language (311). Cixous does not say this merely to denigrate a masculine economy, which is, she argues – if seen outside the exaggerations of patriarchy – naturally a part of writing and reading. "Castration," she says – the symbolic rule of discourse conceived on the male model – "is fundamental [to writing], unfortunately" (Conley 156). "Isn't it evident," she asks, "that the penis gets around in my texts, that I give it a place and appeal?" ("Laugh" 319). The concept of castration is necessary, she goes on somewhat at odds with Gilles Deleuze and Felix Guattari, because it would be "humanly impossible to have an absolute economy without a minimum of [masculine] mastery" (Conley 139), a rule of exclusion (symbolized by castration) to organize the dynamics of writing. The problem she sees, simply, is that the male economy has been promoted beyond the functional need for "repression" in writing to impose very restrictive rules on the deployment of power over women and which always favor men.

In the feminine economy there are no strict rules of dismissal but the play of writing as an "openness," containing "that element which never stops resonating," an undecidable inscription of "white ink" on white paper that writes itself free of masculine rules of decidable order and (hierarchical) contrast ("Laugh" 312). The "openness" of such writing is evident in Cixous' own style, as when she writes that

> We the precocious, we the repressed of culture, our lovely mouths gagged with pollen, our wind knocked out of us, we the labyrinths, the ladders, the trampled spaces, the bevies – we are black and we are beautiful. ("Laugh" 310)

In such writing Cixous forces expository sense into the economy of poetic association and controls the "excess" of imagery through repetition and nonlinear (non-male) accretions. Virginia Woolf also speaks of such writing in contrast to "male" ("shadowed," or violently imposed) writing. This is Kristeva's conception, too, of *jouissance*, the poetic discourse "beyond" the masculine text of reason and order. For all three critics, further, there is the assumption that the feminine economy of excess does not need re-creation exactly, to be made anew, because it has always persisted in the margins and gaps (as the repressed) of male-dominated culture. It follows, therefore, that women, and in theory even men, can find the "*sortie*" from, and the "beyond" of, patriarchal culture precisely by looking for and acknowledging the feminine economy that *already* exists within, along side, and around the margins of male discourse – hence the importance of the "*sortie*" ("excess" and "exit") as the controlling metaphor of Cixous' discourse.

We can see that Cixous participates in the tradition of oppositional critique that dates back to Aristotle by looking at her handling of the man/woman binarity. In her analysis, she couples two propositions that form a "contrary" relationship, as in the opposed but simultaneous existence of man and woman. The pairing of man/woman in a contrary relationship, moreover, forms the axis of possible significations running from the possibilities of courtship and marriage to their contraries in incest and homosexuality. We can posit a second level in her analysis in a supposed square of opposition and find the third term of patriarchalism – the "Father" as the designation of power in the man/woman opposition, the signal that man will be the controlling term. The Father as indicator of ideology, therefore, creates a perspective on and, in a sense, "understands" the first level of reference, interprets and limits it, by identifying the patriarchal principle of hierarchy that organizes it. The fourth term then completes this ideological reading with "Mother" – female sexuality and power. At this furthest reach of the square, "Mother" repeats and alters the category of "woman," stands in opposition to "Father," and gives final expression to (even while it challenges) the patriarchal values this discourse is generated from. In this way, the fourth term marks a new authority emanating from but, at the same time, alien to this discourse. The

economy of Cixous' man/woman opposition can be projected as
follows:

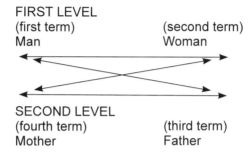

FIRST LEVEL
(first term)   (second term)
Man   Woman

SECOND LEVEL
(fourth term)   (third term)
Mother   Father

Here "Mother" comes into the square as the instance of what was
suppressed all along through the insistence in the discourse on
various formal oppositions. As an historical phenomenon, the
square shows "Mother" to be the core of a specific proposition
emerging as a rupture in the historical fabric, a "rupture" that has
left its trace but is not yet representable as a specific and recognized textual practice.

It is in this way that Cixous' reading of the man/woman opposition demonstrates the economies of relationship engendered by
oppositional binarity. The result for Cixous is a gendered hierarchy
of values inscribed by the square's four terms – themselves rising
from and thus "escaping" the unintelligibility of "mere" differences, unorganized and non-politicized heterogeneity. It follows
that reading the pattern of these values, articulated according to a
rule made evident in the square's operation, constitutes an ideological critique of gender. What we are viewing in Cixous' method of
reading, as with Aristotle, Jameson, Said, Greimas, and the modern
"oppositional" critics generally, is an ideological approach to the
problematic of decipherment. The fourth term – equivalent to
"female sexuality" or "feminine political power" – is not on the
order of a mere logical necessity, ideology being reducible neither
to logical entailment (simple rationality) nor to pure contiguity. As
a cultural phenomenon, rather, Mother is potentially a manifestation of "history" – the diachronic emergence of the unthought and
the initially unreadable.

Cixous goes on in both "Laugh of the Medusa" and "Castration
or Decapitation?" (also in "Sorties" in *The Newly-Born Woman*) to

explore the oppositional logic relating the masculine economy to the "overflow" of erotic "excess." In "Castration or Decapitation?" she emphasizes the extent to which the Man/Woman opposition "cuts endlessly across all the oppositions that order culture" (44). "Everything...that's spoken," she goes on, "everything that's organized as discourse, art, religion, the family, language, everything that seizes us, everything that acts on us – it is all ordered around hierarchical oppositions that come back to the man/woman opposition..." (44). This primary opposition, she concludes, "makes it all work." Therefore, "it's on the [concept of the] couple that we have to work if we are to deconstruct and transform culture" (44). Cixous in this way argues for the primacy of a formal sexual logic, the "couple" (Man/Woman) as an orienting polarity of texts, and in this concentration, repeated throughout her work – prominent in these essays but equally so in "Sorties" – she shows the extent to which she assumes a basic oppositional matrix as fundamental to culture. She commits herself to the implications of this approach as she posits a strategy for reading the essence of the feminine in a formal sense and making "opposition" – for good or ill – her primary instrument of analysis.

Ironically, though, essentialism – or unproblematic "meaning" as discrete and non-relational – is one of the myths that Cixous tries to expose. In any other context Cixous would not believe in absolute essences or grant their authority. Theoretically, then, Cixous' feminine discourse – based on an essential "femininity" that can be investigated in relation to an essential "masculinity" – is problematic. Jones also points up, understandably, that in positing an idealized femininity, "French feminists [such as Cixous] make of the female body too unproblematically pleasurable and totalized an entity" (368). The female body, in this view, actually houses the erotic "essence" supposedly distributed throughout feminine discourse. Jones argues persuasively and probably decisively that Cixous' version of *femininity*, based as it is on an essentialist conception of gender, is not really viable in theory or practice.

At best, Cixous exemplifies the resistance to male "desire" with her own writing – that is, by opposing the "body" and materiality (the style) of her own discourse to masculine writing practices. In effect, Cixous wagers the "body" of her eroticized writing against the repressions of masculine textuality. But if we judge from the testimony of other feminists, the overall success of this performance – in light of the difficulty of altering any cultural discourse – is questionable. Sandra M. Gilbert judges Cixous' "imaginative [utopian] journeys across the frontier of prohibition" to be pure utopian "voyages out into a no place that must be a no man's and no woman's land" (*Newly-Born Woman* xvi) – a provocative performance but perhaps not sufficiently connected with other cultural practices to have a significant impact.

Jones' major objection to Cixous is the global one that Cixous' ultimate appeal is to oppositional thinking. This is a problem for Cixous as cultural critic, Jones argues, because any term conceived in binarity necessarily inscribes, and even legitimizes, the oppositional network – the differential system – it is articulated in. If Cixous strategically advances feminine writing over, in opposition to, masculine discourse, as Jones says, Cixous merely succeeds in reversing "the values assigned to each side of the polarity, but . . . still leaves man as the determining referent, not departing from the male-female opposition, but participating in it" (369). Jones' point is that the fight with – or opposition to – men could have the effect of making patriarchal culture even stronger. This is the predicament of the Foucauldian intellectual, as Jim Merod comments, who "is inscribed within the dominant culture and within the operations of power which he wants to contest. He is [,therefore,] in some undismissible sense, an agent of that power" (Merod 158). Cixous' discourse – potentially an agent of what it opposes – inadvertently returns to and re-enforces the masculine discourse, the values of patriarchy, it was supposed to subvert and go beyond. Cixous-as-oppositional-reader, as Jones summarizes, misunderstands the inherent dangers of oppositional criticism and, accordingly, is lured by the appearance of analytical clarity into the trap of accepting an underlying patriarchal ethos. Cixous' oppositional reading, it follows, is confined and neutralized in effectiveness by the patriarchal frame she unwittingly employs.

This difficulty is yet another version of the impasse often faced by contemporary "engaged" theorists. Intellectuals, like Cixous, who wish to think *and* act, or at least to theorize the impact of their reading and writing, have great trouble finding an avenue to action uncompromised by internal contradictions. They cannot even theorize a mode of action that does not subvert what they set out to achieve. This paradox is particularly disturbing because, especially in Cixous' case, it so vividly challenges the prospect of deliberate and rational intervention, of any political action. In short, the "failure" of Cixous' project, given her reliance on oppositional reading, does not bode well for the possibility of effective cultural opposition – for change from within an institution. Even without subscribing to oppositionality as a policy, one must see that the impossibility of effective opposition – which is so if opposition automatically cancels itself by restoring legitimacy to the dominant discourse – raises the specter of paralysis and quietism, of no response to cultural and political oppression. And since this danger does not plague only the self-identified "oppositional" critic, the radical cultural theorist (like Foucault), or the political strategist of the left (like Baudrillard), the "failure" of Cixous' oppositional project, in important ways, puts the possibility of intervention itself into question. Can a cultural discourse be opposed from within, or is all such calculated action self-canceling and defeated in advance?

Susan C. Jarratt argues, contrary to my claim here, that the immediate problem in understanding Cixous is not her supposed essentialism. We need to remember, Jarratt warns, that "because [Cixous] envisions a possible future in which difference is not tied ontologically to sex, her practice [potentially] can be described as strategic rather than essentialist" (71). Jarratt reads Cixous' formulations as localizable, historical interventions and not as universal pronouncements. I think that Cixous *can* be read in this way, too. But the fact remains that Cixous' discourse does suggest totalized female and male economies, and Cixous founds these notions of gendered discourse on the "fact" of female and male bodies. Also, Cixous' emphasis – often her whole point in cultural intervention – falls on the metaphoric modes of substitution of replacing a closed (male) discourse with an open (female) discourse. In this model, the "true" discourse for the dissemination of knowledge is the open one, and the discourse in error is the closed one.

Gayatri Chakravorty Spivak addresses these same issues concerning patriarchal values and the possibility of cultural change. By contrast, however, Spivak does not draw on the same conceptual totalizations, and Spivak does not resist the idea of unwitting collaboration between versions of feminist critique and the patriarchal values (Jones' charge against Cixous). Spivak freely admits that there is such complicity on the part of feminist and all cultural critique. This complicity is unavoidable, and she ventures that the

ideal of pure and efficacious intervention is an impossible notion
defeated in advance. By contrast, Spivak's own feminist critique is
an attempt to theorize the position of the subjugated person
generally within postcolonial discourse, and then the woman in
history as colonized (divided and compromised) subject. Historically, Spivak views the woman in the West and East as occupying
the position of the "subaltern," or the oppressed, and in this
Spivak draws on both Antonio Gramsci's ideological critique of
hegemony as well as (even if unintentionally) the tradition of
oppositional thinking in Western thought that I associate with
Aristotle.

In third-world discourses such as that of colonized India, for
example, "woman" as a cultural position is situated as subaltern,
that is, in a position on the periphery of culture and political
relations. The inherent strategy of the dominant discourse is not
merely to separate women from power but to position them
against a colonial and hegemonic "center" so as to insure self-
limiting and -negating strategies whenever women attempt to act
on their own behalf. Spivak's theorizing, however, also reflects a
larger critique of the gendered subject in the West and especially its
political relations within postcolonial culture and patriarchy. Spivak's own theoretical counter-move against neo-colonialism, especially in her most recent work (I think especially of the essay "Can
the Subaltern Speak?"), is not so much to "oppose" male privilege,
say, as "women" against "male" oppression, because doing so, as
Cixous' case tends to show, all too predictably may replicate the
categories and positions of discourse that were problematic in the
patriarchal values to start with. The scenario of a monolithic collectivity of women poised against an equally monolithic patriarchal
system may actually be one of the intended emplotments of patriarchal culture.

Spivak moves, instead, to locate the feminist gesture – as exem-
plified by Hélène Cixous – as part of a critique of the Western
subject as it can be reflected in patriarchal narratives. This is a
move that she intends fundamentally to redirect the feminist project in order to address what Alice Jardine and others have discussed recently as the limited range of Anglo-American feminism
particularly during the 1960 and 1970s. Spivak's recasting of feminism also addresses the frustrations of the feminist project in
recent bleak appraisals such as Sandra Gilbert's "Life's Empty

Pack: Notes Toward a Literary Daughteronomy" and many French feminists in the late 1980s and early 1990s who consider themselves to be a part of a movement that is either "post-" or even "anti-" feminist.

High on Spivak's itinerary is to situate "feminism," or her reconstituted version of it, within a postcolonial critique of imperialism that, in turn, resituates the female subject historically and ideologically. This radical practice constitutes her strategy for third-world feminist discourse within three frames, (1) situating the social subject within a critique of social contradiction, (2) situating third-world feminist discourse in relation to neo-colonial discourse and the West's divided subjectivity, and (3) finally, suggesting how a third-world female subject is constituted within postcolonial discourse, the final frame within the first two.

Spivak's idea of feminism derives from her conception of the female subject – or any subject – as constituted in contradiction. By contradiction here she means largely what Marx and Derrida mean by it in the subject – a "subject" divided in terms of the conflicting value systems that make it up. To illustrate her point she takes the famous example from *The Eighteenth Brumaire of Louis Bonaparte* where Marx discusses a split running through French society. In his discussion of a specific strata of nineteenth-century French peasant-class culture, Marx makes two conflicting observations. He says that "in so far as millions of families live under economic conditions of existence that separate their mode of life...*they form a class*," a kind of totality in terms of class. Marx then goes on to say that "in so far as... the identity of their interests fails to produce a feeling of community...*they do not form a class*" (cited in "Can the Subaltern Speak?" 277). Marx advances these observations to illustrate a structural contradiction of class in the most radical sense. And Spivak understands this formulation to suggest the divided constitution of class representation at any one moment. French peasant-class culture is and is not a class – and this irresolvable contradiction is not the ambiguity of a moment of crisis, although the conditions and exact site of contradiction will change, but the formulation of a structural division inherent to the concept of class and the social subject. The social subject in Marx's example exists simultaneously on opposed sides of an ideological divide – divided against its own interests.

The same is true for the subaltern subject (the positions of articulated value found on the "second level" of Aristotle's oppositional
square), in this case, the Indian woman. Historically British
attempts in the nineteenth century to protect women from male
violence in India, ritual suicide, dowry violence, widow suicide,
etc., succeed in suggesting how the Indian woman is supposedly
"saved" and then incorporated into the refinements of colonial
culture. However, excluded from active participation in and from
access to power in the society she is a part of, she becomes both a
victim and an agent of colonial oppression. Insofar as the Indian
woman is subject to the culture of the colonizer and necessarily
"desires" the ends that constitute her as a colonized subject – in
effect, collaborating with the system she is part of – she does not
join with other oppressed people and does not struggle against her
situation. She is part of the problem of colonial oppression. In this
way, framed in two dimensions at once, the Indian-woman-as-
subject manifests the same contradiction of class that Marx identified in the subject of nineteenth-century French peasant-class
society.

An example of the Indian woman as divided, subaltern subject
can be seen vividly in the Indian practice, as Spivak notes, of *sati*,
the ritual of widow sacrifice in which "the Hindu widow ascends
the pyre of the dead husband and immolates herself upon it"
(297). Often described in terms of passionate love and great
devotion to a man, this rite up through the middle nineteenth
century – as Spivak goes on – "was not practiced universally and
was not caste-or class-fixed" (297). However, in complex manip-
ulations of Hindu culture, the British outlawed *sati* in 1829 on
what must be taken, to a large degree at least, as a humanitarian
gesture designed to halt the practice of female suicide. In this
instance of colonial intervention, however, Spivak shows that the
specifics of British rule and the interdiction against *sati* expose a
contradiction, a vivid but not uncommon replication of the hegemonic regime already in place – in this case, the very hegemonic
male practices the new law against *sati* was supposed to be
replacing. Within the colonial experience, that is, the outlawing
of *sati* was just another instance, as Spivak argues, of "White men
saving brown women from brown men" – the white colonists, in
effect, vying with and defeating brown, Indian men for the sexual
allegiance of brown, Indian women (297). In the process, the

woman as subaltern subject, to the degree that she accedes to the British, is re-alienated by being replaced on the periphery of British culture.

Spivak's concern with *sati* as a practice, finally, is a concern with the gendered subject constituted in contradiction and *as* an ideological contradiction – as if, as she says of the subject of *sati*, "knowledge *in a subject* of its own insubstantiality and mere phenomenality is dramatized so that the dead husband becomes the exteriorized example and place of the extinguished subject and the widow becomes the (non)agent [the subaltern] who " 'acts ... out' " the extinction (300). The practice of *sati* and then its banning therein both situate the woman as subaltern, that is, situate the subaltern as such, and then reiterate it so that the woman is subjugated only then to be in a position to be subjugated again, and thereafter to be in a position to be resubjugated, and so on. Whether the resulting sexual economy is played out between Indian husband and wife in the *sati* practice or between Indian wife and British governors in colonial practice, it is clear that the "legally programmed symmetry in the status of the subject," as Spivak says, wherein the woman is an "object of *one* husband ... obviously operates in the interest of the legally asymmetrical subject-status of the male.'

It must be said, finally, that "the self-immolation of the widow," as Spivak concludes, "thereby becomes the extreme case of the general law [of the subaltern] rather than an exception to it" (303). In this way, the contradiction of the subject exposes an ideological aim. Spivak adds that "it is not surprising, then, to read of heavenly rewards for the *sati*" – scenarios in which "ecstatic heavenly dancers, paragons of female beauty and male pleasure[,] ... sing her praise" (303). In virtually an identical way the British offered cultural rewards of legitimacy and British identification for the "good" Indian wife who responded to white administrators to forego *sati* and, in so doing, rejected Indian husbands – that is, rewards for those who rejected Indian for British culture.

As I have already been discussing, Spivak's rationale for defining third-world feminist discourse within the critique of colonialism comes out of her understanding of Western history and the contradiction inherent in the subject. Aligning herself with Marx and Derrida, she reasons that attempts by Western intellectuals such as Michel Foucault and Gilles Deleuze to analyze the third-

world subject solely in terms of power or the operation of econom-
ics – as if the investigators are themselves free of ideology and its
representations – actually succeed in reconstituting the same
discourse and the same oppressed subject. Foucault and Deleuze
inadvertently posit the existence of a privileged angle of intellectual observation – a *transparent* and essentialist mode of investigation. This happens at the moment when Foucault and Deleuze
attempt to stand back and let the subaltern person "speak for
herself," that is, the moment when the white anthropological
investigator chooses merely to listen and record the supposed
self-presentation of oppression. By contrast, and in opposition to
Foucault and Deleuze, Spivak is intent upon recognizing the
intellectual subject's ideological stance at those moments of merely
listening. She then argues against the possibility of such purely
disinterested inquiry and in favor of avowedly interested and
ideologically committed intellectual participation. She is, thus,
against the interventionist project as Foucault and Deleuze define
it precisely because she wishes to take account of and interpret the
constructed colonial subject-as-male-intellectual as it faces the colonized *other* figured in the subaltern female subject.

Spivak here is promoting a theory of neo-colonial discourse that
highlights the oppressed person or class not as merely denied a
voice, as being silenced, but precisely as *constructed* in the subaltern
position to speak through ventriloquism. This happens as the
oppressed person is given a position and a subaltern voice defined
by and standing in a certain relation to the master discourse.
Spivak's own task then as a postcolonial intellectual must be to
rethink the position from which "opposition" may emanate. Implicitly she must retheorize the whole machine of oppositional analysis that heretofore was thought to function as a counter to the
dominant discourse. But now the oppositional analysis is aimed
historically at the very cultural foundations that created the colonial "contradiction" of an oppressed female subject. Spivak's aim is
to situate the very idea of opposition ideologically and to show that
there is no unmarked position of pure victimage from which opposition may be initiated in ideal terms. Her own historical and
ideological critique does begin to define a voice other than that of
patriarchal culture insofar as she locates strategies for critiquing
colonial and neo-colonial practice. The nature of third-world domination necessitates that she inquire into, as she says, "how the

third-world subject is represented within Western discourse" (271). The inquiry into the colonial and neo-colonial phenomenon must also become an inquiry into the question of the representation of power in Western culture generally, particularly capitalism, which in turn must be related to the development of the Western subject and its strategies for self-representation.

As regards Spivak's understanding of the gendered subject, she is clearly suggesting a discourse in which the subaltern is not the actual subjugated woman, the person, and yet at the same time the subaltern cannot be conceived outside of specific gender markings based on actual women in real historical settings. The subaltern, in other words, and this point must be made emphatically, is a position and a structural necessity within the gendered discourse of colonialism, the female subaltern subject being a designation for an "other" constructed precisely to be masterable by the dominant subject of colonial discourse. From a postcolonial perspective, then, female gender is an ideological marker within a complex chain of colonial politico-sexual relations. And in Spivak's view, the gendered subject, thoroughly ideological in its implications, is produced out of a base of material relations that, in turn, advance and continually reduplicate a mode of production, a set of relations that distribute and govern power. It is an inevitable consequence of colonialism to produce the subaltern, just as it is an inevitable consequence of Western subjectivity, from Aristotle through the present, to produce the woman-as-the-subaltern.

The "subaltern" is merely the subject position constructed by colonial discourse specifically for its own strategic ends, a mere place holder that in itself cannot be brought to life, liberated, or empowered except through ventriloquism. The subaltern as such cannot be recuperated. Instead, the dominant discourse speaks through the subaltern subject, and so Spivak has arrived at the same point of ideological collaboration evident in Cixous. And, once again, this paradox is deeply disturbing because it does directly challenge the Western prospect of detached and rational intervention, certainly Western schemes for systematic liberation and social renewal. Finally, if the subaltern cannot speak, if an oppositional theorist such as Spivak cannot maneuver to allow the speech of the "other," then the itinerary for an oppositional program may be compromised before the fact, and there will be no purposeful intervention as such within the cultural matrix.

But as a postcolonial critic and a feminist (in her reconstituted version of feminism), Spivak's response is that the apparent impossibility of opposing the dominant discourse from within, virtually of rewriting patriarchal narrative, is a specter created by neo-colonialism. On the contrary, Spivak's argument is in line with that of Nancy Hartsock, saying that "when we look closely at the economic roles of women we see the ways capitalism, patriarchy, and white supremacy reinforce one another and how the ideology of individualism provides a philosophical justification for these structures" (Hartsock 11). Accordingly, Spivak's own three-part itinerary for oppositional discourse begins with a critique of neo-colonialism and capitalism and the Western project of disinterested inquiry (as figured in patriarchal values) to create a detached and superior observer. She then formulates a strategy for intervention based on the three-part critique I have been discussing.

Spivak's activist strategy aims to avoid the institution of ideal subject positions, the grand strategy of patriarchalism. Spivak's critique institutes truth and error as functional dimensions built into the divided subject, as phases of function rather than as unrevisable characteristics. "Truth," for example, is not a commodity or activity awaiting discovery at some moment in the history of female economy (as Cixous suggests) but one of the constructions of the subject-as-a-contradiction at a particular moment. "Error," likewise, is not avoidable for a social subject who can never be in full possession of its own material conditions and interests.

Cixous' and Spivak's critiques highlight current theoretical dilemmas of cultural studies, that of working through the impasses of patriarchal culture, the curved paths and frequent detours, even failures and retreats, of productive critiques. I am suggesting that in a strategy for displacing such values, Cixous and Spivak together show us ways of reconfiguring patriarchy within the social context of gender relations. Specifically, Cixous demonstrates the "textual" nature of "female" and "male" as categories in all cultural texts. Spivak then argues for the necessity of analyzing those categories within the social and ideological – ultimately political – frames that give those categories coherence and meaning. The act of superimposing patriarchal narratives within specific historical and social frames, and the process of critique doing so is a part of, will not automatically dismantle the postmodern remnants of patriarchalism. Produced in this superimposition, however, are the ripe conditions for further critique. This ongoing critique of patriarchal culture, hinted at by Cixous but realized more fully by Spivak, runs in two directions – (1) toward an ideological critique of the Western subject and (2) toward post-semiotic critiques of the gendered subject, principally those influenced by feminist thought. By suggesting the sequence of Aristotle/Cixous/Spivak, I mean to highlight the issue of the subject as what is *known* in Aristotle and the critique of the gendered subject as the *knowing subject* in Cixous and Spivak. The power to control the positions of speech and of what can be said – as Edward W. Said has said about authority in general and as Cixous and Spivak demonstrate about patriarchal authority specifically – "must be analyzed" before any effective social critique can take place (19). Moreover, Cixous and Spivak demonstrate the extent to which a cultural theory that can encompass and critique patriarchalism must focus on a textual practice with a social impact, a cultural phenomenon in terms of its textual function *and* social value.[1]

1. An expanded version of this article appears in chapter 5, "Reflections on Post-Paternal Culture," in my *The Paternal Romance: Reading God-the-Father in Early Western Culture*, (U of Illinois P, 1993). I have also borrowed comments from my "Woman As Oppositional Reader: Cixous on Discourse" in Susan L. Gabriel and Isaiah Smithson, eds., *Gender in the Classroom: Power and Pedagogy* (U of Illinois P, 1990) and "Gayatri Chakravorty Spivak and the Ethos of the Subaltern," by Robert Con Davis and David S. Gross, *Ethos: New Essays in Rhetorical and Critical Theory*, Eds. James and Tita Baumlin (Southern Methodist U. P, 1994).

Works Cited

Bové, Paul. *Intellectuals in Power: A Genealogy of Critical Humanism.* New York: Columbia UP, 1986.

Butler, Judith. *Gender Trouble: Feminism and the Subversion of Identity.* New York and London: Routledge, 1990.

Cixous, Hélène. "Castration or Decapitation?" Trans. Annette Kuhn. *Signs* 7 (1981): 41–55.

—— "The Character of 'Character'." Trans. Keith Cohen. *New Literary History* 5 (1974):384–402.

—— "The Laugh of the Medusa." Trans. Keith Cohen and Paula Cohen. *Critical Theory Since 1965.* Ed. Hazard Adams and Leroy Searle. Tallahassee: Florida State UP, 1986.

—— and Catherine Clément. *The Newly-Born Woman.* Trans. Betsy Wing. Minneapolis: U of Minnesota P, 1986.

Conley, Verena. *Hélène Cixous: Writing the Feminine.* Lincoln: U of Nebraska P, 1984.

Fuss, Diana. *Essentially Speaking: Feminism, Nature, and Difference.* New York and London: Routledge, 1989.

Gilbert, Sandra M. "Life's Empty Pack: Notes Toward a Literary Daughteronomy." *Critical Inquiry* 11.3 (1985):355–384.

Hartsock, Nancy. "Political Change: Two Perspectives on Power." *Building Feminist Theory: Essays from QUEST.* Intro. Charlotte Bunch. New York and London: Longman, Inc., 1981. 3–19.

Jardine, Alice. *Gynesis: Configurations of Woman and Modernity.* Ithaca and London: Cornell UP, 1985.

Jarratt, Susan C. *Rereading the Sophists: Classical Rhetoric Refigured.* Carbondale and Edwardsville: Southern Illinois UP, 1991.

Jones, Ann Rosalind. "Writing the Body: Toward an Understanding of *l'ecriture feminine.*" *The New Feminist Criticism: Essays on Women, Literature, and Theory.* Ed. Elaine Showalter. New York: Pantheon, 1985.

Kamuf, Peggy. "Replacing Feminist Criticism." *Conflicts in Feminism*. Ed. Marianne Hirsch and Evelyn Fox Keller. New York and London: Routledge, 1990. 105–111.
—— and Nancy K. Miller. "Parisian Letters: Between Feminism and Deconstruction." *Conflicts in Feminism*. 121–133.
Merod, Jim. *The Political Responsibility of the Critic*. Ithaca and London: Cornell UP, 1987.
Miller, Nancy K. "The Text's Heroine: A Feminist Critic and Her Fictions." *Conflicts in Feminism*. Ed. Marianne Hirsch and Evelyn Fox Keller. New York and London: Routledge, 1990. 112–120.
Said, Edward W. *Orientalism*. New York: Vintage Books/Random House, 1979.
Spivak, Gayatri Chakravorty. "Can the Subaltern Speak?" *Marxism and the Interpretation of Culture*. Ed. Cary Nelson and Lawrence Grossberg. Urbana and Chicago: U of Illinois P, 1988. 271–313.

10

Hélène Cixous: A Space Between — Women and (Their) Language

Pamela A. Turner

In art criticism, writing and performing are treated as categorically different. Writing relates to a concrete product, the inscribing of symbols on a page. Performance is treated as an ephemeral activity, as symbolic expression in a space. Writing is of the mind; performing is of the body. Writing is private; performing is public. In line with these distinctions, no scholar that I have found has dealt with the theoretical work of French feminist Hélène Cixous in any way other than as writings. The emphasis of the general corpus of feminist analysis has been almost totally on what she is trying to say rather than what she is trying to do. However, in at least one piece, "The Laugh of the Medusa," it is the action that Cixous both takes and suggests that has caught my attention. In her search for a new woman's voice, Cixous has managed to cloud the difference between writing and performing, making symbiotic the relationship between them. I would suggest that this relationship forms the basis of possibility for Cixous' petition to "write from the body." Previous attention on the Cixousean body as bio-sexual or psycho-sexual being by feminist critics has not left room for discussion concerning the "Medusa" body as that which takes action.

"The Laugh of the Medusa" is a performance on paper, an embodiment of its own subject. It is an attempt to define a working space between two oppositional poles, just as performance is the play in space between the real and unreal, the known and unknown, the sensual and social. Cixous' piece is a playing out of her basic dilemma: how women can create and leave a feminine history without also harnessing or impeding it with the fixed quality of a masculine discourse.

The language of "Medusa" is circular, personal, conversational, self-referential, ephemeral, and insistent. It actively assumes an audience. Yet, it also appropriates the ground of what is theory, thereby moving outside the boundaries of the exclusive or expressionistic. "Medusa" is an essay rife with the images and techniques of a performative mode, from the use of conceptual space as a concrete place of (re)creation to the play of meaning which blurs the lines dividing and identifying actor and audience.

In my response to Cixous, I would like to show how the essay is a performance in both the rhythm and movement of the piece and through the use of theatrical metaphor. Further, I will demonstrate that, consistent with the practice of performance, she is carrying out the experiment while she creates the instructions. Cixous is dancing her dilemma through writing as she expresses the need to write away the loss of women in the space of history. She expresses and becomes her dilemma, just as in performance, by asserting and then diffusing through a stylistic mix of what feminist critic Ann Rosalind Jones calls the theoretical and the imaginary (249).

For our purposes, performance is to be differentiated from acting. The latter is an action of interpretation while the former is one of realization. Acting is part of a social system that is male defined. Acting is the contextual presentation of human behavior and interaction through the artistic and psychological framework of a non-presenced, yet dominant, other party. (I use non-presenced in the sense that even an actor doing his own play or working by his own direction is imposed upon by a vision that is not of the moment of acting.) Performance, on the other hand, refers to that which is immediate and self-referential, both source and birth product of the conditions of the moment. Performance must be both about and by the performer. It is the actual state of creativity, a concept which refers to some type of re-organizing and change. Further, performance is a reduction to only those forces present between the beginning and end of performance time. Clearly a performer brings certain sociologies and psychologies to the performance site, but these pre-conditions lose all power to impose or dominate her in favor of a percolating blend of creation and re-creation which marks the performance process.

The woman as actor is nothing new. Women have always served as social actors, rehearsing (never really ready) the various roles as defined and imprinted by man through his desire and his fear. The nature of woman has been described through the wearing of a series of representational masks meant to cover a blankness beneath, too numerous and foreign to avoid chafing, yet too impositional and protective to remove. "Femininity is frequently associated with the masquerade, with false representation, with simulation and seduction" (Owens 59). Women have served as symbolic representatives of something else which is neither them nor of them. They are an allegory, they play "the part." Like actors, they have interpreted the idea of another, pretending to believe the truth of their presentation only to be told by the author that it all feels like (only) a play.

In calling on women to both create and discover their history through a new feminine language, Cixous is recruiting them as performers. She is suggesting a dissolution of both the play and the "characters." This is consistent with Richard Palmer's description of performance as primarily that which is freed from an imposed scenario. Instead, woman practices truth as she feels it, through performance which is concurrently what it expresses, what it discovers and the act of "Celebration of what is being brought to experiential fullness through performance" (20). In performance, woman's body is materialized, revealed, presenced, rather than dematerialized, made absent behind the curtain of a mask. Through performance, the notion of woman as body which symbolizes absence or lack has been reversed. Woman, who has been characterized as (with) spaces to invade and fill, and to cover with a mask of false substance, is now enjoined to invade, fill and inscribe space. This new strength in action also provides an answer to Sandra Gilbert and Susan Gubar's now (in)famous question: "If the pen is a metaphorical penis, from what organ can females generate texts?" (6–7). The answer is with and from the whole body, re-organ-ized and complete.

As a twentieth century phenomenon, performance has always been a transition art, a bringing together of disparate factions and a means of auditioning certain possibilities. The aspect of possibility serves to define the nature of performance. The performance part of even what is called Performance Art (with its various props and installations often setting the stage) nonetheless defies the creation of any lasting object which can be called art. The perform-er cannot be objectified. Her work is about the movement of bodies in space and content in flux. The performance artist is both revealing a thought-image and finding out what it is. As a way to clarify this point, I use the work of Vito Acconci. In the late 1970s he began to remove his body from the sculpture-like installations with activ-able parts which he still identified as Performance Art. His continued use of this description confirms it, in my mind, as a two-part process: an Acconci installation is only sculpture, though sculpture in a state of expectation, until a human body arrives and gives either physical or responsive movement to it. The perfor-mance part in then the fleeting quality of the overall experience, the completion of it and the validation of the ideal of possibility.

Forerunners of performance, the Futurists and the Dadaists, intended to question the preciousness of the art object. Using their bodies, they became the object which made art of itself, thereby de-objectifying, all the while presenting a text which ques-tioned the very process in which it was engaged. Under director Oskar Schlemmer, Bauhaus stage workshops of the 1920s used performance as a means to bring together all the arts into a cel-ebration of multiplicity. Because performance acted as a mediator to the arts, it was neither subject to nor confined by any of them. A public confrontation form, "performance has always developed along the edges of disciplines...a permissive open-ended medium, with endless variables" (Goldberg 24). This unfixed quality of a marginal form leads us back to Hélène Cixous and her search for just such a conceptual space to write (with) the body.

Cixous is describing performance as she recites what women must do. "Woman must put herself into the text...by her own movement" (245). In performance, particularly postmodern, the emphasis is on staging, a direct assault on the primacy of the authoritative text: performers have reclaimed their own interpret-ive bodies. Cixous would have women reclaim their own bodies by writing with and through them (body as mediator). Women can only write with their bodies because feminine language cannot be separated from feminine being if it is to remain in the hands of women. As some feminist writers, such as Helene Vivienne Wen-zel, have taken Cixous' "writing the body" quite literally, emphasizing only the sexual/erotic intent, I would suggest that it is an expressive reversal: challenge the symbolic order by making writing into performing. As the nature of woman's body has been mediated through male desire and passive (re)production, in performance it becomes its own mediator through personal desire and action. As women must be substantialized through writing, so their voice is literalized as that which speaks from the body. Cixous suggests the body of woman as a cosmopoetic system, both art and artist, both creator through the birth of feminine history and destroyer through the aborting of female role.

Like Shiva, women must destroy in order to create, all the while looking forward. "The future must no longer be determined by the past" (245). In performance, the future is determined by the present; the past has left the performer and taken root within the minds of the viewer. Therefore, it is inscribed but not binding. One cannot page back for a reminder of what was said. The past is disowned by the performer in favor of the shape of the future and endless possibility after a "production of forms...inscribing a resonant vision" (246). As a woman engages in the process of discovery, that process becomes real, takes form and allows for an empowerment toward continuance. There is no need to save what has taken place, to page back, because it is inexhaustible, therefore lasting. Then "we extend ourselves without ever reaching an end" (248) to "foresee the unforseeable, to project" (245) making "dizzying, precipitous flights between knowledge and invention" (263). A performer uses who she is to serve as the basis for what she can be. These small bouquets of fragments from Cixous appropos writing form a litany to the goddess of experiment and revelation. Woman is urged to leap forward, experiencing and celebrating the leap rather than establishing the form of the discovery. In this position of flight, a transformation will occur that results in a feminine knowing. Performance becomes a controlled yet delirious self-transformation that reveals essence rather than disguising truth.

As expressed by anthropologist Victor Turner, "through the performance process...what is normally sealed up, inaccessible to everyday observation and reasoning...is drawn forth" (13). Cixous would will that everyday observation and reasoning be set aside as patriarchal hegemony and that the unsealing of women by woman begin. She alludes to a refusal of the past, but not of female history. The past is a record of women as non-men, the evolution of the ideal of woman. The past is about the *describing* of women. Female history will serve as a connection between what women have done and who they are; it is about the living of women that is inscribed on all women. Woman is (re)born through the bodies of many mothers. As performance is a resistance of death through the endless recreation of life so the individual story must become part of the re-creation of all women: "She can merge... without annihilating herself" (259). Performance like "writing is precisely working (in) the in-between, inspecting the process of the same and of the other without which nothing can live, undoing the work of death" (254).

Like the performer, woman is capable of being many selves, for she is part of a feminine memory, a movement and relation through/with time and experience

> which knows neither closure nor death... [H]er language does not contain, it carries; it does not hold back, it makes possible. When id is ambiguously uttered... the wonder of being several – she... derives pleasure from this gift of alterability... alive because of the transformation. (260)

Woman must perform through writing a being of self and of others like her, allied to self at the same time, "a movement that gathers and separates... in order to be more than herself" (248). Cixous directs women to reiterate their difference from men and their uniqueness within the continuity of femininehood.

Cixous wants to move to the place occupied by performance, the liminal state of possibility, without establishing a closure or fixing of women's experience that would replicate the masculine language. This, again, is her dilemma. Julia Kristeva has suggested that writers such as Cixous challenge the symbolic order by establishing a return to the pleasures of the pre-verbal identification with mother and a rejection of the logic (language) of father (Jones 249). I believe that Cixous wants to solve her perplexity by finding a space that can exist post-mother and pre-father, meaning that she does not wish to reject language completely, only that which separates her from the relation with the feminine. She seeks a language that is communicative and connective rather than definitive and divisive. Women's history must be presented, not represented. It must evade the "false theatre of

phallocentric representationalism" in favor of a performance realized by a

> multiple and inexhaustible course with millions of encounters
> and transformations of the same into the other and into the in-
> between, from which woman takes her forms. (254)

Her occupation with space, which I have given place through a
relation to theatre, is also part of Cixous' desire to leave traces
rather than tracks. This inbetweenness she mentions is precisely
that woman-space that has always meant alienation: a patriarchal
separating of woman from the feminine and a fixing of her as
female in relation to male. This separation makes women both
liminal and marginal. Liminal (as borrowed from Victor Turner)
refers to a place within two fulfillments, a stage of being. In the
positive sense, one is in both a state of becoming and of un-becom-
ing, a transition. In the negative sense, one is neither this nor that,
neither man nor "real" woman. The marginal here refers not to a
state of being but to a position of social placement in a world which
is organized into an inner ring (rule-making, power-taking) and an
outer ring (rule-heeding, power-lacking). Those in the inner
ring ensure that those in the outer ring remain outside and
that this lesser ring remain identified by its relation to the greater
ring.

Imagistically, then, women are assigned to two spaces: a crevass
of being and the fearsome forest of society. They occupy a liminal
sphere in-between two realities, fully reconciled to neither, playing
a role that leaves what Cixous has identified as a space between the
self and the projection of that self. In addition, women live in a
layered world in which each stratum not only distances woman
from self, but from the world around her. This serves to place her
also in a marginal state where her position as the mysterious Other
creates a fearful wall that pushes her outside of society-making.
Woman is socially marginal and personally/egoistically liminal.

Cixous' plan is that woman become socially central yet remain
egoistically liminal in an altered sense. This is the start of a new
language. The feminine liminal would establish this in-between
space not as ground for fragmentation or for alienation, but as a
state of becoming that upsets the phallocentrism of fixed systems.
The cooptation of the liminal state for women is another reversal in
Cixous' scheme. The need for woman to write is one of producing

herself, of mining the dark continent and creating maps with permutable boundaries.

Despite the apparent solution that the idea of performance brings to Cixous' search for an enabling space in-between, there is the concern that the first stage of this (my) interpretive new language merely alters the "real truth" by re-defining an unchanging situation. The concept of liminality, at least in anthropological and theatrical terms, is contextualized by the notion of temporality. A liminal state is meant to be impermanent, the leaving of one condition and the straining toward another. If, as I have laid out, Cixous suggests that becoming be ushered in as the new reality for women, then it would seem that she is also abolishing the future in favor of a never-ending present: "Extend[ing] ourselves without ever reaching an end" (248). The resonance and form of the new feminine vision and language could then be infinite and static, therefore in danger of meaninglessness. What we are left with is the realization that Cixous has no solution to the contradictions inherent in a call for the reworking of liminality but that the concept of performance describes the nature of it. In fact, she eliminates the poles of contradiction by reversing their relationship to a newly privileged in-between. Such stasis would seem a poor position for change.

'Medusa" has also been placed in the theatre space as it can be characterized by the dark, cave-like stage and backstage. As Cixous speaks of woman's dark continent, the uncharted territory, she evokes the theatre in its most powerful sense, that of creating magic in the dark, of drawing forth the very essence of human nature and need through the daemonic powers of the actor-performer. Theatre begins with a waiting in the dark for the appropriate moment of expression, as the lights slowly give form to the shadows. As with the moment of pure darkness in the theatre before the lights are raised, woman is dark and dangerous, her inner being threatening to explode into chaos. "Your continent is dark. Dark is dangerous. You can't see anything in the dark, you're afraid" (247–48).

Dark is used to advantage in theatrical performance as a means for focusing attention, essentializing truth, causing sensation, and hiding that which should not be seen. A fear of the dark is the fear of the unnameable, the unseeable, that leaves the victim momentarily detached from the stabilizing force of language. In terms of performance, then, the dark has meaning in Cixous' essay through the differing relation to it by performer and (whom she makes her) audience. As presented here, the woman is related to the dark. She embodies the dark. Therefore, she is the performer who has control of the dark (of her female essence) and can use it to hide or to enhance and showcase her performance through the use of controlled (writing) (en)light(enment). She can use her own knowledge of the dark as transformative chaos, "by breaking the codes that negate her" (249) as she becomes negation itself, causing a "radical mutation of things…a material upheaval when every structure is for a moment thrown off balance and an ephemeral wildness sweeps order away" (249). This metaphorical "waiting to go on," the standing in the darkened wings, is the state which Cixous suggests women have endured throughout masculinated history. The ephemeral wildness, the performance of woman through writing, must finally make use of that darkness as the theatre does.

The use of darkness by the performer would make of man the audience in so much as he is no longer the director of the show. Man's fear of woman's dark makes him susceptible to rather than in control of the transformations possible there. He would be cloaked by the performative language of woman and, as such, be positioned "within" that new symbolic system. In the past, "woman has always functioned 'within' the discourse of man"; now she must engage in battle to "dislocate this 'within,' to explode it, turn it around, and seize it" (257). Theatre subverts reality. In this fantasized (and yet another) reversal of the patriarchal reality, where once woman was the "servant of the militant male, his shadow" (250), the shadow now takes control, becoming the reflection of woman's dark continent, her story made tangible.

Cixous sets up the fear of performing by women against the imperative to perform. Along with this she creates the theatrical model for the binary of receiver and presenter, or audience and actor, passive and aggressive. In fear, "every woman has known the torment of getting up to speak…ground and language slipping away…a transgression…to speak…in public…her words fall…upon the deaf male ear" (251). Here the woman has negated, or at least twisted, the necessary binary as she is turned into an audience where she would be performer; the male response, his ear the organ of receptivity, is rendered useless, refusing to be activated. Through the fear of performing, a woman negates the entire performance situation. Instead, she only emphasizes the need and effect of performance by making an absence where the presence of performance should be. In speaking of a deaf male ear, the would-be performer is acknowledging that the audience is not an audience, is not her, is not (receptive) like her, is not female. As a result, the idea of receptivity has been forefronted in both its theatrical context (audience) and its social one (female).

In contradistinctive challenge, Cixous suggests that women are natural "performers" in terms of style:

> She doesn't "speak," she throws her trembling body forward; she lets go of herself; she flies... it's with her body that she vitally supports the "logic" of her speech... she physically materializes what she's thinking; she signifies it with her body... she *inscribes* what she's saying. (251)

In this description are those elements which act to reify and physicalize the thoughts and experiences of the performer. Also present is a notion of the patterning and choreography of performance, as when a woman speaks it is "never simple or linear or... generalized: she draws her story into history" (251). The past is organized through the emotive pattern of the present to take hold in the future. Performance is meant to seem of the future; each performative gesture and sound is apparent precursor of what is to come from it, after it. Yet performance is in the present; it is ephemeral; it lasts as only a trace of experience, leaving the performer and entering the imagination of the audience. Apropos of this is Cixous' description of women's speech which evokes that "first sound" of mother and is "that element which never stops resonating... [and] retains the power of moving us" (251).

Cixous, herself, sounds the call to action, to performance, a breaking out of silence that is symbolically reserved for women and into the act of "emancipation of the marvelous text of her self... and... transformations in her history" (250). She encourages the woman as performer rather than actor, since the performer can only create as and through what she is: "Her flesh speaks true" (251). An actor, on the other hand, acts a role through a body "which has been more than confiscated from her, which has been more than turned into the uncanny stranger on display . . . the dead figure" (250). It is the character imposed by an authority outside the text of self. "We must kill the false woman who is preventing the live one from breathing" (250). Women's bodies have been the site of man's performance about what woman must be. Through the urging of Cixous, the body of woman would evolve from passive stage to active self-performer.

From the evolution of the fearful non-performer to the emancipated self-performer there surfaces again Cixous' dilemma in a different wrapping. Like the need to exist between the eliciting and fixing of woman's history is the desire to locate a space that is both audience and performer, an interchange of giving and taking. In a grander plan, Cixous wants woman to be audience as well as performer, receiving what it is to be feminine from women and adding her own story to the larger fabric that can then emerge as woman being with women seeing. In this case, the response of a participatory audience will affect and enrich the meaning of performance. The multiplicity of woman (many facets of a female self) and between women (many versions of the female as self) will blossom and grow and lead to new/old performances.

Cixous has written in a language that is old and which suggests it be made (a)new. She exhorts those with "lovely mouths gagged with pollen" (248) to create a new language. And yet, by its very nature, language is a missile of the voice; erupting from the ungagged mouths, it becomes outgoing, aggressive. The art of writing is of validating narrative by making it concrete; the body is also the concrete form in performance. So again, the female reader is pressed by Cixous into a confused state in which she is asked to find a place in which the aggressivity of language may be reconciled with a reversal of the system that aggressivity represents.

Performance is a partial response to Cixous' dilemma through yet another lens, in that it has the recirculating quality of relationship between audience and performer: without an audience there is no performer; without a performer, the word audience is an absurdity. The body as a tool is concrete, while the content of the communication leaves only an unfixed impression of the performance. Performance equals possibility, the place between is and is not. As she describes what writing is, so she has described what performance does: "Writing is precisely *the very possibility of change,* the space that can serve as a springboard for subversive thought, the precursory movement of a transformation of social and cultural structures" (249). Writing serves as the instigation, performance as the action. Performance is the activity of possibility. It is the actual state of potential, of transformation, a space in time in which social and cultural structures are reordered and re-symbolized through the mediation of the movement, thought and force of the performer. The performer is whatever she says she is in whatever way she shows she is. She is the authority sharing power through the receptivity of the audience. She has made a new language and then abstracted it through performance so that she at once says the (female) unsayable and then lets it slip away again into the impression held by the audience.

As Cixous speaks of flying, that state of being that is not fixed on earth, yet is related to the concreteness of what is not air, so performance is that becoming which hovers between expression and impression. "To give form to its movement" (253), performance and writing allow the saying. But as it is "impossible to *define* a feminine practice of writing... for this practice can never be theorized, enclosed, coded" (253), so it is impossible to capture and hold the product of performance. In this way, authority cannot be imposed on the performance and it reifies only "a process of becoming in which several histories intersect with one another... personal history blends together with the history of all women" (252).

The Cixousean performer empowers herself as owner of the female body. As the performer must control the body in order to perform, so the woman must write through the body that is the key to her feminine story. The new language suggested by Cixous is one of ownership. Within that ownership, of body, of language, are several implications of what I have called reversal: the private made public, the writing becoming performing, the birth of a female history through the aborting of a female role, and the revolving door of audience-performer relationship and meaning. The state of becoming, of in-between, is privileged over the oppositional poles of fixing and fluxing. The continuum of present dissolves the meaning and effect of the past. Woman becomes a presence rather than an absence and mounts the steps of the new stage. She inscribes space rather than embodies space, transforms into giver from receiver. Cixous' new feminine would diffuse woman rather than reduce her. Cixous' essay creates an opening rather than the closure of its printed page.

Works Cited

Cixous, Hélène. "The Laugh of the Medusa." Trans. Keith Cohen and Paula Cohen. *New French Criticisms*. Ed. Elaine Marks and Isabelle de Courtivron. New York: Schocken Books, 1981. 245–67.

Gilbert, Sandra M. and Susan Gubar. *The Madwoman in the Attic: The Woman Writer and the Nineteenth Century Literary Imagination*. New Haven, Connecticut: Yale UP, 1979.

Goldberg, Roselee. "Performance: A Hidden History." *The Art of Performance*. Ed. Gregory Battock and Robert Nickas. New York: E. P.Dutton, 1984. 24–36.

Jones, Ann Rosalind. "Writing The Body: Toward An Understanding Of L'Écriture Feminine." *Feminist Studies* 7 (1981): 247–63.

Mitchie, Helena. *The Flesh Made Word*. New York: Oxford UP, 1987.

Owens, Craig. "The Discourse of Others: Feminists and Postmodernism." *The Anti-Aesthetic*. Ed. Hal Foster. Port Townsend, Washington: Bay, 1983. 57–82.

Palmer, Richard. "Toward A Postmodern Hermeneutics of Performance." *Performance in Postmodern Culture*. Ed. Michael Benamou and Charles Caramello. Madison, Wisconsin: Coda, 1977. 19–32.

Showalter, Elaine. "Feminist Criticism in the Wilderness." *Critical Inquiry* 8 (1981): 179–205.

Turner, Victor. *From Ritual To Theatre*. New York City: Performing Arts Journal Publications, 1982.

Wenzel, Helene Vivienne. "The Text As Body/Politics: An Appreciation of Monique Wittig's Writings in Context." *Feminist Studies* 7 (1981): 264–87.

11

Hélène Cixous and the Need of Portraying: on *Portrait du soleil*

Christa Stevens

It is striking how often Hélène Cixous mentions the genre of the portrait in her titles.[1] *Portrait du soleil*, *Portrait de Dora*, "Le vrai portrait de Nelson" (in *Manne*), "Le dernier tableau ou le portrait de Dieu" (in *Entre l'écriture*), also "Autoportraits d'une aveugle" (*Jours de l'an*), "Oteportraits d'Hommère en Lioncles" (*Partie*), or even "Portée de l'inconnue" (in *La*), tell us that this writer, at any particular stage of her literary project and independent of the genre (fiction, theatre, essay) she practices, seems to be driven by a desire, if not an urge, to make portraits. This need to portray is not restricted to the entitling alone. In many other texts, portraits interrupt the movement of the narrative, introducing a new poetical moment, as in *Le Livre de Promethea*, where the "portrait de Promethea en H" constitutes a real framing out of text, as it is the only fragment with a title.

In this article, Cixous' art of portraying will be approached as an example of her ethics and poetics. I will focus on *Portrait du soleil* (1973), for this book displays the representational problem most dramatically, coupling it to a search which is the moving force behind Hélène Cixous' work: the search for the adored but mortal Face, the figure of the lost Father (*Coming to Writing* 1 – 3).

I. Poetics and ethics of portraying

As included in Cixous' overall poetical quest for "the Other," the
art of portraying expresses the very desire to represent this Other,
or more precisely, to give presence to his otherness, to difference.
In this desire, however, the Cixousian portrait would in itself
appear to seriously contradict the longstanding tradition of the
literary genre of the portrait. Its history in fact reflects the importance of representation and the visual in Western – phallocentric –
thought and writing, where portraying, i.e. the making of distin-
guishing marks in "just discernment" (whose discernment?),
proves an inclination to identification, appropriation and mastery.
Cixous' work is characterized by an overall suspicion of Character
and Ego, and a preference for multiple, eccentric and therefore
"uncharacterizable" forms of subjectivity, as well as that of the
immediate representational forces of language and textuality over
figurative re-presentation. If we take this and the following into
account – her recurrent "Incantation[s] against the images" (163),
her thematics of darkness, interiority and touch and, finally, her
apprehension of reality as a limitless, elusive (and therefore unpor-
trayable) "pluréel" ("plureality") (*Prénoms de personne* 5) – her
attachment for the art of portraying foregrounds most provocat-
ively the representational problem (See also Stevens, "Portraying
the Feminine").

In this respect, Cixous may evoke the portrait also as a counter-
example: with its pretentions of "analyzing a human being, of
circumscribing him, of making up his portrait, the sum of his
being, its true representation," ["de prétendre l'analyser, le cerner,
en faire le portrait, la somme, la représentation"] (*Un K.* 41), the
portrait represents the Law, Authority, and can therefore be
unmasked as a marionette taking part in the phallocentric machine.
This kind of portrait imposes itself as a mold, socially and ideologically encoded and controlled, and in this way presents itself as
reality: "*hold still*, we're going to do your portrait, so you can begin
looking like it right away" ("The Laugh of the Medusa" 263, my
emphasis).

Is it surprising, then, that Hélène Cixous, while tracing her
portraits, marks at the same time their limitations, if not their
impossibilities? The titles of her portraits function, in this respect,
as real poetical programs. "Le vrai portrait de Nelson" ["The real

portrait of Nelson"], for instance, poses the political-ethical question of truth, authenticity and "fidelity," which is so precious to this writer ("Le dernier tableau" 188). Opposing the "real" to the "false," which is a reference to traditional representation, this title literally inscribes the responsibility of the other subject hidden behind the intended "subject of the portrait," the portrayer herself: "[elle] ne change pas le corps de l'autre en fantasmes" ["[she] does not change the body of the other in fantasies"] (*Illa* 72).

This problem can be illustrated as follows. The portrayer is explicitly named in a title like "Portrait de Promethea en H," which provides Promethea's portrait with a point of view, that of the portrayer. Moreover, the double value of the genitive *de*, both objective and subjective, mirrored by *en*, allows this portrait to be read as a double(d) one where, in a mutually constitutive way, the portrait of the one (Promethea) is also the (self) portrait of the other (H), where H constitutes herself in her portraying of Promethea, becoming her other other in the other. So a portrait, as this title indicates, is always a "Theatre of the Eye/I," telling in the portrayed the story of the portrayer; and this story is, as the letter H "figures," both "ladder" and "axe,"[2] made of approaches and separations between the portrayer and her model.

"Portrait de Dora," in its turn, already ambiguous because of its double genitive, is a very misleading title. As it bears a name, we might expect a mapping out of the young woman called Dora, something like her faithful photograph which guarantees her uniqueness and undeniable identity. It is this same name, however, which makes that "Dora," at any moment her portrait is drawn, escapes from identification and classification and does not "hold still." Her name functions, as the narrator explains in *Portrait du soleil*, the text from which *Portrait de Dora* is taken, as "monnaie marquée au niveau socio-économique" ["money that is marked on the social-economical level"] (110), as a coin of *gold* (D-*or*-a) symbolizing the economical and libidinal value the young girl Dora represents both for her adulterous father and friends and for her analyst Freud. Cixous depicts how Dora, while circulating as an object of sexual and emotional investment between the other characters, assumes in each of her relationships with them other positions and other identities. It is this drifting, excessive part of her subjectivity which makes this portrait of Dora also a portrait *by* Dora: by escaping from the close embrace and the controlling eye of her nearest and dearest, she draws at the same time a fine picture of them and their lies, blowing up the system of the social and sexual conventions upon which they rely.

The titles "Portrait du soleil" and "Portrait de Dieu," finally, inscribe the impossibility of portraying. For who can pretend to have seen the sun, to have looked at the face of God, without being struck by blindness? Heliocentrism is, as Jacques Derrida reminds us, just one of the occurences of phallo-logocentrism in Western mythology and philosophy: the sun is merely a metaphor for the Subject, the Father, the Law, including the law of representation and figuration itself, for it is the sun which permits such symbolic oppositions as day and night, visible and invisible, presence and absence (Derrida, "La Mythologie Blanche," *Marges* 299; see also Hanrahan, "Une Porte"). A "portrait of God," in its turn, reminds us of the biblical God who prohibited representation ("Thou shalt not make unto thee any graven image . . . ."), to begin with His own representation.

In striving to make these portraits, Cixous is not only crossing the border-line of representational interdiction, but also defying the authority and law that govern it. Moreover, for these portraits imply that it is possible to look (in)to what otherwise cannot be looked at, to make visible the invisible, they also unveil the hidden "truth" of these models which is their very invisibility, i.e. the mere fact of their absence. And as these particular models, these originals stand, as we have seen, for the Subject, the Father, the Origin, these titles state at the same time the very absence of this absolute Origin and of his or its representatives. They reveal the very "essence" of their nature as a "non-essence," a "non-truth." As Gilles Deleuze would have said, the sun and God are to be qualified as "*devenirs*": their essence is that of a becoming, which means that they will never be complete(d). In consequence, they cannot be determined in a form, nor singularized in a whole: they will always be "inbetween," indefinite (*Critique et clinique* 10 – 11). So in conclusion we can say that these portraits of Cixous denounce Representation and the reality principle ("Life," "Truth," "biography," "sense") it is supposed to illustrate (by identification, imitation, Mimesis). In this sense, Representation is not only a falsification, but also an illicit appropriation of Truth and Origin, of Sense and Essence, by the instance which imposes itself as the unique and absolute Referent – or, in other languages, God, Ideology, the Absolute Signifier, etc.

> Que les formes reçues soient abîmées..., que les modèles soient lacérés et jetés aux ordures..., je ne prends pas la ressemblance pour moi-même.... Je n'habite pas parmi les images. (*La* 163-64)

> May the established forms be worn down..., may the models be ripped and torn and discarded..., I don't see a resemblance to me as part of me.... I don't inhabit images.

With this disavowal of identifying forms of representation and figuration, Hélène Cixous seeks to escape from the treadmill of reproduction of the Same and of the fetishization of the subject-model by its recognizable, explicable, knowable and conscious aspects. For this reason, her portraits are distanced from their pictorial equivalents: as a *representation* of "reality," paintings can only be simulacra of this reality. Cixous is very preoccupied with this paradox: the aim of representation to give presence to the other, to the model, in fact excludes the model. It may even "kill" the model, take the life out of her, metaphorically or literally, as is shown in Poe's *The Oval Portrait* to which Cixous often refers. In this tale indeed, a great painter loses his wife when he transposes onto the canvas her beauty, captivating as "Life itself!" (549). Aware of this crime which can also become the writer's (*Three Steps* 30), Cixous wants in her portraying to save the living and to give presence to it. This new portrayer's task may be an almost impossible one, for in order to approach the indescribable, unidentifiable, unknown aspects of the "pluréel," she will have to withdraw herself from what she already knows, to project herself out into "what does not yet exist..., into the unheard-of" ("Character" 383). The unknown, the dark and her own blindness will thus be her guides.

But the impossible unveils its own possibility: these portraits of Cixous actually exist, as promises the performative structure of their titles. But given the absence of the model, what then is the "real" subject of these portraits? Let's try to answer this question by focusing on the title *Portrait du soleil*, by taking its "subject," the sun, as does Cixous, in its concreteness: as the diurnal star.

The sun, as it travels along its daily orbit, is an exemplary object of portraying which does not "hold still." Besides, sunset, clouds and eclipses make of it an object that regularly disappears and ceases to exist. Shadows, reflections and mirrorings underline its presence as a reflected, mediated one. The radiation of its heat shows it to be manifestly beyond the realm of the visible. How then could this ever-moving, eclipsing, escaping sun be fixed and framed within a portrait? Any portrait of the sun would therefore be merely a simulacrum, an act of illicit appropriation; and in consequence, the "appropriator," its real subject.

But the sun is also an agent of representation, as suggests the double genitive of the title, and as is proved also by its religious, mythological and philosophical connotations. As a portrayer in itself, the sun does not hold still either. The varying moments of its orbit deprive vision and representation of a stable point of view as well as of a single, fixed focal point. Vision and representation therefore are implicated in the incessant movement of "différance" (Derrida, "La Différance," *Marges*), where no image, no portrait, is able to impose itself as the only, truthful, definite one. On the contrary, it is constantly deferred in the oscillating movement of its constituents, the portrayer and his model. This oscillation, i.e. the way portrayer and model approach/let themselves be approached (by) each other,[3] forms the ethics of this art of portraying. Its aesthetics can be found in the cyclic, quasi-zodiacal movement with which the narration flows, as a sun indeed following its course, from one subject to another, from one scene into another:

> Je traverse à la course... dans une envolée de fantasmes, sans viser personne, traversée par ma course, au rythme exact du soleil sans qu'ombre me précède ou suive.... (190)

> I ran over... in a flight of phantasms, unseeing, driven along by my speed, shadowless under the precise beat of the sun....

We may also find an example of this "style of the sun" (153) in the disseminative force which sustains this text. Any glimpse of a portrait or a description finds itself, by means of homophonic, metaphoric or intertextual allusions, caught up in a chain of signifiers which disrupts and decentralizes the initial image which was constituting itself and even takes it out of the realm of the visible.

Blindness is another aspect a portrait of the sun inevitably evokes. To portray the sun, daring to face its blinding effects, implies that the enunciation of such a portrait is also situated in blindness: its drawing proceeds in the dark. What then is the "real" subject of this "blind" portrait? Is it its invisible, because dazzling, object, or is it its blinded portrayer – here I refer to Derrida's statement that a drawing of a *blind* is also a drawing *by* a blind (*Mémoires d'aveugle* 10). This question evokes another one: what is the subject of blindness, i.e. what kind of object can constitute itself in blindness, what "model" emerges from darkness, when it is by definition hidden from view, deprived thus of objective existence? Blindness would then belong to the realm of interiority, even of anteriority. For the blind(ed) portrayer of the sun could only "see" and represent her blinding model by the figures she already possessed of him by imagination, projection or remembrance. As a result, this sun belongs to the interior, to subjectivity, whereas this blindness does not constitute a separation with a context or with an exteriority: on the contrary, it is a return to the self, the inner "I/Eye,"[4] in its different figurations. Which means, finally, that this portrait is also a self-portrait.

Blindness evokes also the initial "decree of blindness" (*Coming to Writing* 3) issued by the "subject" of this portrait. Hélène Cixous, fashioning in her portraits a graven image for herself, challenges this decree by taking precisely blindness as her point of departure. Darkness, infernal night and interiority are important motifs in *Portrait du soleil* and shape the background from which this portrait will detach itself. For the dark leads inevitably towards the day, to the light which makes vision possible and objects visible, towards *la prim'ombra*, as Dante saw in Purgatory, "the first shadow" in which he recognized the rising of the sun; and if the day begins with a shadow, so a shadow gives birth to an image (see Minazzoli, *La première ombre* 12). It is notable that if portraying can be considered as this voyage to the light, the notion of "portrait" has stayed close to its etymological signification, for *pro-trahere*, "pour traire," means to draw forward, to reveal, to decipher.

Let us continue our reading of the "portrait" as a signifier by taking a closer look at its second syllable, *-trait*, so that we can find another relationship between darkness and writing. The *trait* refers to the act of writing and drawing as well as to its concrete, graphical results. Similarly, the act of writing in *Portrait du soleil* is often compared to drawing ("Je vais dessiner...") ["I am going to draw"] (31), to engraving and even carving, for the hand which writes also turns out to be a knife that cuts ("Le couteau est confondu avec ma main") ["The knife merges with my hand"] (40). At the same time, this knife, *couteau*, rhymes with *écriteau* (193), which functions therefore as a "porte-manteau" of *couteau* and *écrit(ure)* and defines this text as a lacerated, carved, opened up surface.

These metonymical and homophonical displacements have a metadiscursive value, for they offer other ways of reading the text. First of all, by this focusing on the *trait*, the text stresses its graphic dimension, the materiality of its drawn signifiers. In fact, by using italics, capitals, greek alphabet, columns, the whole scale of punctuation marks etc., this text of Cixous presents itself as a traced surface and, moreover, as an object which demands to be looked at. And as a correlative to this textual "exhibition," we find a certain "blindness" on the level of the signified, in the sense that referentiality and figurability have no pertinent function.

Secondly, the accent put on the *trait* as a drawn, carved and carving sign opens up this textual surface to its underlying, interior dimensions. Here reside its *pentimento* and palimpsests, its *inscriptions* and other textual layers which are to be uncovered and explored. The *traits* of the signifiers here reveal themselves to be merely *traces*: unidimensional, linear left-overs of a layered, disseminated textuality.

This conception of the signifier as a trace, finally, leads us back to the very gesture of writing-painting. An essential aspect of the signifier should therefore be found in the tracing moment itself, in the spatial instant of its realization. *Portrait du soleil* foregrounds, as we have seen, the act of writing itself. The writing-cutting hand, presented in its immediacy, even becomes autonomous:

> je voulais dire la peau, mais ce qui est écrit est écrit... ça glisse, ça échappe, c'est très fort. (31)

> I wanted to say the skin, but what is written is written..., it slides, it slips away, it's powerful.

This remark of the narrator defines writing as a conscious activity but disturbed by effects and unconscious impulses provoked by the gesture of writing itself. Writing, therefore, is not a matter of manipulating language, but of the writing hand wandering, or even slipping off the blank page: the text traces itself, as if without any intellectual, i.e. visual control of the writer. The *trait* marks writing as a passage through an unknown terrain, deprived of any reference points. This tracing, this projecting of lines as if into nowhere, progresses therefore in obscurity. This is very similar to what happens in pictorial drawing, for painters-designers qualify their working indeed as a groping blindly, "in the dark, in the deepest night" ["dans l'obscurité, dans la nuit la plus ténébreuse"] (Paul Klee, cited by Tisseron, "Le dessein du dessin" 94). And Derrida states that in its initial moment, when the pencil point touches the surface, the tracing, the inscription remains invisible. The *trait* invents itself, it does not follow something presently visible, even when there is a model in front of the artist. So even when a drawing is reproductive, figurative, representative, in its initial moment, it does not belong to the mimetic. Which implies that it is not the model that the artist retraces, but perception, visibility, through memory, if not memory itself (*Mémoires d'aveugle* 49 – 50; 53 – 54).

Hélène Cixous sees this portrayer's "blindness" as constitutive of her own work. Writing, for her, is a question of "truths." Not of "the Truth," which is a phallocentric construction, but of unknown truths, secret ones, truths that exist because we can feel them, without ever knowing or "seeing" them. Blindness, and all its risks, is therefore a reading position: that of the reader, but also that of the creator who, like indeed a portrayer of the sun, the symbol of the invisible, because unbearable truth, has to go toward what she cannot bear to see and understand. This is also her own blindness:

> We go toward the best known unknown thing, where knowing and not knowing touch, where we hope we will know what is unknown. Where we hope we will not be afraid of understanding the incomprehensible, facing the invisible, hearing the inaudible, thinking the unthinkable, which is of course: thinking. Thinking is trying to think the unthinkable: thinking the thinkable is not worth the effort. Painting is trying to paint what you cannot paint and writing is writing what you cannot know before you have written: it is preknowing and not knowing, blindly, with words. (*Three Steps* 38)

Writing, therefore, proceeds in the dark, hesitating, off the beaten track, and, just like the blinded portrayer's adventure, without a guiding model:

Ecrire chemine dans le noir vers ces vérités. On ne sait pas. On
va. Je suis ce que je sens les yeux fermés. ("De la scène de
l'Inconscient" 15)

Writing advances in the darkness towards these truths. One does
not know. One just goes. I am what I feel with eyes closed.

But the dark does not exist without the light; nor does hell without
paradise. "On écrit pour sortir de cet enfer en direction du jour
caché" ["One writes to get out of this hell in the direction of the
hidden day"] (*Id.* 21). In this hidden light, we hope to see the other
face of the sun. For we must not forget that the sun is not only that
blinding, threatening god-star, but also radiating light and heat,
profusive, fertilizing, "foyer de tendresse et de vie" ["source of
tenderness and life"], as writes Rimbaud ("Soleil et chair" 6).
Which means that its portrayer can face him directly, walk, as
did the blind Orion, in its direction and regain vision. For the
blind are also said to be visionary.

II. Portraying and remembrance

"La leçon d'anatomie" (40-43, hereafter *Lesson*) in *Portrait du soleil*
is inspired by one of Rembrandt's paintings of the same title.[5] It is
in this explicit reference that the question of the portrait intervenes,
for Rembrandt's *Lesson* is meant as a portrait of a chirurgeon,
Deyman, in the full exercise of his skill and mastery.[6] But this
portrait of Rembrandt contains also another "subject," which we
risk remaining blind to, in spite of its striking evidence: it is also a
portrait of the corpse opened up and dismembered, which we
know was the convicted Johan Fonteyn. So Rembrandt's *Lesson* is
also a portrait of a dead man, if not of death.

In Cixous' *Lesson*, the art of the portrait intervenes in the description of a living statue and of Rembrandt's painting. These two
descriptions move freely into a long narrative fragment which
evolves around scenes of eroticism, death and memory. Moreover,
it involves the relationship between "Jeor" and the narrator, and is
therefore an exploration of different attitudes, or in more Cixousian
terms, libidinal economies, towards vision, knowledge and representation.

The anatomical reference invokes the question of the (por)*trait* and thereby defines this art *a priori* as "surgical." In the Derridean, i.e. etymological sense of this term (*chirurgia* [lat.] – *kheirourgia* [gr.] meaning "manual operation"), this implies that by referring to anatomy, to the writing-cutting hand, the text makes clear what it is made with, the manual operations that constitute it, the body of its instruments (*Mémoires d'aveugle* 12). Moreover, this "handmade" text makes clear that this hand is a cutting one: "Je tirai comme un trait de gauche à droite" ["I cut as if at the stroke of a brush from left to right"] (40), just one of the many acts described in the book where the cutting mimics the writing.

In fact, the examples of the equation writing-cutting are abundant. On the very first page the word "oran*je*" (my emphasis) figures, a strange word because of its orthography, which the narrator explains as the cutting of a word engendering writing:

> La première fois que j'ai coupé un mot c'était elle. Je l'ai coupé en deux morceaux inégaux, un plus long, un plus court. J'épluche cette orange en février 1970. (5)

> The first time I cut a word it was her. I cut it in two unequal pieces, one longer, one shorter. I'm peeling this orange, my orange, in February 1970.

Portrait du soleil contains also a series of erotical fantasies on the cutting of throats. These scenes involve Dora, the character which Cixous takes from Freud's famous analysis. As the Freudian Dora suffered from aphonia and a nervous cough ("*toux*"), which are all symptoms that concentrate on the throat, the amorous cutting scenes represent on a metonymical level the desire Dora was not able to enunciate.

The first syllable of *port*rait reveals itself also to be related to the cutting metaphor. *Porte*, the door, constitutes an important motif in this text of Cixous. The narrator often describes herself sitting before a door, waiting for it to open. These doors, succeeding one another as the narration proceeds, opening up to a behind, an inside which reveals itself more and more, are merely a metaphor for textuality, for the multi-layered text which demands to be peeled, just like the *oranje* of the first page. The implications of this opening up, of this penetration, which is therefore a metaphor for reading, becomes clear when this opening of doors is compared to a ripping open of the belly. Moreover, it affects the narrator herself, as if she were dissected herself:

Voilà, c'est cette porte qui m'ouvre brusquement, à la façon des . éventreurs. (21)

There it is. The door that suddenly opens me up, just like Jack the Ripper.

This reciprocity belongs to the same Cixousian ethics we saw at stake for the "subject of the portrait": one subject does not go without the other. This is made clear, for instance, in one of the occurrences of the chain of signifiers engendered by Dora's cough: *toux* < *tout-toucher*, which inscribe themselves in the text even before the character Dora herself makes her appearance. Because of its graphics, the carved-carving mark of its "x," ("lames croi-sées"; "crossed swords"), the dissemination of *toux* inevitably affects the author's own name and subjectivity:

Il me semble saisir de vagues échos sonores. D'une toux. Ce mot est porteur de lames croisées: x x, comme mon nom. (19)

I think I sense some vague echos. Of a cough. A sharp cough like the clash of swords evoked by the sound of my name.

At the end of the book, the sound and the carving image of *toux* reappear in the term "ta*tou*ée" (193) by which the narrator refers to her book, as if to affirm the idea of the text as a scarified surface and of writing as a carving in the flesh. And the act of tattooing has the same ethic display: it does not distinguish between a tattooing and a tattooed subject: "que l'autre a tatouée de moi de lui sur mon front" ["that the other has tattooed of me of him on my forehead"] (193). They mutually constitute each other.

So the writing-cutting metaphor imposes itself in this text. It causes wounds: from the first sentence ("Il faut choisir une *sang-uine*"; "One has to choose a blood orange") to the last ("Et main-tenant, de quel *sang* signer ça?" [my emphasis]; "And now, sign this with whose blood?"), this text is bathed in blood. But this blood, "ancien, bien connu, trop salé, inapaisable, surchauffé" ["old, familiar, too salty, insatiable, overheated"] (6) continues to flow, it lives, it is remembering: "le sang remonte les âges" ["the blood creeps back through the ages"] (5).

This remembering, in fact, is very crucial to the *Portrait du soleil*. As a signifier it circulates in the text through the name of *Rem*brandt. Once it is explicitly shown:

J'ajoute que 'remembrer' est un mot anglais dont tout le monde à Vienne sait ce qu'il veut dire. (130)

I add that 're-member' is an English word and everybody in Vienna knows what it means.

In this Viennese, i.e. Freudian, psychoanalytic context, the English-French "remembrer" evokes not only memory, but also reconstitution, that of painfully scattered fragments of childhood. It evokes the French "remembrement," the putting together again, and is therefore directly related to anatomy, which is dismembering. "Remembrer," in its two significations, is also a definition of portraying. A portrait has a rememorizing function, but is also the reconstitution of the "pluréel" reality of its model into a coherent image. As for the *trait*, "remembrer" repairs its tracing, separating movement, to foreground its compository, weaving, healing dimensions. The duality between separation and reparation determine the economical organization of *Portrait du soleil*: it cuts the text in pieces, but permits it also to slip from one subject to another. It explains its disseminative structure as an opening up to other textual layers, to be reconstructed by reassembling dispersed parts. It explains also why the cutting of the *oranje* engenders subjectivity, not only because it lets flow the *jus*, anagram of "sujet"/subject, but also affects the writing subject, for *oran-je* refers back to Cixous' place of birth, Oran, and her "je" (see Hanrahan 48). And it explains why the *toux*, this dispersed, silent, carving memory of Dora, inevitably evokes *tout*, the necessity of wholeness, reparation, and *toucher*, the touching that strives against separation.

"La leçon d'anatomie" belongs to a series of fragments and sketches where the narrator finds herself in a situation of waiting, of watching. Her starting point is that of a blind person. For she is waiting to see, see scenes that her "mémoire dégorge" (27), see the spectacle that is hidden behind the door. She wants to have eyes, "des yeux désarmés" ["unshielded eyes"] (27), even if these eyes are false ones or only imaginary ones, like in dreams, or belong to someone else, like in the *Lesson*, where Jeor looks for her, as if to make the seeing bearable. What she wants to see has to do with the secret, the secret of life and death, of love and loss, and with understanding. "Je saurais tout" ["I would know everything"] (6). This knowing expresses the desire for wholeness, for remembering, for the reparation of a separation:

> Je traverserai l'orange, j'irai m'assoir sur les genoux de Jeor et je passerai mes bras autour de son cou, le ciel autour de nos corps sera de ce bleu phosphorescent qui coule dans son vase de verre en l'absence du soleil. (6)

> I will go through the orange, I will sit down on Jeor's lap and I will put my arms around his neck, the sky around us will be of the same phosphorescent blue that flows in the glass vase in the absence of the sun.

This description tells a childhood memory, but it also contains a portrait, a family portrait, because of its pictorial reference: we recognize in it the "Virgin, the Child Jesus and Saint Anne" of Leonardo da Vinci.[7] In Cixous' portrait, the "sun" is significantly replaced by a daughter, and the double mother-figure by "Jeor," a figure who belongs both to the narrator ("je") and the sun ("or"). In fact, the name of Jeor constitutes a complex of crossreferences, referring to the I/"je" of the narrator and her Other: in Hebrew, it signifies "light" and it sounds like "George"/je-or-je, the first name of Cixous' father she lost so young and whose death is at the source of her writing (*De la scène* 16).

As a lesson, this fragment promises insight, which it couples, by anatomy, to the inside, the inner, oneiric, bloody space towards which Cixous' quest is oriented since her first book *Dedans*. So the point of departure in the *Lesson* is blindness: a blindness that, as we shall see, the text allows, paradoxically, by its very "surgical" writing. For the surgeon, as Derrida reminds us, at the moment he makes his first cut, does not look at his hands, at the point where his scalpel will make its cut, nor at the body before him: he proceeds in the dark (*Mémoires d'aveugle* 64).

So the hand replaces sight; this is what the *Lesson* is going to teach. This passage is about "une idée de Jeor, qu'il a développée avant de s'endormir sur le lit entre mes âges" ["an idea of Jeor that he developed before falling asleep between the sheets of my (p)ages"]. It tells a dream, an imaginary scene, colored by eroticism and memory ("le lit entre mes âges"; "between the sheets of my (p)ages"). Its main issue is seeing, coupled to knowing: "Cette façon de *regarder* tracerait de nouvelles *perspectives* dans le lieu de notre existence....Il y aurait une *connaissance* encore *jamais vue*, une *révélation* digne des *dieux*, il y aurait cette *connaissance* identique à notre corps et *sans jour*" ["This way of looking would trace new perspectives in the place of our existence....There would be a knowledge that has never been seen before, a revelation, worthy of the gods, there would be that knowledge, identical with our body and opaque to the light of day"] (41, my emphasis). Here speaks another Prometheus, rivaling the gods, reaching for the impossible: to see through the secrets of life – and death.

Jeor's project concerns a statue made out of the bodies of himself and the narrator, by which he expresses a longing for his lost other half, for an original wholeness, which is in turn a longing for (sexual) in-difference. This longing is also a mythical one, referring to Aristophanes' tale of the androgyne (Plato *Banquet*) as well as to that of the Hermaphrodite in Ovidius' *Metamorphoses*.

> On se tiendrait par quelque point de nos corps, par exemple par la langue ou le sexe. Ensuite on développerait les corps; on retirerait un organe que l'on élèverait vers la lumière, puis on le poserait, à côté, puis on retirerait un autre organe....On poserait un inconnu (l'organe). Puis on juxtaposerait un deuxième inconnu et ainsi de suite. On tiendrait les artères entre deux doigts, on les placerait. (40-41)

> We would hold each other at some point of our body, for example with the tongue or the genitals. Then we would unfold our bodies; we would take out an organ and hold it up to the light, then we would put it aside, then we would take out another organ....We would put down something unknown (the organ). Then we would place a second unknown thing next to it and so forth. We would hold the arteries between two fingers, we would put them down.

The verbs of this passage all belong to the manual vocabulary, expressing holding, grasping, even mastery. Apparently Jeor knows, without looking, where to hold, what to take. But the more he looks and sees, the less he knows. He started his lesson by naming two organs of the body ("la langue ou le sexe"; "the

tongue or the genitals"), but cannot distinguish between them
anymore, referring to them by their generic name, "organe," to
qualify them finally as "inconnu" ["unknown"]. So not only seeing
and knowing, *voir* et *savoir*, do not always go together, but their
incompatibility also illustrates the failure of Jeor's project as a
search for in-difference, for it leads to neutrality, ignorance and
blindness.

The ambivalent consequences of his enterprise become more
clear when we consider the work of the fingers. The fingers exercise a double function of separation and reparation. They open up
the body, remove and hold up the organs as if before a projection
screen, a last distanced vision. But the fingers are especially the
instruments of death, as the following passage shows. Note its
vocabulary that shows the tension between separation and reparation (my emphasis):

> Je vis *entre* ses doigts une *section* d'artère *détachée* d'une *jonction*
> pulmonaire, et je sus qu'il était mortel, et j'en eus une colère
> étouffante. (41)

> Between his fingers I saw a piece of artery detached from a
> pulmonary junction. I knew then he was mortal, and I was
> seized by a suffocating anger.

But the fingers have also a reparatory function. They weave
("tissage"), repair, make a new work, and significantly this work
is a statue: something that not only can be seen, but also touched.

Already implicitly introduced by the "re-membering" fingers,
the importance of the "remembrer"-motif is emphasized in the
description of Rembrandt's *Lesson*, even though at first in a negative way:

> Rembrandt avait mis le corps entier dans un carré: ce cadavre était
> deux fois mort, fait pour les yeux, pour les attirer et les repousser
> et les tromper avec exactitude. Rembrandt avait peint sur la même
> ligne horizontale les plantes des pieds insérés dans le texte contre
> l'abdomen ouvert jusqu'aux côtes et vidé, sur la même ligne les
> mains écrasées au bout des bras en raccourci, ce n'était ni animal
> ni humain, ni beau ni laid, c'était une leçon inscrite dans un carré,
> une géométrie de mort, avec des contours, des proportions, des
> mesures. Je comprenais cela. C'était juste. (42)

Rembrandt had put the entire body in a square: this corpse was twice dead, laid out for the eye, to attract and repel it, to deceive the eye with precision. Rembrandt had painted on the same horizontal line the footsoles, fitted in the text against the abdomen which was laid open up to the ribs and emptied, on the same line the crushed hands at the end of the shortened arms; it was neither animal nor human, neither beautiful nor ugly, it was a lesson, inscribed in a square, a geometry of death, with contours, proportions, measures. I understood that. It was right.

"Remembrer" does not consist, as does Rembrandt according to this reading, in preserving the wholeness ("entier") of this body, for this has flattened and reduced the body. Rembrandt's painting is also criticized for its provocative, horrifying precision. As a mold, a smooth and perfect extract of the "real" body, Rembrandt's figure in fact "kills" the concrete body. For his figure is emptied ("vidé"), deprived of interiority, not only in its concept, as a dissected corpse, but also in its pictorial representation, as it is articulated "sur la même ligne." So, being merely a surface instead of a universe, it hardly covers the painter's canvas ("insérés dans le texte"). This accurate geometrical reconstruction, following prescribed contours, proportions and measures, remains blind to difference, to the concrete body, to the inside and blood. Such a portrait mystifies the (living) body and kills it.

Being very similar to Rembrandt's *Lesson*, Jeor's dreamed statue is disapproved of by the narrator. For her, the revealing precision which takes the body out of its intimacy, becomes literally unbearable:

> Aussi lorsque Jeor me fit voir sous un jour de précision les couleurs, les formes, les fonctionnements, j'éprouvai qu'il me tranchait les paupières, et que je ne pourrais plus jamais jouir de la nuit et de l'obscur toucher. (42)

> And when Jeor had then made me see in the sharp light of day the colours, forms, functions, I felt that he pierced my eyelids, and I would no longer be able to enjoy the night and the blind touching.

Jeor's enlightening activity is blinding. The final vision it promises is only another perfect extraction from the concrete body, comprehensible, recognizable, for it is overexposed in the precise, exterior light of science. To this imperative blinding vision, for it takes away other visions, the narrator prefers another blindness: that of darkness and interiority, where touching replaces visuality and where the absence of any model opens up to invention, imagination and memory. A "corps fictif," a fictive body which cannot be figured out, an almost invisible presence, becomes her aim:

> Je me rendis compte à cette occasion que mes explorations en rêve avaient toujours désiré un corps fictif: moi aussi j'avais désiré ses poumons et ses entrailles, mais voilés, vagues et doux. (41)

> At this point I realized that the explorations in my dreams had always longed for a fictive body: I, too, had wanted his lungs and intestines, but veiled, vague and soft.

This imaginary body is approached in the dark, there where it cannot be seen: it reminds us of "les muqueuses de l'anus que je pouvais toucher mais ne voyais pas" ["the mucous membrane of the anus that I could touch but not see"] (41). These erotic–anal mucosa introduce the interior, for they are composed of exterior skin and interior flesh. Moreover, as they are "soyeuses et fuyantes... fuyantes et invisibles et farouches" ["silky and elusive..., elusive and invisible and savage"], they invite what Luce Irigaray would call an "ethics of touching," where touching is neither active nor passive and involves two subjects, inspecting and respecting each other's difference ("L'Invisible de la chair" 151 – 152).

So these touching fingers venture, instead of the eyes, into the unknown, into otherness. Their only guide is a "mémoire tactile," a tactile memory which functions as a "remembrement":

> les poumons et les entrailles m'apparaissaient alors comme les prolongements raffinés de ces tissus, également enveloppés et invisibles et fuyant mes doigts. (42)

> the lungs and intestines seemed to me then like the refined extensions of these tissues, also wrapped up and invisible and slipping from my fingers.

This memory evokes the materiality of the living tissue, of corpore-ality and interiority, consisting of layers which touch each other and can be touched, caressed, dis-covered. Being "invisible," they escape from a reduction to the recognizable, the knowable, and therefore from indifference and subjugation; fleeing ("fuyant"), they are an agency as well as the fingers that touch them. Not knowing of a model, of "truth," this tactile memory makes at each exploration new discoveries; its creative power assures, in this dream-night, that the "remembrement," replacing an in-different eye/I and its surgical, dead-end activity, can take place.

This *Lesson*, therefore, is also an allegory of reading. The anatom-ical, cutting metaphor, with the unbearable sights and dead figures it engenders, functions as a warning against representation and mimesis as the reproduction of sameness. But anatomy constitutes also an invitation to touch the text, to enter its inside, there where it is living tissue, containing within its layers secrets which are yet to be discovered. Reading, then, is "re-membrer," in its two significa-tions: reassembling what in a text is dispersed, following the traces by which it appeals-peels itself, and being, as the reader, re-mem-bered in this activity, allowing the inner I/eye to be touched by the appeal of the unknown.

As for the narrator, this appeal will lead to a final revelation when she prepares herself to "read" the peels thrown away by Jeor. This reading is a moment of kissing, even of erotical caressing ("je les baisais"; "I kissed them"), as well as a moment of remem-brance, in the two senses of the term, the reading of the dispersed body-text ("toutes les *lettres* de l'âge"; "all the letters of the age"), conjuguating both memory ("âge") and "re-membrement" ("toutes").

This remembrance evokes a short scene situated in 1940, when the narrator was only three years old. This childhood memory is in fact a primal, and therefore lost scene, representing a child at the center of her own universe and the others, the Other, surrounding her in "adoration" for her. This adoration scene is constituted around the statue, which has significantly changed from a double statue into a single one, formed by the narrator only. Jeor is detached from the statue, as an "adorer" around the sun. But according to the Cixousian ethics, the adorer becomes himself the adored, a "god" whose white costume gives him the appearance of a sun.

"Je me retire dans mes enfances" ["I am withdrawing into my childhood"]. The narrator's separation from Jeor, her withdrawal holds a sexual connotation if we take into account the pictoral reference of Jeor's statue, which is one of the anatomical sketches of Leonardo da Vinci, with the title "de coitu."[8] This drawing represents a man and a woman having sexual intercourse; their standing position and their intertwined legs perfectly remind us of Jeor's double statue.

The sexual withdrawal then announces the disunion of the narrator and Jeor and, as a "retrait" indeed, cuts their dual unity into two halves. But this cut, paradoxically, is healing. It inaugurates a process of "re-membrement" engendering wholeness, where the narrator becomes "cette somme sculptée, ruisselante, lisse" ["the smooth, fluid, sculptured contours of the oneness of the body"], and her other half "total, infranchissable, gardé, abandonné, confiant, replié sur lui-même" ["complete, impenetrable, watched over, abandoned, trusting, withdrawn into itself"] (43, my emphasis). Making the former "lovers" both whole and withdrawn in themselves, the "trait" completes the separation as well as it heals the wounds caused by the anatomical-sexual act – a paradox which illustrates the inevitability and need for separation.

This withdrawal is accompanied at the level of representation by a refusal of visibility and figuration:

Quel dieu voit-il quand il se regarde dans la glace? Il ne se regarde pas. Il n'a pas besoin d'image, ni de peau, ni d'apparence, mais de cette somme sculptée, ruisselante, lisse qu'il me donne à toucher. (43)

What god does he see when he looks in the mirror? He does not look at himself. He does not need an image, nor a skin, nor an appearance, but the smooth, flowing, sculptured line of the oneness he gives me to touch.

This eclipse of the "god," of the adored adorer, refers back to the narrator's search to see, to catch a glimpse of the adored, but absent face. This impossible portrait makes her search futile; apparently the Face does not have a visible form. It offers ("donne") itself to her as something to be touched and, moreover, to be touched in herself, in the very corporeal living statue she forms. This touching is a reference to autoeroticism, to a state or "re-membrement" where desire and the imaginary can only undo the destructive forces of separation, death and oblivion. But this body-statue refers also to the text, whereas the withdrawal into "mes enfances," this sinking away ("je m'enfance"/enfonce) (61) evokes the deeper layers of textuality. The emphasis put on touching, therefore, reminds us that reading is a continual and pleasurable act of re-membrement, of reconstitution, based on the reader's desire for wholeness, for presence and representation. The reader thus is another Isis, the ancient-Egyptian goddess who reassembled the dispersed fragments of the body of her murdered husband, Osiris, to bring him back to life. For this is also the aim of the narrator, weaving her impossible portrait in the certainty that in the tortuous texture of allusions, wandering signifiers and slipping narratives, the Face will reappear.

What then is the lesson of this *Leçon d'anatomie*? The very surgical act it foregrounds, the allegory of Anatomy it constitutes, rejects the art of portraying-tracing in its distinctive and mortal consequences, but approves its possibilities to go "inside," to cross the borders between exteriority and interiority, between the visible and the invisible, between the there and the not-there. For this interior universe is the realm of the "encore"/en corps, of the still being there, where absence is animated, distance healed, and the Other re-membered.

The love story the *Lesson* illustrates is above all a story of loss: a loss the narrator seeks to undo in the very gesture of tracing-writing. For this gesture mimics the act of separation, whereas the *trait* it leaves functions as an objectification of the trace left by the absent Other (Tisseron 101). The *Lesson* therefore is an *histoire d'oeil/deuil*, allowing the carving narrator to see disappearance with her own eyes, to look loss in the eyes, to "rendre gorge" (43), to give back George. (See also *Coming to Writing* 5.) But this tracing is implicated in a gesture of touching, kissing, caressing; it refers to a hand that not only cuts, takes and encloses, but that also points out, "sees" with its fingers and draws-transcribes blindly what it discovers: otherness. The portrait such a tracing-touching creates is neither achieved nor absolute, and its making is a continuous act of re-membrement, involving two caressing subjects. A door for the living indeed.

Notes

I would like to express my gratitude to Roy Bicknell for his careful reading of this article and the English translations of Cixous' texts.
1. This article is a revised and expanded version of two papers held at the symposium "Lectures de la différence sexuelle," 19 October 1990 and at the seminar of Hélène Cixous of 1 December 1990, both at the Collège International de Philosophie and the Université Paris VIII-Vincennes in Paris.
2. The H in fact can be *seen* as a passageway between two shores or a ladder, permitting the descending-ascending movement, the exploration of the lowest and deepest: it's the figure for writing. We can also *hear* this H, which in French makes *hache* (axe), which figures another breakdown at the deepest level. In English *hache* sounds like *ashes*, reminding us of the value of the residual, the remainders, the non-value. See *Three Steps on the Ladder of Writing* 3 – 4.
3. Like in the following title of Cixous: "L'Approche de Clarice Lispector. Se laisser lire (par) Clarice Lispector."
4. Note that the figure of the Eye functions in many representational systems as a symbol of both God and the Sun.
5. "De anatomische les van Dr. Jan Deyman." Amsterdam: Rijksmuseum, 1656.
6. As a matter of fact, Dr. Deyman is quite absent from Rembrandt's painting. He's the figure standing at the head of the corpse, of which we can only see the hands. This misrepresentation is due to the fact that the picture is only a fragment left of the original.
7. Around 1510, Paris, Louvre.
8. Anatomical drawings, Royal Library, Windsor Castle. The references to da Vinci in *Portrait du soleil* are related to Cixous' reading of Freud, especially that of his *Eine Kindheitserinnerung des Leonardo da Vinci* (1910).

Works Cited

Cixous, Hélène. "L'Approche de Clarice Lispector. Se laisser lire (par) Clarice Lispector." (1979). *Entre l'écriture*. Paris: des femmes, 1986. 113–138.

——. "The Character of 'Character'." *New Literary History*. 2 (Winter 1974): 383–402.

——. *"Coming to Writing" and other essays*. Ed. Deborah Jenson. Cambridge: Harvard UP, 1991.

——. "De la scène de l'Inconscient à la scène de l'Histoire: Chemin d'une écriture." *Hélène Cixous, chemins d'une écriture*. Ed. Françoise van Rossum-Guyon and Myriam Díaz-Diocaretz. Saint-Denis: Presses Universitaires de Vincennes, Amsterdam: Rodopi, 1990. 15 – 34.

——. "Le dernier tableau ou le portrait de Dieu". *Entre l'écriture*. Paris: des femmes, 1986. 169–201.

——. *Illa*. Paris: des femmes, 1980.

——. *Jours de l'an*. Paris: des femmes, 1990.

——. *Un K. incompréhensible: Pierre Goldman*. Paris: Christian Bourgois, 1975.

——. *La*. Paris: des femmes, 1976.

——. "The Laugh of the Medusa" (1975). *New French Feminisms*. Ed. Elaine Marks and Isabelle de Courtivron. Brighton: Harverster, 1981. 245-64.

——. *Le Livre de Promethea*. Paris: Gallimard, 1983.

——. *Manne aux Mandelstams aux Mandelas*. Paris: des femmes, 1988.

——. *Portrait du soleil*. Paris: Denoël, 1973.

——. *Prénoms de personne*. Paris: Seuil, 1974.

——. *Three Steps on the Ladder of Writing*. Trans. Sarah Cornell and Susan Sellers. New York: Columbia UP 1993.

Deleuze, Gilles. *Critique et Clinique.* Paris: Minuit, 1993.

Derrida, Jacques. *Marges de la philosophie.* Paris: Minuit, 1972.

——. *Mémoires d'aveugle. L'autoportrait et autres ruines.* Paris: Réunion des musées nationaux, 1990.

Hanrahan, Mairéad. "Une porte du *Portrait du soleil* ou la succulence du sujet." van Rossum-Guyon and Díaz-Diocaretz 45–53.

Irigaray, Luce. "L'invisible de la chair." *Ethique de la différence sexuelle.* Paris: Minuit, 1984. 143–171.

Minazzoli, Agnès. *La première ombre. Réflexion sur le miroir et la pensée.* Paris: Minuit, 1990.

Stevens, Christa. "Hélène Cixous. Portraying the Feminine." *Beyond Limits. Boundaries in Feminist Semiotics and Literary Theory.* Ed. Liesbeth Brouwer. Groningen: Rijksuniversiteit Groningen, 1990. 83–96.

Tisseron, Serge. "Le dessein du dessin: geste graphique et processus du deuil." *Art et fantasme.* Ed. Claude Wiart. Seyssel: Champ Vallon, 1984. 91–105.

12

Ariane Mnouchkine / Hélène Cixous: The Meeting of Two Chimaeras

Rosette C. Lamont

Meeting Hélène Cixous in New York on her first trip to the United States three years after the 1968 French student uprising was like breathing the heady air of social revolt. I called on her (the appointment was made over the telephone) at the Central Park South hotel where she had elected to stay while *en mission* to the United States as an envoy of the Ministry of Foreign Affairs to the French Cultural Services. I had no clear image of what she looked like or what to expect. I knew of course her reputation as one of the leading French feminist theoreticians, her connection with the newly formed publishing house, Des Femmes, and the fact that she was the youngest scholar in France to have earned the prestigious degree, Doctorat D'Etat, with a dissertation on James Joyce. She was teaching in the Department of English and American Studies of Vincennes, a new campus (now transferred to St. Denis) of the multi-branched Université de Paris, then known as a hotbed of young Communists, Maoists, and all the "ists" and "isms" of revolutionary fervor. Cixous was proud of being a radical, although politically she was mostly involved in redefining feminism in a series of essays and pamphlets. As a novelist, her style was *recherché*, influenced by that of the author of *Finnegans Wake*. Those who did not appreciate her writing defined it as a new form of *préciosité*. She had not yet tried her hand at writing plays.

The Department of Romance Languages of Queens College (CUNY) had been able to secure her presence for one lecture. It was my special duty to shepherd our lecturer through the maze of the subway system and bring her safely to the department office. Standing in the hotel lobby, I kept on wondering how she would look. Was she tall or short? Good-looking? What I should have but never expected was that she would be delivering her talk dressed in the latest Parisian style of the post-student revolution: Hot-Pants. The woman who appeared before me was tall, slender, with long legs covered by black tights. Her shorts came all the way up to the edge of her hips, and her thick, dark hair was cut very short. Her North African Jewish looks were strictly pre-Diasporic, tinged with that aura of displacement formerly referred to as "exotic" before the word became politically incorrect.

In those early days, Cixous was still quite shy, but as we rode the F train she relaxed, and we chatted through the hour-long trek from Manhattan to the campus. Since in Paris everyone uses the *Métro*, she was not taken aback by our mode of travel and was fascinated by the speed of the express train skipping the local stops. I recall that her lecture was as controversial as her way of dressing and that her analysis of Joyce did not meet with the approval of the Joyce specialists of our English Department.

Although she was an ardent feminist, the young Cixous was not averse to a bit of flirtation. In France, she had the reputation of being *"une grande consommatrice d'hommes"* ["a devourer of men"]. It was also rumored that only a short time before, she had been a girl who did not know how to dress. It had taken a lover, it was said, to shape and alter her appearance, giving her what the French today call *"le look."* In turn, she was going to give a new look to the many girls, students and disciples, who worshipped her.

For many years now, Cixous' appearance seems modeled on the bust of Nefertiti, discovered by a German expedition at Amarna in 1912 and described by Camille Paglia in *Sexual Personae*: "Nefertiti is the opposite of the Venus of Willendorf. She is the triumph of Apollonian image over the humpiness and horror of Mother Earth. Everything fat, slack, and sleepy is gone.... The radiant glamor of the supreme sexual persona comes to us from a palace-prison, the overdeveloped brain" (66–67). Paglia points out that the proper response to the "intolerably severe" Nefertiti bust is one of fear (67). Unlike her feminized spouse, Akhnaten, whose round belly gives him a pregnant look, Nefertiti, that "half-masculine vampire of political will," has come down to us as a bodiless pillar, a "caryatid" who bears the "burden of state upon her head": "visually, she had been reduced to her essence" (Paglia 69).

The Western Nefertiti, according to Paglia, is Leonardo's *Mona Lisa*. Far from seeing her as mysterious, and gently soft, Paglia compares her to the Gorgon. Her expression is one of "blankness" which, like Nefertiti's bust, creates fear in the viewer. For Paglia, the world's most famous painting is "Zeus, Leda, and egg rolled into one, another hermaphrodite deity pleasuring herself in mere being" (154). Soft-voiced, feminine on the surface, Cixous has a will of iron. Her sensuality may well be Dionysian, but she has also become a master and a sage to a generation of young women seeking their paths. As a teacher, she operates in the tradition of Socrates with the difference that the ephebes who often literally sit at her feet are girls. Shaped by the French intellectual tradition, her mind is Apollonian. One might well salute her in the very terms used by Michelangelo for his friend, Vittoria Colonna: "a man, a god rather, inside a woman," an "hermaphrodite Muse" that "makes mythologically intelligible his depiction of the Sybils as half-male viragos" (Paglia 162).

Throughout history, there have been women of genius whose complexity forced a fearful kind of admiration; they became known as magnificent monsters (the French always called their great actresses "*monstres sacrés*"), or chimaeras. By standard definition, the chimaera is a fire-breathing creature endowed with a lion's head, a goat's body, and a serpent's tail. The latter is much like a phallic appendage. This symbol issues from the collective unconscious; it is one of the strange yet familiar archetypal images. The colossal stone figure of the Sphinx near the pyramids at Giza is the embodiment of such an archetypal image. In classical mythology, the Sphinx had the head and breasts of a woman, the body of a lioness, and eagle's wings. The Egyptian Sphinx has a regal, masculine head atop a lioness' body. The mythological Sphinx is female.

In the course of a series of lectures given at New York University a number of years ago, Cixous reminded the students that the being encountered by Oedipus following Laius' murder at the crossroads was *"une Sphinge,"* a woman-beast who questioned him in song-like riddles. She is, in fact, the interpreter of chthonian mysteries – like the mysterious Mother Faust seeks out in the utter darkness of the void in order to extract from it the image of the Eternal Feminine, the beauteous Helen of Troy. In this haunting scene, Goethe dramatizes the heroic task of the poet who delves deep into his own subconscious to unearth buried archetypes, giving them new life in his verse. The mythological story of Oedipus follows a similar pattern. The future king of Thebes must guess the Sphinx's wise riddle about the ages of Man in order to survive and triumph over the scourge. When he does, the creature falls dead, and the hero comes down bearing the mortal remains of the monster, a lion's skin. Thus, he wins a throne, the love of the queen, power over his people, and eternal damnation. Having blinded himself to truths that transcend logic, he will suffer the consequences. Cixous, however, is much less interested in Oedipus, and even less so in the Freudian Oedipus complex, than in the female Sphinx erased by the male victor. *La Sphinge* becomes for her the symbol of the superior woman defeated by the single-minded, ambitious male. She, at any rate, has kept clear of meeting a wandering, wondering Oedipus.

Perhaps the most important meeting in Cixous' life will prove to be with another chimaera, another magnificent monster, the creator of Le Théâtre du Soleil and of a whole style of retelling familiar masterpieces. Although other directors have staged Cixous' plays, most notably Simone Benmussa who directed *Portrait of Dora*, the association with Ariane Mnouchkine proved profoundly creative. In this case, Cixous composed plays geared to the actors of the company, and the two women arrived at an astonishingly harmonious and daring dramaturgic form. Two plays in particular will be the subject of this essay: *L'Histoire terrible mais inachevée de Norodom Sihanouk, roi du Cambodge* and *L'Indiade ou L'Inde de leurs rêves.*[1] Both plays are the result of a passion the two women shared for Eastern culture and their pain over the bloody, fratricidal, auto-genocidal wars that maimed a highly civilized corner of the globe.

Like Peter Brook, who seems to joke, but is quite serious when he declares: "I'm not a director who travels, but a traveller who directs plays," Mnouchkine and Cixous are inveterate explorers. Like Brook, they embarked on study voyages with members of their acting and technical staff. They decided to write a modern "history," in the Shakespearean sense, about the "unfinished" life of Norodom Sihanouk, before Mnouchkine embarked on her four-year Shakespeare project: *Richard II* (1981); *Twelfth Night* (1982); and *Henry IV* (1984). Originally, Mnouchkine planned to write the text herself, but she realized that she could not carry out the task of authorship. In Cixous, she found the poetic voice and scholarly discipline needed for this demanding enterprise.

Mnouchkine and Cixous chose Cambodia as the *locus* of their cooperative effort for two reasons: their desire to present a noble, gentle people – the Khmer – whose culture they admired, and their equally powerful wish to show the wanton destruction of a people and a culture by power-mad ideologues. Saloth Sar, whose *nom de guerre* is Pol Pot, caused the death of three million Cambodians and was only too successful in his project to return Cambodia to "Year Zero." In the course of a four-year reign of terror, millions were assassinated, sadistically tortured, or died of starvation. Five of Sihanouk's children, along with fourteen of his grandchildren and other relatives, were murdered by the Khmer Rouge in the madness of their campaign to impose a Maoist, purely agrarian society on Cambodia in the 1970s. In the first mass rally held after the Prince's return to Phnom Penh, he declared: "In a war, a person is shot and killed instantly. In my family's case, they were tortured and clubbed to death." A Cambodian student of mine told me that her mother was hanged, flayed, and the skin of her face peeled off by a rapier. For Cixous, a half-Algerian, half-Viennese, Jewish woman, Pol Pot's insane project echoed the mass murders of Nazi death camps and the mass grave of the Babi Yar ravine near Kiev. The same can be said of Mnouchkine who told me that her paternal grandparents died in deportation. French-born, Ariane Mnouchkine is the daughter of a British mother, June Hannen, (Mnouchkine learned her English at home and at Oxford University where she was an active member of the Oxford University Drama Society [OUDS] and the Experimental Theatre Company [ETC]) and a Russian-Jewish father, born in Petrograd in 1908, the distinguished founder of Ariane Films (1945) and the head of the French Film Academy from 1988 to his death in 1993. Cixous and Mnouchkine are "citizens of the world," both by ancestry and existential choice. When journalist, Frederic Ferney, interviewing Mnouchkine about her forthcoming *Atrides*, asked the provincial question, "Doesn't Aeschylus represent an absolute foreignness?," she answered: "We have everything to learn from what is foreign. We place our bets on the pedagogical value of difference" (*Le Figaro*, 11/13/1990).

Each member of Mnouchkine's cast is international, multilingual, multicultural. Over the years they developed similar intonations in their French (even French actors such as Georges Bigot, the company's unforgettable Sihanouk). This accent has nothing to do with realism or even with the actors' original national languages; it is part and parcel of the Brechtian distanciation between signifier and signified. Moreover, what distinguishes Mouchkine's stagings is her adoption of a mixture of Asian dramaturgic forms and styles for her Shakespeare productions, and, appropriately, for her modern "history plays," *Sihanouk* and *L'Indiade*. Although previously she drew primarily on Persian and Indian art for her inspiration, the postmodern idiom she invented for her recent Greek cycle is an amalgam of Japanese Kabuki and Sanskrit *kutiyattam*. The latter is a synthesis of many arts and developmental periods built upon the Sanskrit tradition which eventually gave rise to *kathakali*, India's major dance-drama from the state of Kerala.

What Mnouchkine has sought, above all, is a sharp break with the French neoclassical tradition, what she describes as "Greeks and Romans wearing bed sheets." She adds the following explanation: "I am certain that there was a time when Greek plays about the Trojan war were performed in Oriental-style costumes, particularly when Alexander the Great reached the Orient." Indeed, according to historical accounts, 5,000 Greek artists were brought to India to entertain the soldiers, and Greek tragedies were performed in the Indus Valley. Today, unconventional, intercultural performances of the classics are a theatrical trend throughout the world. Take, for example, Tadashi Suzuki's *Trojan Woman* and Spanish director Travora's *Bacchae* in which he uses flamenco foot work as a metatheatrical language. In New York, we were treated at La Mama to a *Hippolytus* in Kannada by the Mysore-based Rangayana repertory company, directed by a Greek, Vasillios Calitsis. Like her Eastern colleagues, Mnouchkine wants to develop a dialogue between ancient performance cultures as well as between those cultures and our own.

For both Cixous and Mnouchkine, their route as travelers and artists is a form of spiritual quest. The task they have undertaken is that of returning to the source, the unconscious, and then setting its archetypal images upon the scene of history.

The Terrible but Unended Story of Norodom Sihanouk: King of Cambodia

Wearing austere black, four men and a woman stand at the edge of the vast, square, beechwood stage of Ariane Mnouchkine's Théâtre du Soleil at the Cartoucherie de Vincennes, a former munitions store-house offered by the French government to the Mnouchkine company in 1970. The five are the leaders of the Khmer Rouge: Saloth Sar, Khieu Samphan, Hou Youn, Ieng Sary, and Ieng Thirith, Sary's wife. These Sorbonne-educated intellectuals, steeped in Marxism and the philosophy of terrorism, have taken advantage of the King's exile – the result of a coup d'état fomented by Sihanouk's conservative cousin, Prince Sirik Matak, and General Lon Nol during their sovereign's diplomatic voyage through the Soviet Union and China – to launch an offensive against the corrupt, dispirited forces of Lon Nol's American-supported army and air force. Clearly, America's assistance has failed.

In fact, we now know that corruption increased with massive aid as the Cambodian army grew from 37,000 soldiers to more than 200,000. Hungry soldiers often resorted to pillaging villagers, particularly since their commanders failed to pay existing troops in order to pocket the money. After the invasion of American and South Vietnamese forces, a full-fledged civil war developed. From 1970 to 1975, the Khmer Rouge grew from 3,000 guerillas to 30,000. In 1972, Lon Nol declared himself President, but when the final Khmer Rouge offensive began on New Year's day 1975, he was vacationing at the beach resort of Lampong Som on the Gulf of Thailand. Phnom Penh fell on April 17.

This is the moment dramatized by the Cixous/Mnouchkine team. The four male leaders and the one woman raise their binoculars to observe the capital on the other side of the river. Their nostrils fill with the sweet scent of success. However, the breezes blowing over the Mekong also carry the stench of rot and death. Pol Pot is facing the most challenging problem of his entire career as a revolutionary, that of organizing the peace. The leaders debate with ruthless objectivity the matter of administrating "a crocodile that will tear (them) to shreds."

Phnom Penh is a city peopled by an urban middle class, and, following the Khmer Rouge's murderous advance through the devasted countryside, an uprooted peasantry. Only one solution presents itself to the leaders: "We've got to empty out the trash can, kick it over." This suggestion comes from Ieng Thirith, an Oriental Lady Macbeth. The leaders are ready to execute two and a half million occupants, driving them out into the rice patches. "They'll eat what they grow!" When Hou Youn, a former minister in King Sihanouk's 1966 coalition government, raises his voice in protest against this final solution, he signs his own death warrant.

Hélène Cixous' nine-hour modern history play, based on the reign and fall of the King of Cambodia, bears the unmistakable stamp of Shakespeare's histories and comedies. A beautifully researched text, it is in no way didactic. Cixous has always been concerned with the texture of language. Her historical drama is written in a style at once poetic and direct. It is the passionate portrait of a well-intentioned monarch and the troubled waters of history he was unable to sail. At this moment, he is still being tossed on the trecherous seas. Both writer and director were intrigued by the complex character of Sihanouk: a patriotic ruler; a father to his people; a seemingly religious man, often invoking Buddha's name to this day; a wily charmer; an avid reader of world literature; a sensitive musician. They saw in him a fellow artist who also enjoyed the game of politics and diplomacy, a game he might not be able to win in the end. His remains, after all, an "unfinished story."

As the two friends began their work on the play, they came to the startling realization that the subject met with indifference, even resentment. France's colonial wars, followed by America's later involvement in Vietnam, had turned young people into unquestioning Vietnam sympathizers. Cambodians were viewed as enemies rather than victims. Mnouchkine felt strongly that she had to alter this perception.

The Cixous/Mnouchkine spectacle is both political and poetic theatre. Mnouchkine often emphasizes in interviews the importance of transcending realism, of being in tune with the mythical world. Yet, because of the physical nature of theatre, myths and ideas must be incarnated. The quirky character of Prince Sihanouk is at the very core of this vast historical fresco. Both prince and artist, he sees the invisible and may enter into conversation with it. For all major decisions, Cixous' Sihanouk relies on consultations with his father's ghost, rising from a temple jar like some masked jack-in-the-box. In Cambodia's ancient land, contact between the living and the dead is an essential component of daily reality. Thus, two wonderfully comical crones, the green-grocer, Khieu Samnol, and her Vietnamese friend, Madam Lamné (clearly for women, personal attachments are stronger than political quarrels), lend their creaky, rusty bicycle to the dead king, Norodom Suramit, so that he may join his living son in Peking. As this amiable specter cycles off on the rusty wreck, wending and winding his way between the pit and the first row of benches, the humble vehicle is transformed into a Pegasus. In the Cixous/Mnouchkine shows, the quotidian is raised to the level of myth.

Cixous' treatment of Americans in this play is even-handed. If Kissinger comes off as a caricature – he and Pol Pot were played by the same actor – John Gunther Dean is presented as a noble, generous, suffering man. Addressing the paralyzed, power-mad Lon Nol on the eve of Cambodia's demise, the ambassador exclaims: "Don't you see you're committing suicide? I who love this country would like to avert the Communist takeover. I've wept for this land and for my own!" Later, in conversation with the visiting Republican senator, Paul McCloskey, Dean utters with profound feeling and wisdom, "Can it be that we don't recognize pain because, as Americans, we have not suffered enough? We would need to confront gas chambers to admit to ourselves that evil intends to rule our planet."

The whirlwind of history blows through the play, carrying the ensemble of actors on and off-stage as an entity. It is the gestural metaphor for ceaseless socio-political change. Yet, there are also oases in space and time. In a beguiling scene, which supposedly takes place on the night of Sihanouk's birthday, while the King of Cambodia is still in power, he walks out into the palace garden, accompanied by his loyal Penn Nouth. He intends to instruct his minister in the names he has invented for the stars studding his heavenly meadow: "You see this bright one, over there, it's the child prodigy Mozart. Further, we have Pandit Nehru, and this one is Charles de Gaulle." "What about William Shakespeare, your majesty?" questions the cultured minister, adhering to the rules of this fine game. Sihanouk hesitates for a moment before venturing: "He's a bit too great...a whole empire...a gigantic giant. I prefer gigantic dwarfs!"

Indeed, as often in Shakespeare, the little people are given meaty parts in Cixous' drama. One of the deepest, most abiding human relationships in the play is that linking two poor, slightly ridiculous old women who care for one another and manage to remain together throughout the war. Madam Lamné goes as far as to assist her friend in rehearsing the brutal credo of the new revolution, so that they may pretend successfully that they have been indoctrinated. "Our duty is to teach our grandchildren to hate. Each one of us must kill ten Vietnamese, and instruct future generations in doing the same. All hail to the Marxist-Leninist revolution!" The fact that a Vietnamese woman is doing this coaching introduces the right note of irony. Only the dignified death of Khieu Samnol will separate the two friends. Toward the end of the play, Madam Lamné tells her companion, "The most beautiful thing in my life was knowing you."

As one hears these words, one cannot help thinking that they are a message delivered in public, that of Cixous to Mnouchkine, and perhaps also, at that time, of Mnouchkine to Cixous. The play celebrates the tie of friendship which gives meaning to the besieged lives of two women caught in the sweep of political change. It is their message of love and tolerance, a message addressed to the world. It is also the message of two great chimaeras whose love and respect for one another created an unforgettable work of art. The play was the major triumph of the 1985–86 Paris season: L'Indiade.

No longer centered on a single figure, such as the beguilingly crafty Sihanouk, L'Indiade (the title echoes the most famous of all epics, the Iliad) is also concerned with the whirlpool of political intrigue. It explores the struggle for independence by diverse religious and ethnic Indian communities where, in the process, unity is compromised by partition. Carved from India's body, the state of Pakistan severed Western Punjab from Eastern Bengal. As Cixous states in her preface to the published text: "August 1947 marked an implacable surgical operation."

Two polar figures represent the struggle between purity and political expediency: the saintly Mahatma Gandhi, played as a clever holy fool by Andreas Perez Araya, and Nehru, given great dignity by Georges Bigot, who played Sihanouk in an entirely different vein. In his well-cut, white European suit, Nehru is a thoroughly westernized gentleman, whereas the half-naked, hairless, toothless Gandhi could try out for the part of Lear's Edgar.

L'Indiade begins even before the audience settles down on the tiered, thinly-upholstered benches facing the vast, low-platformed stage. As the audience scrambles up to their unmarked seats (at the Cartoucherie it is always "first come, first served"), actors, dressed as Indian villagers, trickle onto the village square (the stage), sweeping away the morning dust and sprinkling it with fresh water. Filtered through an airy canopy, the morning light suggests the start of an ordinary day in the dry, poor subcontinent of Southern Asia.

While this is going on, a Bengali itinerant female beggar, Haridasi, runs up and down the aisles, asking members of the audience to identify themselves by name and nationality so that she might introduce them properly to her friends, the villagers. Since the audience of the Cartoucherie is unfailingly international, or at least European, the breakdown of national barriers is established from the start. To be addressed by Baya Belal, playing Haridasi, in highly accented Indian English, contributes to the sense of estrangement already experienced by people at the moment they step into the huge foyer with its back wall covered by a map of India. Part of the *dépaysement* was the strong smell of curry in the same foyer, as costumed, made-up actors, who would later be seen on the stage, served this spicy dish to an audience that had travelled to Vincennes on an empty stomach. Paris seemed to have vanished in the distance.

For the audience, the voyage begins the moment they enter the vast entrance hall of the Cartoucherie. Once they have claimed a seat, often by putting down a coat, they make their way down to the floor level in order to watch the actors, seated at low tables, apply the make-up that will transform them into the characters they are to play. The communal dressing-room is visible through a flimsy curtain made of split, open panels. It is located directly under the tiers of benches. This is all part of the Théâtre du Soleil's "politique d'accueil." Ariane Mnouchkine is always present, often standing at the high and wide carriage-entrance or moving through the lobby, greeting friends, meeting strangers, and visiting foreigners. Her community of actors, musicians, technicians, and administrators is also always present, creating a bond of complicity and friendship with the public, establishing a relationship full of joyful respect and trust. It is as though, coming into the Cartoucherie, we had all embarked on a very informal ocean-liner, ready to sail to a foreign land. Inside the ship we will all be cared for, fed, entertained. Above all, we will learn something we needed to know. Yet no-one plays the role of teacher or guru; we learn together by doing, by being.

In a short essay entitled, "Qui es-tu?" ["Who are you"], which concludes the handsomely published text of L'Indiade, Cixous describes this process of initiation, these rites of passage that will take interpreters and viewers in the same direction. We must lose the distinction between "I" and "Thou," she explains, realizing that they are one and the same. The example she uses is of the process of transformation in applying make-up. She writes:

Every day the actors disappear in the mirror, un-know and un-make themselves. You must no longer recognize yourself. This takes a long time. At last, you are no longer there, and now, in the night of imagination, you go in search of the other's face. For an hour, an hour and a half, you swim in the amniotic dark, trying to bring to light the new-born, slowly creating the visage of the "Thou." Suddenly my actor friends are not there – instead there are Indians. Part of the voyage has been accomplished.

For Cixous, the writer, this process is particularly important since, as she says, she writes with her body ("J'écris avec le corps"). To write or to act, you must leave the upper floor of forgetfulness, where you forgot the meaning of childhood, and rush below to that level where "hearts open to the earth, a soil irrigated by water and blood, nourishing our roots." Writing poems, novels, even essays, is a solitary task. However, Cixous discovered the writing of plays is not. The author, she says, is the first spectator of the work, seated at the core of the envisioned community, looking at other members of that community move upon the stage. She describes this in terms that are familiar to students of French feminism, physicalizing the mental process:

To "write" a play, I must first "go" to the theatre by stepping behind thought. I close my eyes and, ensconced in the very depths of my body, I watch the characters I create come to life. Facing the paper I write on, I grow agitated, utter wild exclamations, dissolve in tears. This means that it is already theatre, and that I am not condemned to solitude by this act.

L'Indiade is teeming with people and their passions; it is truly an epic, an *Iliad*, except that Homer's battles have become struggles of the mind, clashes of diverse political and religious appurtenances. We are not shown combat, the life and death struggles of great heroes, but we are told that the decisions taken by statesmen result in violent happenings. Looking backward, after having seen Mnouchkine's tetralogy, *Les Atrides*, we realize that the central preoccupation is much the same as in the previous play, *Sihanouk*: absurd, devastating fratricidal wars. Again and again, in interviews, Mnouchkine states that we do not murder enemies but brothers, that the blood knot between kith and kin is indeed soaked in blood. But what is even more striking today is how relevant this modern history play is to contemporary events in Europe, those of that divided land once known as Yugoslavia. There, also, partition means bloodshed; freedom has come to mean freedom to rape and kill.

Theatre, as Antonin Artaud taught us, is the time of the plague, the time of cruelty. Cixous calls it the *locus* of crime and of forgiveness. She writes, "We do not kill only what we hate, we also kill what we love." In "The Deadly Sins/Anger: The Fascination Begins in the Mouth," Mary Gordon raises many a puzzling, unanswerable question:

> The events in the former Yugoslavia seem to me to characterize perfectly the results of deadly anger. We outsiders are tormented and bedeviled by unimaginable behavior from people who seem so very much like ourselves ... And yet, a kind of incomprehensible horror has grown out up precisely because of an anger that has gone out of control and has fed on itself until all human eyes are blinded by the bloated flesh of overgorged anger. People, who five years ago, ate together, studied together, even married, have sworn to exterminate one another in the most bloody and horrifying ways ... This is the deadly power of anger; it rolls and rolls like a flaming boulder down a hill, gathering mass and speed until any thought of cessation is so far beside the point as to seem hopeless. (31)

Indeed, partitioned India and divided Yugoslavia became theatres of death and blood. Gandhi's philosophy of passive resistance could not stop the "flaming boulder" of anger and hate. The unified India he envisioned did not come to pass. The symbol

Cixous uses for irrational forces is that of Moona Baloo, a trained
female bear which eventually goes mad and mangles those who
come too close, including her trainer. In a short essay, "And What
About the Female Bear?" Cixous states: "There can be no play
about Man without a Female Bear. It is as essential to the meaning
of the work as Gandhi."

Only a great chimaera would compare the saintly Gandhi with a
female bear. The one character in the play who serves the function
of a one-woman chorus and Cixous' message-bearer is the illiterate
Bengali folk poet and seer, Haridasi. In the short prologue to the
play, spoken as the audience settles on the benches, she makes the
following declaration, one that challenges the ethnic/religious
struggle of colonized, then partitioned India:

> Do you know how many races there are among men?
> Only two races, and a third:
> One is the race of men,
> The other, the race of women.
> The third is of beings half-male half-female.

Haridasi, the natural poet, is evoking an ancient, universal arche-
type: the chimaera.

As noted earlier, a chimaera is not only hermaphroditic, but part
human, part beast. Marrying brute beast, the female bear, and the
holy man, Gandhi embodies the chimaeric image, one that does not
exist in nature, but rises nevertheless from the depths of the collective unconscious. In this context, we might consider contemporary sculptor, Louise Bourgeois' comments on her piece, "Nature
Study," originally entitled "Chimaera": "This title is of course
ironic, since no such creature exists in nature." Bourgeois' sculpture depicts a composite, headless creature, a lioness with three
sets of round, voluptuous human breasts and an erect male penis.
This mythical beast is endowed with claws or eagles' talons. As
Bourgeois explains: "Life is not easy for such creatures. They have
many enemies, ready to tear them to shreds, to behead them."
Cixous might well have spoken these words.

I began this essay with a personal recollection of the Cixous I met
in 1971 when she was already celebrated as a brilliant young
scholar – the youngest *Docteur d'Etat* France had ever had – a
theoretician of feminism, and the writer of Joycean novels whose
principal subject was language. However, in this critic's opinion,

Cixous' major talent lies in the field of drama. To fully come into her own, she needed to meet, love and work with another chimaera, the theater director Ariane Mnouchkine. Their association proved and continues to be highly productive.

Recently, Cixous translated *The Euménides* for Mnouchkine's *Atrides* tetralogy. The final play of Aeschylus' trilogy conveys the ultimate message of the poet/pedagogue, his praise of democracy's golden mean and of the insauration of the Athens tribunal, the council of the Areopagus. *The Oresteia* has been called a rite of passage from savagery to civilization, but if the humanized gods of reason can guide human beings to a superior realm of feeling, the Furies also cling to a truth of their own. They raise an essential question which remains unanswered: If matricides are to be pardoned, what will be the fate of the civilized world? As Robert Fagles and W.B. Stanford point out in their foreward to the Fagles' translation of *The Oresteia*: "The Navelstone is hemorrhaging again, and this means another Olympian violation of the Mother and the Fates." It is this violation that dictates the flow of images, the gestural motifs, the echoing laments throughout the cycle.

In staging *The Euménides*, Mnouchkine concretized the struggle between the light and the dark in ways that are original, yet faithful to the text. The play reflects that secret mysteries of Eleusis which sprang from the autumnal harvest rites that celebrated the reunion of Demeter and her abducted daughter, the queen of the underworld. As envisioned by Mnouchkine, the "younger gods" of light and reason, Apollo and Athena, clothed in radiant, white robes, institute a higher moral order by defeating the forces of darkness. Yet no justice can be achieved if the chthonian deities are excluded. These must be remembered with respect. In the Mnouchkine production, the Furies are harmless victims, three Brechtian *clochardes*. In drawing them into the dance, Athena wins them over, transforming them into *Euménides* (the Kind Ones.) However, her tetralogy has no happy ending. As the *clochardes* vanish, other members of the chorus invade the stage; they are beasts – part lion with huge manes, part ape, part growling, fanged dogs. They run down-stage, ready to devour the audience. These are creatures of our collective nightmares: horrifying, yet weirdly familiar.

The Euménides may be the talkiest of the four plays, but the text, as translated by Cixous, breathes with the ample rhetoric of Greek

culture at its height. Aeschylus presents the earthly paradise of a
great *polis* with its regulated life and courts of law, but the military
hero who fought in the battle of marathon knew only too well how
fragile this order was, how close it always comes to destruction.
The grandchild of Russian Jews (on her father's side) who died in
deportation, Mnouchkine is fully aware of the transient nature of
civilized living. This is also true of Cixous, half Sephardic-Algerian
(her paternal roots), half Viennese Jew. In bringing Aeschylus'
sublime text to the stage, the two artists created their greatest
work to date, a masterpiece that will undoubtedly be considered
one of the summits of the theatrical endeavours of this century's
final decade.

For their next project, the Mnouchkine/Cixous team announced
a play about recent French history, the Vichy regime under the
German occupation. It was certainly a fitting project for the 50th
anniversary of Europe's liberation from the Nazi yoke, and it is a
pity that this plan was abandoned. In June, 1994, the Théâtre du
Soleil presented Cixous' *La Ville parjure ou le réveil des Erinyes* [*The
Forsworn City or the Furies Awakening*]. It deals with the recent
political and moral scandal of the AIDS-tainted blood transfused
to hemophiliacs as a calculated risk. Cixous' test is a cry of horror,
a denunciation of the duplicity and greed of the establishment –
members of the medical profession, powerful hospital administrators, and even government officials. Since millions of francs
were involved, a decision was taken not to "waste" French blood
reserves, although it became clear that these were 100% contam-
inated by high-risk donors and compromised by the French inability to heat plasma. Thus, the French National Transfusion Center,
headed by Michel Garretta, and the AIDS Hemophilia French
Study Group, created by Dr. Jean-Pierre Allain, continued their
"business as usual" procedures, infusing death with the life-giving
fluid. Both men have been sentenced to four years in prison, but a
new trial may reopen in criminal court. Using the facts carefully
researched by the journalist Anne-Marie Casteret, and presented in
her book, *L'Affaire du Sang*, Cixous put together an indictment
rooted family in the political scene, yet transcending time and
place thanks to Mnouchkine's retention of the Greek Tetralogy's
basic set. Thus, the theme of tainted blood becomes a symbol for all
forms of racism and persecution, for genocidal murder whether in
Nazi death camps or in Bosnia.

The play begins in the walled city where Agamemenon's army is awaiting the winds that will permit it to sail to Troy. Yet here, the two-sided enclosure which, in previous productions, suggested a bullfighting arena, is now made up of tombs, small monuments bearing Greek and Hebrew inscriptions, and frescoes not unlike those of Pompei. In more ways than one, this is the last stop, a vast necropolis where squatters make their home amid the bones of the dead. Indeed, homeless beggars appear, dressed in earth-tone rags. They come in limping, dragging their bundles. As they occupy the tombs, their oil lamps shine in the night, and their voices whisper, ghostly and sorrowful. They form the chorus of the new play whose connection to the *Atrides* cycle is further emphasized by the name of the cemetery guard, a gnarled crone perched upon scaffolding erected against the left wall, clearly a columbarium: this teller of the tale is "Aeschylus." Behind an upstage ornate fence, much like that of the Palais de Justice, a wall with a blind, bricked-up window reminds us that Justice is always blindfolded.

A prematurely grey-haired, pale young woman, the Mother (Renata Ramos Maza), settles on a mat she spreads at the center of the stage. She speaks of fleeing the forsworn city, but first she hopes to hear a request for a pardon from those who betrayed her trust, causing the death of her two young sons: doctors, lawyers, ministers, "wolves dressed in white gowns," shepherds who bleed their flocks. As she curls up on the mat, the ghosts of her two boys visit her in a dream. Two black-clad, black-hooded puppeteers, supposedly invisible according to the Bunraku tradition, each walking the puppet of a male child, enter behind the wrought-iron fence. Hélène Cixous and Ariane Mnouchkine suggest in this poetic fashion (Mnouchkine often combines various forms of Oriental, or Near Eastern theatre) that a crime was committed against leukemia-stricken children, infected by the transfusion of AIDS-tainted blood; the children were the unfortunate puppets in a medico-political in-fight.

The most poetic character of the play is Night, played by the company's tall dancer, Shahrock Meshkin Ghalam, who also played Apollo in *The Euménides*. Night's uncanny presence is evoked in Ghalam's slow, graceful crawl along the outside of the gate where, once on top, he remains perched like a wondrous bird.

Unlike Athena and Apollo, Maitre Maguerre and Maitre Brackman, in their flowing black robes, are a travesty of justice. They

fear disorder more than injustice. They are ready to grant the
mother reparations, but not an admission of their clients' guilt.
Soon, the three cackling Furies make their entrance, sent by Athena's democratic state. After 5,000 years underground, they have
resurfaced. "Look at the state of the planet," they shout. "Nothing
new except for the telephone." Cixous always keeps her sense of
humor. The Furies have a job to do in this modern so-called
democracy: they must bring the public servants to trial. In her
introduction to the play, Cixous tells a fable: "One day the lambs
found out that their shepards were actually wolves." Mnouchkine
and Cixous are the beautiful chimaeras who give voice to the
Furies' indignation. The play, which on weekends was given over
the matinee and evening with a break for a lovely buffet dinner,
served, as always, by members of the cast, could only gain by
judicious cuts. Although Cixous' text is poetic, this work is on the
didactic side, particularly its second part. Some scenes are played
in almost total darkness, an innovation for Mnouchkine who favors
dazzling lighting. Jean-Jacques Lemêtre's music, with the composer performing on instruments built or reconstructed for him,
always deepens and widens the spectacle.

The same month (June 1994), Cixous was represented in two
theatres at once. Her other play was written at the request of the
experimental, postmodern director, Daniel Mesguich. Entitled
L'Histoire (qu'on ne connaîtra jamais) [The History or Story One
Will Never Know], it is an amalgam of Snorri Sturison's *Younger
Edda*, the *Nibelungenlied*, and Wagner's *Gotterdämmerung*. It focuses
on the secret rivalry, jealousy, and murderous hate of two powerful
queens: Sigfrid's wife, Kriemhild, who will betray the secret of her
husband's vulnerability to the villainous Hagen, and Brunhild,
spouse of King Gunther, the gold-rich monarch of the Rhine.
Throughout the text, all manner of questions are being raised.
Was Brunhild Sigfrid's first love? Did he conquer her only to forget
her? Does she still pine for him? These questions remain unanswered, since the world of legend is stuck with the malady of
forgetfulness. Cixous suggests that historical facts are not retained
in any sequential or logical order in legend's poetic universe. They
leave a faint, puzzling trace, an ache like that experienced in a
severed, amputated limb.

For comic relief, and metatheatrical effect, there is a *Commedia*
character, a bald-headed, ancient woman (played by a young man

who shaved off his hair), who pops in and out of the prompter's box. His/her name is Edda, which in Icelandic means "great-grandmother" as well as "poetics." Although the poet is treated with respect, Edda is the butt of numerous jokes. She has the last laugh after her death when she is able to somersault and levitate at the same time, then, spreading her withered thighs, she urinates on the heads of those below who mistake this downpour for ill-smelling rain.

Cixous' new play is about many things: being a literary artist, the conscience and consciousness of one's age; being a teacher, a transmitter of half-forgotten fact and of the forgotten truth of God's word. It is principally about the pain of love and loss. It is as though the author had learned the bitter lesson of final repara-tion, irretrievable parting. Although still strikingly handsome, she has also glimpsed in the mirror time's cruel claw upon her face. And there must be deep pain at the thought of her "divorce" from Ariane Mnouchkine. This may account for the fact that their most recent endeavour was less successful in the eyes of the French and German press (although attendance was as strong as ever, with people crowding not only the benches but the aisle steps).

A new road lies ahead for the writer. Cixous' texts are dazzling as they come to life upon the stage, but they also stand up as works of literature upon which to carefully meditate. They were so when the two chimaeras worked in a state of deep communion. At present, the conjunction with Mesguich heralds all kinds of possib-ilities. *L'Histoire (qu'on ne connaîtra jamais)* was first presented in Paris at the Théâtre de la Ville and then at the National Theatre of Lille. Mesguich, who is known for the liberties he takes with texts, was completely faithful to Cixous' work, although he allowed his imagination to create wonderful images. One in particular comes to mind: Brunhild and Kriemhild circle around each other in a kind of *pavane*, their long trains, one golden, the other silver, slide over one another like snakes shedding their skin, then form a knot, a ring, perhaps the Nibelungen ring. At the Symposium which followed one of the Lille performances, Cixous stated graciously: "Daniel comes up with these wonderful gifts to my text."

The philsopher, Jacques Derrida, one of the panelists, presented his own gift in his summation: "This is drama of vast proportions because it tackles the very notion of what constitutes history. The writer deals with unrecorded history, facts buried in the soil of legend. Indeed, what do we know about the past, what is the nature of the knowable? Forgetfulness lies at the very core of memory."

Notes

1 *L'Indiade* was published by the Théâtre du Soleil, and sold as an extension of the program.

Castaret, Anne-Marie. *L'Affaire du Sang*. Paris: Editions La Decouverte, 1992.

Cixous, Hélène & Catherine Clément. *La Jeune Née*. Paris: Union Générale d'Éditions, 1975.

The Euménides. By Ariane Mnouchkine. Dir. Ariane Mnouchkine. Paris: Théâtre du Soleil, December, 1992.

Fagles, Robert & W.B. Stanford. Introduction. *The Oresteia*. By Aeschylus. Trans. Robert Fagles. New York: Viking Press, 1975.

Ferney, Frederic. Interview with Ariane Mnouchkine. *Le Figaro*. 13 November 1990. 33.

Gordon, Mary. "The Deadly Sins/Anger: The Fascination Begins in the Mouth." *New York Times Book Review*. (June 13, 1993): 31.

L'Histoire (qu'on ne connaîtra jamais). By Hélène Cixous. Dir. Daniel Mesguich. Paris: Théâtre de la Ville, June, 1994.

L'histoire terrible mais inachevée di Norodom Sihanouk, roi du Cambodge. By Hélène Cixous. Dir. Ariane Mnouchkine. Paris: Théâtre du Soleil, 1986.

L'Indiade ou l'Inde de leurs rêves. By Hélène Cixous. Dir. Ariane Mnouchkine. Paris: Théâtre du Soleil, 1987.

Paglia, Camille. *Sexual Personae: Art and Decadence from Nefertiti to Emily Dickinson*. New York: Vintage Books, 1991.

La Ville parjure ou le réveil des Eringe. By Hélène Cixous. Dir. Ariane Mnouchkine. Paris: Théâtre du Soleil, June, 1994.

13

The Self and "Other(s)" in
Cixous' *Sihanouk*

Cynthia Running-Johnson

It would seem that Hélène Cixous' play, *The Terrible but Unfinished Story of Norodom Sihanouk, King of Cambodia* (1985), marked a turning point in her work: movement from the body to history, from the self to others. Through theater she was, as she put it, venturing away from "those rare, desert places where only poems grow" to enter "the land of others" where "the self remains imperceptible" (*L'Indiade* 253).[1] *Sihanouk*, commissioned by director Ariane Mnouchkine to be part of the Théâtre du Soleil's cycle of history plays,[2] takes as its framework the period from 1955 to 1979 in Cambodia; it covers Sihanouk's various exiles from his country and the rise of the Khmers Rouges. Cixous followed *Sihanouk* with two works which also evidence openness to the international political scene: her play, *The Indiade or the India of Their Dreams* (1987) and her long prose-poem, *Manna* (1988).[3]

Sihanouk appeared at a propitious moment, at least as far as the reception of Cixous' work by scholars in this country was concerned. The publication and mise en scène of the play corresponded to the burgeoning of cultural studies, especially in the U.S., and seemed a response to critics of her earlier theoretical concept of "écriture féminine." They were – and still are – accusing her of denying "les autres" in her apparent privileging of "woman" over "women" in all of women's diversity of class, race, culture, and sexual orientation. They have seen her as trapped in the essentializing category of the feminine "other," or as caught up in post-structuralist games which remained detached from the concerns of the exterior, material(ist) worlds.[4]

Although Cixous' "theoretical" work has generally been perceived as being too close to the body – like a too-clingy, too-"feminine" slip, some have suggested that Cixous, in her silky subtlety, has been giving us all the subversive slip.[5] I have more often been of this second opinion. Although troubled by the essentialism of her notion of the "feminine," I have also found Cixous' theoretical writings – such works as "The Laugh of the Medusa," *The Newly-born Woman*, "Coming to Writing," her plays *The Name of Oedipus* and *Portrait of Dora*, and her various shorter pieces on theater – to exceed the frames that are placed around them. Like critic Anu Aneja, I admire Cixous' subversion of the traditional division between poetry and theory and see potential in Cixous' linking of work on language with political change.

Sihanouk, appearing at a time when Cixous was presenting herself as turning from the "le féminin" to "l'humain,"[6] is a strange hybrid of the two tendencies: of focus on "l'autre" – a term coming out of her concept of "écriture féminine," indicating the acceptance of and engagement with that which is different; and concern with including "les autres," which more precisely refers to individuals or groups of people. In my essay, I will examine the author's movement outward in this play – explore the ways in which she includes "les autres"; look at this change in direction in relation to her theoretical writing of the seventies; and, finally, discuss the success and desirability of Cixous' project to inhabit a space in which "the self remains imperceptible."

In Cixous' theoretical/theatrical writings appended to *The Indiade*, the author links her movement away from the region of "le moi" with theater. It is only on stage, she says, that she can permit others to speak, that her "self" does not monopolize the creative space. She began her escape from "le moi" with her earlier dramatic pieces, notably *Portrait of Dora* (1976) and *The Name of Oedipus* (1978). In both it was a question of rewriting myth – modern myth in the case of Freud's Dora, ancient myth (with important modern and contemporary resonances) in the other. In the two plays, although the author shifts the frames through which the stories have traditionally been seen, the rewriting still inscribes

itself in certain hierarchal structures.[7] But Cixous' choice of drama
as an arena for interrogating these myths is an important aspect of
her movement toward "les autres." Drama's possibility of involving other participants – creators of a production of the play as
well as its audience – moves the interior, psychoanalytic aspects of
those "universal" stories outward from the self, into the open.[8]

With *Sihanouk*, which appeared seven years after *The Name of
Oedipus*, Cixous moved from writing a potential production to
collaboration with a particular director. Although the writing of
the play was not the fruit of the Théâtre du Soleil's improvisation,
it involved close work with Mnouchkine and, as the published text
notes, included modifications by the troupe during the rehearsal
period. As Cixous explains in the essays following *The Indiade*, she
was enchanted by the work of the company, fascinated by the
actors' "mothering" of her characters and dialogue. And it was
she who had chosen to make her work available to that additional
creative activity – to the activity of others.

As far as the text of the play itself is concerned, Cixous' most
obvious inclusion of "les autres" in *Sihanouk* lies in her use of a
different culture – an eastern rather than a western culture – as a
setting. This choice (Mnouchkine's and hers) corresponded to
a general interest in the culturally "other" in French theater at
the time. The major production of the year, for example, was
Peter Brook's and Jean-Claude Carrière's telling of Indian creation
myth, *Le Mahabarata;* and the Festival d'Avignon that summer
featured theater and dance from India. *Sihanouk*, which is in fact
two plays in one, called "Première Epoque" and "Deuxième Epoque" (an eight-hour production in Mnouchkine's hands), is
"autre" in time as well as location, a chronological depiction of
events from the fifties through the seventies. In addition, it not only
follows Sihanouk, as the title would indicate, but other actors on
the southeast Asian scene. The sheer number of "others" in the
play is impressive: over fifty characters, half of whom play quite
substantial parts in the action by the conclusion of the "Deuxième
Epoque." The roles include the various and often warring elements
of the Cambodian government(s), the leaders of China, the Soviet
Union and Vietnam, and American political and military men such
as Kissinger and Laird. Sharing the stage with the famous figures
are lesser-known or invented characters including Sihanouk's wife,
mother and the mother's best friend, two village women, a war

orphan, the ghost of Sihanouk's father, and the growing number of additional dead. Cixous thereby shows the "other" of official History: the voices of the people as well as of the ruling groups.[9] By including characters outside of the historical "names," she is able to increase the number of women characters, as well.

It is through the outsiders in the group of characters – outsiders because of their class, sex, nationality or exile from the world of the living – that the author is able to propose different social relations among people, as well. In contrast to the incessant changing of loyalties on the level of Cambodian international politics, the fast friendships among the "excluded" are striking. The relationship of love and generosity between Khieu Samnol and her friend Madame Lamné, both market vendors, for example, counters the coldness or madness of most of the politicians and military men. (It is the Khmers Rouges who are the most negatively presented in the play; in Khieu Samnol's words, "they're so strange and unnatural . . . they don't know how to live, or laugh, or taste anymore" [54 – 5]).[10] The two women keep each other physically and emotionally alive during the years of want and political oppression of the reign of the Khmers Rouges and take an orphan, Yukanthor, under their wing, as well. A similar relationship exists between two other of the main women characters, who come this time from the upper class: Sihanouk's mother, Kossomak, and her friend, Mom Savay, who also happens to have been her husband's mistress.[11] The two pairs of women cross class lines and interact at certain points, providing additional help to each other: in the first play, Kossomak is inspired by a conversation with the two village women to call her wandering son back to Cambodia (III, 4), and in a lively scene in the second half of the work, the queen concocts a scam which insures that Khieu Samnol and Madame Lamné will avoid starvation (IV, 4).

Members of the ever-increasing number of the dead also display these characteristics of fidelity and generosity – often accompanied by a charming naïveté, as in the case of Sihanouk's father, Suramarit. Consulted by his son on political matters, Suramarit seems less concerned with the changing political tides than with whether or not the men in power have wives (being married is, to him, an indication of their humanity) and whether Sihanouk has remembered to bring him the daily paper. Finally, Sihanouk himself, different from most of the other public figures in the play, has traits that one may associate with an "other" societal way of being. Although able to modify his political allegiances with the best of them,[12] his major concern is the well-being of his country and of his compatriots – a heartfelt, even bodily identification with Cambodia, as translated in the following lines: "I can no longer stop from being Cambodia. I have myself become these rivers, these streams, these mountains, and all of the country-people who inhabit me" (165). Even the leader's political shrewdness seems more associated with the down-to-earth attitudes of his country's "others" in this play – characters such as the two village women – than with the almost machine-like, dangerously utopian dreams of leaders like Khieu Samphan. The Khmers Rouges official imagines early on in the play "a perfect society" in which "we would erase everything. We would clear out the towns. We would start the world anew. . ." (60–61) – a vision whose beginning, at least, is realized in the second play, in the communists' disastrous evacuation of Phnom Penh.

It is noteworthy that the characteristics of the societal "others" in this play correspond to those which Cixous had, in the seventies, associated with her concept of "écriture féminine": generosity, acceptance of that which is different, profusion (here, profusion of sentiment), movement and energy.[13] Appropriately, the language of the "good" characters often takes on those same traits – a sometimes playful, sometimes poetically dense speech, reminiscent of Cixous' libidinal, "feminine" writing. Sihanouk, for example, spars cleverly with his political adversaries, at one point expanding on the American ambassador's reference to Cambodia as "your little country"(64) to emit a string of "petit"s as a linguistic demonstration of how "[y]ou are methodically shrinking us": "First Cambodia is little, then it is very little, the next day I read that it is extremely little, there it is, minute, it's the pocket-sized kingdom, it's an eleventh toe, it's a speck in your eye, it's a crust, it's invisible! . . . But I am here, Sihanouk is here, Cambodia exists!" (65).[14] This accumulation of "littles" finally and paradoxically produces, of course, the opposite effect of enlarging Sihanouk's – and therefore, perhaps, Cambodia's – presence in the perception of the assembled politicians on stage. More often, certain more serious speeches by Sihanouk, his counselor Penn Nouth, the queen Kossomak, the Princess, and the Khmers Rouges leader Houn Youn (after his "conversion" to the more benign world of the

dead) display a particular sensitivity to the sound and connotations of words. Penn Nouth's invocation at the end of the first play
– when Sihanouk has decided to accept the help of the communists
– exemplifies this use of language, with its repetitions and rhymes
("pas"/"là-bas"; "sillon"/"étions"/ "reviendrons"), and with its
assonance ([ã]) and alliteration ([v], [s] and [r]):

> . . . [V]ous qui veillez sur le Cambodge,
> Génies des arbres et des eaux,
> Génies des routes et des sillons,
> Ne vous en allez pas, restez là-bas.
> Grandes et petites puissances,
> Vous qui nous aimiez tant
> Lorsque nous étions riches et heureux,
> N'oubliez pas de vous rendre le soir
> Au bord du fleuve
> Et de nous rappeler.
> Nous reviendrons, nous reviendrons.

> . . . [Y]ou who watch over Cambodia,
> Genies of the trees and waters,
> Genies of the roads and furrows,
> Do not leave, stay where you are.
> Great and small powers,
> You who loved us so
> When we were rich and happy,
> Do not forget to go every evening
> To the banks of the river
> And call us back.
> We will return, we will return. (190)

Cixous' play with language is often, at the same time, metapoe-
tic: her highlighting of the figure of the metaphor in the play is
striking. *Sihanouk* is filled with comparisons and allegorical stories
involving natural elements – in correspondence, one would sup-
pose, with the integrality of such elements in eastern culture: in
oriental art, religion, and both literary and everyday language.
Cixous draws attention to these nature comparisons through repetition, in some cases to underline and make more profound the
tragedy of the situations which she is describing, in others to
complement the tragedy of the play with humor. In the case of

tragedy, it is the metaphor of the river – "le fleuve" – that is most noticeable and effective in *Sihanouk*. It flows throughout the play, used largely to describe the Cambodian people – most often, their suffering. In the "Deuxième Epoque," for example, one of the dead describes the mass exodus from Phnom Penh as follows: "On route 6 flows the slow, blind river, the human river," where he sees Khieu Samnol and Madame Lamné "[f]loating on the crowd like two dead leaves" (313).

More frequently, nature metaphors are a source of humor, usually through their accumulation or their misinterpretation by the characters. In a scene near the beginning of the play, Sihanouk is announcing his abdication of the throne in order to run for prime minister in the next government. His language consists of a series of comparisons involving various animals which, echoed by the chants of the musician, pile up to the point of ridiculousness. Near the end of the scene, one of the rival nobles is speaking of Sihanouk's placement on the Cambodian throne by the French fifteen years earlier:

SIRIK MATAK: You weren't so proud then, and you clung to the throne that was being stolen from us, screeching like a wildcat.

SIHANOUK: A cat! You lie, snake! I am a tiger and my mother is a lioness! Go on, renounce the crown; it's flying too high for you, up there with the eagles. (46)

As Sihanouk exits the room at the end of the scene, the musician adds to the menagerie by intoning, "Leaving is the Maddest of the Mad Who is the Strongest of the Strong in this kingdom. The lion-est, the hare-est, the eagle-est" ["le plus lion, le plus lièvre, le plus aigle"] (48). In an earlier scene, the character Khieu Samnol comments on her own misunderstanding of a metaphor and thereby underscores the refreshing openness and warm humor of her character. When her son, communist official Khieu Samphan, was young, she says that it was predicted, "'If your child does not fall under the claws of a wild beast, he will fly very high.' And to this day, I thought he would be an airplane pilot!" (53). Later in the scene, after her son expresses his idea of wiping out the existing Cambodia to create a new, perfect society, she says, creating a metaphor of her own: "I wish he would have become an airplane pilot, instead. At least up there they fly on real clouds!" (61).

The poetic element of Cixous' text appears not only in her language but in the scenic aspect of *Sihanouk*, as well. Near the beginning of the play, the two village women give their old bicycle to the wandering ghost of Sihanouk's father, who appears on it several times in the course of the work. His pedaling across the stage on the rickety machine scenically represents his freedom in death and reinforces his quaint charm, providing a breathing space in the lengthy parade of political events. Memorable also is the image of Sihanouk and the Princess flying above the clouds near the end of the first play, imagining how their life might have turned out had Sihanouk not been placed on the Cambodian throne. Sihanouk describes the clouds and, according to a rare stage direction, the clouds appear on stage, their denseness mirroring his feeling of separation from his compatriots:

> O my people. O my children! . . . Ah! But where are my people? Where are my people going? And where am I going? When will I find them again? The clouds are so thick, like frozen ground dividing us from the living land. ([Sihanouk and the Princess] exit and the clouds do, as well). (166)

Although I have described at some length these moments of poetry, it must be said that, when one considers the play as a whole, they are relatively few, lost in the morass of expository, prosaic dialogue. The characters whom I have linked with the "feminine," representatives of an alternative economy based upon acceptance rather than exclusion, appear quite infrequently. And it is obvious that they have little or no control over the larger – mainly disastrous – events on the political scene. At the end of the play, Sihanouk is left wandering, firmly pushed out of the country by Pol Pot; the characters belonging to the "petit peuple," Madame Lamné and her adopted son, are watched by the dead as they escape to Thailand. The only hope is expressed – typically, for Cixous – in terms of writing, of language and the voice. In Sihanouk's last lines, he speaks of writing the story/history ("l'histoire") of Cambodia, a story which, as his wife says, as the title of the play indicates and as the world has seen in the meantime, "is not finished" (404). In the final scene, peopled by the assembled dead and two surviving members of "le peuple," Suramarit and

Kossomak speak of the necessity of preserving "our language, our sweet Khmer tongue" (407); and the queen hopes that the spreading of the news about Cambodia will cause others to come to its aid: "There are so many of us, we the people of the Cambodian dead, so many that maybe if we all yell together then, maybe, the faint cry of all our people will be heard by someone, there amidst the loud noise of the living. . . " (411). Although a certain optimism emerges at the end, then, the overall effect is one of sadness. The qualities of the "good" characters may correspond to those which Cixous connected with the "feminine"; but, largely relegated to a position of ineffectuality, these characters do not have the subversive effect which Cixous saw as the outcome of the "feminine" practice of writing and being in the world.

Of course, it is impossible for the author to escape the course of past history and politics in a play which is created for the purpose of treating those subjects. Because Cixous has taken as her framework a situation in which the ordinary people of the country had no say in political events, it is only natural for *Sihanouk* to reflect that reality. But, at the same time, Cixous quite inexplicably reinforces the oppression represented in the play with restrictiveness on other levels of the text, as well. The author chooses to devote most of the script's 411 pages to the details of the long, quite complex political story, and includes comparatively few of the scenes or passages which let her poetic voice be heard. Certain aspects of the text correspond to her political/aesthetic view of a non-hierarchical style of writing: she uses the character of Sihanouk as a link among the various scenes but does not center the story on him; and she builds the plot around a period of Cambodian history that contains dramatic events such as the evacuation of Phnom Penh by the Khmers Rouges without culminating in a single climax. But the excessive length of the play moves it into a more burdensome mode. Might it not be said that the apparent refusal of the play to come to an end, even at the end, as Sihanouk (again) discusses the possibility of yet another return to Cambodia is, in fact, a sign of an impulse to mastery? A frustration of "jouissance" – a multiple frustration – rather than a celebration of "feminine" multiplicity? In her play, Cixous constantly criticizes the hegemony, the ruthlessness of the American government, then of the Khmers Rouges; and yet her own text often seems controlling, forcing us through numbness or a sense of duty to stay with the script until the play is finished.

In the context of the play as a whole, even the characters whom I have seen as reminiscent of Cixous' "feminine" contribute, to a certain degree, to the claustrophobic aspect of the work. The exaggerated difference established between the good characters and the bad – a strange choice in a work which shows such concern with historical accuracy – lends *Sihanouk* a moralizing tone that becomes more oppressive as the play goes on.[15] The kind of satirical presentation of excessive power seen here (for example, in the portrayal of a figure like Kissinger as outrageously mad and puppet-like), a representation which may have shocked or delighted in past decades, has now lost its force.

Sihanouk might be contrasted with Jean Genet's play, *Les Paravents*, in terms of its degree of dogmatism and associated dramatic effectiveness. *Les Paravents*, another long work which also takes as its subject struggles for power in a former colonialist region, avoids moralizing and, instead, more productively interrogates differences through the presentation of its main characters. The characters Saïd, Leila and the Mother exist outside the binary of politically and morally good and bad, and even, in the case of the first two, outside the division between dead and alive: they escape both groups by simply disappearing by the end of the play. The ambiguous result is much more satisfying than the morally simplistic *Sihanouk*.

Cixous' decision to not only include but let dominate the political "Others" – those of (official) History – in her text finally, then, works to suppress "the other," reducing the profusion and liveliness of her writing. At the same time, however, Cixous does treat another aspect of History – one which she knows more intimately – with more nuance and, therefore, more success: she engages with her own literary/theatrical tradition. Part of Cixous' interrogation of her cultural past consists of references to western dramatists: Shakespeare and, less directly, the "modern classic" author, Genet. As Liliana Alexandrescu has shown, both covert and more subtle allusions to Shakespeare abound in the text, from the pointedly appropriate quoting of Hamlet's and Polonious' conversation on the shapes of clouds (IV, 3, "Deuxième Epoque") to the *Hamlet*-like presence of the father's ghost. Genet's voice echoes in the naïvely poetic tone of much of the dialogue and in the non-psychological

representation of the characters. More specific parallels between
Sihanouk and *Les Paravents* are also evident, including their eastern-
colonial setting, their length, and the accumulation of the "living"
dead on stage. Cixous' reference to these dramatic creators serves
to underline the ways in which her text varies from the classic
form. For example, although she divides each play into the traditional five acts, she organizes the action less conventionally, with a
circular rather than mounting structure – Sihanouk ever returning
to his state of wandering exile rather than definitively rising or
falling, succeeding or failing. Cixous' use of metaphor is a more
generalized reference to literary tradition, in this case not limited to
the west; here, too, as previously shown, she embroiders on the
past, in her extensive commentary on and playing with the figure.
Through her highlighting of metaphor and her reference to preceding theatrical models, Cixous is examining her position as a
contemporary writer – her equivocal position vis-à-vis past practices and conventions.

   This element of the text places her at an interesting point in the
context of current artistic discourse and production. The present
scene has been cogently described by art critic Mark Stevens in a
review article on two contrasting exhibits from the spring of 1993 –
the Whitney Biennial and a show by painter Susan Rothenberg.
Although Stevens comments on specifically visual art in his piece, I
believe that what he says is transferable to dramatic and literary
artistic creation. In his opinion, the artists displaying work at the
Whitney are over-concerned with the value of their pieces as political and moral statements and do themselves the disservice of
ignoring the work that has preceded them; they are forced to rely
solely upon themselves rather than on tradition and thus to be
"nothing less than astonishing" (38) – which they unfortunately
are not, in his opinion. Rothenberg, on the other hand, is engaging
with tradition rather than bypassing it, "welcoming the past into
her work in the hopes of finding a present" (42). (This is Stevens'
way of dealing with the contemporary confrontation that is too
often and too easily put in terms of aesthetics vs. politics.) In
Sihanouk, Cixous, similar to Rothenberg, both refers to her lit-
erary/dramatic tradition and creatively moves beyond it; but she
does not do so to the same extent as the painter has. Cixous seems
dogged at every step by the overwhelming weight of her subject,
by her exaggerated concern with presenting the complexity of the

political situation and by her didactic portrayal of certain characters' moral degradation.

It would seem, then, that Cixous might have done better in
Sihanouk to affirm rather than deny her "self," her past – which
includes the poetry of her "écriture féminine." The author might
have been advised to let herself be carried by her own river of
writing, to permit her historical "moi" to productively show itself
rather than working to make it "imperceptible"; to avoid dimin-
ishing the "other" by welcoming too many of the "Others." However, Cixous certainly must be applauded for venturing into such a
new and vast territory: the domaine of History – of an "other"
history, especially, in conjunction with Mnouchkine and her
troupe. And the play is fascinating as a record of the cultural and
artistic moment in which it appeared – a period which, as Stevens'
article would indicate, has continued to more recent years. Cixous'
text, an ambitious effort to establish dialogue between genres
(poetry and theater), between the past and the present, there and
here, and politics and art, shows the complexity of negotiating
those differences.

Notes

1. Translations from French to English in this essay are my own.
2. *Sihanouk* was the first of a series of plays by the Théâtre du Soleil which were to be a "history of our time" (Kiernander 188). These productions had been prepared by the troupe's mise en scène of three Shakespearean history plays: *Richard II* (1981), *La Nuit des rois* (1982), and *Henry IV* (1984). *Sihanouk* (1985) was followed by another commissioned "documentary" work by Cixous, *L'Indiade ou l'Inde de leurs rêves* (1987). An additional collaborational play about women poets in Stalinist Russia, entitled *Voile noire, voile blanche*, was announced several years ago; but with a parting of the ways between Cixous and Mnouchkine, it was not staged.
3. *The Indiade* takes as its subject the later life and times of Ghandi, and *Manna* is based upon the figures Winnie and Nelson Mandela and the Russian poet Osip Mandelstam.
4. See Anu Aneja and Robert Con Davis, who summarize and, in the case of Davis, uphold the major critiques of Cixous' "écriture féminine," particularly concerning the relationship of Cixous' concept to the social.
5. See Anu Aneja, who created part of this metaphor.
6. At a seminar held on Cixous' work at the University of Utrecht in May 1987, the author said that her interest was no longer concentrated on "la féminité" but, rather, "l'humanité."
7. See, for example, Jeannette Savona.
8. Cixous describes these "others" of dramatic creation in the following lines from her essay, "L'Incarnation": "Theater is the palace of others. It lives off of the desire of the other, of all others. And on the desire of the desire of others: the audience, the actors" (*L'Indiade* 260).
9. In her essay, "Le lieu du Crime, le lieu du Pardon," Cixous describes the possibilities that drama offers her as writer. In her fiction, she says, she could not give an "illiterate countrywoman" (a reference to Khieu

Samnol or Madame Lamné in *Sihanouk*) the chance to talk "without taking [the woman's speech] back, in one fell swoop of my own, without burying her in one of my well-made sentences"; in theater, however, she can let this woman speak (*L'Indiade* 253). Similarly, theater gives her the possibility of including men in her work. Whereas in fiction it is the body that speaks – and she, as a woman, can only write (about) woman's pleasure – in theater, "it is the heart which sings, . . . [and] the human heart has no sex" (265-66).

10. Morag Shiach notes the intersection of Cixous' and Mnouchkine's own political journey as French leftists during the seventies with that of various factions in Cambodia at the time: the initial support of the left for the Khmers Rouges (many of whom had studied in France) and its subsequent disenchantment with the group's increasingly violent solutions (126-27). That rejection is reflected in the play in Cixous' treatment of the Khmers Rouges as "unnatural": efficaciously cruel at their worst and tragically misguided at best.

11. It is interesting that in both pairs of women there is an inherent motive for the two members of the couple to dislike each other: for the queen Kossomak and Mom Savay to feel jealous of each other because they shared Suramarit, for Khieu Samnol and Madame Lamné to distrust each other because they come from different, sometimes warring, countries, Cambodia and Vietnam. The mutual loyalty of the women is all the more striking for these reasons.

12. After joining with the communists at the end of the first play, Sihanouk says, "All of these good reasons [for our union with Hanoi] / Are worth more than a fragile sincerity" (207).

13. For Cixous' discussion of "écriture féminine," see especially "The Laugh of the Medusa" and "Coming to Writing."

14. The passage in French is as follows:
    D'abord le Cambodge est petit, ensuite il est très petit, le lendemain je lis qu'il est extrêmement petit, le voilà minuscule, c'est le royaume de poche, c'est un reste inutile, c'est un onzième orteil, c'est une poussière dans votre oeil, c'est une croûte, c'est un rien! . . . Mais je suis là, Sihanouk est là, le Cambodge existe! (65)

15. See Anne-Marie Picard for a commentary on what she sees as the tautological and didactic nature of Cixous' next play, *The Indiade*.

Works Cited

Alexandrescu, Liliana. "*Norodom Sihanouk*: l'inachevé comme lecture shakespearienne de l'histoire contemporaine." *Hélène Cixous, chemins d'une écriture*. Ed. Françoise van Rossum-Guyon and Myriam Díaz-Diocaretz. Amsterdam: Rodopi, 1990. 187-204.

Aneja, Anu. "The Medusa's Slip: Hélène Cixous and the Underpinnings of *écriture féminine*." *LIT* 4.1 (1992): 17-27.

Cixous, Hélène. *"Coming to Writing" and Other Essays*. Trans. Sarah Cornell, et al. Cambridge: Harvard UP, 1991.

___. *L'Histoire terrible mais inachevée de Norodom Sihanouk, roi du Cambodge*. Paris: Théâtre du Soleil, 1985.

——. *L'Indiade ou l'Inde de leurs rêves, et quelques écrits sur le théâtre*. Paris: Théâtre du Soleil, 1987.

——. "The Laugh of the Medusa." Trans. Keith Cohen and Paula Cohen. *New French Feminisms*. Ed. Elaine Marks and Isabelle de Courtivron. New York: Schocken Books, 1981. 245-67.

Davis, Robert Con. "Cixous, Spivak and Oppositional Theory." *LIT* 4.1 (1992): 29-42.

Kiernander, Adrian. "The Orient, the Feminine: The Use of Interculturalism by the Théâtre du Soleil." *Gender in Performance: The Presentation of Difference in the Performing Arts*. Ed. Laurence Senelick. Hanover, NH: UP of New England, 1992. 183-92.

Picard, Anne-Marie. "*L'Indiade*: Ariane's and Hélène's Conjugate Dreams." *Modern Drama* 32.1 (1989): 24-38.

Savona, Jeannette Laillou. "In Search of a Feminist Theater: *Portrait of Dora*." *Feminine Focus: The New Women Playwrights*. Ed. Enoch Brater, 1989. 94-108.

Shiach, Morag. *Hélène Cixous: A Politics of Writing.* London: Routledge, 1991.
Stevens, Mark. "Brushes with Art." *New Republic* 17 (May 1993): 36-42.

Works Consulted

Canning, Charlotte. "'The Critic as Playwright: Performing Hélène Cixous' *Le Nom d'Oedipe*." *LIT* 4.1 (1992): 43-55.

Cixous, Hélène. "Aller à la mer." *Modern Drama*. Trans. Barbara Kerslake. 27 (1984): 546-48.

——. "From the Scene of the Unconscious to the Scene of History." Trans. Deborah W. Carpenter. *The Future of Literary Theory*. Ed. Ralph Cohen. New York and London: Routledge, 1989. 1-18.

——. *Le Nom d'Oedipe*. Paris: Editions des femmes, 1978.

——. *Portrait de Dora. Hélène Cixous: Théâtre.* Paris: Editions des femmes, 1976.

Négron Marrero, Mara. "Comment faire pour écrire l'histoire poétique-ment/ou comment faire pour ne pas oublier." *Hélène Cixous, chemins d'une écriture*. Ed. Françoise van Rossum-Guyon and Myriam Díaz-Diocaretz. Amsterdam: Rodopi, 1990. 205-12.

van Rossum-Guyon, Françoise. "A propos de *Manne*. Entretien avec Hélène Cixous. Ed. Françoise van Rossum-Guyon and Myriam Díaz-Diocaretz. 213-34.

14

Bringing a Historical Character on Stage: L'Indiade

Liliana Alexandrescu

It's the gift theater gives the author: incarnation.

-Hélène Cixous[1]

Theater as religion

"I need heaven for theater to exist. And for the terrestrial scene to be reflected in the celestial" (247). So begins Hélène Cixous' collection of essays, *Écrits sur le théâtre*, published as a sequel to *L'Indiade*. The immense panorama that she spreads before our eyes, stretching to the horizon and beyond – "clouds, sky, sun of the human heart" – puts us at once in the center of a vision of lived history on the scale of the sacred. Indeed, in the definition Cixous gives us, theater is the space where the individual experiences his existence "as an atom in space, as a moment of Time, as a question in the millenial dialogue between man and the Gods" (248). We are looking at a religious approach to theater here, seen as a mystery and secret rite, revealing to us the hidden meaning of our acts and histories, "the faces hidden behind faces" (254). Thus man in the *Indiade* "is not without the stars" (248). It is through his rapport with the stars, the celestial authority, that he grasps the extent of his terrestrial dimension. "I confess that theater is a form of religion," Hélène Cixous declares in her chapter, "Le lieu du Crime, le lieu du Pardon" (256). What takes place in theater is the Passion, but the Passion according to Oedipus, according to Hamlet, according to Woyzzeck, "according to me" (253).

It is while reflecting on writing for the theater in her article, "De la scène de l'Inconscient à la scène de l'Histoire," that Cixous discusses good and evil, heaven and hell. In the beginning, there is hell, the feeling of being formless, insignificant, wicked: "Our wickedness is one of the breathtaking themes that occupy the realm of writing" (Van Rossum-Guyon, *Chemins* 226).[2] But what is heaven? Cixous asks. We write in order to leave hell for what proves to be the present. For that is what heaven is: coming to live in the present. Our happiness means being in the absolute present: "Here I come back to the problematics of theater"(*Chemins* 226). For theater, as an expression of the spiritual incarnated in the perishable, is always in the present, tightly bound in its portrayals to the ephemeral substance of the body. Working in theater means accepting the fragility of the present, confining oneself to its con-solidation and becoming the "prophet of the present." But living entirely in the present requires an unceasing effort "of being there." Admitted for an instant into heaven – this "balcony over the hells of earth" – the writer must plunge again and again into these hells, the burning source of his prophecies. "That is why I sometimes say: 'Heaven is hellish'" (*Chemins* 22). A world in which the text is so saturated with religious expression naturally has its saints, angels, and miracles. In the *Indiade* it is the She-Bear who, chained or unchained, drags us through arduous tracks which may lead us to Paradise: "by caressing the She-Bear, we scratch at the gates of the Lord" (249). As for the Angel of this hagiography – the angel "who is perhaps no more than a plumed bear" – he is there too: he is "that bear without a single hair which is Gandhi" (250–251).

Questioned as to her relationship with faith and Christianity, Hélène Cixous denies having a religion. She admits, however, that she is not without links to a space that approximates religious space. A Jew, she rejects the image of Christianity which was, in her childhood, an inimical image. Nevertheless, the words she places in Gandhi's mouth carry a Christian resonance: love one another. This seeming paradox becomes congruous when we remember that Jesus' *Sermon on the Mount* was a turning point in the development of Gandhi's thought. But Cixous' are not explicit allusions to Christianity: they "are rather images" (*Chemins* 222). Nonetheless, the resulting world vision is so clearly imbued with Catholic Christian thought that a Bossuet would not disavow it. Certain passages from the *Écrits sur le théâtre* make us think of Saint Theresa of Avila and her spiritual exercises:

"Il m'est arrivé de me presque mourir en donnant vie à Toi.... Comment arrive cette perte de vie? Cela se passe ainsi: on écrit une scène, de tout son coeur. Le coeur devient la scène. Le monde exterieur a disparu. Plus d'espace, le temps disparaît ....Les larmes je leur fais barrage. Humble scribe d'une douleur mondiale que je suis, je ne dois pas avoir de coeur, seulement des oreilles pour recueillir les plaintes des désespérés, et pour les transcrire. Pas de pitié, car autrement pas d'écriture....Et à la fin le coeur de l'auteur qui est resté immobile et impassible comme la scène du Théatre, pour laisser s'inscrire la Passion, le coeur grossi de larmes interdites, éclate. Pas avant la fin. À la fin le barrage cède, et sous le flot, l'on perd conscience." (*L'Indiade* 277–278)

"There were times when I almost died giving life to You....How does this loss of life occur? It happens so: you write a scene, from the bottom of your heart. The heart becomes the scene. The external world disappears. No more space, time disappears....I stop the flood of tears. Humble scribe that I am of a universal pain, I should not have a heart, only ears to gather the laments of the hopeless, and to transcribe them. No pity, for otherwise there can be no writing....And finally, the author's heart, which has remained still and impassive, like the Theater stage, to allow Passion to make its mark, the heart swollen with forbidden tears, bursts. Not before the end. At the end, the dam gives way, and under the flood, you lose consciousness."

Irresistably before me rises, in the superhuman flight of her marble folds, Bernini's Saint Theresa, ready to be pierced by the arrow of the divine messenger, her soul transported by ecstasy, her body abandoned, her face raised, transfigured in a mortal and blessed expectation.

Theater as History

The question of history in theater is not simply a question of period and subject, but also one of form, of literary genre. "I was not born a playwright," declares Hélène Cixous (*Chemins* 24). When one is a "writer of fiction," to be able to engage theater, one must do one's apprenticeship, what Cixous calls the "less and less of me, more and more of you." This apprenticeship first comprehends the *inside*, that space where one comes to know the mythologies, where one rediscovers all that happens at the bottom, that which is suppressed, that which is "always on the level of the epic" (*Chemins* 24). Then, one can hope that the me, after this plunge, will agree to give way and become, not the hero of the scene, but the scene itself, "the place, the situation of the other," which is specifically "the scene of History" (*Chemins* 25). Thus, while saying, "Gandhi is the one person who I will never be," Cixous recreates Gandhi on stage by drawing on her own ambivalence to give expression to the Other (*Chemins* 232).

In 1971, while she was composing her first grand historical fresco, *La Pupille* (a stage version of a prose work, *Révolutions pour plus d'un Faust*), Hélène Cixous was haunted by the image of a story similar to Macbeth, made of sound and fury. Even while assuming in it a coherence at the level of the tale, she was mistrustful, feeling that she was a receptor as far removed from the scene of the action "as an ethnographer of myths he is analyzing" (32). This displacement will be overcome, Cixous argues in the preface to *L'Indiade ou l'Inde de leurs rêves*: when the author claims that her heros' souls are cut from the stuff of myth, she will have entirely taken upon herself their superhuman tension. She will no longer be the observer but the interpretor of the dreams and destinies of another people of another continent. It is with the play *La prise de l'école de Madhubai* (1984) that Cixous broaches for the first time the subject of India in theater. Its central figure is Sakundeva, a woman of extraordinary character who is transformed, through her daring and force, from a slave to a rebel and queen. Here for the first time, Cixous introduces the heroic material which will engender her two grand theatrical epics *L'histoire tragique mais inachevée de Norodom Sihanouk, roi du Cambodge* (1985) and *L'Indiade* (1987). In the introduction to *Prise de l'école de Madhubai*, entitled "Le droit de légende," Hélène Cixous gives us a definition of theater writing bound in space, both interior and exterior: writing for the theater is "taking distance from oneself, leaving, traveling a long time in the darkness... until one reawakes transformed" into someone else at the other end of the world (4). Thus, she continues, if I can remove myself, "my soul and me," all the way to India, this means that human beings are not so separated and impenetrable as all that and that feelings "survive in many Indias of the planet" (4). We observe in passing that India, in this context, is already in the process of becoming a measure of humanity. The theater is precisely the place which ought to show us our true dimension "in keeping with the mysteries," our depths, our heights, "our interior Indias"(6). For, according to Cixous, the theater must be "the realm of legends" for us. On stage, people like ourselves, but transfigured, are present to remind us that, if we choose, we can still be the stuff of legends today (7).

Seen from all sides, the figure of History in theater stands out more and more clearly at the center of Hélène Cixous' universe and thought. Her meeting with Ariane Mnouchkine and the Théâtre du Soleil hastened its crystalization. As Mara Negrón Marrero explains in her study on Cixous' theatrical oeuvre, "That *Sihanouk* saw the light of day was also thanks to the existence of the Théâtre du Soleil. It expanded [the play's] poetic course maintaining its original goal: the march toward the other" (*Chemins* 208). Soleil's "créations collectives" – *1789* and *1793* (1970–73) and the subsequent *L'Âge d'or* (1975) were meant to broach the question of history solely through theatrical means, without author or text: "make no more of a spectacle than what it is: a moment in the quest of a theater for the present."[3] "We want to tell our history to make it go forward – if this could be the role of theater" (*L'Age* 14). Nevertheless, in 1981, finding themselves at a turning point in their quest, Mnouchkine and her company came up against a difficult question: how to come to grips with modern themes and resolve their confrontations with the immediate world on stage, that magic place where "the transformation of the real into poetic metaphor" happens (Moscoso 6). In other words, while keeping a distance from yet permitting a flashing perception of the instant, what methods must we apply in order to understand and portray the modern epoch for ourselves: "What forms of narrative could be born of the history of our times?" (Moscoso 6). In the face of this uncertainty, Mnouchkine's provisional solution was to immerse

everybody in the teachings of the greatest master of theater: Shakespeare. Between 1981 and 1984, in addition to its own works, the
Théâtre du Soleil also played "the Shakespeares": *Richard II*,
Twelfth Night, and *Henry IV*. To do these, the company delved
into Japanese theater: Nô and Kabuki, those grand and primeval
epic forms which permit the imagination to go beyond familiar
Shakespearean stereotypes of Western thought. Thus, two ways
met in a single search: the ways of the East and the ways of the
present. Mara Negrón Marrero calls this convergence "the conniv-
ence between the dreams of Hélène Cixous and those of Ariane
Mnouchkine" (*Chemins* 209). We know the results: *Sihanouk* and
L'Indiade.
    To the Soleil's question about the forms of historical narrative in
theater, Hélène Cixous' answer is the epic.

J'ai toujours pensé que l'Histoire ne pouvait être traitée que
poétiquement dans le texte (à moins d'être historien), qu'elle
devait être chantée, qu'elle devait être une épopée comme *l'Il-
liade*. L'Histoire avec sa figure humaine: le Destin. Mais est-ce
que l'épopée a encore droit de cité aujourd'hui? Au théâtre oui.
C'est encore le lieu où il y a de l'épopée, où il y a encore ce que
l'on pourrait appeler de la légende. (*Chemins* 28)

I have always thought that History can only be treated poetically
in a text (unless you are a historian), that it should be sung, that
it should be an epic, like the *Iliad*. History with its human face.
Destiny. But does the epic still have the right of acceptance
today? In the theater, yes. It is still the place where the epic
exists, where there still is something of what one might call the
legendary.

However, because of her own physical, social, and historical safety
in relation to the subjects she treats, because she is out of danger,
the writer experiences a sort of guilt, of bad conscience: "you write
while we die." Feeling responsible for all the "phantoms of
peoples" who climb back to the surface of her narrative,
Hélène Cixous asks herself constantly: "Which History is mine?
Of which History am I a witness? How does one combine
History and text?" (*Chemins* 26). This passionate questioning
meanders through her shadows and doubts. On one hand, the

epic, the most primitive genre, is an "extremely political" genre, it is "the chessboard on which a human group battles" (*Chemins* 232–33). On the other hand, Cixous sees politics as a social damnation:

> Je suis otage, comme nous tous, des scènes politiques, de l'Histoire, mais je n'écris pas cela, j'écris plutôt de ce qui reste librement humain à travers la captation ou la capture du politique. (*Chemins* 216)

> I am a hostage, as are we all, of political scenes, of History, but that is not what I write; rather, I write about that which remains freely human throughout the betrayal or capture of politics.

Cixous resolves this dilemma through her characters. When it comes time to act, Gandhi, the "divine warrior," settles the question and simply takes the most effective decision: "Let us go down from the level of the sublime to the political floor. Have they declared war on us? We will declare peace!" (*L'Indiade* I.2, 57).

History in the present tense

One of Pirandello's *Six Characters in Search of an Author*, forced to submit to the repetition of a painful scene on the grounds that it took place in the past, protests vigorously: "No, it is taking place now and always... at every instant of this torture, which is mine and which renews itself, always alive and present" (114). In theater, both for the actors and their characters as well as for the audience, there is no past; there is only the moment itself and their simultaneous presence in the course of the dramatic action which has thrown them together. To this double essence of theater – to exist simultaneously in real life and in the make-believe, to this physical and immediate quality of a performance – Hélène Cixous returns again and again.

Already in connection with her first historical play, she said:

> Le théâtre est au présent. Doit toujours être au présent. C'est sa chance. À chaque moment le present éclate. Le présent est d'un noir brillant. On avance le coeur battant de ne pas savoir ce qui va arriver. Et cet imprévisible qui nous tient en haleine, nous

soulève, nous transporte au-dessus de nous-mêmes, c'est la vie même. ("Le droit" 5)

The theater is in the present tense. It ought to be in the present always. That is its luck. The present thunders at any moment. The present is a brilliant black. We go forward, our hearts beating fast because they do not know what is about to happen. And this unknown, which keeps us breathless, excites us, transports us above our very selves, is life itself.

For anyone who wants to write for the stage, the discovery of theatrical time seems indispensable. A text inscribed across pages and meant for individual reading has another sense of time: that of the book, and a book has "all the time in the world, even eternity." Theater is written in a vertical manner and its tense is *the immediate*. Anyone who has ever seen a play knows that it will end: "we live our life, our death immediately" (*Chemins* 32). Therefore, we are in a hurry. Playwriting should be supple, quick, condensed. Each blow, played in the theater, is felt instantly by the spectator. Since theater is in the "present absolute," History, the assembled past, from the moment it is put on stage and manifests itself through the vulnerable, perishable bodies of the actors, finds itself in the present (*Chemins* 227) . We are suddenly the contemporaries of heroes who have been miraculously resuscitated – of Antigone, Orestes, Bajazet, Richard II, or of the last viceroy of India, Lord Mountbatten – encompassed in their time and they in ours. And in this world which starts again, "pure of our memories," ("Le droit" 4) in the rustling black of the theater, we do not know more about the characters than they know themselves. As Cixous explains, "In theater, as I write it in my historical plays, the characters are blind" – they do not know where their steps are taking them, what is going to happen to them – "in this sense we are contemporaries" (*Chemins* 32). And because we are our own contemporaries, we too are blind.

Present and Legend

"I need the theater to tell me its stories as legends" (*Chemins* 253). But how is one to combine history and text, the present and legend? Their relationship is difficult: they lack the effect of distance with its reliefs and chasms. It is up to poetry to project on them its own limelight, to make choices, to build hierarchies, to treat the present as a past and *vice versa*. Dramatic poetry thus works on contemporary history inside this dialectic of closeness and distance. A performance, now near the end of our own century, is often made to reflect on the epoch. Certain events – the Vietnam war, the war in Algeria, troubles in China, Cambodia, India, and Africa – have provoked several waves of reaction. In this sense, we have been able to ascertain, in a Europe sickened by its own history, a shift in interest toward the history of other continents, toward Africa, especially toward Asia. In the post-colonial context, Montesquieu's question, "How can one be a Persian?," acquires a new accent: "How can one take it upon himself to write about the Khmers?" (*Chemins* 24). The voyage to the East, whether physical or mental, becomes a frequent temptation for a European theater eager to explore other cultural spaces.

> Pourquoi l'Asie, l'Orient? Parce que c'est moi, parce que c'est le monde différent de moi qui m'apprend moi, ma différence qui me fait sentir ma/sa différence. Et aussi parce que l'Asie est religieuse dans son âme, parce qu'on salue en joignant les deux mains...parce qu'elle est noire devant le blanc incolore, parce qu'elle est notre préhistoire et notre passé présent. Parce qu'il y a des masques: en Asie on croit aux masques, au visage-âme, à l'autre....
>
> C'est une réalité qui existe par milliards. Parce qu'il y a tellement de mort et donc tellement de vie....En Asie, on révère le fruit et le grain à partir de quoi tout commence y compris l'amour, l'écriture et le théâtre. (*Chemins* 33)

Why Asia, the Orient? Because it is myself, because it is a world different from myself, which teaches me myself, my difference, which makes me feel my/its difference. And also because Asia is religious in its soul, because there one greets by joining the two hands... because it is black before colorless white, because it is our prehistory and our present past. Because there are masks: in Asia one believes in masks, in the face-spirit, in the other....

It is a reality that exists for billions. Because there is so much death and yet so much life....In Asia one reveres the fruit and grain, from which everything, love, writing and theater included, begins.

The Western fascination with exotic regions and the political tragedies that take place there is sustained in a host of writings, experiments, projects, and works on both small and large scale. At the Théâtre du Soleil there are, of course, Ariane Mnouchkine's grandiose productions of Cixous' plays, *Sihanouk* and *L'Indiade*. At the Ivry Theater, Antoine Vitez created the production, *La Rencontre de Georges Pompidou avec Mao Zedong* – 'Fragments of a series of works on the grotesque cruelty of modern history' (1979) and, later, at the National Theater of Chaillot, *Tombeau pour 500,000 soldats* (1981). In his search for different mythologies and different codes of communication, Peter Brook together with his troupe stayed for a time at Persepolis in Iran (*Orghast*, 1971), made a tour of Africa, and, inspired by the myths of India, put on a monumental *Mahabharata* (1985). The German writer Peter Weiss, author of the famous *Marat/Sade* (1964), wrote *Gesang vom Lusitanischen Popanz* or *Song of the Lusitanian Bogey* (1967) for musical theater on the theme of the Portuguese exploitation of Angola and Mozambique. A year later, he wrote the *Viet Nam Diskurs* (1968), which includes, among its cast of white characters, figures such as Winston Churchill and the Presidents Eisenhower, Kennedy, and Johnson. In the United States, Peter Sellars, *enfant terrible* of young American theater, staged John Adams' opera, *Nixon in China*, (based on a libretto by poet Alice Goodman) in 1987 at the Worthan Theater Center in Houston. Here, legendary distance is achieved not solely through writing style, but by means of music. The story is literally *sung* by the principal characters like Pat and Richard Nixon, President Mao and his wife, Chiang Ch'ing, Prime Minister Chou En-Lai, and Henry Kissinger.

We can ask ourselves as a matter of principle if these characters, so close to our political reality, have the necessary degree of transparency, of the unreal, to become *legendary*. Perhaps a certain geographical displacement, a certain temporal distance, or certain extreme situations in their existence allow them to prevail upon our imagination and to suspend, upon appearing on stage, "the struggle between the spirit of legend and the spirit of realism" (*L'Indiade* 264) Three centuries ago, Racine, wishing to write a play about a drama in the seraglio – Prince Bajazet's condemnation to death by his brother in 1638 – asked himself the same question. In the two prefaces to *Bajazet* (1672), he undertook to present an entire argument in favor of the modernity of the tragic subject: "It is an adventure which happened at the seraglio not more than thirty years ago" when a certain Count de Césy was Louis XIV's ambassador to Constantinople (*Oeuvres* 5). The ambassador, from afar, had often seen Bajazet, who was allowed at times to walk along Seraglio Point, by the shores of the Bosphorus. On his return to France, the ambassador related this "tragic adventure" which became the source of Racine's tragedy: an eye witness account, at least in part. Racine assured those who might be shocked that he dared to put on stage "a story so recent," that not one line of dramatic literature forbade him to do it. Nevertheless, he thought that if one took so modern a subject for tragedy, one must choose one's heroes from the history of another country.

Les personnages tragiques doivent être regardés d'un autre oeil que nous regardons d'ordinaire les personnages que nous avons vu de si près....L'éloignement des pays répare en quelque sorte la trop grande proximité des temps. Car le peuple ne met guère de différence entre ce qui est ...à mille ans de lui et ce qui est à mille lieues....Nous avons si peu de commerce avec les princes et autres personnes qui vivent dans le sérail que nous les considérons, pour ainsi dire, comme des gens qui vivent dans un autre siècle que le nôtre. (*Oeuvres* 9)

Tragic characters should be seen with another eye than that with which we are accustomed to look upon characters whom we have observed at such close range....The distance of countries makes up in a way for the too close proximity of the time period. For people hardly notice the difference between what is...a thousand years removed from them or a thousand leagues....We have so little to do with the princes and other people who live in the seraglio, that we consider them, so to speak, as people who live in another century than our own.

Racine's final argument in favor of modernity is, paradoxically, the example of the Ancients. Aeschylus, he says, introduced in one of his tragedies Xerxes' mother while she was still living, and staged in Athens the dispair at the Persian court after defeat. "And," adds

Racine, "this same Aeschylus took part himself in the Battle of Salamis, where Xerxes was defeated" (*Oeuvres*10). The distancing about which Racine talked was in fact an adjustment in the perspective in which the characters moved, an adjustment in the manner of giving them an imaginary dimension greater, more expressive than life: "The Turkish characters, modern though they may be, take on dignity on our stage. We quickly learn to see them as Ancients" (*Oeuvres* 9). Hélène Cixous suggests a similar adjustment between two time periods in a passage from her introduction to *L'Indiade*: the unprecedented characteristic of this story, she says, is that in the middle of the Twentieth Century there lived in India beings belonging "to spiritual epochs which, for us, ended centuries and millenia ago" (*L'Indiade* 14). The distance that separates these two realities becomes a voyage for her. Hélène Cixous is "the author who leaves herself behind in order to reach India" by means of the theater, which is the trip itself and, at its end, "a world different from the one we know" rises before our eyes ("Le droit" 4).

Characters and Players

From whatever angle we broach the problem of the character in theater, it always implies two levels of creativity: that of the writer and that of the stage actor. Where the two meet, the play unfolds. But while on stage facing the audience, the actor stands alone, a disconcerting creature, real and unreal, a product of art and nature, a phoenix eternally consumed and reborn in the flames of the footlights in an interminable series of spectacular lives. Having absorbed all the dramatic potential of the text, allowing himself to be possessed by the fictional existence he is in the process of creating, he forgets himself; he is only his character. "It is not the character who becomes real in the actor, it is the actor who becomes *unreal* inside his character," said Sartre (368). Similarly, in his *Dictionnaire du Théâtre*, Patrice Pavis comments, "The theater character – and therein lies his deceit but also his force of persuasion – seems to invent his words. In fact, just the opposite is true: it is his words that invent the character" (293). Hélène Cixous, too, feels this existential force of the word. In theater, she says, all that remains silent in reality and in books – the Word – is given sound:

"I must write as the ardent body speaks" (*L'Indiade* 261). The words the author puts into the mouth of his character must be "the same words moving and thinking lips form and give life to" (*L'Indiade* 261). This physical aspect, down to the corporeal peculiarities of her text on stage, intrigue and charm the author who, until then, was confined to her workroom. Yet it is in solitude, on paper, that the creation of characters takes place:

Voici comment m'arrivent les personnages. D'abord ils naissent. Ils naissent par la poitrine. Le coeur est gros.

Ils ne sont d'abord qu'une phrase, un soupir, un sourire, oui c'est ainsi qu'ils se présentent. Et trois répliques plus tard, les voilà soudain entiers, debout, en pleine destinée, en plein leur histoire.... Là-dessus les voilà qui deviennent mes proches, ma famille de supplément....Ils restent et se mêlant à nous, ils deviennent comme d'anciens vivants réels, qui, leur vie finie, se retirent - pour toujours dans nos mémoires.

Cela, cette survie, nous la devons aux comédiens. La vie qu'ils ont donné au personnage, nul ne peut la reprendre. C'est comme l'amour maternel, absolument donné. (*L'Indiade* 262-63)

This is how my characters come to me. First they are born. They are born through the chest. The heart is pregnant.

At first they are no more than a phrase, a sigh, a smile; yes, that is how they appear. And three rejoinders later, there they are, suddenly complete, standing, in the midst of their destiny, in the midst of their history....Thereupon they become my intimates, my complementary family....They stay and mix with us, they become like real beings from the past who, their life over, retire – forever in our memories.

This survival we owe to the actors. No one can take back the life they have given to the characters. It is like a mother's love, given unconditionally.

Thus the creation of a character on stage is like a birth; the author, the players, are "the mothers." It is interesting to compare Cixous' passage on maternity, from the pen of a woman playwright, to the following passage on virility born of a masculine mentality and signed by Alfred Jarry, the author of the famous *Ubu roi*. In his *Douze arguments sur le théâtre* he writes:

Le théâtre, qui anime des masques impersonnels, n'est accessible qu'à qui se sent assez viril pour créer la vie: un conflit de passions plus subtil que les connus ou un personnage qui soit un nouvel être. Il est admis par tous qu'Hamlet, par exemple, est plus vivant qu'un homme qui passe, car il est plus compliqué avec plus de synthèse, et même seul vivant, car il est une abstraction qui marche. Donc il est plus ardu à l'esprit de créer un personnage qu'à la matière de construire un homme." (12)

The theater, which gives life to impersonal masks, is accessible only to those who feel themselves virile enough to create life: a conflict of passions more subtle than the common, or a character who would be a new manner of being. Everyone agrees that Hamlet, for example, is more alive than an ordinary mortal, for he is more coherently complex, in fact the only one truly alive because he is a walking abstraction. Thus it is more difficult for the spirit to create a character than for matter to construct a man.

Here *virility* is associated with spirit, while *matter* is a substitute for the womb which generates the human species. For her part, Hélène Cixous links maternity not only to femininity, of course, but also to the giving of oneself, to sanctity. In her view, the actor breaks free of himself in order to give life to another; he is "always a little bit saint, a little bit woman" (*L'Indiade* 265). Womanly too is the stage director, the one who brings the characters and players on stage, who "brings them into the world." Asking herself with oratorical coquetry, "Will the author Hélène Cixous boast of her sanctity," she replies, "no"; because an author, even if she loses one *self*, multiplies herself into twenty characters, "a heady consolation" (*L'Indiade* 265). It is the player who is a saint, he, who through a tireless effort in humility, gives himself up in exchange for one character: "Resigning of myself, submitting to You....Love thy character as thyself and more than thyself" (*L'Indiade* 268). We find ourselves again in the full mystique of theatrical work, seen as asceticism and as spiritual exercise.

On the other hand, in the empire of their fictions, the carnal impulses, the eroticism, the sexuality of the characters are often the prime movers behind their most exalted acts, with great repercussions. History is made "of stories of husbands, lovers, fathers, daughters, mothers, sons, jealousy, pride, desire" (*L'Indiade* 255).

And the epic of all epics, the *Iliad*, gives us the most brilliant example: "Faces launch fleets of a thousand sails and destroy cities" (*L'Indiade* 255). But can an author, man or woman, create characters of the opposite sex and make them real? In theater, "yes," replies Cixous, thanks to the actors and actresses who give to the playwright their bodies which he no longer needs to invent.

C'est le cadeau que le théâtre fait à l'auteur: l'incarnation. A l'auteur homme, il permet de créer des femmes qui ne seront pas feintes, et à l'auteur femme il accorde la chance de créer des hommes parfaitement constitués. (*L'Indiade* 266)

It's the gift theater gives the author: incarnation. It allows a male author to create women who are real, and to the female author it offers the possibility to create perfectly constituted men.

One category of theatrical character is that of the *historical character*, constructed according to a real model. This prototype, complete with a biography, a known physical appearance and an already ascertained moral status (positive or negative), seems at first sight, because of his very reality, resistent to the creative process. Everything that makes up his private and public life, preserved in the archives of History, have frozen him into a sterotypical image, imprisoned him in a mold. To give him back his heartbeat, his look, his movements, in a word, his life, we must begin by releasing him from his own effigy. And then, perhaps, as in the case of Suramarit, Sihanouk's father, he will come down from his pedestal and start talking to us.

In spite of the difficulties of this confrontation with a preestablished image, the heroes of History have often tempted dramatic authors. Beginning with Antiquity, every epoch has presented authors with brilliant examples, both of good and evil, of grandeur and decadence. What is the source of this force of attraction, this magnetism of historical personalities? I think in the first place and at the most general level, that their force has to do with the fact that they are *famous*, that they have escaped anonymity, that they are extraordinary. It is their *glory*, the Ancients would say, their *celebrity*, we would say, which makes them fascinating. It is in essence the same sort of attraction – a mixture of curiosity, envy, and admiration – that takes us to Madame Tussaud's, to the Grévin Museum, or even to the Moscow mausoleum where rest the

remains of Lenin, that sad embalmed doll of the October Revolution. These phantoms, frozen forever in certain attitude, guardians
of the secret of their success or damnation, are imposed upon the
public's attention; they have put their stamp on certain events, and
thus they are worthy of being reproduced and exposed. We look
upon them with a certain unease, due to their physical pseudo-
presence, as we try to comprehend the enigma of their fame. A
similar confrontation, though of another order, takes place in the
theater.

At the creative artistic level, what attracts an author to an historical character is that he has come to the end of his journey and
transformed it into destiny. He is thus the possible carrier of a
message which must be discovered, interpreted, and expressed.
Since these once powerful characters are no longer so when made
to go on stage – even if they still live, disgraced or exiled (Nixon,
Sihanouk) – one can "play" with their stories, as with hypotheses
about the human spirit. One can, finally, laugh wickedly at the
expense of tyrants once terrible like Hitler or Stalin (consider
G. Tabori's *Mein Kampf* or David Pownall's *Master Class*). For laughter, as Hélène Cixous says, too, is the "supreme sign" of freedom:

> Nous rions. Même si telle scène est tragique: c'est que la source
> du comique, c'est justement l'absolue liberté d'expression. Fût-il
> au fond du malheur, l'homme dont la langue est libre peut
> affronter les dieux. Et c'est cela qui nous fait rire: que chacun
> dise, dans sa langue noble ou populaire, leurs quatre vérités aux
> forces du destin et de l'humanité. (*L'Indiade* 276-77)

> We laugh. Even if a scene is tragic: for the very source of comedy
> is the absolute liberty of expression. Even in the depths of dis-
> pair, a man whose tongue is free can mock the Gods. And it is
> precisely this that makes us laugh: that everyone tells, in his
> noble or common tongue, the bald truth behind the forces of
> destiny and of humanity.

In the opposite sense, if suddenly Gandhi rises before us, we join
him on the road of his legend and we cry again at the announcement of his assassination which took place half a century ago:
"Extraordinary things happen under the theater sky....We still
have our tears, may they be blessed!" (*L'Indiade* 260). Revenge
after death or the recapture of a sublime moment, such an histor-

ical episode evoked on stage often helps us to rethink and decipher our own epoch. Summoning the Homeric heroes to his aid, Giraudoux wrote *La guerre de Troie n'aura pas lieu* (1935) almost on the eve of the second world war.

At the same time, because they once really did exist, historical characters are evidence for us of the reality of the tragic. Their stories are not invented; they can therefore, in principle, be repeated with other protagonists, for example, with potentates of our own recent or ongoing history. A modern American Shakespeare could see in the fate that has dealt so severely with the Kennedy family the subject of a new series of "tragedies of kings." Their misfortunes, their fall, are just so many warnings.

> Il y a toujours le moment d'hesitation: et si je tuais? Et si je me trompais? Et si j'étais un monstre? Et si j'étais aveugle? Ce moment nous est donné au Théâtre, c'est l'instant tragique où tout pourrait être changé. (*L'Indiade* 258)

> There is always that moment of hesitation: and if I killed? And if I was wrong? And if I was a monster? And if I was blind? This moment is given to us in Theater, it is the tragic instant when everything could turn out differently.

But more than being reference points for us, in a way, through the miracle of their reincarnation, historical characters in theater represent a triumph over death. Appropriating for themselves the actors' stature, their gestures, faces, voices, their entire physicality, for a time they recover on stage their former earthly existence in flesh and blood. Thus they grant us, partially, "our oldest desire: to be able to cross the boundary of death alive and well" (*Chemins* 30). This "resurrection" of forgotten or faraway heroes in the bodies of the players creates for them a fictional and immortal double who can survive indefinitely thanks to successive reincarnations. Faced with an historical model, the actor assumes it and wraps himself inside it, as if within a "great phantom," said Diderot in *Paradoxe sur le comédien*, making him move from inside.

Cixous followed the actors' search step by step in the course of rehearsals at the Théâtre du Soleil:

> Je vais vous raconter certains de leurs secrets.
> Il s'agit de sacrifice....Un sacrifice obstiné, répété, laborieux.

C'est un travail d'humilité inlassable qu'il faut accomplir pour se faire admettre par Toi, pour deviner le lieu de Toi....On ne sait pas, on se met à la disposition du personnage: on l'attend. Qu'il vienne! Le comédien devient le serviteur d'un maître. Ce maître est la vérité du personnage....
Cela commence le matin, par des gestes qui semblent simples et sans mystère, et qui sont cependant magiques. Au Théâtre du Soleil, ils arrivent tôt les chercheurs de Toi. Et ils ne savent pas qui ils seront. Ils sont encore les comédiens du Théâtre du Soleil, ils ont encore leurs noms propres, ils ont encore leurs vêtements, leurs mémoires d'aujourd'hui....
Voici que le signal est donné: qui veut devenir qui? Qui veut aujourd'hui chercher Gandhi...? (*L'Indiade* 268-69)

I will tell you some of their secrets.
It is a question of sacrifice....A stubborn, repeated, difficult sacrifice. They must complete a labor of tireless humility in order to be accepted by You, to find their way to You....They do not know, they put themselves at the disposal of the character: they wait for him. That he would come! The actor becomes the servant of a master. This master is the truth of the character....
This begins in the morning, with gestures that seem simple and unmysterious, and that are nevertheless magical. At the Théâtre du Soleil, these searchers for You arrive early. And they do not know who they will become. They are still the actors of the Théâtre du Soleil, they still have their own names, they still have their own clothes, their memories of today....
Now the signal is given: who wants to become who? who wishes to search for Gandhi today...?

A *half-naked fakir*: Testimonies for a Portrait

In a speech to the House of Commons on the negotiations between Lord Irwin and Gandhi in February 1931, Winston Churchill expressed his shock at the "humiliating spectacle of a half-naked fakir striding up the steps of the Viceroy's palace to negotiate and parley on equal terms with the representative of the King Emperor" (*Gandhi* 82). This incredible arrogance hid, in fact, a political fear: Churchill realized Gandhi's true dimension and the enormous consequences his peaceful but stubborn struggle against English domination could entail: India's independence and, consequently, for the English crown, the loss of the most precious jewel of Britain's colonial empire.

Others, also from the English side, reacted differently to this unique personality of our century. Gandhi's stay in London in the autumn of 1931, on the occasion of the conference on India's new status which culminated in the Irwin-Gandhi pact, vividly impressed English public opinion. The *Times* devoted several articles to him wherein the exotic figure of Gandhi passes, in his usual loincloth and shawl, standing out all in white against the gray London sky as in a period film: "Although the rain fell heavily all day, his comings and goings clad in loincloth and robe of white khaddar (home spun India cloth) and with sandals on his feet were watched by crowds." At a union meeting, one of the speakers said to him: "You are so sincere that you make some of us suspicious, and so simple that you bewilder some of us" (*Times* 9/14/31, *Gandhi* 39). Lord Irwin himself, recalling in his memoires this historical encounter with Gandhi, wrote:

> The man himself was larger than any of the attempts made to paint his portrait. There was a directness about him which was singularly winning, but this could be accompanied by a subtlety of intellectual process which could sometimes be disconcerting. To appreciate what was passing in his mind it was necessary, if not to start from the same point, at least to understand very clearly what was the starting point for him; and this was nearly always very human and very simple....He was the natural knight-errant, fighting always the battle of the weak agaist suffering and what he judged injustice. (Alexander 20)

On his arrival in New Delhi to guarantee the transfer of power, Lord Mountbatten, the last Viceroy of India from March to August, 1947, met Gandhi and Jawaharlal Nehru, "Gandhi's chosen son." Gandhi's influence, he noted, was felt on two levels, spiritual and political. "Those closest to him always felt that the spiritual leadership, which had earned him the title of Mahatma, was more important" (Mountbatten 85). Mountbatten's biographer, P. Ziegler, asserts that he was fascinated and charmed by the "old prophet," as he affectionately called Gandhi. On Gandhi's death, he told his mother, "I had become so fond of dear old

Gandhi that his assassination was a real personal blow as well as an immense anxiety" (Ziegler 471). This man, whom Gandhi had appreciated for his honesty and loyalty, would in his turn perish, assassinated in 1979 in an attack by the I.R.A. His veneration for Gandhi was such that he wrote one day: "I think history will link him with Buddha and Mahomet, and the Indians include Christ in this classification" (Ziegler 471).

For Americans, the figure of Gandhi had different connotations. Some have compared him to Lincoln, the father of a nation, the founder of a political era, acting as a principle of equality for all – black or white – before the law; Gandhi himself founded modern India and fought for the rights of the Untouchables. On the other hand, by the Nineteenth Century, Hindu mysticism had entered certain American intellectual circles and influenced writers like Henry David Thoreau who, with his friend Ralph Waldo Emerson, translated the *Bhagvad-Gita* (the Hindu "bible") and several *Upanishads*. Thoreau would one day pay back this spiritual debt: after reading Thoreau's, *Civil Disobedience*, Gandhi conceived of and developed his own brand of non-cooperation and civil disobedience on a national scale after 1920.

The missionary E. Stanley Jones, who lived in India for many years, conversed several times with Gandhi, and he even visited him in the communal village he had created in Sevagram: "In a bamboo thatched hut, plastered with mud, sat the Mahatma, and from there he ruled India. He ruled India, though he didn't hold an office – he ruled it by spiritual power" (159). Louis Fischer, author of the book on which Richard Attenborough based his 1981 film on Gandhi, had also known the Mahatma personally. In 1942 he spent a week in the bosom of the Sevagram community. He draws a portrait of Gandhi at the age of 73: "He seemed bigger than I had imagined him. He wore only his famous loincloth and sandals, thus presenting a contrast between immaculate white and luminous brown" (Fischer 156). He was wellbuilt, with a muscular torso, a slender waist, and long slim legs with very prominent knee joints. His body did not give one the impression of advanced age, on the contrary "[h]is skin was smooth and had the bloom of health" (Fischer 156). His facial features, however, did betray his age. His entire expression came "from his eyes with their kind and friendly look, from his lower lip, which expressed self control, strength, and compassion, and from his eternal smile, which exposed his gums" (Fischer 156). On seeing him again in 1946, he found him in poor physical condition. Nevertheless, Gandhi still liked to joke and laugh, as before, and essentially, noted the American, "he is the same: the karma yogi, the man of action who strives constantly toward a goal" (Fischer 171).

A less familiar text on Gandhi seen up close by a contemporary is that of Romanian writer and religious historian, Mircea Eliade, who was born in Bucharest and died in Chicago, where he taught at the university from 1957. In Calcutta, while working on his doctoral thesis on yoga, the young Eliade was present at the March 29, 1928 lawsuit brought against Gandhi who was accused of having incited his compatriots to burn their English-made clothes in order to encourage local production and manner of dress. He is witness to Gandhi's arrival in the packed hall:

> Finally Mahatma Gandhi was announced by the uproar outside. Ovations and whispers. Making a way for himself through the crowd, appeared a small brown man, looking darker in his white linen shawl, which only covered half his chest. Bare feet in sandals, uncovered head. His face looks tortured, furrowed: his small eyes shine like melted lead, the great circles around them hidden by large glasses....I listen while he speaks. Suddenly he seems someone else....Here comes Pandit Nehru, a sort of brown tiger, with a firm, square jaw.... The Mahatma stops speaking and sits down. A strange, belated emotion takes hold of me. His eyes were now looking far into the distance, so far that, had I not known him, I would have thought he was blind. (55)

In his *Memoires*, Nehru described Gandhi's manner of speaking: simple, precise, without a superfluous word. It was the total sincerity of his speech that impressed people most; he let the great reserves of his strength be seen:

> This little man of poor physique had something of steel in him, something rock-like, which did not yield to physical powers, however great they might be. And in spite of his unimpressive features, his loincloth and bare body, there was a royalty and a kingliness in him which compelled a willing obeisance from others. Consciously and deliberately meek and humble, yet he was full of power and authority....His voice, clear and limpid,

would purr into the heart and evoke an emotional response. (*Gandhi* 58-59)

His enormous popularity did not affect Gandhi's modesty: he defended himself against the sometimes idolatrous veneration of which he had become the object, and against the title Mahatma (great soul) which had been bestowed upon him. In contrast, he laughed every time his old friend and companion in arms, the poetess Sarojini Naïdi, called him by the nickname she had given him, "Mickey Mouse!" (Tariq Ali 38).

To end this series of testimonies, I would like to call on the voice of someone who did not love Gandhi but who nevertheless judged him with exemplary impartiality: George Orwell. In his essay, *Reflections on Gandhi* (1949), he tries to demythify the Mahatma, balance his faults and qualities in order to bring him back to human size. The lines he devoted to Gandhi are among the most far-seeing and chivalrous homages ever paid to him:

> Saints should always be judged guilty until they are proved innocent, but the tests that have to be applied to them are not, of course, the same in all cases. In Gandhi's case the questions one feels inclined to ask are: to what extent was Gandhi moved by vanity – by the consciousness of himself as a humble, naked old man, sitting on a praying mat and shaking empires by sheer spiritual power – and to what extent did he compromise his own principles by entering into politics, which, of their nature are inseparable from coercion and fraud? ... Inside the saint, or near-saint, there was a very shrewd, able person....His character was an extraordinarily mixed one, but there was almost nothing in it that you can put your finger on and call bad, and I believe that even Gandhi's worst enemies would admit that he was an interesting and unusual man who enriched the world simply by being alive....One may feel, as I do, a sort aesthetic distaste for Gandhi, one may reject the claims of sainthood made on his behalf (he never made such claim for himself, by the way)...but regarded simply as a politician, and compared with the other leading political figures of our time, how clean a smell he has managed to leave behind! (525–31)

The Embodiment of a Hero

When he was a child, Gandhi was given permission one day to watch a play put on by a group of itinerant actors. Recounting this memory in his *Autobiography. The Story of My Experiments with Truth* (1927-1929), Gandhi added: "This play – *Harishchandra* – captured my heart. I could never be tired of seeing it....It haunted me and I must have acted *Harishchandra* to myself times without number. 'Why should not all be truthful like Harishchandra?' was the question I asked myself day and night. To follow truth and to go through all the ordeals Harishchandra went through was the one ideal it inspired in me"(7). A century later, this childhood dream would be realized in a very unusual way. After having played his part in History, the little spectator of old would himself become a fictional hero, and others would dream of his sublime model.

Written in French and played first in Paris, *L'Indiade ou l'Inde de leur rêves,* is attached nevertheless – by its heroic inspiration, by the fullness of its development in time – to the grand tradition of Indian epic theater. The play is divided into five acts and a prologue, with lyric moments (commentary on an event, historical contemplations) which are recited or sung. The action begins in Bombay in 1937 and ends in New Delhi in 1948 with the announcement of Gandhi's death. It unfolds in episodes, alternating known characters with invented or anonymous ones who represent the common people, urban and rural. Thus, in the cast of characters, alongside names such as Nehru, Patel, Jinnah, Sarojini Naïdu, and Mountbatten, we find, for example, Haridasi, a wandering ascetic, Bahadur, the bear trainer, Rajkumar and Siddiqui, peasants, Inder, a rickshaw wallah and untouchable, and Mourad Khan, the man who sings the song of Partition, plus an entire crowd of servants, porters, officers, soldiers, and street people, men and women in colorful costumes designated sometimes as "a typical Indian (or Indian woman)." The man who goes through all the walks of life of this dramatic structure, from the political summit to the most humble human level, is Gandhi. We see him on stage, tireless, one minute talking to ministers, party leaders, British officials, and the next, going out on the street to talk to just anyone, to stroke Moona the bear, to rub the tired feet of an untouchable, and, finally, to climb again the stairs of the government palace and sit directly – a half naked fakir – on the Viceroy's throne.

This last scene (II.4) is also one of the most important of the play. From the point of view of action, it marks the apogee of conflict, the result and the outcome, patiently prepared, of opposing opinions, interests, and passions. We find ourselves in New Delhi, in 1947, on the eve of the transfer of power to the Indian authorities. Standing on stage in his white uniform – modern archangel of this Visitation – Lord Mountbatten, the Viceroy, meditates in solitude on the historical act that is to take place the next day, fearing all the unknown implications that such an act hides: hopes, rivalries, dangers, unforeseen consequences. It is one of those moments when action has been suspended, when everything is about to happen but has not happened yet, when the characters try to find their way among the shadows. "The theater that I love I would call *theater of the eve*, in Shakespeare, the eve of battle, or the eve of a decision" (*Chemins* 231-32). And indeed, Mountbatten will impart his anxiety and doubts in a Shakespearean monologue:

O India, grosse de tempêtes et de merveilles,
Tu attends le coup en tremblant
Comme une bête qui sait et ne sait pas son sort...
C'est par de telles nuits que dans les pièces de
Shakespeare s'embrassaient les amours condamnées.
C'est par de telles nuits que les rois devinaient la
défaite, les reines sentaient venir la mort.
Les cieux prenaient feu soudain...
Être le dernier Roi de cet Empire!
Le couronné découronné
Et être en même temps l'accoucheur et le bourreau!...
Selon mon coeur, je ne puis plus maintenant servir
dignement que l'Angleterre.
Pour l'Inde, je ne vois que désordre et division. Car
les leaders indiens ont déja brûlé chacun les vaisseaux de
l'autre....
Haute nuit, qui balances comme les branches d'acacias
tes milliards de lustres au-dessus de l'Enfer et du Paradis,
Toi et moi nous savons que c'en est fait du rêve de Mahatma
Gandhi.
Je pense à lui, antique déité sans dents, vieille mère sans
mamelles,
dernière preuve de l'existence des dieux et de leur impuissance à

faire admettre leurs prophètes dans notre siècle politique.
Pauvre vieil oiseau déplumé, pardonne-moi.... (*L'Indiade* IV.1,
147-48)

O India, heavy with storms and marvels,
You await the blow, trembling
Like a beast which knows yet does not know its fate....
It was on nights like this that condemned lovers
Kissed in Shakespeare's plays.
It was on nights like this that kings forsaw their
doom, that queens felt the imminence of death.
The skies suddenly burst into flame....
To be the last king of the Empire!
The crowned uncrowned
To be both midwife and executioner!
My heart tells me that from this day forward
I can serve only England with honor.
For India I see only disorder and division.
Her leaders have already burned each other's ships. ...
Deep night, you, like the acacia branches, balance
Your million lights above Hell and Heaven,
You and I, we know that it is done with Mahatma Gandhi's
dream.
I think of him, ancient toothless deity, old, breastless mother,
final proof of the gods' existence
and of their vain attempts to introduce their prophets into our
political century.
Poor old featherless bird, forgive me....

The following scene (II) will bring victory and defeat to Gandhi:
the independence and the partition of India by Jinnah's separation
of Pakistan. Concurrently, this scene creates a great tension between
the text and its acting. The dramatic account is quick, dense, com-
pact: within four pages everything has been said. The scenic account
carries the intent of the writing to its greatest intensity and makes it
explode. Directions such as "Enter Gandhi" produce a triumphal
image on stage: Gandhi runs up the stairs and takes his place in the
Viceroy's empty chair. Two pages later, Jinnah, the champion of
separation, having rejected the unity of India for the last time, gets
ready to leave. Gandhi rises from his chair, throws himself face
down to the floor, crawls toward Jinnah, wraps his arms around

his knees, immobilizing him, clings to him, seizes him, and stammering pleads in a terrible embrace. After this desperate struggle, Gandhi is thrown again to the ground and Jinnah leaves.[4]

At the Théâtre du Soleil, having drunk Indian tea and eaten Indian food (prepared and served in the foyer by Ariane Mnouchkine and her actors), we all sat waiting, as soon as the play began, for Gandhi to appear, with a mixture of impatience and fear: what if his physical appearance disappointed us? What if the actor, Andrés Pérez Araya, did not live up to our expectations? What if he could not convince us of the miraculous presence of this legendary character, Gandhi – not on screen but here, in the same space we inhabited? The play would be barren in its very core. At last, he appeared, preceded by an uproar, carried in by the crowd, as if by a great wave, and placed on the stage floor. And we, the spectators, were immediately relieved. This familiar image: the white loincloth, the bare feet, the modest iron-rimmed glasses, the toothless smile, the relaxed, benevolent attitude – it was he, just as we had seen him in history book pictures or in documentary films, just as we had imagined him. A calm force emanated from this fictional body, which the actor had fashioned in imitation of his real prototype. Once we had passed this threshold, we could freely abandon ourselves to the fluctuation of events, let ourselves be borne on a flying carpet to the India of their dreams...

Thus have we arrived at this especially difficult problem of giving shape to an historical character: the *resemblance*, the physical credibility, from which the credibility of this type of fiction begins. We can reject a direct confrontation, in this sense, as being too concrete, and resort to suggestion: that is what the Italian director Ettore Scola did, for example, in his film *La Nuit de Varennes*. The moment the French royal family – Louis XIV, Marie-Antoinette, the Dauphin, and the Dauphine – in its flight from the Revolution, stops and takes lodgings upstairs in an inn, the camera follows the stairway but stops at the landing; it only lets us see, through a partially open door, the king's legs and a fold of the queen's dress. Or, as Peter Weiss did in *Marat/Sade*, one could substitute, in the text itself, for the figures of the heroes, pseudo-identities, second degree identities, by allowing them to be played by madmen in a so-called lunatic asylum. They could keep only the most visible props of their original guise: Marat, his bath; Charlotte Corday, her knife, and so on. But one might also wish, as Peter Sellars did in his production of the opera *Nixon in China*, to recreate a recent historical reality in minute detail in order to make it more striking. He was thus constrained to reproduce on stage, as closely as possible, the physical appearance of the characters portrayed. Thus – we are told by a commentator – when the former president and his wife, inside the stage scenery, get off the airplane in Peking, "audiences in America drew their breath, so 'real' were these Nixons" (Steinberg 15). If we are dealing with personalities of our own century, I think, this is our only choice: in fact, through their doubles, we reinforce the effect of fiction by provoking the shock of instant recognition of *unreal* bodies.

Present at the metamorphosis of the actors into the characters of her text, author Hélène Cixous marvelled: "Underneath the charm of the costumes and the make up, underneath the masque, what rises to the light is the truth, that is, the best or the worst" (*L'Indiade* 254). The make up, seemingly a technical gesture or a skill, is in fact a test. Leaning before their mirrors, the actors, brushes in hand, search for "the face of the other" and, in the process of successive touch-ups, gradually bring it to the surface: "A face has been formed atop the former face" (*L'Indiade* 270). Thus, the final touch in adjusting the corporeal envelope of the character has been made: the actor has become someone. And he is as moving as the face of an infant, because we associate him with the exit from nothingness, and with miracles, says Cixous. "Here too: the infant is perhaps an ugly old man, ragged and toothless; still, he is as beautiful as a new-born babe. And so the actor can be proud of the child he has brought into the world and which is himself. He smiles gently to greet the appearance of this new-comer"(*L'Indiade* 270).

Translated from the French by Cornelia Golna

Notes

1. *L'Indiade,* 266. Unless otherwise indicated, all subsequent parenthetical references in the first paragraph refer to *L'Indiade.*
2. Subsequent references to this text will be cited as *Chemins.*
3. *L'Age d'Or,* Texte programme. (Théâtre du Soleil, 1976), 20.
4. I would like to thank Ms. Marguerite Sandré, who kindly sent me from Paris Bernard Sobel's videotape (1989) - issued by the Théâtre du Soleil for internal use only - of the performance of *L'Indiade ou L'Inde de leurs rêves.* (I saw the play myself on the evening of October 16, 1987.)

Works Cited

Alexander, Horace. "Gandhi through Western Eyes." *Gandhi.Film* 20: 20–21.

Cixous, Hélène. "Le droit de légende." *L'Avant-Scène.Théâtre* 745 (March 1984): 4-5.

———. *La Pupille. Cahiers Renaud-Barrault* 78 (1971): 1–136.

———. *L'Indiade ou l'Inde de leurs rêves et quelques écrits sur le théatre.* Paris: Théatre du Soleil, 1987.

Dalhuizen, L.G., ed. *Gandhi. Film en werkelijkheid.* Leiden: Coördinaat minderhedenstudies (Bouwstenen voor intercultureel onderwijs, AVS), RUL, 1991.

Eliade, Mircea. *Biblioteca maharajahului.* Bucharest: Editura pentru turism, 1991.

Fischer, Louis. *Gandhi. Zijn leven en zijn boodschap.* Trans. Bram Moerland and Alexandra Gabrielli. Wassenaar: Mirananda, 1983.

———. *Gandhi. His Life and Message for the World.* New York: New American Library, 1954.

Gandhi, Mohandas K. *An Autobiography. The Story of My Experiments with Truth.* Boston: Beacon, 1957.

Jarry, Alfred. *Tout Ubu.* Paris: La Librairie Générale Française (Le Livre de Poche), 1962.

Jones, E. Stanley. *Mahatma Gandhi. An Interpretation.* London: Hodder & Stoughton, 1948.

Moscoso, Sophie. "Notes de répétition." *Double Page.* No. 32. Le Théâtre du Soleil: Shakespeare 2e partie. Paris: Éditions SNEP, 1984. 6–11.

Mountbatten, Earl of Burma. "Reflections on the Transfer of Power and Jawaharlal Nehru." *Gandhi. Film.* 85 : 84–85.

Negrón Marrero, Mara. "Comment faire pour écrire l'histoire poétique/ ou comment faire pour ne pas oublier." Van Rossum-Guyon & Diaz-Diocaretz. 205–212.

Orwell, George. *The Collected Essays, Journalism, and Letters of George Orwell.* IV. Ed. Sonia Orwell & Ian Angus. New York: Harcourt, Brace & World, 1968.

Pavis, Patrice. *Dictionaire du Théâtre.* Paris: Éditions Sociales, 1980.

Pirandello, Luigi. *Six personnages en quête d'auteur.* Trans. Michel Arnaud. Paris: Gallimard, 1977.

Racine, Jean. "Bajazet." *Oeuvres.* III. Paris: Alphonse Lemerre,1874–75. 5-10.

Sartre, Jean-Paul. *L'Imaginaire. Psychologie phénoménologique de l'imagination.* Paris: NRF, Gallimard, 1940.

Steinberg, Michael. "Real Characters in Opera." *Nixon in China.* John Adams. Amsterdam: De Nederlandse Operastichting, 1988. 15.

Tariq Ali. *The Nehrus and the Gandhis. An Indian Dynasty.* London: Picador, 1985. Théâtre du Soleil. *L'Âge d'Or.* Texte programme (Théâtre Ouvert). Paris: Éditions Stock, 1975.

van Rossum-Guyon, Françoise and Myriam Diaz-Diocaretz, eds. *Hélène Cixous, chemins d'une écriture.* Presses Universitaires de Vincennes PUV (L'Imaginaire du Texte), RODOPI (Faux titre, 49), 1990.

Ziegler, P. *Mountbatten, the Official Biography.* London: Collins, 1985.

15

Men More Than Men

Violette Santellani

Having attended several rehearsals of the Théâtre du Soleil at the Cartoucherie of Vincennes in July, 1987, to view the performance of Hélène Cixous' *The Indiade or the India of Their Dreams*, I was able to see Ariane Mnouchkine at work with her actors during production.

It is this experience – particularly the work done in both rehearsals and in public performances – that this reading takes as its point of departure. It was in this first incarnation of the author's words and images that my eyes touched these men in a state of parturition: these men, more than men, able to live more than a single experience of being man. Because of a certain state of history and of love, they went as far as becoming the woman they could have been had they been born "other," had they been born to know the act of bringing forth into the world with its ruptures and – by way of this very flexibility – to rediscover deeply buried in themselves the newly born child open to all possibilities, still undetermined.

The actors who inspired these few notes: Baya Bélal as Haridasi, Andres Pérez Araya as Mahatma Gandhi, Georges Bigot as Pundit Jawahardal Nehru, Simon Abkarian as Ghaffar Khan, J-F Dusigne as Jinnah, Myriam Azencot as Sarojini Naidu.

One further word on the place and time in which these experiences of being could take form: India between 1937 and 1948; from the gestation, in the hearts of several men with contradictory desires; from the new India, liberated of the British yoke; to the assassination, both a sacrifice and punishment, of Mahatma Gandhi.

In the prologue, Cixous "opens" her text with the verbal viaticum of the old woman wanderer named Haridasi:

There are only two races, and a third:
One is man,
The other is woman,
The third is half-man half-woman. (20)

Haridasi, in her ancient and simple wisdom, asks the essential question: that of origins. A drama will play itself out, immense. Why? How did all of this begin? How, before these times, did one, here in India, reckon with these differences?

Haridasi is of here, of now, but also of other times and of everywhere. Like everyone she is in a state of expectancy. But who is expecting the child here? Who is pregnant with the future India?

Principally men.

And, as always, this pregnancy is the natural consequence of a story of desires.

Of course, as we shall see, it doesn't have to do with ordinary men, simply circumscribed with a definitive mastery of a few indispensible possessions.

Gandi, Nehru, Ghaffar Khan, Azad, Patel are precisely part of this third category where being is no longer one, cut off from two, but at once one and two, at once one and the other, at once many others still...

Tonic cocktail, boiling, wherein the proportions of masculine/feminine libidinal economies modify and mix with each other to no end, according to the urgency of the action, the blazing of desires, the assault of doubts and terrors sent from the unconscious. These five men recognize themselves all as sons of a same symbolic mother, their land: millenial India, immense mosaic of races and religions. All are heavy with expectancy, more or less serene, all dreaming of the miraculous child: the new India, independent, and liberated from the British yoke.

Yet over this scene of love which is also a political scene, emblematic flip side of this race of men, looms Jinnah, head of the league. He too wants a free India, freed from the British, but he wants it Muslim. With a line on the map, that is to say with a knife in reality, he wants to separate Muslims and Hindus who, up until then, had lived here together.

"For a thousand years," Gandhi will tell him,

> we have lived together, making war and making peace with each other. For a thousand years we have been asking ourselves: does he love me? does she love me? He no longer loves me! No, it's I who no longer love him. And yet how to live without you all, without you? Sometimes, in the fullness of love, one believes one no longer loves oneself. (81)

As a pregnant woman idealizes the child she is expecting, Jinnah too dreams. In his fantasies, the new India merges with the mother, with the lover. In reality, the death of his beloved wife has cemented an extreme solitude inside of him. Cut off from the others, inhabited by a terrible disease, a cancer which pulls him towards his tomb, his soul distorted by resentment, it's in his own terms that he dreams of the India to come:

> See, I hold the sacred two-edged sword above India. See, I let it go. Now it will fly proudly like a royal eagle above the breathless flanks. How moving and alluring is this immense terrestrial flesh upon which he will descend one of these days like a divine lover. Then the [decree] will fall on the continent and here, here, there, there, with a line which will not tremble; the knife will do its work of separation and deliverance. (68)

Knife, sex, phallus... The blind Jinnah does not see that his scene of love, his scene of birthing is a scene of murder. No pregnancy possible here, with its largos, its states. No parturition, no multiplication, but a partition which will break apart, dismember from all sides: mother and child.

Jinnah "being-without" – without love, without other, without future – and surrounded by sinister doubles or enemies can only conceive, in the act of birth, of a monsterous chimera which in reality will lead to the massacre and separation of twenty thousand men.

Walled up within refusal, his heart definitively closed to any opening, as stiff and dry as his raging body, already in reality beyond the limits of humanity, Jinnah presents himself as a monolithic being. Difference can move him no more, nor can it move within him aptitudes to become other, to meet the other, to return to the shores of Life.

Yet, it's precisely this that Gandhi ceaselessly offers him.
Gandhi, the most transparent human figure to knock on
blindness' door.
"If today you permit me," he says, "I'm going to speak to you of
love" (81).
"No! No! No!" answers obstinate Jinnah who, in turn, receives
like blows, like a rape, a murder, these words trying to open the
space of the other: "Don't tell me your dreams any more...Men
don't love each other. We are inacceptable one to another" (83).
In his logic of separation, there is no reparation possible. However, because as a visionary he is the bearer of the whole human
memory, Gandhi foresees the terrible consequences, for the
moment and for generations to come:

> You have only spoken to me of separation... All night I thought
> of you, of us, of what is lying in wait for our India. I had dreadful
> visions. I saw a body torn apart, the mother disemboweled, India
> sliced up like meat! A nightmare! Let's wake up! (80)

The expected child is in danger. In this terrible wait, the hoped-for
deliverance threatens to destroy. So Gandhi, sublime mother, like
the biblical mother before King Salomon, faced with the inexorable
will of Jinnah who wants to cut the child in two – half India,
half Pakistan – Gandhi offers the possession of India: new,
independent, whole to the false, monstrous mother, head of the
league:

> Listen to me: your Excellency, I beg you, give India alive to Mr.
> Jinnah and don't put it to death! Don't split it up, for the love of
> God, give it to Jinnah. (160)

Yet Jinnah has no need of saving the integrity of that which is
human, alive. Bearer of death, he persists in seeing only ruse where
there is gift of the living, whole child. So before the imminence of
disaster, from the mother he had been the instant before, Gandhi,
in Ariane Mnouchkine's production, becomes the lover crazed with
desperation; and increasing tenfold his old man's strength, he
seizes his beloved Jinnah in his arms, clutches him, and – like
every loving person can do – weeping, clinging to him who leaves;
Gandhi the wise man, Gandhi the great immolates his own love by
attempting to touch, to actually open the heart of the other. Yet

Jinnah remains horrified before the force of love and the metamorphosis of the one he calls "crazy." And because he is the bearer of death, eaten away by cancer, he cuts himself loose and hurls with a voice that's choked and torn: "You want to immure he who is no longer of your world. But you don't see that I am dead? ... Let me go. Don't cling to me or I will drag you into my tomb!" (162).

When Jinnah disappears from the scene, Gandhi – the saint, the genius of India, he who has already undergone so many sufferings, so many dangers – is, on the ground, no more than a child in tears, curled up into himself, lost, alone, because with the other the thread of trust was broken.

Discreet witness until that moment, Nehru then comes forward from a corner of the stage and very softly, with much respect and sweetness, finds a mother's gestures to take the broken old man into his arms and cradle his pain. With infinite compassion, he kisses the bald skull of Gandhi, once more as fragile and trusting as a newborn.

When Gandhi rises, Nehru remains on his knees, as if in prayer, before God, before humanity.

Nehru, and in particular Gandhi, are exemplary of these beings whose virtual palette can't limit itself to the only sexual difference biologically established at birth. For them, all the roles of life between birth and death are possible: father, mother, masculine lover, feminine lover, son, daughter, even fragile nursling. These changes are made very quickly in reality, according to the urgency of the moment, which is also the urgency of the theater. And it's in the theater, on the stage where the vital strength of these men is deployed, unthreatened by castration because unsubjected to stifling "masculine" predetermination.

As for living, it's infinite.

Gandhi finds all the courage, all the passageways. Nehru is open to all possible paths.

Thus, it's with gestures of an abrasive comicalness, but with words thrown like stones, that Gandhi defies British power; like young David, reckless because confident of his rights, he scoffs at and chases great Goliath – Viceroy of India – who, furious, orders him to be silent:

Not another word? Fine. So two words? Quit India! ... Your Excellency! Two words: Quit India! (60).

In this immense field of liberties, beyond categories, Gandhi meets and entices, between Paradise and Hell, all who live, all who suffer, all who rejoice too: For instance, there is Moona, the bear he plays with and near whom he falls asleep. It is a vision of innocence which makes Haridasi say:

Two baby Moonas.
One is covered with hair.
The other is a naked moona. (125)

Gandhi, who does not know the confinement of genders, also escapes that of ages.

While the massacres between Hindus and Muslims begin, while India becomes the monstrous mother, the Mahatma gives the irresponsible parents another chance. He decides to fast until death if his people don't cease the killings.

He who amongst the Untouchables he calls "bitter children of God" (bitter, in French, is "a-mers" which resonnates with the meaning "sans mère" or without mother); he who, indefatigable mother, cleans, feeds, listens, consoles, amuses; he, the mother who bears, becomes again a dependent fragile foetus and gives his chance to India – in turn, to bear him, feed him, save him.

While, disarmed by love, the people break the chain of murders, old Gandhi, almost dying, goes out with child-steps, tottering in his embryonic night and stammers: "If only you knew how delicious it is to be born at the age of 78. Does my laughing show?" (197).

And the reign of the human could begin...

But that wouldn't allow for the strange, obscure ambivalences which divide men.

Nehru is the pure, pathetic example of this.

The arrogant sparring match with Jinnah, the impatience, the lack of political clairvoyance, make him – like Peter the Evangelist at the dawn of the eve, before the Passion – renounce the one he loves, in whom he believes: the Mahatma.

Before the minister Pattel who accuses him: "Admit that you lean towards a just partition Panditiji?," he answers, "In truth, with all my force, with all my desire, I reject it" (150).

For whom, in fact, will this child be; who will be born to him this night?

Nehru, in the grips of opposing desires, no longer knowing if he wants to hold on or let go, save or let die, implores old Sarujini, "Stay with me! I am so afraid! Ah! The Partition haunts me like an atrocious temptation... I am so afraid, my God! I'm frozen with fear! I am crazy with fear!" (151).

Bringing into the world a child...a work...a country, comes through pain, through doubt, through error, too. Sometimes the mother, crushed under the weight of her little one, shrinks, shrinks and becomes more fragile, more miniscule even than him.

The great Nehru, slipping under the feet of grandmother Sarujini, rolls himself up like a foetus to forget the instant of imminent birth, the decision. In the morning, it's the demons who will have won: "Without being able to do otherwise, I betrayed," he confesses sorrily (170).

The Indiade, a play which recounts the epic of men in their quest for the human, is also a story of crime and punishment.

Nehru – this man who is also a woman, whose heart and body are open, permeable, who hasn't put on iron armour like Jinnah to resist love, whose being lights up and radiates as soon as it has received gandhian waves – Nehru as in the most sublime stories of passion, is also the one who, in withdrawing his faith and trust, kills the one he loves, whom he admires the most.

Thus will his own bell toll. It is, in fact, from his mouth that the people learn of the tragedy: "Mahatma Gandhi is dead. His assassin is a Hindu" (207).

Nehru too is Hindu. The crime is shared. The punishment will be this eternal separation from the one who was at once his mother, his father, his fiancée, his little one.

Of course you have guessed that in this play by Hélène Cixous, the phallocentric schemata of the theaterical code have been shaken. The males, with whom the audience identifies, are men "beyond gender," but are alive, are possible, are real because incarnated before our eyes by the actors.

And, in fact, Cixous writes, the "actor is always a bit saint, a bit woman: one must give life by withdrawing oneself. Moreover everything is woman in the theater: woman the director, giver of birth to characters and actors!" (265).

Yes, Ariane Mnouchkine, from one rehearsal to the next, with patience, with impatience, with strength, with humility, with love, carries each actor in a circle of trust. She throws out images, metaphors: threads that catch and which permit one to pass through, without dying completely, from an amniotic night state where there is nothing more – neither man nor woman – to this particular state of transparency where one will be born once more to incarnate oneself.

So on the stage, it's a story of waiting, of watching, of night, of pain, of tears, of passages – but also of laughter, of jouissance and lightness. When the miracle of being in the right state of one's character produces itself for the actor, his playing becomes as beautiful and as physical as a dance.

Nehru, Gandhi, and the other characters of whom we have not been able to speak here can't be limited to a determined sex. Of course they are genetically men; but in them functions the dissemination of libidinal virtualities. Only Jinnah dooms himself to opposition and thus duality, duel. The others cross this line between birth and death that is called existence in the whole stretch, the richness of their living being. So there can also be mission and transmission, death, birth, transformations, resurrection.

Their "male femininity" is, according to the author's own terms, always sharper; knights of the round earth, they possess all the virtues of integrity, of combativity, of honor which, throughout the battles they have undertaken, make them say, in the heart of defeat which is only a more difficult step towards victory: "Courage, let's trust man."

Therefore, the production of *The Indiade or the India of Their Dreams* really invites us to a reflection on the origins of the human structure. A play of the deepest ontological character, it sets us, ourselves, in motion.

The actors, who have lived and played it, know.

"We'll never come out of this play intact" said one of them.

Notes

1. This play was produced by the Théâtre du Soleil on September 30, 1987 at the Cartoucherie, Paris-Vincennes, France.

Works Cited

Cixous, Hélène. *L'Indiade ou l'Inde de leurs rêves, et quelques écrits sur le théâtre*. Paris: Editions du Théâtre du Soleil, 1987.

16

The Critic as Playwright: Performing Hélène Cixous' Le Nom d'Oedipe

Charlotte Canning

In 1975 Hélène Cixous asked "How, as women, can we go to the theater without lending our complicity to the sadism directed at women, or being asked to assume, in the patriarchal family structure that the theater reproduces *ad infinitum*, the position of victim" ("Aller" 546)? The question still poses a difficult and important challenge for feminist theater practitioners, critics and spectators. In her strategic answer the roles of critic, spectator, and artist meet. She heralds the "arrival of Woman," one who "stays beyond the bounds of prohibition," and whose coming will allow women to go to the theater and "feel themselves loving and being loved, listening and being heard, happy as when they go to the sea, the womb of the mother" ("Aller" 547–48). Cixous proposes a joint effort in the recreation of theater as a feminist venture. There must be new artists to create it, new spectators to experience it, and new critics to address it. She mentions her play, *Le Portrait de Dora*, as "the first step" of her own journey toward the new theater she wishes to see and create ("Aller" 547).

What is important in Cixous' essay about theater is that there is a
synthesis of roles. She writes from a critical position, yet is
informed by her practical experience as a playwright. Her plays
draw upon her knowledge as a theorist and critic, and her theoretical and critical writings are largely shaped by literary works of
fiction. Morag Shiach commented on this textual contiguity when
she wrote, "the most important source of her [Cixous'] critical and
... theoretical positions seems to lie in the work of what amounts
to an alternative canon of literary writers who challenge the
dominant order of representation and ethical values" (3). All of
Cixous' work is marked by connections across disciplinary borders
and a blurring of traditionally distinct forms. She actively rejects
labels like "feminist" or "theorist.'[1] Instead she writes across
boundaries to create hybrid forms of writing. In her criticism/
theory there are long passages of lyric writing more often associated with poetry or fiction. Her drama is shaped and determined
by her theory and criticism. But maintaining the categories of
fiction, theory, drama, criticism, and poetry ignores Cixous' own
focus – the creation of a mode of writing that transgresses the
dictates of traditional disciplinary boundaries and hierarchies.

One way Cixous found to escape some of the limitations of
literature-based criticism was to turn to the theater and performance. Many of the writers she draws upon, Kleist or Genet for
example, wrote for the theater, and Cixous finds it a challenging
mode for her own critical project. Morag Shiach noted how Cixous
is able to use theater to resist the hierarchies of patriarchal meta-
physics.

> The attraction of a medium that can give concrete form to such
> spatialized thought is clear, and Cixous, in collaboration with a
> number of different directors, uses the spatial dimensions of
> theater in quite conscious and transgressive ways, in order to
> open up multiple points of view, to complicate the relations
> between language and character, and to provide a framework
> for the mythic narratives she wishes to develop in her historical
> dramas. (106)

Writing plays for performance provides physical, visual, and aural
elements not available in written criticism, theory, or fiction.

It is important to note, however, that performance criticism and
literary criticism are not the same. The criticism that is embedded

in Cixous' theatrical texts bears more resemblance to theater criticism than literary criticism. Cynthia Running-Johnson holds that a theater critic inhabits a contradictory position in the theater: "Critics occupy an ambiguous – a multiple 'feminine' place, both inside and outside what is happening before them onstage" (181). Critics, she maintains, are both "inside" because they have specialized and expert knowledge that the average spectator does not and "outside" because they are always aware of their knowledge and their purpose; they attend the theater in order to produce published criticism. Running-Johnson ultimately considers the critic another component of the performance, allowing the audience and the production to extend their encounter beyond the moment of performance.

Cixous' plays mimic the unique role of performance critic. She presents spectators not with characters, plot, and action but with critical and theoretical positions animated and shaped by the possibilities of theater and live performance. This forces spectators to experience her plays at a remove; denied realistic identification with the characters as people, they are forced to recognize them as critique. A character is read as a "site of articulation," not as a material person (Shiach 15). In her play *Le Portrait de Dora*, written in 1972 as a radio play and rewritten in 1976 for performance, she used Freud's famous case study to critique Freud, Freudianism, and the patriarchal culture that produced them. Jeannette Laillou Savona sums up *Dora* as "an interesting, although difficult, attempt to produce an unconscious female subject which also may be perceived as social and historical" (105). In *Le Nom d'Oedipe*, first performed at the 1978 Avignon Theater Festival, Cixous engages the Oedipus myth, a story inextricably embedded in Western culture. She inherits the Oedipus of Sophocles, the Oedipus of Freud, and the Oedipus of narrative, as well as the Oedipus of what is possibly the strongest taboo in western culture, incest. Dramatizing her critical and theoretical ideas provides Cixous with opportunities for critique not available to her in the standard critical format. Through the dramatic text she can actively subvert narrative and character, as well as taboo. Production furthers these possibilities by physicalizing what is written and adding visual and aural elements impossible to create or reproduce on the written page.

Interrogating an actual production of one of Cixous' plays could produce concrete examples of how her work functions as criticism and theater. Throughout the Fall of 1991 I served as "text analysis consultant"[2] on a production of Cixous' opera, *Le Nom d'Oedipe*, in translation at the Yale School of Drama (YSD). This piece proposes to examine that production as an example of how Cixous transgresses the boundaries of theater and criticism, offering new ways to produce both. Revisioning the Oedipus myth through a feminist eye, she uses the myth to foreground narrative, and woman's construction in the patriarchy. Naming and production supported and strengthened the feminist critique through visual, physical, and aural means.

Using a non-linear and non-traditional narrative structure, *Le Nom d'Oedipe* scrutinizes the relations between Oedipus and Jocasta, particularly as they play out patriarchal and heterosexual prescriptions affecting female desire and agency. Names and naming are identified as an important instance of these prescriptions. As Rosette Lamont points out in an essay about *Dora*, naming is a crucial power usually conferred on men and critiquing that power exposes the operations of patriarchy.

> In Freud's Vienna, indeed in all of Western culture, men had the double power to confer a name or conjure it away. Women had no name other than the one they received at birth from their father, relinquishing it only to assume that of their husband. Today's feminists say that the name was a mask placed over a woman's face; it made of her existence an eternal disguise. What's in a name? An independent person's identity. Depriving a woman of her name is a way of displacing her identity, indeed of effacing it altogether. (84)

Naming is, from the first moment of *Oedipe*, introduced as the crux of Jocasta's tragedy. Throughout the play the characters' positions in regard to naming ultimately determine the choices they make and the fates they suffer.

Oedipus' name is also the name given to conventional third-person narrative as it is constructed in Western discourse. As posited by feminist theorists, including Teresa de Lauretis and Kaja Silverman, the focus is on the male subject who is ubiquitous and active and the passive female subject whose desire is mediated through the male subject of the narrative. Teresa de Lauretis writes:

The desire is Oedipus's, and though its object may be woman (or Truth or knowledge or power), its term of reference and address is man: man as social being and mythical subject, founder of the social order, and source of mimetic violence; hence the institution of incest prohibition, its maintenance in Sophocles's Oedipus as in Hamlet's revenge of his father, its costs and benefits, again, for man. However, we need not limit our understanding of the inscription of desire in narrative to the Oedipus story proper, which is in fact paradigmatic of all narratives. (112)

Women are consequently positioned as the prize or reward at the end of the quest or travail. This points back to Cixous' question quoted at the beginning of this piece: how can women attend to theater without supporting structures of oppression? She meets the challenge on its own turf, so to speak. As de Lauretis points out, the Oedipus of Freud is the Oedipus of Sophocles, already inscribed in dramatic narrative and "sharply focussed on the hero as the mover of the narrative, the center and term of reference of consciousness and desire" (112). Through a disrupted and disruptive Oedipal narrative Cixous wrestles with all the Oedipuses. In *Le Nom d'Oedipe* Jocasta is a prize who refuses to construct herself as the

> properly Oedipalized female subject [who finds] relief from her crippling sense of inadequacy only through a heterosexual, procreative cathexis and by aligning herself with the qualities of passivity, exhibitionism, and masochism. (Silverman 143)

Instead, Jocasta is " 'the mother who exalts in orgasm'. . . . Chanting and intoning, she subverts a syntactically-ordered male-centered and generated language in pulsating verses in praise of incestuous passion" (Miller 208).

The play opens with Jocasta exhorting Oedipus to ignore the cries of the city. Finally she entreats him: "Do not be Oedipus, today you are not the one they are calling. Do not be the one they beg, disown the dying, the envious, disown the name they throw to you" (*Oedipe* 3–4)[3]. If he can abandon his role as the always already narrativized Oedipus she promises him: "I shall tell you our true names" (*Oedipe* 4). Seizing the power that should be his, she offers

them new names, names of her choosing, not his. He declines her offer, pointing out that it is his duty and responsibility to answer the call of the city. From the first moment she is either aware that he is her son or has already abandoned roles that would divide them. She is also not unaware that her project is most likely doomed and that he will leave her: "I have already heard this silence" (*Oedipe* 7). Jocasta does not seem bound by the demands of linear time. She is not experiencing her narrative as a passive object awaiting enlightenment or rescue by a male subject. Instead she makes demands on him and moves through time so that past, present, and future exist almost simultaneously.

Her love and her need for him physically lead her to cast the city in the role of the other woman. In fact, Cixous seems to offer Thebes as the conventional woman in an Oedipal narrative. In *Oedipe* Jocasta is far too desirous and demanding to play the role of the passive woman who waits for the hero's return. Instead it is the city, absent, disembodied, and characterized as "his daughter, the one he loves, his lover," who waits for him and seemingly demands nothing (*Oedipe* 15). When asked what the city offers that she cannot, she replies:

All that he does not want from me.
Her needs, her distress, her fragility.
Her voice – so weak. Who could resist it?
She draws him. He is drawn.
I understand it. Such a voice. The softness
Of a sad humid breeze. Irresistible.
Weak *and* strong. (*Oedipe* 16)

Jocasta knows that it is the city that keeps him from her and that he remains caught in the name of Oedipus which dictates his actions and his allegiances.

Oedipus is seemingly deaf and blind to what Jocasta offers him. When Jocasta begs him not to leave he tells her that he "must go to what I fear most" (*Oedipe* 20). The voice he follows is identified as the Sphinx by the chorus: "he only has ears for the horror of the Sphinx" (*Oedipe* 21). Love is not enough, he believes. Instead he must pursue the mystery. Oedipus is caught in a prison of his own vision of himself. "I am not a man of doubts and disguises" (*Oedipe* 22). He forces himself to move along a linear trajectory that he

believes will bring him to the Truth. Jocasta blames herself for
being "unable to wean" and divert him from the inevitable track
of the Oedipal narrative, unable to stop him from striving for the
"source" (*Oedipe* 22). She suggests the option of ignoring the oracle
and refuses its authority to dictate their lives. But in the next scene
Oedipus is entranced by Tiresias, interrogating him and demanding his story.

The scene is not, however, the climax of the play. It is the fourth
scene of fourteen and undercuts the narrative structure of the
original story. Gaining the knowledge of his origins is not what
destroys Oedipus; it his inability to look beyond them or to construct a narrative for himself that is not dictated by the Oedipal
narrative. Miller point out, "His *name* determines Oedipus and
delimits him.... The myth of 'Oedipus' imprisons Oedipus. The
more he knows, the more Oedipus falls apart, disintegrating into
the myth of himself" (208). Jocasta understands this about Oedipus, as in the next scene she asks "And now my lover son, who is
waking? Now, who will you be?" (*Oedipe* 29). She is constantly
offering him options that would allow both of them to escape
Oedipal prescriptions; but while he demands solutions he cannot
see that it is his very demand, his very investment, that dictates his
situation.

OEDIPUS: How to be free to fear.
JOCASTA: Man is allowed not to fear.
OEDIPUS: I fear I no longer understand myself.
JOCASTA: It is not forbidden to live
         Without consulting the gods. (*Oedipe* 42)

Oedipus is completely unable to hear her suggestions, to hear
the substance of what she is saying. She foregrounds his self-
recriminations and passivity while struggling for the autonomy
and agency he is automatically granted by the privilege of
gender. But as Miller points out, Oedipus cannot hear her
because "[h]e can only respond to predefinitions of himself, to
preordained credentials and titles" (209). Ignoring the gods
and fear would not work into his conception of the path he must
take.

Oedipus' torture over his situation issues directly from his belief
in naming. Jocasta offers him love "with my flesh and soul. Without names" and with complete access to her body. "I did not name.

I did not hide. I gave" (*Oedipe* 52–53). He, however, cannot relinquish the knowledge that she is his mother: "If fate had allowed my mother to be..Words...hardly breathe" (*Oedipe* 52). He is unable to surrender his view of Jocasta as his mother because it would mean abandoning his own self-construction. If he is not Oedipus, he is nothing, he is no one, he is unmanned. "I lack myself. Separated from my name. Less and less here" (*Oedipe* 62). Oedipus finally leaves Jocasta because he cannot name her, cannot cast her in an Oedipal role. She begs him to say her name as he leaves but he refuses because she no longer has one for him. She has, at least partially, escaped the system he embraces. "No name can name you anymore" (*Oedipe* 68). She accepts that this is impossible for him, that if he cannot place her within the patriarchy, he cannot name her, and instead asks him to speak his own name. He complies despite his resistance. When she forces him to yell his name, he adds "the name of Oedipus no longer names anyone" (*Oedipe* 70). If Jocasta refuses her Oedipal role then perhaps it is impossible for him to be Oedipus.

Finally, despite her struggle for an active desire, her perception of a system outside the patriarchal/Oedipal one, and her position as the focus of the play, Jocasta dies. She has failed in her goal to "deliver him from names. All the names that pass for gods" (*Oedipe* 72). Judith Miller sees the ending as ultimately liberating.

> In a poetic apotheosis made possible by rejecting linguistic laws of gender and number and sociological ones of kinship and accepting instead the alchemy of the verb, a new being emerges at the play's close. Oedipus incorporates Jocasta and, as she says, matching a singular French verb to a plural pronoun, "Nous continue." Oedipus no longer uniquely male becomes a dual-sexed person, psychologically bisexual.... (210)

However, it is difficult to reconcile "the new being" with the physically male body it inhabits and with the dead woman in his arms. In fact, the new being looks suspiciously like the old being.

The ending is more productively viewed as indicative of the problems of working within a system, versus completely abandoning it. Shiach quotes a remark Cixous made about *Dora*, to characterize that play's ending. The text, Cixous stated, is one of "rebellion rather than revolution" (117–18). As long as Jocasta is invested in the system of Oedipal patriarchy she is doomed. While she was able to resist, or at least foreground the "impossibility of singular identity, of fixed origins," she was also "compelled by the power of naming and thus reproduce[d] herself as the woman [in the patriarchy]" (Shiach 117). Jocasta is not a feminist heroine who destroys the Oedipal narrative but one who is able to significantly disrupt it, and whose disruptions throw its problems, limitations, and oppressions into sharp relief. The tragedy is not as in Sophocles, or even in Freud, of a man who breaks a taboo, but of the oppressive situation of women denied desire and agency.

In production interpretation is made tangible. Jocasta's contradictory status, as a site of rebellion and as an oppressed woman in a masculinist culture, can be forcefully realized, as it was in the December, 1991 Yale School of Drama production. Directed by Marya Mazor for her MFA thesis, staged movement, music, costume and scenic design worked together to present a critique in collaboration with the production team.

Structurally, *Le Nom d'Oedipe* disrupts the conventional Oedipal narrative. The story line no longer follows a linear and chronological path, scenes in the present tense are mixed with scenes that seem to be memories of Jocasta and Oedipus before the plague descended on Thebes. Verb tenses are never constant, leaping from past to present to conditional, always unmooring the text from any definite time or sequence. In production, a crucial visual disruption that echoed the textual ones was the splitting of each major character into a part for two performers. Jocasta, Oedipus, and Tiresias were each played by two actors, one who sang the role and another who spoke. It is not easy to determine what the differences are between the sung and the spoken lines in the written text. For the purposes of the YSD production it was decided that Singing Oedipus and Singing Jocasta would be semi-deconstructions of the characters, while the speaking roles would represent the characters' more public or conventional selves. The split served a crucial purpose, preventing the audience from reading the story as a traditional narrative. This participated in a larger French avant-garde project to disrupt realistic representation. "To break up character and unity, linked to a linear conception of time, is a political gesture necessary to bring about social change" (Conley 25). It became extremely difficult for the spectator to construct an easy, realistic identification. The absence of realistic and unified coherence confounded a traditional Oedipal narrative, making it impossible to read the characters as people. Instead they were realizations of feminist critiques.

Equally, in the script, the spoken and sung lines are not delivered in a linear manner. Instead speaking and singing overlap and voices vie with one another or provide indistinct background sound. Mazor decided in each instance which part of the text was to be emphasized and then used the other parts to weave in and out, creating a stimulating and provocative aural text of sound and music. Mazor chose not to use the music originally composed for the opera, opting instead to have Yale directing student and composer Loni Berry create new music for the production. Berry, an African-American, drew upon the rich heritage of African-American music, including gospel, rhythm and blues, and soul, for his composition and in doing so translated the play into a distinctly American idiom. This unmoored the play from its relentlessly white European roots by invoking other non-western or oppressed cultures and the histories of the interactions of those cultures with the west.

The sense of dislocation introduced by the music and by the double cast characters was furthered by Mazor's casting choices. She cast across racial and ethnic identities. No specific racial interpretation was laid over the casting – Singing Jocasta was cast with an African-American performer (Melody Garrett) but not because the part was considered more appropriate for an African-American woman. Instead, Mazor wanted to take full advantage of the diverse talent pool available to her in the graduate actor training program and not limit herself to an all-white cast. The casting was something the (predominately white) production team wrestled with throughout the process, challenged to do so not only by the composer, but also by a desire to predict the ways in which the audience might read the casting. There is no easy interpretation of the casting as it was not done according to a systematic apportioning of the roles. Speaking Jocasta was a Latina woman, Mary Magdalena Hernandez; Speaking Oedipus an African-American man, Michael Potts; and Singing Oedipus a white man, Malcolm Getts. The chorus was five women, three white, two

African-American. The casting helped prevent the audience from constructing a teleological, Oedipal narrative based on similarities by confronting them with the unalterable visual differences of race/ethnicity and physical separation. The casting foregrounded the transgressions in the text by adding visual and non-verbal elements that further unmoored character as a fixed and stable site of meaning. The stress moved from a realistic identification between character and actor to a more visual emphasis on the physical presence of bodies onstage enacting textual relations with characters who were places of critical and theoretical articulation.

The costume design was an important element in the deconstructive approach of the play. Choosing to support the idea, as Miller puts it, that the play both "deconstructs an old myth and reconstructs a new but incomplete one," the costumes, designed by Elizabeth Michal Fried, worked with the doubled casting to present an equally doubled view of the characters (211). The speaking characters wore costumes that best interpreted their conventional roles while the singing characters' costumes deconstructed those roles by making actual the unspoken and the unacknowledged.

Speaking Jocasta was the perennial bride, forever waiting for the promised joys and fulfillment of marriage. Dressed in an Edwardian bridal grown, the costume was highly ornate and obviously expensive. White taffeta was adorned with rosettes, bows, pearls, and pleated ruffles and shimmered under the light. Hernandez's hair was elaborately styled and piled high on her head, and she wore long white gloves. The dress had a long train, also ornately decorated, making it almost impossible for the performer to move without help. The dress, typical of the Edwardian period, was physically restricting. Hernandez could not raise her arms, sit with ease, or take deep breaths – prevented from doing so by her tightly laced corset. The costume was intended to invoke the position of women both within heterosexual norms of marriage and within class. It was apparent from the first moment onstage that Jocasta was both of her class and position and trapped by it. Singing Jocasta made what was implied in Speaking Jocasta's costume literal. Garrett was encased in a metal corset that closed with large metal buckles and a metal hoop skirt that also closed with the same buckles. Her skirt had a long mesh train, making it

Figure 1. The Name of Oedipus, *Yale School of Drama, from left to right: Michael Potts, Melody Garrett, and Magdalena Hernandez. Photo by Gerry Goodstein.*

impossible for her to walk without assistance. She was physically imprisoned. Visible under the corset and hoops were an off-white chemise and bloomers. The production's interpretation of Jocasta's position was quite clear, she was imprisoned by her role as wife and mother, just as she was imprisoned by the dictates of the story.

Speaking Oedipus, on the other hand, was encased in a prison of a very different sort. Dressed in a military uniform, he was bedecked in medals and ribbons, making clear his allegiances to the state and his official role. He was envisioned as the perfect dictator or ruler. Singing Oedipus wore nothing but a simple loin cloth, intended to signify his unreadability and his lack of self-vision outside the defined role of Oedipus.

The chorus wore simple slips and overcoats, allowing them to change their look easily. They were understood as a

Figure 2. The Name of Oedipus, *Yale School of Drama, from left to right: Mary Magdalena Hernandez, and Michael Potts. Photo by Gerry Goodstein*

traditional chorus that interrogates the main characters and comments on the action. The two Tiresiases were also simply clothed in large robes with hoods evoking monks' habits or prophets' robes.

Monica Raya's scenic design provided an open and neutral playing space for the action. The stage sloped gently away from the audience and into a pool of water that was about nine inches at its deepest. The color palette consisted of blues and grays and the stage was surrounded on three sides by grey scrim through which figures could often be perceived. The only objects on the stage were a life-size chaise lounge made from metal and mesh downstage right and a similarly shaped but upholstered chaise in miniature scale upstage in the pool of water. Center stage left was a miniature neo-classical door, about a third the size of a regular door. The door was a visual pun on the play as a revisioning of a classical text.

Figure 3. The Name of Oedipus, *Yale School of Drama, from left to right: James Kall, Melody Garrett, and Brendan Corbalis. Photo by Gerry Goodstein.*

Mazor's staging combined all the elements of design and casting to create highly stylized and static movement and blocking. The four main performers moved little throughout the performance. Foregrounding Cixous' non-traditional narrative, Mazor chose non-traditional methods of interaction between the characters. Heightening the potential failure of Jocasta's project to abandon

the Oedipal narrative and Oedipus' inability to see his imprison-
ment within that narrative, the characters never addressed each
other directly. Conversations, already fragmented and non-devel-
opmental in the written text, were completely released from realistic conventions. Rarely moving, the characters addressed no one
but the space in front of them as they lamented, pleaded, or
explained. Speaking Jocasta never moved from her downstage
center position throughout the entire first act (see Fig. 1)[4]. Her
only movements were gestures with her head and hands, otherwise she was frozen, staring straight ahead. Singing Jocasta was
similarly frozen in place upstage and stage right of Speaking
Jocasta and she sang in agony to no one, except perhaps the
audience. She did not acknowledge the presence of any of the
characters, not even Speaking Oedipus when, in scene six, in a
rare moment of unrestrained movement, he pleaded with both
Jocastas to understand the pain he felt over Laius' death. At one
point he closed his hands around Speaking Jocasta's neck, almost
but not quite touching her, while she stared fixedly ahead, seemingly unaware of his presence (see Fig. 2). Emotional expression
was also highly controlled and stylized. Always in the singular,
fear, pain, joy, rage, and sensuality were never overlapped or
complex. The acting was not according to a "method" approach
aimed at realistic emotional content, but a demonstration of the
signs of emotions, more easily identifiable and foregrounded as
representation.

Only the chorus moved about the whole stage, able to react
while making eye contact, questioning, and disagreeing with
Speaking Oedipus and Jocasta. They had a freedom of movement
denied the other characters. In the second act the Chorus' movement pattern changed and they continually circumnavigated the
stage, carrying candles, and singing their dirge-like pronouncements. They were frozen in one set of movements while they
waited for Jocasta's death.

Both Jocastas looked slightly different for the second act. Both
had their hair down and Speaking Jocasta no longer wore gloves.
While Singing Jocasta resumed her position upstage, Speaking
Jocasta began in her Act One position but then, winding herself
up slowly in her train she lowered herself on the metal/mesh
chaise. There she shifted position constantly, writhing, sitting, or
lying as though searching for the best position in which to die. The

death scene provided Mazor with a powerful visual moment suggested only by the production's interpretation of the text. As Speaking Jocasta was lulled to her death by Tiresias, Singing Jocasta, for the first time, began to move slowly upstage. When she stopped moving one of the two Tiresiases crossed to her and, as Speaking Jocasta said "I do not know your name. I have never known it, I will never known it, the one that will not wake me up...." he began to open the metal closures on Singing Jocasta's corset and hoop skirt (*Oedipe* 101). With each opening she reacted sharply as if in pain and finally as the last one opened she stretched as if released from prison (see Fig. 3). Turning, she moved upstage to the pool of water where, dressed in her chemise and bloomers, she lay face down in the water. This moment was extremely elongated and made Jocasta's death simultaneously a triumph and failure. While it was clear that her death was her failure to break free from the system that oppressed her, it was also a brief moment of liberation and choice. This created a strong sense of contradiction. When Oedipus returns and cradles her in his arms, the two speaking characters downstage on the chaise and the singing characters upstage in the pool, it is the first time they have touched in the play and there was both a sense of loss, that Oedipus had not returned in time to save her, and a sense of appropriateness, that because she could not save herself she died.

Ultimately, Cixous, like Jocasta, both rejects and is compelled by the power of names. Cixous resists the determination of names and labels – "I am not a feminist" – but she constantly engages her writing with mythical characters such as Medusa, Electra, and Tiresias, using them to stand in for and represent complex theoretical and critical positions. Similarly Oedipus and Jocasta stand in for the complexities of desire, narrativity, and gender. But perhaps this is a productive approach. Teresa de Lauretis points out in the conclusion to her study of desire and narrativity:

The most exciting work in cinema and in feminism today is not anti-narrative or anti-Oedipal; quite the opposite. It is narrative and Oedipal with a vengeance, for it seeks to stress the duplicity of that scenario and the specific contradiction of the female subject in it, the contradiction by which historical women must work with and against Oedipus. (157)

There is nothing more Oedipal than the story of Oedipus himself. Jocasta is destroyed by her contradictory position in the Oedipal narrative but she was also denied many of the solutions that "historical women" have sought; solidarity with other women, refusing to accept society's compulsory heterosexuality, or abandoning the oppressive situation. Instead, Jocasta operates as a critique of the system that kills her and as a productive articulation for material women seeking to eliminate the patriarchy.

In *Le Nom d'Oedipe* Cixous performs simultaneously the roles of critic and playwright. As a critic she uses the story of Oedipus to critique its position in Western society. Through the myth she foregrounds the construction of women within patriarchy, narrative, and theater. Reading *Oedipe* through "Aller à la Mer" positions the play as a powerful critique of the operations of theater. As Merope Palvides notes in her essay, "Restructuring the Traditional," theater theorist Frances Ferguson called Sophocles' *Oedipus* "a crucial instance of drama, if not the play which best exemplifies this art in its essential nature and its completeness." She also adds that Aristotle based his theories of drama on *Oedipus* (152). Thus, when Cixous challenges the reception and interpretation of the Oedipus myth, she is also challenging the history of theater. Her feminist revision of the story also serves as a feminist critique and revision of theater itself. "Cixous argues that such political theater would have to emphasize proximity, involvement, rather than distance that supports an illusion of unity and coherence for most dramatic performance" (Shiach 110). Her theater can be understood as a relentless search for a way out of the oppressive voyeurism imposed by the traditional Oedipal narrative.

The simultaneous critical and theatrical operations identified here depend on more than the possibilities of the written text. They require live performance to fully realize the potential of critique as theater and of theater as critique. Cixous' criticism is much more productive when read in conjunction with her plays, and her plays are impossible to perform without reading her criticism. As she herself said, "If I go to the theater now, it must be a political gesture, with a view of changing, with the help of other women, its means of production and expression" ("Aller" 547). Desiring change and realizing it requires both a critic and a playwright, both written and performed textual operations. Hopefully this piece has demonstrated the possibilities in Cixous' work for finding both.

$$\boxed{\text{Notes}}$$

1. Toril Moi comments on Cixous' rejection: "Cixous believes in neither theory nor analysis...; nor does she approve of *feminist* [emph. Moi's] analytical discourses: she is after all the first woman who flatly declared that 'I am not a feminist' and later went onto say that 'I do not have to produce theory'. Accusing feminist researchers in the humanities of turning away from the present towards the past, she rejects their efforts as pure 'thematics.' According to Cixous, such feminist critics will inevitably find themselves caught up in the oppressive network of hierarchical binary oppositions propagated by patriarchal ideology." Moi goes on to say that the rejection of the term "feminist" has more to do with the struggles within the French women's movement than with a rejection of the ideas of feminism. Moi uses the term feminist to describe Cixous and her work, believing that the term as construed in the U.S. is an adequate description of Cixous' politics. In this, I have followed her lead (103).
2. The position was that of dramaturg, but Yale School of Drama policy did not allow anyone who was not a student to be listed in the program in an already existing production position.
3. Page numbers of *Le Nom d'Oedipe* refer to the production copy of the script and not the published manuscript.
4. For performance purposes the fourteen scene play was divided into two acts, with one fifteen minute intermission. The division was made between scenes nine and ten.

Works Cited

Cixous, Hélène. "Aller à la Mer." *Modern Drama*. Trans. Barbara Kerslake. 27 (1984): 546–48.

———. *Le Nom d'Oedipe*. Trans. Christian Makward. *Plays by French and Francophone Women: A Critical Anthology*. Ed. Christiane Makward and Judith G. Miller. Ann Arbor: U of Michigan P, 1994.

Conley, Verena Andermatt. *Hélène Cixous: Writing the Feminine*. Lincoln: U of Nebraska P, 1984.

de Lauretis, Teresa. *Alice Doesn't: Feminism, Semiotics, and Cinema*. Bloomington: Indiana UP, 1984.

Lamont, Rosette C. "The Reverse Side of a Portrait: The Dora of Freud and Cixous." *Feminine Focus: The New Women Playwrights*. Ed. Enoch Brater. New York: Oxford UP, 1989.

Miller, Judith. "Jean Cocteau and Hélène Cixous: Oedipus." *Themes in Drama: Drama, Sex and Politics*. Ed. James Redmond. Cambridge: Cambridge UP, 1985.

Moi, Toril. *Sexual/Textual Politics: Feminist Literary Theory*. London: Methuen, 1985.

Palvides, Merope. "Restructuring the Traditional: An Examination of Hélène Cixous' *Le Nom d'Oedipe*." *Within the Dramatic Spectrum*. Ed. Karelisa Hartigan. Lanham, MD: University Presses of America, 1986.

Running-Johnson, Cynthia. "Feminine Writing and Its Theatrical Other." *Themes in Drama: Women in Drama*. Ed. James Redmond. Cambridge: Cambridge UP, 1989.

Savona, Jeannette Laillou. "In Search of Feminist Theater: *Portrait of Dora.*"
    Feminine Focus: The New Women Playwrights. Ed. Enoch Brater. New
    York: Oxford UP, 1989.
Shiach, Morag. *Hélène Cixous: A Politics of Writing.* London: Routledge,
    1991.
Silverman, Kaja. *The Subjects of Semiotics.* New York: Oxford UP, 1983.

About the Contributors

Liliana Alexandrescu was born in Romania, and has lived and worked in the Netherlands since 1974. She earned a degree in French Literature from the University of Bucharest and in Theater Research and Stage Direction from the Institute of Art History. In addition to acting as co-editor of the *International FIRT/SIBMAS Bulleten*, since 1975, Ms. Alexandrescu has been the director of FRI Theater group at the University of Amsterdam. She has published on modern and ritual theater.

Anu Aneja studied Franch at Jawaharlal Nehru University in New Delhi, India. She received her M.A. and Ph.D. in Comparative Literature from Pennsylvania State University under Professor Christiane Makward. She is currently an Associate Professor in the Humanities & Classics Department of Ohio Wesleyan University, where she teaches courses on Postmodernism and Women of Colour, among others. Professor Aneja's recent translation of Cixous's *L'Indiade* into Hindustani is due out in 1997.

Mireille Calle-Gruber, Professor of French Literature and Writing at Queen's University (Ontario), is the author of a number of articles and books on literary theory (notably, *L'effet-fiction. De l'illusion romanesque*, Nizet, 1989) on the "new novel, and particularly several pieces on Michel Butor and Claude Simon, as well as on écriture féminine (*Photos de Racine*, with Hélène Cixous, Édition des Femmes, 1994). Her third novel, *La division de l'intérieur* is due out in 1996 (Montreal: L'Hexagone), and she has signed with L'Harmattan for a book entitled *Une écriture de l'altérité. Les partition de Claude Ollier*.

Charlotte Canning is an Assistant Professor in the Department of Theatre & Dance at the University of Texas, Austin. She is the author of *Feminist Theaters in the U.S.A.: Staging Women's Experience* (Routledge, 1996).

328 ABOUT THE CONTRIBUTORS

Marie-Lise Charue, Ph.D. candidate in the Department of Modern and Classical Languages at the University of Connecticut is currently writing her dissertation in Medieval Philosophy with Professor Anne Berthelot.

Robert Con Davis, a professor at the University of Oklahoma, teaches American studies, cultural studies, and critical theory. ahe is the co-editor of the criticism and theory textbook, *Contemporary Literary Criticism* (Longman), not in its fourth edition. He has co-written *Criticism and Culture: The Role of Critique in Modern Literary, Theory* (Longman) and *Culture and Cognition* (Cornell). His most recent book is *The Paternal Romance: Reading God-the-Father in Early Western Culture* (Illinois).

Claudine Guégan Fisher is a Professor of French at Portland State University. She has published *La Cosmogonie d'Hélène Cixous* (Amsterdam: Rodopi, 1988), and has edited a collection of essays on the Québec writer, Gaétan Brulotte called *Gaétan Brulotte: une nouvelle écriture* (1992). Her research interests include contemporary literature, feminism, and Québec writers, and she has published numerous articles in those fields.

Rosette C. Lamont is the author of *Ionesco* (1973), *The Two Faces of Ionesco* (1993), *Ionesco's Imperatives: The Politics of Culture* (1993), *The Life and Works of Boris Pasternak, De Vive Voix*, and *Women on the Verge*. She received her doctorate from Yale University in 1954, and is currently Professor of French and Comparative Literature at the Graduate School and Queens College of the City University of New York. A correspondent for many publications including *Theater- Week*, Professor Lamont has also won many awards, including a Guggenheim Fellowship.

Sissel Lie is Professor at the University of Trondheim, Norway, teaching French literature. She was Visiting Professor at the University of Washington, Seattle, in the fall of 1996. In addition to short stories and novels (one novel, *The Lion's Heart*, was translated into English in 1990), Professor Lie has also published articles, books, and anthologies on women's cultural history and on French and Norwegian writers. One of her essays appears in *The Body and the Text* (Ed. H. Wilcox et al, 1990).

Marilyn Manners teaches Humanities at the University of California, Los Angeles. She has edited *Emergences*, the journal of the Group for the Study of Composite Cultures, and published articles on contemporary feminism and cultural studies.

Martine Motard-Noar is an Associate Professor of French at Western Maryland College. She has published a monograph on Cixous entitled "Les Fictions d'Hélène Cixous: Une autre langue de femme" at French

Forum Monographs (1990), and chapters on Cixous in *Images of Persephone* (1994) and *The Contemporary Novel in France* (1996), both at the University Press of Florida. She is currently working on Marie NDiaye, Marie Redonnet, and Sylvie Germain.

Catherine Nevil Parker, Managing Editor of *Lit: Literature Interpretation Theory*, is a Ph.D. candidate in English at the University of Connecticut where she is working on a dissertation in twentieth century American literature.

Aileen Phillips (translator) Completed O.B.H. at the University of Chicago betorc undertaken groduale studres with Hélène Cixous at the University of paris VIII. She has been a member at the reasearch seminar since 1979.

Anne-Marie Picard is a tenured professor at the University of Western Ontario in London, Canada. She has published numerous articles on French women's writings, especially on Marguerite Duras, Colette, and Hélène Cixous. She works on the production of the gaze in the visual arts, literature, and philosophy (Dalhousie French Studies, 1995), the Imaginary of theory (*Texte*, University of Toronto, 1996), and the body and its words (*Le Corps et ses lettres*: Nuit Blanche, Québec City, 1996). She is currently preparing a book on a theory of the reading subject using psychoanalysis and a clinical experience on pathologies of reading in children at Saint-Anne Psychiatric Hospital (Paris), and is doing research on the production of the critic as subject in pre-structuralist French literary aesthetics and criticism (1840–1940).

Cynthia Running-Johnson is an Associate Professor of French at Western Michigan University. In her work, she has examined drama and prose by French-language authors notably Jean Genet and Hélène Cixous, in relation to feminist theory. She is currently investigating intersections between the visual and literary arts, researching art critical writings by contemporary French authors of poetry and fiction.

Violette Santellani was born in the south of France where she completed her M.A. studies to become a teacher of literature and history. She has worked as a member of the research seminar since 1982. She currently teaches literature at a graphic art school in Paris.

Christa Stevens is a researcher in Women's Studies at the French Department of the University of Amsterdam. She is currently finishing her thesis on Cixous's *Portrait du soleil*, which will be published under the title *Portes et portraits*. She is co-editor of *(En)jeux de la communication romanesque* (Amsterdam/Atlanta: Rodopi, 1994). She has written essays and reviews on contemporary French literature and on francophone African and Antillian literature.

Judith Still is Professor of French and Critical Theory at the University of Nottingham. She is the author of *Justice and Difference in the Works of Rousseau* (Cambridge, 1992) and co-editor, with M. J. Worton, of *Intertextuality* (Manchester, 1990) and *Textuality and Sexuality* (Manchester, 1993). She has also translated Djanet Lachmet's *Lallia* and co- translated, with J. M. Collie, Luce Irigaray's *Elemental Passions*.

Barbara A. Suess is a Ph.D. candidate in English at the University of Connecticut, where she is working on her dissertation on gender and Yeats's verse dramas. She has published in the field of twentieth century Irish literature, and is editing a critical volume of essays on Anne Brontë. She is also an editorial assistant for *Lit: Literature Interpretation Theory*.

Pamela Anne Turner is a playwright, teacher, and scholar in Atlanta, Georgia. She holds a Ph.D. from Emory University in Performance Theory and Intellectual History. She teaches Theatre at Georgia State University and Agnes Scott College, and Playwrighting at the Academy Theatre. Her most recent play, *Voices*, was part of the 1996 Centennial Olympic Games Cultural Olympiad.

Index

331